Approaching Language Variation through Corpora

Linguistic Insights

Studies in Language and Communication

Edited by Maurizio Gotti,
University of Bergamo

Volume 167

PETER LANG
Bern · Berlin · Bruxelles · Frankfurt am Main · New York · Oxford · Wien

Shunji Yamazaki & Robert Sigley (eds)

Approaching Language Variation through Corpora

A Festschrift in Honour of Toshio Saito

PETER LANG
Bern · Berlin · Bruxelles · Frankfurt am Main · New York · Oxford · Wien

Bibliographic information published by die Deutsche Nationalbibliothek
Die Deutsche Nationalbibliothek lists this publication in the Deutsche Nationalbibliografie; detailed bibliographic data is available on the Internet at ‹http://dnb.d-nb.de›.

British Library Cataloguing-in-Publication Data: A catalogue record for this book is available from The British Library, Great Britain

Library of Congress Cataloging-in-Publication Data

Approaching language variation through corpora : a festschrift in honour of Toshio Saito / Shunji Yamazaki & Robert Sigley (eds).
pages cm. – (Linguistic Insights : Studies in Language and Communication, ISSN 1424-8689 ; Volume 167)
Includes bibliographical references.
ISBN 978-3-0343-1264-6 – ISBN 978-3-03-510495-0 (eBook)
1. English language–Variation–Japan. 2. English language–Japan–Data processing.
3. Language and languages–Variation–Japan. 4. Discourse analysis–Japan.
5. Computational linguistics–Japan. 6. Japan–Languages. I. Yamazaki, Shunji, editor of compilation. II. Sigley, Robert, editor of compilation. III. Saito, Toshio, honouree.
PE3502.J3A66 2012
427–dc23

2012038053

ISSN 1424-8689 pb. ISSN 2235-6371 eBook
ISBN 978-3-0343-1264-6 pb. ISBN 978-3-0351-0495-0 eBook

Hochfeldstrasse 32, CH-3012 Bern, Switzerland
info@peterlang.com, www.peterlang.com, www.peterlang.net

Contents

Section 2. Descriptions of Synchronic Linguistic Variation

Section 3. Descriptions of Diachronic Linguistic Variation

Section 4. Descriptions of Social and Stylistic Variation

Emeritus Professor Toshio Saito

TOSHIO SAITO (born 1933) received his BA, MA, and PhD from Osaka University, where he worked as professor and dean of the Faculty of Language and Culture until 1996 when he became Emeritus Professor at Osaka University. After teaching three years at Himeji Dokkyo University, he took the position of professor and dean at Daito Bunka University until his retirement in 2003. He served as president of the Japan Association for English Corpus Studies (JAECS) for eight years from 1993 to 2001. He was awarded the Emperor's medal, the Order of the Sacred Treasure, in recognition of his long-term contribution to education and research in 2011.

Saito's main research interest has been in English historical/diachronic linguistics, especially in syntactic developments from Old English to the present day. His papers, written both in English and Japanese, include studies of the syntactic development of relative pronouns, interrogative pronouns, gerunds, infinitives, and changes in word order. His first published paper, "The Development of the Relative Pronouns in Modern Colloquial English" (1961), was a statistical survey based on a one-genre corpus (though not an electronic corpus) of 49 British plays from 1560 to 1958. All his papers on syntactic change were based on manually collected data up until the release of the Helsinki Corpus in 1991.

His diachronic research on these specific syntactic features also led him to investigate the possibility of more general stylistic change in English writings. In the 1970s he spent several years studying the issue of whether English prose constitutes a continuous tradition of influence from Old English onwards (the "Continuity of English Prose" issue), as propounded by R. W. Chambers in *On the Continuity of English Prose from Alfred to More and his School* (1932), subsequently translating Chambers' book into Japanese, along with I. A. Gordon's *The Movement of English Prose* (1966).

This research also led him to realize the importance of the Middle English metrical romances in the history of English literature. Accordingly he organized a small ME romance research group in 1977, which has so far translated about forty romances into Japanese, published in 4 volumes. One vital part of the process of translating these works was the preparation of concordances. With that aim, together with Mitsunori Imai, he set up a large scale KWIC concordance compilation project, "Osaka University Concordances to Middle English Metrical Romances" in 1985, using a mainframe computer installed at Osaka University, and successfully compiled a database of fifty major romances. The project group published *A Concordance to Middle English Metrical Romances* (1988), in two volumes, including four romances labeled as Matter of England, and the seven Breton lays, but then had to abandon publishing the concordances to the rest of the romances because personal computers and concordance programmes had become so readily available that, they concluded, "no more paper concordances were necessary."

While Saito spent the 1967-68 academic year under Randolph Quirk at University College London (UCL), the Survey corpus of contemporary English did not attract his attention. In the 1980s, however, reports of the ongoing compilation of computer-readable historical/diachronic corpora, such as the Century of Prose Corpus and the Helsinki Corpus, provoked his interest in corpus linguistics. He later organized and chaired a symposium on "English studies and computers" at the 1990 Convention of the Modern English Association, which resulted in his editing a collection of papers, *Studies in English Language and Literature and Computers* (1992) [in Japanese], the first of its kind in Japan. The publication of this book was instrumental in the founding of the Japan Association for English Corpus Studies (JAECS) in 1993. This organization, which he presided over for 8 years, started with about 60 members, and has now grown to more than 400 members. This organization promoted corpus linguistics in Japan through inviting eminent corpus linguists, such as Jan Svartvik and Graeme Kennedy in 1997, Geoffrey Leech in 1999, and Douglas Biber and Randi Reppen in 2000 to deliver lectures at semi-annual conventions.

His next major project was the text (written in Japanese), Toshio Saito, Junsaku Nakamura, and Ichiro Akano (eds), *English Corpus Linguistics: Basics and Practice* (1998; revised edition 2005), which is still the best introductory book on English corpus linguistics written in Japanese. Then, together with Shunji Yamazaki and others, he published a Japanese translation (2003) of Biber, Conrad and Reppen (1998) *Corpus Linguistics: Investigating Language Structure and Use.*

One further outcome of Saito's work with JAECS, following on from the preparation of supporting reference works, was the fostering of a thriving English corpus research community in Japan. The obvious next step was to present the work of that group to the global corpus linguistics community. To this end, an edited collection of papers was compiled to show the state of the art in Japan to corpus linguists elsewhere in the world; this volume was published as Toshio Saito, Junsaku Nakamura and Shunji Yamazaki (eds), *English Corpus Linguistics in Japan* (2002). This work completed the circle back to Europe with the help of Jan Aarts (who was Saito's classmate at UCL, and helped in promoting the book proposal) and Geoffrey Leech (who provided the foreword).

After his term as president of JAECS, he has had a continued advisory role in the association, and has been engaged in studying syntactic developments mainly in Late ME and Early ModE, using the Helsinki Corpus, the PPCEME, the PPCME2, the COPC and other diachronic corpora.

The present volume in his honour, combining the contributions of scholars from Japan, Europe, and elsewhere, constitutes a culmination of this goal of integrating Japanese corpus research into the global research community.

GEOFFREY LEECH

Foreword

In this book the reader will find a celebration of the achievements of Toshio Saito, pioneer of corpus linguistics in Japan, who took the lead in founding the Japan Association of English Corpus Studies (JAECS).

Corpus linguistics has advanced immeasurably since I first met Saito in 1968, early in his career and in mine, when we were both under the tutelage of Randolph Quirk (now Lord Quirk) in the Department of English Language and Literature, University College London (UCL). At that time Saito was spending a year as a visiting student at UCL, while I was a very junior lecturer in the same college.

Quirk, as founder and director of the Survey of English Usage at UCL, was then building up his corpus of contemporary English, spoken as well as written. This was a major project which had already attracted international attention, and which in retrospect may be seen as the beginning of the corpus revolution that has transformed the way in which English language research has been carried out in recent decades. Quirk's corpus (which at first existed only on paper) began a year or two before Nelson Francis at Brown University, USA, initiated the first computerized corpus of English in 1961.

Neither Saito nor I were immediately inspired by Quirk's corpus work to begin our own corpus creation. Nevertheless we must have both caught from Quirk a latent 'corpus bug' which came to fruition when our careers had progressed further. I moved to Lancaster where, in 1970, I began with colleagues to create the LOB corpus – imitating the American model of Francis's computer corpus. Saito, on the other hand, had already undertaken an early corpus study in his first published paper 'The Development of the Relative Pronouns in Modern Colloquial English', the result of his Osaka University MA project, in which he studied the language of 49 British plays 1560–1958. As this topic shows, he was from the start primarily a scholar in diachronic linguistics, and during his tenure of a Chair of English at Osaka University (1980-1996) he developed the use of computers and concordances as tools for improving the empirical basis of historical English studies.

The Middle English metrical romances occupy an important though neglected position in English writings. Saito founded a research group which went on to translate some forty romances into Japanese, and to publish them in four volumes. For this Herculean enterprise, the use of concordances, and hence of computers, was a virtual necessity. The final result was a corpus of fifty romances.

The diachronic study of English took another step forward with the creation of the historical Helsinki Corpus, by Matti Rissanen and associates, between 1984 and 1991. This ground-breaking compilation attracted Saito's intense interest: here at last was a true marriage of diachronic linguistics with corpus linguistics. He organized and chaired a symposium on English studies and computers at the 1990 Convention of the Modern English Association, and edited the collection of papers *Studies in English Language and Literature and Computers* (published in Japanese by Eichosha in 1992), the first book on this topic in Japan. The publication of this book led to the founding of the Japan Association for English Corpus Studies (JAECS) in 1993. Ably supported by other founding fathers of JAECS, Mitsunori Imai, Junsaku Nakamura and Ichiro Akano, Saito became its first president – a position he held for eight years. JAECS began with a membership of about 60, which has since increased to over 400.

It is worth reflecting on the importance and success of this foundation of JAECS. To my knowledge, it was the world's first, and for a long time the only, national academic association for corpus linguistics. True, the organization known as ICAME (International Computer Archive of Modern and Medieval English) was founded earlier – in 1977 – and has acted as an international association for corpus linguistics ever since then. However, it has never had institutional membership or subscriptions, and has only relatively recently acquired a constitution. JAECS, on the other hand, was from the start a national association, and its then unique status has only rather recently been matched by the American Association of Applied Corpus Linguistics (AAACL) founded in 1998, and the Spanish Association of Corpus Linguistics (AELINCO) founded in 2008. In 2003 JAECS was awarded collective honorary membership of ICAME.

JAECS has been highly influential in popularizing corpus linguistics in Japan. One important move in this direction was the publication by Saito and his co-editors of an introductory book in Japanese on corpus linguistics: Toshio Saito, Junsaku Nakamura and Ichiro Akano (eds) *English Corpus Linguistics: Basics and Practice* (Kenkyusha 1998; rev. 2005), which is still the best introduction to corpus linguistics written in Japanese. Another means of raising the profile of corpus linguistics in Japan has been the invitation extended by JAECS to visiting corpus linguists such as Jan Svartvik, Graeme Kennedy, Douglas Biber, and Randi Reppen to give special lectures. I have also benefited from the hospitality of JAECS more than once during visits to Japan, and with other visitors from European and English-speaking countries, have been granted honorary membership of JAECS.

In 1996 Saito retired from Osaka University, and in 1999 he took up a chair at Daito Bunka University in Tokyo. Here, his colleague Shunji Yamazaki, with Saito's advice and encouragement, has worked hard to provide funding for various corpus linguistic projects such as sponsored visits from overseas scholars.

What Saito wanted to do most for JAECS was to edit, with colleagues, a collection of papers to demonstrate the state of the art in Japan to corpus linguists around the world. The outcome was a volume edited by Saito, Nakamura and Yamazaki entitled *English Corpus Linguistics in Japan*, published by Rodopi in 2002.

The present volume may be seen as a successor to this earlier volume. Whereas the earlier volume showed the range, variety and quality of corpus research on English in Japan, the present volume is a tribute paid by internationally known scholars, both within and outside Japan, to Saito in recognition of his determination and success in building up corpus-based English linguistics in Japan. The Preface by Yamazaki and Sigley, which follows, gives details of the contributing authors and the contents of the book, but it is worth special mention that the contribution of Saito himself is an excellent example of his meticulous historical scholarship in English syntax. In this paper he makes use of the most advanced and complex tools for diachronic English syntactic research: in particular, the Penn-Helsinki Parsed Corpus of Early Modern English (PPCEME). He thus demonstrates that, from the earlier and more primitive days of computerized diachronic linguistics he has moved on to take advantage of the more powerful and advanced corpus resources available at the present day.

The contributors to this book need no further introduction from me. Collectively, they illustrate leading trends in contemporary corpus studies of variation and change in English.

Geoffrey Leech
Lancaster University

SHUNJI YAMAZAKI / ROBERT SIGLEY

Preface: Approaching Variation

The present book is a single-volume collection of research papers using corpora to explore variation in the use of English. "Corpora" are defined here as "systematically-collected samples of authentic language production", and "variation" is defined inclusively as "different preferences for use under different conditions". Together, the papers represent many different dimensions of variation, including: differences in (frequency of) use under different linguistic conditions; differences between styles or registers of use; change over time; differences between regional varieties; differences between social groups; and differences in use by one individual on different occasions.

Corpus-based study of language, as a methodological approach, is primarily observation-based. Whether the level of interest is phonological, lexical, grammatical, stylistic, or social, the starting point in all cases is a description of authentic examples of language use. Such observations are typically subsequently aggregated in a description of distribution patterns, whether in terms of probabilities (frequencies of occurrence in different linguistic, textual, or social environments), or in terms of the most typical or frequent possibilities of usage (constructions, combinations or collocations) observed in our data. Explanations may then be proposed for the observed distribution patterns, and those explanations may be tested by further more detailed description, or by observations on fresh data. Our observations may be used to challenge existing ideas and models of language, and to construct improved or radically different models; hence the end point of corpus-based research may be somewhat more theoretical. Nevertheless, the most prominent distinguishing feature of this field of research is a solid grounding in observed facts; and one of the most consistently observed facts about language use is the rich potential for variation.

Even the most cursory observation of a large sample of usage will confirm that there are different preferences for language use under different conditions. Such variation appears to be an inseparable part of language use; and evidence regarding such variation is the main contribution of corpus-based approaches to language. Any observation-based study of language use must be able to describe and explain correlates of variation: whether as part of the synchronic language system (as seen in the "variable rule" tradition, studying isolated linguistic variables in the narrow sense of meaning-preserving alternations of form in pronunciation, word choice, morphosyntax, or grammar); or when investigating change over time in functions within the language system; or stylistic variation across text types; or differences in use by different groups of language producers.

In consequence, this is where corpus linguistics differs most consistently from more traditional approaches to the description of language use: rather than trying to dismiss variation as irrelevant to some ideal rule system, corpus linguists typically try to engage directly with the observed variation. Many different dimensions of variation can potentially be investigated using corpora, including anything that we can describe in distributional terms.

However, the dimensions of variation that we can most easily investigate are determined by the type of data available in the corpus. Several dimensions fall out immediately from the purpose of a corpus, as a systematic sample of observed authentic language use that seeks to represent some selected language producer(s), in selected genre(s), of some selected dialect(s) of a language. It follows that corpora are typically nested samples, in which dimensions of language variety (dialect), social group, style or register, and time period may all be present. In practice, for different purposes of collection, some of these dimensions may be controlled to varying extents: thus, the collection protocols and aims for a specific corpus determine the extent to which each of these various dimensions can be utilized in that corpus. The main objective of most of the general corpora so far made widely available has been to represent some standard variety of contemporary English (such as "edited written American English" in the case of the Brown corpus), keeping time and dialect constant. Most such corpora are subdivided by text type, allowing controlled internal comparisons of usage by register or style. Cross-comparisons between parallel corpora of this kind allow controlled study of regional or time-based variation (e.g. Brown against LOB for American vs. British writings, or LOB against FLOB for 1961 vs. 1991 British English). By contrast, the time dimension is the main focus of the Helsinki Corpus, which is primarily intended for study of language change (though information on region, genre, and writers of texts is also available).

One of our aims in editing this volume was to represent a wide range of different approaches to variation within corpus linguistics, firstly by representing studies on as many different dimensions of variation as possible. Accordingly, the papers in this collection are grouped into four broad sections corresponding to different dimensions of interest. However, an equally important aim of this collection is to illustrate that researchers, regardless of their specific focus, also need to keep other possible sources of variation in mind in order to fully interpret corpus data. As such, any classification of papers by primary dimension of focus is inevitably somewhat arbitrary, because it is extremely difficult to interpret results for one dimension of variation independently of all the others. For this reason, the first section consists of several papers that explicitly address the multidimensional nature of variation observed in corpus data. These papers introduce, and suggest solutions for, specific methodological problems in the use of real language samples.

A recurring theme in the papers collected here (but most explicitly stated in Johansson's initial survey) is that researchers need to make careful, informed selections from the data available, in order to make maximally controlled comparisons, and thus to be able to interpret their findings. Johansson illustrates this point with reference to specific linguistic variables, in particular the distribution of the modal *shall*. The next paper, by Sigley, continues this theme, using a broader stylistic measure of "formality" to conduct general comparisons of the "standard" corpora modelled on LOB and Brown, in order to assess how far these corpora, and each text category within these corpora, can be treated as fully parallel samples. Both Johansson and Sigley note that the variation between registers within each corpus is much greater than overall differences between different standard varieties of English, and so register needs to be carefully controlled in order to study regional variation. Sigley also notes ways in which the textual distribution of a linguistic difference between corpora may be used to choose among competing explanations for that difference.

Furthermore, even within one dialect, it is generally necessary for researchers to think in terms of cumulative and interacting effects from different situational, social, or linguistic factors. This point is amply demonstrated by Hoffmann and Sigley's analysis of variation between *that* and Ø in the mandative subjunctive, which compares the results of overall frequency comparisons with the output of a variable-rule model. Hoffmann and Sigley raise the important issues of how variables should be defined for study (they favour an empirical approach, comparing usage in different linguistic environments, and grouping together environments that follow similar constraints), and of how confounding factors, or associations between proposed causal factors, can be identified and corrected for in order to more accurately interpret findings (using a logistic regression model).

The second section consists of case studies primarily describing features of language usage in different linguistic environments in modern English. Even so, the three studies included in this section illustrate three very different approaches to the study of linguistic function, in that they make use of different types of information about the distribution of tokens in a corpus. Kennedy's comparison of the usage of ten common verbs denoting mental processes in the British National Corpus uses semantic features of collocations to illustrate distinctions in word meaning. Fukaya's study of variation in the use of *when* and *though* concentrates more on grammatical features of surrounding constructions to illustrate syntactic function, and considers the observed uses of these words in terms of a functional continuum between syntactic properties defining prototypical behaviour for the grammatical categories of conjunctions and subordinators. Finally, Yamazaki's investigation of variation in the distribution of comparative and superlative forms across text category in LOB, Brown, FLOB and Frown uses the distribution of competing forms across text category, time, and regional variety to map the progress of ongoing linguistic change.

The time dimension is more directly a focus of the papers in the third section, which investigate change over time in corpora representing different historical periods of English. Each of the first three studies focuses on a small number of closely related variables. Rissanen describes the variation in use of the adverbial subordination markers *þe* and *þæt* in Old English texts. Saito investigates competition between different constructions using gerund forms in Early Modern English. Iyeiri uses a corpus of texts from Chaucer and Caxton to document the beginnings of grammatical and semantic changes in usage of the verb *pray*. In contrast, Tsukamoto takes a multi-feature approach, using observed patterns of change in a much wider range of variables to attempt to define the boundaries of, and distinguishable periods of development within, Middle English.

The papers in the final section illustrate variation in usage for different purposes, or by different groups or individuals, in society. Using selected components of the International Corpus of English, Peters compares variation in choice of pronoun case in different regional varieties of English, and finds evidence for the influence of pragmatic factors in some registers less subject to prescription. In terms of methodology, the final two papers are more focussed case studies, with a more careful interpretation of individual examples of usage. In an application of corpus approaches to a literary work, Hori describes the stylistic differences between the constructed voices of a male and female character in Hemingway's short story 'Hills Like White Elephants', with reference to other literary sources and to spoken data from the British National Corpus. Finally, Stubbe analyses the use of verbal feedback devices in a sample of conversational data drawn from the Wellington Corpus of New Zealand English by gender and ethnicity. Her careful functional analysis of the data indicates the importance of context in determining how verbal feedback is used, and highlights some of the problems with interpreting variation in relation to gender and the use of interactive discourse variables in corpus data.

Despite the wide range of variation displayed here in topic and method, the main aim throughout this collection is to present practical solutions, in an approachable manner (grounded by real case studies), for methodological and interpretational problems common in such research. We have been especially concerned with making the research methods followed, and the reasons for choosing them, as transparent as possible, to educate and inspire future researchers. The present work is not intended as a textbook in its own right, but as an important stand-alone resource book suitable for students undertaking their first research projects. It thus aims to bridge the gap between introductory corpus linguistics textbooks, and more specialised anthologies of research.

Acknowledgements

The Editors would like to thank the contributors for their patience and understanding, and Geoffrey Leech for his support and advice.

Section 1
Evaluating Approaches: Some Methodological Issues

STIG JOHANSSON

Interpreting Textual Distribution: Social and Situational Factors

1. Beyond free variation[1]

There was a time when social and situational factors of language use tended to be overlooked in mainstream linguistics:

> It is customary (except in works devoted specifically to this question) to abstract from synchronic variation in language, either by restricting the description of a language to the speech of a particular group using a particular 'style', or by describing the language in terms of such generality that the description is valid (in intention at least) for all 'varieties'. Some degree of 'idealization' is involved in either of these two procedures, and this may be necessary at the present stage of linguistic theory. (Lyons 1968: 50)

Variation was not denied, but the main focus was on describing language structure in isolation from the conditions of use. With the development of variationist sociolinguistics, pioneered by Labov (1966, 1972), it became increasingly apparent that language use is conditioned to a great extent by social and situational factors and that these cannot be ignored in language description. What some may have rejected as 'free variation' turned out to be highly patterned.

The availability of computer corpora has greatly advanced our knowledge of language variation. Whereas studies within the quantitative sociolinguistic paradigm were often concerned with individual linguistic features elicited in an experimental situation, computer corpora have provided easy access to a vast amount and a broad range of authentic texts. Given these data sources and the associated analysis tools, it has become possible to analyse language variation in great

---

1 For comments on an earlier version of this paper, I am grateful to Bengt Altenberg, Lund University, my colleagues Johan Elsness and Hilde Hasselgård, University of Oslo, and Geoffrey Leech, University of Lancaster.

depth and on a scale which was not possible before. Interpreting linguistic variation may not be straightforward, however. In this paper I focus on research on publicly available corpora of present-day English texts, many of which were specifically designed for language comparison. In the conclusion, I suggest some directions for future research.

2. The Brown family

To start with two of the earliest and most influential English corpora, *The Brown Corpus* and *The Lancaster-Oslo/Bergen Corpus* (LOB), these were designed to be representative of printed American and British English texts, respectively. The aim of the LOB Corpus project was to assemble a British English counterpart of the Brown Corpus. Rather than concentrating on limited categories of texts to be used for specific purposes, both corpora were intended to provide a general representation of written text categories for use in research on a broad range of aspects of the language. To facilitate comparison, an attempt was made to match the British English material as closely as possible with the American corpus. Both contain 500 text extracts of about 2,000 words each, or about a million words in all. The year of publication (1961) and the sampling principles were identical, though there were necessarily some differences in text selection (Johansson *et al.* 1978). The basic composition of the corpora is summarised in Table 1. The two corpora have been extensively used both for inter- and intra-corpus comparisons.

Text categories	Number of texts in each text category	
	Brown	LOB
A Press: reportage	44	44
B Press: editorial	27	27
C Press: reviews	17	17
D Religion	17	17
E Skills, trades, and hobbies	*36*	*38*
F Popular lore	*48*	*44*
G Belles letters, biography, essays	*75*	*77*
H Miscellaneous / government documents	30	30
J Learned and scientific writings	80	80
K General fiction	29	29
L Mystery and detective fiction	24	24
M Science fiction	6	6
N Adventure and western fiction	29	29
P Romance and love story	29	29
R Humour	9	9
Total	500	500

Table 1. The basic composition of the Brown Corpus and the LOB Corpus (differences are marked in italics).

2.1. Comparing LOB and Brown

Soon after the completion of the Brown Corpus, its compilers published a quantitative description of the corpus (Kučera/Francis 1967), focusing in particular on word frequency and sentence length. After the completion of the LOB Corpus, a similar quantitative account was given (Hofland/Johansson 1982), which included lists comparing frequencies in the LOB Corpus and the Brown Corpus, as well as some discussion of differences on various levels: spelling, word form, auxiliary verbs, and some semantic groups of words. Some sample frequency comparisons are given in Table 2 below.

Word	LOB	Brown	Word	LOB	Brown
behavior	9	96	*railroad(s)*	1	74
behaviour	119	3	*railway(s)*	66	13
spelled	2	6	*holiday(s)*	107	29
spelt	9	0	*vacation(s)*	3	59
downward	11	16	*baseball*	1	57
downwards	16	0	*cricket*	21	3
he/his/him	17603	19412	*man/men*	1789	2113
she/her/hers	8163	6037	*woman/women*	486	468
shall	348	267	*Mr.*	1508	839
should	1,276	888	*Mrs.*	292	535

Table 2. Raw frequency comparisons for the LOB and Brown corpora (data from Hofland/Johansson 1982).

Many of the differences observed confirmed what was already known about British vs. American English language (e.g. the differences in spelling and vocabulary variants known to be associated with the respective national varieties) and culture (e.g. in the popularity of baseball vs. cricket). Such findings served to raise confidence in the use of the two corpora for inter-corpus comparison, and to permit some confidence in cases where results were new and unexpected, such as the marked gender bias, with higher frequencies for masculine forms of pronouns and explicit reference to *man/men* in Brown, and for feminine forms and reference to *woman/women* in LOB (though the title forms *Mr.* and *Mrs.* showed an opposite trend). Both corpora agreed in having generally much higher frequencies for the masculine than for the feminine forms, though the contrast was especially striking in the American corpus.

Using the frequency lists of Hofland/Johansson (1982) as a starting-point, Leech/Fallon (1992) further analysed cultural differences between the two corpora, revealing consistent differences in a number of domains: sport, travel and transport, administration and politics, social hierarchy, military, law and crime, business, mass media, science and technology, education, arts, religion, etc. As for the differences with respect to gender-related terms, they note that "the USA was in 1961 already ripe for the feminist movement which hit it in the later 1960s" (1992: 43). Summing up the analysis, they:

> propose a picture of US culture in 1961 – masculine to the point of machismo, militaristic, dynamic and actuated by high ideals, driven by technology, activ-

> ity and enterprise – contrasting with one of British culture as more given to temporizing and talking, to benefitting from wealth rather than creating it, and to family and emotional life, less actuated by matters of substance than by considerations of outward status. (1992: 44f.)

They are, however, careful to point out weaknesses of this type of comparison, a topic that will be taken up in Section 2.3.

The Brown and the LOB corpora have also been used for a large number of studies comparing aspects of grammar: modal auxiliaries, the subjunctive, verb complementation, the genitive, etc.[2] Some studies which include other members of the Brown family will be referred to in Section 2.4. After the Brown and LOB corpora had been tagged for part of speech, it was possible to compare word-class distributions, as in Table 3,[3] which shows that there is good agreement between the two corpora. The rank order of the word classes is almost identical, and even the absolute numbers are very close. This contrasts with the considerable differences evident between the two broad text category groups of informative prose (categories A–J) and imaginative prose (categories K–R) in the LOB Corpus. The same picture emerges from a comparison of sentence length (Johansson/Hofland 1989, vol. 1: 17), where again, the overall tendencies are very similar in both corpora, while in each corpus there are notable differences between text categories, with a consistently higher average sentence length in informative prose. In other words, differences between the two corpora are less marked than those within each corpus. This brings us to intra-corpus comparison.

---

2 See Altenberg (1991), and the ICAME bibliography archived at: <http://gandalf.aksis.uib.no/whatis.html>.

3 Table 3 is based on Johansson/Hofland (1989: 15). The figures for the Brown Corpus are quoted from Francis/Kučera (1982).

Word class	LOB			Brown
	A–J (%)	K–R (%)	Total	
Nouns	26.9	20.0	254,992	272,984
Verbs	16.4	21.9	179,975	185,393
Determiners	13.0	10.5	125,018	123,321
Prepositions	13.1	9.6	123,440	122,613
Adjectives	7.8	5.7	73,546	72,034
Pronouns	5.0	13.1	71,498	66,879
Adverbs	5.0	7.2	56,083	53,283
Conjunctions	5.5	5.4	55,516	60,328
Numerals	2.2	0.9	19,126	20,853
Infinitival *to*	1.5	1.7	15,837	15,030
WH-words	1.5	1.6	15,718	14,921
Not	0.6	1.1	7,454	6,976
Existential *there*	0.3	0.3	2,794	2,280
Interjections	0.0	0.4	1,109	629
Other	1.3	0.7	11,631	–

Table 3. The word-class distribution in the tagged LOB Corpus (A–J: informative prose; K–R: imaginative prose) and the Brown Corpus (total).

2.2. *Intra-corpus comparison*

Just a glance at the distribution of text categories in Table 1 above makes it clear that there is a need for caution in using the two corpora for intra-corpus comparison, most obviously because the text categories vary greatly in size and some of them are very small indeed.[4] Nevertheless, an intra-corpus comparison may be revealing, at least in connection with common features of the language. Table 3 above shows that there are considerable differences in word-class distribution between the two subsets of the LOB Corpus. In informative prose the relatively more common types were nouns, determiners, prepositions, adjectives, and numerals. In imaginative prose they were verbs, pronouns, adverbs, *not*,

4 Oostdijk (1988: 17) observes that "corpora […] compiled with the intention of representing a cross-section of a language are not suited for the study of linguistic variation since, in selecting a great many samples, they neutralize any variety-specificity." However, the problem may be more accurately characterised as one of range than of number of samples – especially, that these corpora include text types subject to a high degree of standardisation, in which variation may be expected to be minimised. (See also Sigley, this volume.)

and interjections. Most of the differences are evidence of greater complexity at the noun phrase level in informative prose. In imaginative prose the verbs are more prominent (and elements accompanying verbs: adverbs, *not*); the verbs, in fact, outnumber the nouns. There are also considerable differences in word class sequences between the two category groups (Johansson/Hofland 1989, vol. 2: 3); thus, for example, the sequence 'singular noun plus singular noun' is more than twice as frequent in informative prose as in the fiction categories.

An intra-corpus comparison of the most frequent words may also be revealing (Hofland/Johansson 1982: 340ff.). For example, the definite article – the most frequent word in the English language – has a higher relative frequency in all the informative prose categories than in the categories of imaginative prose. By contrast, the modal auxiliary *could* is relatively more frequent in all the categories of imaginative prose than in the categories of informative prose. For less frequent words as well, an intra-corpus comparison may reveal interesting patterns. Tables 4–7 list some of the words most strongly distinguishing text category J (learned and scientific writings) from K–R (fiction): more specifically, the 40 nouns (except proper nouns and abbreviations), lexical verbs, adjectives, and adverbs with the highest 'distinctiveness coefficient' in each group.[5] A number of general observations can be made on the basis of these comparisons. For example, in Table 4, the nouns in J are predominantly abstract, whereas those in K–R are concrete. In Table 5, the verbs in J include a variety of verb forms and process types, whereas those in K–R are almost all *-ed* forms and denote material or behavioural processes. The differences between the adjectives (Table 6) and the adverbs (Table 7) are equally striking.

5 Tables 4-7 are quoted from Hofland/Johansson (1982: 28f.). The distinctiveness coefficient used (1982: 14) is Yule's difference coefficient, $= [f_A - f_B] / [f_A + f_B]$.

Nouns distinctive of Academic writing (J)		Nouns distinctive of Fiction (K–R)	
constants	*oxygen*	*mister*	*dad*
axis	*sodium*	*sofa*	*lawn*
equations	*equilibrium*	*wallet*	*receiver*
oxides	*oxide*	*cheek*	*madam*
equation	*variable*	*living-room*	*jacket*
theorem	*evaporation*	*cafe*	*fool*
coefficient	*contamination*	*wrist*	*pistol*
ions	*approximation*	*darling*	*envelope*
correlation	*alloy*	*sigh*	*shoulders*
electrons	*hydrogen*	*gun*	*door*
impurities	*ratios*	*gaze*	*forehead*
oxidation	*data*	*clip*	*phone*
parameters	*component*	*fist*	*knees*
nickel	*symmetry*	*trail*	*tears*
electron	*curve*	*lounge*	*bedroom*
impurity	*displacement*	*cheeks*	*fingers*
diagram	*computer*	*lips*	*patch*
ion	*cells*	*cigarette*	*skirt*
parameter	*curves*	*stairs*	*eyes*
coefficients	*particle*	*footsteps*	*pocket*

Table 4. Nouns occurring with higher than expected frequency in categories J vs. K–R of the LOB Corpus (listed in descending order of distinctiveness).

Lexical verbs distinctive of Academic writing (J)		Lexical verbs distinctive of Fiction (K–R)	
measured	*occur*	*kissed*	*muttered*
assuming	*stressed*	*heaved*	*stared*
calculated	*illustrates*	*leaned*	*flung*
occurs	*recognized*	*glanced*	*grinned*
assigned	*identified*	*smiled*	*laughed*
emphasized	*testing*	*hesitated*	*shrugged*
obtained	*follows*	*exclaimed*	*jerked*
executed	*observed*	*murmured*	*tapping*
tested	*tend*	*gasped*	*laughing*
corresponding	*demonstrated*	*hurried*	*swung*
vary	*exposed*	*flushed*	*pretended*
bending	*containing*	*cried*	*leaning*
varying	*deposited*	*eyed*	*wondered*
loading	*using*	*staring*	*shook*
measuring	*forming*	*paused*	*kiss*
determine	*indicates*	*whispered*	*straightened*
isolated	*examine*	*waved*	*rang*
dissolved	*associated*	*nodded*	*sounded*
resulting	*indicate*	*frowned*	*gripped*
defined	*obtain*	*shivered*	*smiling*

Table 5. Lexical verbs occurring with higher than expected frequency in categories J vs. K–R of the LOB Corpus (listed in descending order of distinctiveness).

Adjectives distinctive of Academic writing (J)		Adjectives distinctive of Fiction (K–R)	
thermal	*chemical*	*damned*	*worried*
linear	*internal*	*asleep*	*tired*
radioactive	*initial*	*sorry*	*stupid*
structural	*reliable*	*gay*	*polite*
finite	*significant*	*miserable*	*savage*
transient	*continuous*	*dear*	*quiet*
physiological	*relevant*	*silly*	*tall*
numerical	*prior*	*empty*	*lonely*
magnetic	*intermediate*	*stiff*	*glad*
conceptual	*liquid*	*dreadful*	*damp*
residual	*equal*	*afraid*	*dark*
differential	*rapid*	*deadly*	*mad*
stationary	*constant*	*sweet*	*pretty*
statistical	*imperial*	*ashamed*	*quick*
negative	*consistent*	*lovely*	*pink*
relative	*positive*	*faint*	*clean*
experimental	*upper*	*calm*	*sudden*
theoretical	*aesthetic*	*silent*	*desperate*
integral	*statutory*	*nice*	*loud*
mechanical	*external*	*funny*	*ugly*

Table 6. Adjectives occurring with higher than expected frequency in categories J vs. K–R of the LOB Corpus (listed in descending order of distinctiveness).

Adverbs distinctive of Academic writing (J)		Adverbs distinctive of Fiction (K–R)	
theoretically	*widely*	*impatiently*	*slowly*
significantly	*strictly*	*softly*	*desperately*
approximately	*mainly*	*hastily*	*sharply*
hence	*directly*	*nervously*	*away*
relatively	*partly*	*upstairs*	*barely*
respectively	*previously*	*faintly*	*backwards*
commonly	*specifically*	*quietly*	*somehow*
separately	*chiefly*	*abruptly*	*utterly*
consequently	*presumably*	*eagerly*	*aboard*
similarly	*closely*	*upright*	*down*
rapidly	*accordingly*	*tomorrow*	*lightly*
thus	*frequently*	*downstairs*	*quickly*
furthermore	*however*	*gently*	*inside*
sufficiently	*moreover*	*anyway*	*carefully*
therefore	*nevertheless*	*maybe*	*again*
secondly	*unfortunately*	*swiftly*	*off*
ultimately	*briefly*	*presently*	*then*
readily	*considerably*	*suddenly*	*never*
effectively	*purely*	*somewhere*	*sooner*
generally	*originally*	*back*	*scarcely*

Table 7. Adverbs occurring with higher than expected frequency in categories J vs. K–R of the LOB Corpus (listed in descending order of distinctiveness).

An early ambitious undertaking designed to study intra-corpus variation is Alvar Ellegård's Syntax Data Project (Ellegård 1978). Samples from the Brown Corpus, more exactly 16 texts from each of text categories A,

G, J, and N, were analysed manually on three levels – clause structure of sentences, constituent structure of clauses, and word class of individual words – with the aim of providing "an as nearly complete as possible parsing" (1978: 1). Among the project's findings is that:

> The language seems to be remarkably stable as regards such features as the number of clauses per sentence, and the depth of embedding for such clauses. We might have expected the popular [fiction] texts to have much shorter sentences (in terms of clauses) and much less embedding than the literary and scientific ones. There is indeed a slight tendency in this direction, but it is very weak. (1978: 76).

The distribution of clause types is also quite similar, though one might have expected fewer subordinate clauses in the popular fiction texts. The stability is confirmed by the striking similarity between half-samples from the same text category. The most notable differences have to do with the distribution of word classes – e.g. more verbs and fewer nouns in the popular texts – and the length and complexity of phrases – lowest in the popular fiction texts (N), highest in the scientific texts (J), with the journalistic (A) and literary texts (G), as in most cases, occupying the middle ground.

As a final example of intra-corpus comparison, consider the distribution of *shall* in the LOB and Brown corpora, shown in Figure 1.[6] In spite of the overall difference between the corpora (see Section 2.1), the distribution across text categories is very similar: *shall* in category H accounts for the majority of the examples and is about equally common in both corpora; the main difference is found in fiction, where the frequency is much higher in the LOB Corpus, though it is far lower than the figure for category H.[7] Hence, again, we see that differences between the two corpora are less marked than those within each corpus.

---

6 The frequencies for *shall* given here and in the comparisons below include the form *shan't*. There were very few occurrences of *shan't* (e.g. five in LOB, all from fiction; and only one in Brown). The few instances of *shalt* (found in historical quotations, and therefore not representing current English) are not included.

7 For a more detailed account, see Krogvig and Johansson (1984).

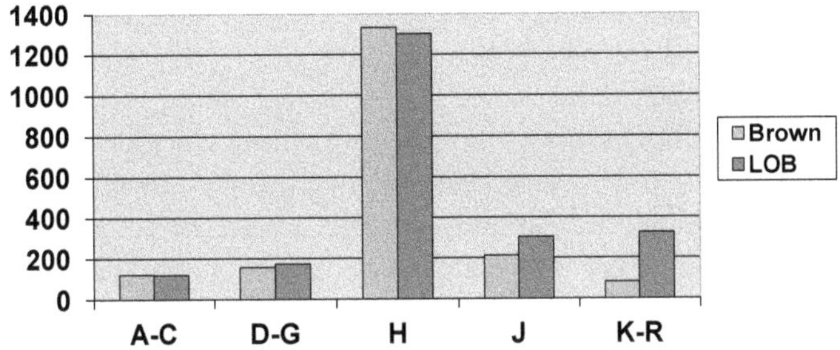

Figure 1. The distribution of *shall* in text categories of the Brown and LOB corpora (relative frequency per million words).

2.3. Provisional conclusion

If we want to use the two corpora for conclusions on the relationship between British and American English, there is a need for caution. In the first place, the corpora are quite small and contain relatively short text samples, which limits their usefulness for studies of lexis and discourse patterns. Second, they lack many important text categories, notably different types of speech. Third, as we have seen, there may be greater differences within each corpus than between the corpora. For this reason, it is hazardous to interpret textual distributions without considering intra-corpus variation. Any study of textual distributions between the corpora should therefore take intra-corpus variation into account.[8]

Differences between corpora are often quantitative rather than absolute. For this reason, there is a need for statistical testing. Many of the items in our lists comparing words in the LOB and Brown corpora (Hofland/Johansson 1982: 471ff.) include chi-square values. We stress, however, that these should only be regarded as a rough guide:

> The only thing we can be certain of is that the absence of a significant chi-square value is a good indication that a difference is accidental. It is far more doubtful whether a significant chi-square value justifies safe conclusions

8 One example of such a study is Nakamura's (1993) quantitative comparison of modals in the LOB and Brown corpora; another is the quantitative analysis of modals in Wilson (2005).

> about frequency differences. The reader is encouraged to look for consistent behaviour of related words. (1982: 39)

Kilgarriff (2001a) has identified several problems in using the chi-square test for this kind of comparison, and recommends the use of other tests, such as Mann-Whitney U. Certainly, there is a need for better statistical measures. However, there is also a more general problem, that statistical significance is at best an unreliable indicator of whether or not differences are linguistically important, or can be given a reasonable linguistic interpretation (as also discussed by Hundt 1998: 123ff). Here it is useful to look for consistent behaviour across individual observations, as suggested in the quotation above. A simple example in Hofland/Johansson (1982: 40) compares the frequencies of the words *firstly, secondly, thirdly, fourthly* in LOB and Brown. Each word count is very low, but the pattern is extremely consistent: every one of these forms occurs with higher frequency in LOB (respectively 14, 29, 10, 3) than in Brown (respectively 0, 5, 1, 0), which strongly suggests some systematic difference in their use between British and American English.

Leech/Fallon's cultural comparison (Section 2.1) provides other examples, as do the lists in Tables 4-7 above, in the latter case to do with intra-corpus comparison. By itself, the distribution of a single word may not mean much; but when viewed together, word distributions build up an interpretable pattern.

Another aspect of the comparison of word frequencies, as found in Hofland/Johansson (1982), is that it focuses on form rather than meaning. Yet we know that homonymy and polysemy are prevalent in the language. Interpreting the distribution of forms, without considering meaning, requires great caution. Ideally, we should study forms in context, a point which applies both to lexis and grammar. It is a problem that the use of electronic corpora may tempt one to look only at frequency distributions, ignoring context, or at concordances, without consulting the wider context. This is not a flaw of the corpus itself, but rather of the way it is used. Electronic corpora make it possible for the researcher to examine both macro- and micro-level patterns, varying the analysis according to the focus of the study.

2.4. Extending the family

The Brown and LOB corpora have served as models for other corpora, as listed in Table 8. The corpora differ not only in regional variety, but also in the time of publication of the texts. In all cases, however, the compilers of the new corpora attempted to follow the Brown and LOB sampling principles as closely as possible. Nevertheless, there were necessarily some differences. Shastri, the compiler of *The Kolhapur Corpus*, points out that the fiction categories differ from those of the LOB and Brown corpora "because of the inherent difference in the Indian situation" (Shastri 1988: 17). The categories 'Science fiction', 'Adventure and Western fiction', and 'Romance and love story' are much smaller, and more texts are included in the 'General fiction' category (K). The sample of imaginative writing in WWC is "a single category of general fiction, not subdivided into specific genres (owing to the paucity of special-genre fiction written, edited and published within New Zealand)" (Sigley 1997: 211; see also Sigley, this volume). Sand/Siemund (1992) report that there were difficulties in matching the texts of the press categories of FLOB with those of LOB, but comment that, nevertheless, they "ranked the comparability of LOB '91 to LOB '61 higher in priority than the possible alternative goal, viz. to create the accurate picture of the British printed press right now" (1992: 120).

Corpus	Abbreviation	Date of corpus texts
Australian Corpus of English	ACE	1986
Brown Corpus	Brown	1961
Freiburg-Brown	Frown	1992
Freiburg-LOB	FLOB	1991
Kolhapur Corpus	–	1978
Lancaster-Oslo/Bergen Corpus	LOB	1961
Wellington Corpus of Written New Zealand English	WWC	1986

Table 8. The extended Brown family.

In the building of comparable corpora, there is necessarily a tension between comparability and representativeness.[9] In the case of the LOB and Brown corpora, it was generally possible to sample in a corresponding manner, though there were problems, such as finding British texts to match American western fiction. In matching the composition of corpora for other regional varieties (whether for the other members of the Brown family, or for the International Corpus of English [ICE]), problems are often greater (see Section 6.1). The tension between comparability and representativeness is something we have to live with, but it means that the researcher must take great care in interpreting the results of corpus comparison. We must consider to what extent observed differences may be due to a sampling bias, and to what extent the corpus findings can be regarded as representative of the varieties the corpora are intended to represent.

As an example, consider first the distribution of *shall* in the Kolhapur Corpus, as compared with the Brown and LOB Corpora. The overall distribution is: 269 tokens in Brown; 354 in LOB; 364 in Kolhapur.[10] Thus the frequency for *shall* is higher in the Kolhapur Corpus than in the other corpora, as noted by Shastri (1988: 18), who speculates:

> This may be due to the predominance of written language over spoken in the Indian pedagogical context. Also, English in India, taught as a second language, tends to retain some of the older usages which might have lost currency in the first language situation.

If we compare the distribution across text categories, we find that the overall tendency is the same as in LOB and Brown; but *shall* is considerably more common in Category H, as shown in Figure 2. The data

9 See the discussion in Leech/Smith (2005: 87ff.), where the issue of representativeness vs. comparability is raised in connection with the planning of Lancaster 1931, a new corpus designed to match LOB and FLOB. It is pointed out that "[t]he next planned extension to our project will be a further prequel of this kind, that is, a matching corpus of British English texts published in 1901, provisionally named Lancaster 1901" (p. 84). As the time span is increased, the sampling difficulties will multiply.

10 The figures for *shall* exclude the negative form *shan't*, which was rare in all the corpora (the highest frequencies being 5 in LOB, and 3 in FLOB; all British English examples came from fiction texts).

from this category needs to be examined in more detail before any definite conclusions can be drawn. Given that different institutions may be represented in official documents for different countries, the difference observed seems likely to reflect differences in some specific institutional norms of usage, rather than any more systematic difference in language. However, within those institutions, Shastri's explanation of the difference may still be valid.

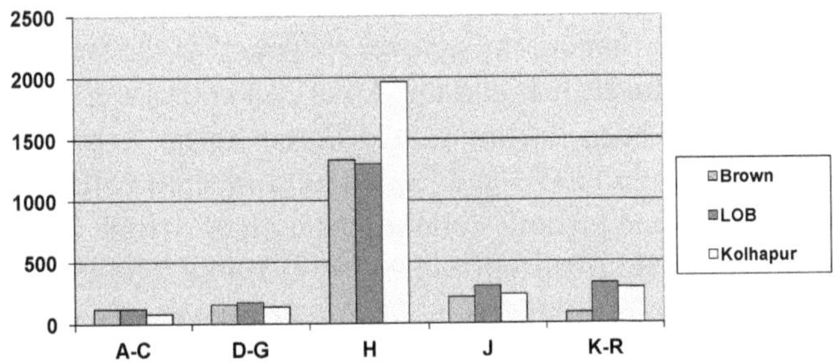

Figure 2. The distribution of *shall* in text categories of the Brown, LOB, and Kolhapur corpora (relative frequency per million words).

If we move on to a comparison of the Brown, Frown, LOB, and FLOB corpora, we find 269 tokens of *shall* in Brown; 149 in Frown; 354 in LOB; and 197 in FLOB. These figures indicate that for both the British and the American corpora, there has been a reduction in the use of *shall* in the period from 1961 to 1991/92. Moreover, the gap between the British and American corpora has grown smaller. The latter might be due to a trend towards Americanisation in British English. But how could we explain the decline in both American and British English?

At this point, we turn to Leech (2004), which examines the distribution of the modal auxiliaries, including *shall*, in the Brown, Frown, LOB, and FLOB corpora. This paper is a model with respect to the care taken in analysing and interpreting the data. Leech lists some "hazardous assumptions: from data description to language description" (2004: 70), which deserve to be quoted in full:

1. That the corpora are large enough and varied/balanced enough to allow us to extrapolate from corpus findings to what is happening in (relevant varieties of) the language in general.

2. That the corpora are sufficiently comparable in terms of samples of the varieties represented, and in using the same sampling methods.

3. That statistically significant results can be attributed to real linguistic differences, rather than to extraneous factors such as cultural shifts or faulty sampling.

4. That the grammatical categories are defined and used in a way that other grammarians or linguists find reasonable.

5. That the extraction of data from the corpora has been acceptably (if not totally) free from error.

Leech finds that there has been a general reduction in the frequency of the modals both in the British and the American corpora, though individual modals have been declining at different rates. A possible explanation of changes in FLOB and Frown as compared with LOB and Brown might be a trend towards colloquialisation of written English, as suggested in papers by Christian Mair (1997, 1998). The study is extended to changes which might be indicative of a development towards a more colloquial style, and there are indeed some striking findings: an increase in the use of the present progressive, of verb contractions, verbless questions, the genitive, etc. But how could we account for the process of colloquialisation? For this we need to turn to theories of the cognitive and social workings of language.

Before leaving Leech's paper, we need to return to *shall* in the Brown, Frown, LOB, and FLOB corpora. Leech suggests that "it is in the nature of corpus research to be provisional" (2004: 75), and he mentions on the same page that "[o]nce the gross frequency changes have been plotted, the next step is to investigate factors internal to the corpora that might help explain these changes (e.g. differential results in the different subsections of the corpus)". A study of the distribution of *shall* shows that the greatest changes have taken place in category H, in which *shall* has been reduced by more than half between the two generations of corpora, although it still stands out as the text category having the most frequent use of *shall*.

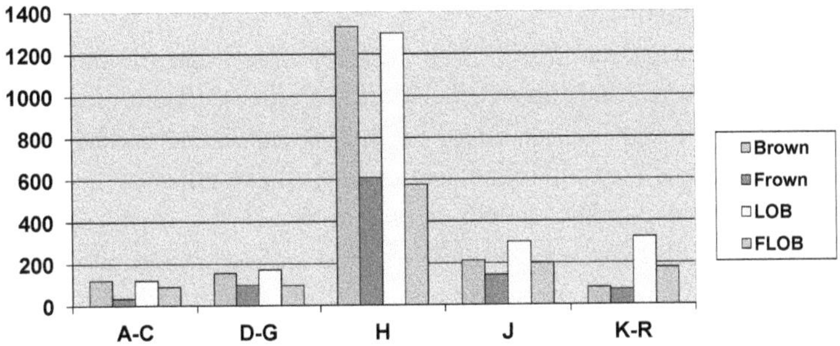

Figure 3. The distribution of *shall* in text categories of the Brown, Frown, LOB, and FLOB corpora (relative frequency per million words).

A closer study of *shall* within category H (Figure 4) reveals that the form is very unevenly distributed, which is not unexpected in this heterogeneous category.[11] The majority of occurrences are concentrated in a limited number of texts. In the LOB Corpus, three texts (H13, H14, and H24, sampling acts, treaties and other official government proceedings) account for 78 of the 95 examples; and in FLOB a single text (H14, a government treaty) accounts for 32 of the 43 examples. Otherwise, the examples are thinly scattered, with no more than three examples in any other text. What this shows is that it is necessary to examine single texts closely before drawing any firm conclusions on developments. A general trend towards colloquialisation is not sufficient to account for the data (see further Section 5). We need instead to investigate what sorts of texts are affected, and in what ways they are changed.

Figure 4. WordSmith dispersion plot for *shall* in Category H of Brown (first line), LOB (second line), Frown (third line), and FLOB (last line).

---

11 Each vertical bar indicates a hit, going from the first to the last text. Where hits cluster closely together, they cannot be singled out individually.

A number of studies have compared members of the extended Brown family, including Hundt (1997, 1998), Mair (1997, 1998), Holmes/Sigley (2002), Mair/Hundt (2002), and survey articles on Australian English (Collins/Peters 2004) and New Zealand English (Hundt *et al.* 2004). Many notable patterns are revealed, e.g. that Australian and New Zealand English are leading the field in the decline of *shall* (Hundt *et al.* 2004: 589). How and why the changes have come about, however, remains something of a puzzle which cannot be solved without a close examination of the distribution in text categories and a close study of individual texts.

3. Speech vs. writing

Form	LOB	Brown	Carroll *et al.* (1971)	Jones/ Sinclair (1974)	Form	LOB	Brown	Carroll *et al.* (1971)	Jones/ Sinclair (1974)
the	1	1	1	1	*have*	26	28	25	25
of	2	2	2	8	*are*	27	24	15	36
and	3	3	3	3	*which*	28	31	41	–
to	4	4	5	6	*her*	29	35	–	–
a	5	5	4	5	*she*	30	37	–	–
in	6	6	6	9	*or*	31	27	26	27
that	7	7	9	11	*you*	32	33	8	4
is	8	8	7	12	*they*	33	30	19	15
was	9	9	13	14	*an*	34	29	39	–
it	10	12	10	7	*were*	35	34	34	–
for	11	11	12	26	*there*	36	38	37	37
he	12	10	11	21	*been*	37	43	–	–
as	13	14	16	40	*one*	38	32	28	28
with	14	13	17	47	*all*	39	36	23	29
be	15	17	21	33	*we*	40	41	36	50
on	16	16	14	23	*their*	41	40	42	–
I	17	20	24	2	*has*	42	44	–	–
his	18	15	18	–	*would*	43	39	–	–
at	19	18	20	35	*when*	44	45	35	–
by	20	19	27	–	*if*	45	50	44	39
had	21	22	29	–	*so*	46	–	–	38
this	22	21	22	20	*no*	47	49	–	18
not	23	23	30	–	*will*	48	47	46	–
but	24	25	31	17	*him*	49	42	–	–
from	25	26	23	–	*who*	50	46	–	–

Table 9. The 50 most frequent words in the LOB Corpus as compared with the ranks of the corresponding words in three other corpora (quoted from Hofland/Johansson 1982: 19; "–" indicates that a word is not found among the 50 most frequent words in the corpus).

A comparison based on the Brown family can only deal with written or, rather, printed texts. What happens if the comparison is extended to speech? A simple comparison of frequency lists shows that there are great differences. Hofland/Johansson (1982) compare the most frequent words in four corpora: LOB, Brown, an American corpus of written texts "to which students are exposed in school grades 3 through 9 in the United States" (Carroll *et al.* 1971: xiii), and a British corpus of spontaneous conversation (Jones/Sinclair 1974). The most frequent words in each corpus are listed in Table 9. The spoken corpus stands out as being strikingly different, not just in relation to the two American corpora, but also as compared with the other British corpus. In fact, the closest correspondences are found between LOB and Brown, and not within the groups of British or American corpora.

The availability of spoken corpora has greatly advanced our knowledge of spoken English and of features which differentiate speech and writing. A major breakthrough was the completion of *The London-Lund Corpus* (Svartvik 1990), which includes a wide range of spoken material collected and transcribed according to the plan for the Survey of English Usage, a project which was designed to collect a corpus of spoken and written texts for use in the description of English (Quirk 1960). Here we are only concerned with the spoken material, which was prepared for computer analysis at Lund University under the direction of Jan Svartvik.[12] Like the members of the Brown family, the London-Lund Corpus (LLC) was made available to the community of researchers through ICAME.[13]

Shortly after the LLC was completed, Bengt Altenberg and Gunnel Tottie initiated a project comparing aspects of speech and writing on the basis of LOB and the LLC. Equal amounts were selected from two sub-varieties: spontaneous conversation from LLC, and expository prose (from categories D–J of LOB), which could be regarded

12 The original London-Lund Corpus consisted of 87 texts of 5,000 words, 34 of which – representing surreptitiously recorded conversation – were published in printed form in Svartvik/Quirk (1980). 13 texts (including one additional conversation text) were added later, after being processed at the Survey of English Usage "in conformity with the system used in the original London-Lund Corpus" (Greenbaum/Svartvik 1990: 14), making the total corpus size approximately 500,000 words.

13 See: <http://gandalf.aksis.uib.no/whatis.html>.

as the archetypal forms of the two media. In the Introduction to the collection of papers from the symposium which marked the end of the project, their choice of data is explained as follows:

> We [...] felt that by restricting our samples to spontaneous conversation and expository prose, we could achieve, at the same time, maximum contrast and maximum comparability – maximum contrast because of the differences in medium as well as formality, and maximum comparability because the speakers participating in the recorded conversations were all educated to academic level, and could be thought of as potential readers or writers of the type of written material included. (Tottie/Bäcklund 1986, Introduction by Tottie, p. 8)

Judging by the findings reported in the papers, this was a good starting-point. Altenberg (1986: 13-40) writes about contrasting linking and focuses on two links where there are marked differences between the corpora: *but* and *anyway*. Drawing on illustrations from the LLC, he shows how *but* can be used for a variety of communicative purposes, such as interactive countering, topic shifting, and topic resumption. Bäcklund (1986: 41-55) examines conjunction-headed abbreviated clauses (e.g. *beat until stiff*), showing that they are used somewhat differently in the two media, possibly related to the difference in the communicative situation. Hermerén (1986: 57-91) surveys the means for expressing modality, including both modal auxiliaries and other structures, paying attention both to form and meaning. Interestingly, he finds that the spoken material is more modal overall, though meanings are differently distributed in the two corpora. In her study of adverbials of focusing and contingency, Tottie (1986: 93-118) arrives at the conclusion that the former are more typical of writing and the latter of speech, which may reflect differences in communicative constraints and situational and communicative needs. Aijmer (1986: 119-129) sets out to answer the question 'Why is *actually* so popular in spoken English?', while Stenström (1986: 149-163) addresses the functions of *really*.

Although frequency figures like those given in Table 7 above are suggestive, they need to be further analysed and interpreted. In the papers I have referred to, quantitative observations, such as the finding that *actually* is ten times more frequent in the LLC than in LOB, are merely a starting-point. What strikes the reader is the focus on meaning and function, and the attention to language use in context. Repeated reference is made to Chafe's (1982) description of informal speech vs.

formal written language as characterised by fragmentation vs. integration and involvement vs. detachment. This gives added significance to the individual observations and provides a general framework within which the findings can be interpreted.

The availability of the LLC led to a spate of studies analysing spoken English or comparing spoken and written English. Apart from those already mentioned, important works include Altenberg's (1984) paper on causal linking in spoken and written English, and monographs on cleft constructions (Collins 1991) and negation (Tottie 1991). This body of work represents a great step forward in the analysis of language variation.

4. Beyond individual features

Douglas Biber's pioneering work, identifying broad functional dimensions of language, represents another important step forward in the study of linguistic variation. Here I will focus on the research reported in his monograph on variation across speech and writing (Biber 1988). The two main distinguishing characteristics of this approach are (1) the inclusion of a wide variety of different categories of spoken and written texts, and (2) that the study includes a wide range of linguistic features rather than selected individual forms or structures. This is done in a highly innovative manner which takes maximum advantage of computational and statistical techniques. A similar study would be inconceivable without access to electronic corpora.

Although Biber's work is very well known, I will give a brief outline of his methodology. The 1988 study includes 17 written 'genres', viz. texts from the 15 LOB categories and 2 collections of letters, and 6 'genres' from the LLC, all in all about a million words. On the basis of previous work on spoken/written differences, Biber identified 67 features for inclusion in the analysis: tense and aspect markers, place and time adverbials, pronouns and pro-verbs, questions, nominal forms, passives, stative forms, subordination features, etc. Frequencies were calculated for each feature in each text and normalised to a text length of 1,000 words. A factor analysis of the co-occurrence of features revealed seven factors underlying the variation across the texts. On the basis of the feature loadings, both positive and negative, Biber interpreted the factors as representing the following textual dimensions: Dimension 1 was interpreted as representing 'Involved versus Informational Production', Dimension 2 as 'Narrative versus Non-Narrative Concerns', Dimension 3 as 'Explicit versus Situation-dependent Reference', Dimension 4 as 'Overt Expression of Persuasion', Dimension 5 as 'Abstract versus Non-Abstract Information', and Dimension 6 as 'On-Line Informational Elaboration'. (Dimension 7 was not considered strong enough to justify interpretation.) Dimension scores were calculated for each text by summing the frequencies of features associated with each dimension. Mean values were then calculated for each genre such that they could be ranked in relation to each other for each dimension. This reveals, for example, that telephone conversations and official documents are at the extreme ends for Dimension 1, with the other genres placed at different positions along the scale. Relations along each dimension were discussed and illustrated by short text samples.

The most significant finding is that there is no dimension which unequivocally characterises speech vs. writing:

> This analysis shows that there is no single, absolute difference between speech and writing in English; rather there are several dimensions of variation, and particular types of speech and writing are more or less similar with respect to each dimension. (Biber 1988: 199)

The relationship is multi-dimensional. Thus, for example, official documents are at the bottom for Dimensions 1 and 2, at the top for Dimension 3, in the middle for Dimension 4, at the top for Dimension 5, and fairly low for Dimension 6. In contrast, telephone conversations are at the top for Dimension 1, fairly low for Dimension 2, towards the bottom for Dimension 3, in the middle for Dimension 4, at the bottom of Dimension 5, and fairly low for Dimension 6. Different genres can therefore be similar, or differ, in a variety of respects. Using the same methodology it is possible to show the range of variation within each genre and relationships between sub-genres.

There is no doubt that Biber's work has provided significant new insight and has given us a new methodology which has proved to be seminal and has inspired many researchers to follow suit. Biber himself and his co-workers have applied the methodology to many different types of studies (see e.g. Biber/Finegan 1991, Biber *et al.* 1998): research articles in different fields, relationships among the sections of research articles, student speech and writing, textbooks, language acquisition, historical change, individual author styles, etc.[14] Whereas the focus of earlier corpus-based studies of variation was on individual features, we now have a way of characterising texts as well as text categories and their relationships.

Considering the achievement, it seems petty to draw attention to possible shortcomings.[15] Perhaps the most obvious problem is that the focus is on surface features which can be relatively easily identified and quantified. Even so there may be difficulties in capturing all tokens of the relevant features, as can be inferred from Biber's (1986: 388) note that

> […] the goal of the programs was to capture 70–90% of the occurrences of a construction, with no obvious skewing in one mode or another.

Many occurrences of features which are part of the analysis may thus be missed. Moreover, as pointed out by Esser (1993: 54f.), the statistical processing of form-based counts does not take account of "the possibility that a linguistic form may serve more than one communicative purpose", which is especially a problem if each function is not evenly distributed across text types. Equally importantly, there is uneven coverage of possible linguistic functions, as Biber himself admits (1986: 388): "Other features were not included because they cannot be analysed automatically – e.g. conjoined phrases and conjoined clauses […] and features representing different types of cohesion and information structure". Prosody is not included. Syntactic complexity can only be observed indirectly. Another relevant point is that the texts on which the analysis is based are not full texts but fairly short samples. All of this may cause problems for the interpretation of the dimensions.[16]

---

14 The method was subsequently applied to cross-linguistic comparison (Biber 1995).

15 For critical discussions of Biber's methodology, see Ball (1994) and Lee (2005).

16 The difficulties in interpreting some dimensions can be seen from inconsistencies in the names given to them. For example, Dimension 5 is named "Abstract versus Non-Abstract Information" in Biber (1988), but "Impersonal vs. Non-impersonal Style" in Biber *et al.* (1998: 155).

To conclude, the approach is very valuable, but must be applied with caution, taking possible limitations into account. What we can hope for is that studies of this type will be combined with analyses of the behaviour of specific features and, not least, with micro-level studies of individual texts. As we learn more about these matters, the multi-feature analysis may be further refined.

5. A corpus-based grammar

Biber's variation studies led him to launch a new major undertaking which resulted in a corpus-based grammar (Biber *et al.* 1999). Whereas the focus in his earlier work was on how a multi-feature analysis can throw new light on texts and text categories, the grammar project aimed at showing how a study which takes texts and text categories as a starting point can yield new insight into the use of forms and grammatical structures. Simplifying, we can perhaps say that the earlier research explored the question of what the distribution of grammatical features revealed about dimensions of variation, whereas the latter research asked what the distribution across 'registers' revealed about grammar. But the most obvious difference is that the grammar takes up a much wider range of grammatical features.

Four main text categories, or 'registers', were identified for description: news reportage, academic prose, fiction, and conversation. Each can be characterised with reference to major situational differences (1999: 16): mode (spoken vs. written), interactiveness and online production, shared immediate situation, main communicative purpose/ content, audience, and dialect domain. Large corpora were compiled for each of these registers and analysed for a large number of grammatical features, with a view to revealing how grammatical choices are made and to what extent they differ across registers. Though the analysis is quantitative, there is a consistent attempt in each case to interpret the findings in relation to the situational variables and other relevant factors.

To take a simple example, the type/token ratio (TTR) – incidentally, a point which is usually not dealt with in grammars – is quite different in the four main registers. It is consistently lower in conversation than in the written registers, and somewhat lower in academic prose than in fiction and news reportage. The suggested explanation is:

> TTR is low in conversation because it is less concerned with the transmission of information than writing. Moreover, conversation is spontaneously produced, with little time for planning and varying the choice of words. Repetition is characteristic of spoken language. It may be used for emphasis, to help the planning of the speaker, or to make sure that the message gets across to the hearer. [...] The TTR differences among the written registers are more surprising. We naturally expect a somewhat higher TTR for fiction, where the focus is more on form and elegance of expression. The high TTR in news reflects the extremely high density of nominal elements in that register, used to refer to a diverse range of people, places, objects, events, etc. At the other extreme, academic prose has the second lowest TTR, reflecting the fact that a great deal of academic writing has a restricted technical vocabulary and is therefore less variable than fiction and news reportage. (Biber *et al.* 1999: 53f.)

Similar patterns are noticed, commented on, and illustrated in all the chapters. Biber *et al.* (1999) thus amply exemplifies the general point that, by corpus analysis, we can discover patterns which were previously unknown as well as document phenomena which we had suspected. The distributions show a remarkable degree of consistency, and it is usually possible to provide plausible interpretations for the patterns observed. The most notable part is perhaps the final chapter on the grammar of conversation which brings together, interprets, and expands on observations which are made throughout the book.

At the same time, there is a need for caution. Many grammatical phenomena cannot be identified in a corpus except by laborious manual intervention, and there is a temptation to focus on matters which can be dealt with more easily. It is a major problem that prosody, one of the most basic aspects of speech, is totally ignored. In a number of cases, e.g. in connection with word order, the analysis is based on a small selection of texts from the corpus. The reader is strongly recommended to consult the analysis notes referred to in the "corpus findings" sections and printed at the end of the book.

A simple example will serve to illustrate problems in interpreting the quantitative findings. A comparison of the modal auxiliaries and the semi-modals shows that they are most common in conversation (1999: 486). In the discussion of the findings it is said that "the greater frequency of both modals and semi-modals is understandable given that these forms mostly convey stance-type meanings" (1999: 487), and a cross-reference is made to Chapter 12. What one must keep in mind, however, is that clauses are shorter and more numerous in conversation than in the written registers, as evidenced by the high proportion of verbs (1999: 65), and the more clauses there are, the more opportunities there are for using modal auxiliaries. Ideally, the frequency of modals should have been calculated in relation to the number of clauses, not merely in relation to the number of words in the sample; but this was unworkable in the absence of a syntactically parsed corpus (like the one produced by Ellegård; cf. Section 2.2). The same point applies to a great many other quantitative observations; frequencies in terms of words per million may well be convenient (as they can be calculated more easily), but they may greatly complicate the interpretation of the findings.

It is probably true, nevertheless, that modals are more common in conversation than in the written registers. Such a distribution would be consistent with the more general frequency of stance markers (1999: 979) as well as with Hermerén's findings (reported in Section 3). These findings also help in the interpretation of the decline of the modals referred to in Section 2.4. Considering that the modals appear to be more characteristic of speech than of writing, it seems unlikely that the recent change in their frequency is due to colloquialisation of written norms (as, if that were so, one would have expected an increase rather than a decline). But the modals are many-faceted, and need to be differentiated by function and use, before definite conclusions can be drawn.[17]

A further point which complicates the interpretation of the corpus findings in the grammar is that the register categories are very broad, each containing a great deal of internal variation. It can indeed be questioned whether the notion of register is applicable at all. It would have been preferable to make distinctions within the registers or, at least, have some measure of dispersion within the registers rather than just indications of mean frequencies. However, to be fair, such a requirement would likely have made the task unmanageable. On the

17 For further discussion of reasons for the decline of the modals, see Leech (2003, 2004), where there are observations on spoken as well as written corpora. Leech (2003) is also significant in including some discussion of semantic aspects of modal decline.

basis of the results that are presented, it should be possible to get a general picture of how grammatical features vary across registers and to build up a profile defining the grammatical characteristics of each of the main registers. The results can be used as a yardstick in the study of grammatical features of texts and as a basis for further research, because much remains to be done in the area of corpus-based grammar studies.

6. Other developments

Below I will briefly refer to some other developments and their relevance with respect to a discussion of problems in interpreting textual distribution.

6.1. The ICE and ICLE families

The International Corpus of English (ICE) was launched by Sidney Greenbaum (1991), with the primary aim of collecting material for comparative studies of English worldwide, both used as a mother tongue and as a second language, and including both spoken and written texts, thus allowing for analysis of variation both within and across corpora. Each ICE corpus was to consist of one million words of English, produced after 1989 and collected in accordance with a common design (Nelson 1996). Ten ICE corpora are currently available.[18] It has proved a considerable challenge to compile comparable English corpora for language communities as different as in East Africa, Great Britain, India, and Singapore, to mention but four of the participating

18 As listed at the ICE homepage, URL <http://ice-corpora.net/ice/>, as of April 2012, component corpora are available for Canada, East Africa, Great Britain (see Section 6.2), Hong Kong, India, Ireland, Jamaica, New Zealand, the Philippines, and Singapore. Components representing only written texts are also available for America and Sri Lanka. Other components in preparation include corpora representing Australia, South Africa, and Uganda.

regions. Leitner (1991), discussing ICE-India, questions whether it is possible for English corpora to satisfy both a local requirement (true representation of texts from a particular area) and a global requirement (comparability across corpora from different areas). In similar vein, the manual for ICE-East Africa (Hudson-Ettle/Schmied 1999) notes that:

> Our intention from the start was [...] to adhere strictly to the guidelines set down by the ICE teams which would enable comparable studies with other ICE components [...but...] When our data collection began in 1991, we soon became aware of:
> a) the impossibility of placing Kenyan and Tanzanian varieties of written English in one basket;
> b) the difficulty of acquiring data for some of the ICE categories;
> c) the rarity of texts of 2000 word length in East Africa.[19]

For example, English radio broadcasts are available in both Kenya and Tanzania, but have a wide audience only in Kenya; and, while educated Kenyans may converse in English, in Tanzania, Swahili is preferred, and English is not generally used for ordinary conversation. Another modification was an increase in the corpus size, to do justice to the very different uses of English in the two countries represented. Similar problems must have arisen in connection with other ICE projects. As such, though the material is no doubt extremely valuable, the user should take great care in interpreting data from the corpora.

Similar caution is advised in the use of the subcorpora of *The International Corpus of Learner English* (ICLE), which is designed to collect data from English language learners from different parts of the world (Granger 1998). Although there is a common overall framework, learning situations inevitably vary in different countries, making it difficult to compile comparable corpora. Again, it is clear that the material is very valuable in opening up new avenues of research, but the user should pay close attention to the learner data included with the corpus and the accompanying description of the status of English in the different countries.

19 See: <http://www.tu-chemnitz.de/phil/english/chairs/linguist/real/independent/eafrica/index.htm>.

6.2. ICE-GB

The British component of ICE needs to be singled out for special comment, as it offers unique possibilities of intra-corpus comparison (see Nelson *et al.* 2002). Not only is it tagged and parsed (and post-edited!), it also comes with dedicated retrieval software which allows the user to carry out very complex searches combining linguistic, social, and situational variables.

Nelson *et al.* (2002: 257 ff.) explain how the corpus can be used to design experiments. Rather than first observing and later interpreting variation in a corpus, the researcher formulates specific hypotheses in advance and tests these with reference to the corpus, thereby reducing the element of interpretation. The hypothesis is either confirmed or rejected. In addition, ICE-GB can of course be used in the same way as any other corpus, with the added advantage that the delicacy of searches can be much greater. We can, for example, ask: In what situations are tag questions used most? Are they used more by women than men? It remains for the user to analyse the material and interpret the function of the tag questions, e.g. as used in the classroom and in legal cross-examination, two situations where tag questions are especially common.

A drawback of ICE-GB is that, at one million words, it is rather small, so that it may not provide sufficient material, particularly if searches are very narrowly defined. In addition, the maximum benefit from the detailed tagging and parsing can only be obtained if users familiarise themselves with the way terms and categories are defined (e.g. to recognise that *up* in *take up* is dealt with as an adverb, while 'particle' is used for other purposes). Without an awareness of these details, it may be easy for users to draw unwarranted conclusions.

6.3. The British National Corpus

What ICE-GB lacks in size, it makes up in depth. The opposite is true of *The British National Corpus* (BNC), which is no doubt the most valuable of the publicly available English corpora (Aston/Burnard 1998). With its 100 million words, its large text samples and broad representation of text categories, including informal speech from different parts of the country, it is suited for many types of variation studies: speech vs. writing, types of written texts, types of spoken interaction (dialogue vs. monologue), types of speakers (age, sex, etc.), and so on. In a recent study of apology formulae Deutschmann (2006) shows how the social and situational categories of the BNC can be put to good use, reaching the conclusion that "the potential for future socio-pragmatic research is boundless" (2006: 217).

As always, there are a number of things the user should keep in mind. Using the social categories requires caution, as shown by Deutschmann (2006: 208f.). While the dialogue material in the BNC lacks the academic bias of the London-Lund Corpus, is much larger, and includes a wider range of speakers, it is less well transcribed and is often difficult to interpret. Prosody can only be deduced indirectly through punctuation. There are inconsistencies in the transcription. For example, the sequence *must have* may appear as any of *must have*, *must've*, or *must of*; similarly, *there're* may represent *there are* or *they are*. There are many errors in word class tagging.[20] All in all, however, these problems do not detract from the great value of the corpus, as long as the user treats the material with care.

7. Future directions

In a recent paper Charles Meyer (2004) asks the provocative question "Can you really study linguistic variation in linguistic corpora?" He puts this to the test with reference to a case study based on some of the ICE subcorpora, and concludes (2004: 339) that "although certain kinds of language variation can be validly studied in a corpus such as ICE, other kinds of variation require different kinds of corpora." With this I whole-heartedly agree. It is the task of corpus users to evaluate whether the corpus is suitable for their research questions. All corpora are not suitable for all types of research questions. It is nevertheless striking how much research has come out of early corpora such as Brown and

20 Note, incidentally, that the word class tagging in BNC differs from that of ICE-GB, not just in the level of delicacy but in the way certain word classes are defined.

LOB, including investigations which the compilers had probably never even dreamed of.

Much earlier Nelleke Oostdijk (1988: 12) observed that "linguists have not been very well equipped to carry out large scale formal empirical analyses which would enable them to systematically vary extra-linguistic factors and examine the accompanying linguistic variation." Part of the problem with many corpus-based variation studies is that researchers have unquestioningly accepted genre categories that have been built into publicly available corpora. Oostdijk asks for a new type of corpus compiled for the specific purpose of variety study and allowing for the systematic varying of extra-linguistic variables.

With time, the corpora available have become more numerous and more varied, opening up new opportunities for research. In addition to multipurpose corpora such as the BNC, we have specialised corpora of textbooks, academic writing, learner language, etc.[21] Problems of interpretation are reduced when the corpus user can choose the best corpus for a particular research question. Corpus annotation and new analysis software aid in the processes of investigation and interpretation. What must not be forgotten is that documentation is vital for the use of the corpora and for the interpretation of the findings: information on the texts, on text categories, on speakers, the kinds of annotation, etc. The BNC sets a good example in this regard.

Research questions have frequently been tailored according to the available ready-made corpora. With the ever-increasing quantity of material available in electronic form, it is becoming easier to tailor the corpus to the research question. Many have started to talk of the Web as a corpus (see e.g. Kilgarriff 2001b and Renouf 2003). I would rather view it as a vast text archive from which different types of corpora can be drawn depending upon the research question. Christian Mair (2006: 370) argues for the use of material from the Web as follows:

> Today [...] the supply of digital text – online and offline – is practically unlimited for English and a small number of other languages, so that restricting

---

21 Among important types of corpora which I have not discussed, we find multilingual corpora such as the English-Norwegian Parallel Corpus (see: <http://www.hf.uio.no/ilos/forskning/forskningsprosjekter/enpc/>) and historical corpora (see e.g.: <http://www.eng.helsinki.fi/varieng/>). For a discussion of some problems in using historical corpora, see Rissanen (1989).

> the scope of one's work to data available in a small number of corpora only would be counter-productive in the analysis of many linguistic problems. Corpus linguists of the future will therefore be a much more heterogeneous community – no longer focussed on a specific corpus but working in a vast and expanding corpus-linguistic environment in which one of the chief skills required will be to identify the resources which are relevant to the problem studied from a vast range of possibilities.

In using the Web it may be difficult to evaluate the material and indeed also to interpret the findings. Christian Mair discusses some cautionary procedures which need to be followed. In my view, the Web is *one* possible source, to be used where it is applicable.[22] The guiding principle is the nature of the research question.

Like many others, Christian Mair talks about 'corpus linguists', and 'corpus linguistics' has indeed become a household word.[23] The terms have been significant in underlining that using corpora is an important new undertaking, but they may have contributed to creating a gulf in relation to other types of linguistic inquiry, such as sociolinguistics. Despite considerable mutual interest in variation, "corpus linguistics" and "variationist sociolinguistics" fail to intersect as much as might be expected. For example, the *Handbook of Language Variation and Change* (Chambers *et al.* 2002) contains only one contribution specifically on corpora (Bauer 2002) – though others, e.g. on discourse variation (Macaulay 2002), do occasionally refer to corpus data. Sigley (2006) suggests that one possible reason for the surprisingly limited interaction of these fields may be that corpus linguistics' emphasis on obtaining representative samples of authentic language is not always easily reconciled with variationist sociolinguistics' emphasis on controlling language tasks in order to allow matched comparisons of individuals representing different social groups. Yet these approaches are not entirely incompatible, as is shown by the example of Cheshire's (2005) study of gender and social class variation in the use of discourse-new markers, using a speech corpus assembled for a sociolinguistic project where social and situational factors were strictly controlled.

---

22 Cf. Bergh (2005: 45): "the Web is best enjoyed in carefully cut slices, preferably based on the raw capacity of Google and spiced according to taste with the fine-tuned facilities of WebCorp".

23 One of those who have been sceptical of the use of these terms is Wallace Chafe (1992).

Cheshire reaches the conclusion that it is necessary to go beyond conventional sociolinguistic frameworks of analysis and she "confirms the view articulated by Pintzuk (2003: 525) that a coherent theory relating grammar and usage can and should be formulated" (2005: 502). Although much new insight on variation has been gained through corpus studies, leading to a better understanding of texts and of the use of language, there is a need to go beyond customary 'corpus linguistic' approaches to variation studies. Now is an appropriate time for linguists of different persuasions to join forces to advance our understanding of language in use as well as for the development of linguistic theory and new models of language variation.

References

Aijmer, Karin / Altenberg, Bengt (eds) 1991. *English corpus linguistics. Studies in honour of Jan Svartvik.* London: Longman.

Altenberg, Bengt 1984. Causal linking in spoken and written English. *Studia Linguistica* 38, 20-69.

Altenberg, Bengt 1986. Contrastive linking in spoken and written English. In Tottie, Gunnel / Bäcklund, Ingegerd (eds), 13-40.

Aston, Guy / Burnard Lou 1998. *The BNC handbook: Exploring the British National Corpus with SARA.* Edinburgh: Edinburgh University Press.

Bäcklund, Ingegerd 1986. Beat until stiff. Conjunction-headed abbreviated clauses in spoken and written English. In Tottie, Gunnel / Bäcklund, Ingegerd (eds), 41-55.

Ball, C. N. 1994. Automated text analysis: Cautionary tales. *Literary and Linguistic Computing* 9/4, 295-302.

Bauer, Laurie 2002. Inferring variation and change from public corpora. In Chambers, J. K. / Trudgill Peter / Schilling-Estes, Natalie (eds), 97-114.

Bergh, Gunnar 2005. Min(d)ing English language data on the Web: What can Google tell us? *ICAME Journal* 29, 25-46.

Biber, Douglas 1986. Spoken and written textual dimensions in English: Resolving the contradictory findings. *Language* 62/2, 384-414.

Biber, Douglas 1988. *Variation across speech and writing*. Cambridge: Cambridge University Press.

Biber, Douglas 1995. *Dimensions of register variation: A cross-linguistic comparison*. Cambridge: Cambridge University Press.

Biber, Douglas / Finegan, Edward 1991. On the exploitation of computerized corpora in ariation studies. In Aijmer, Karin / Altenberg, Bengt (eds), 204-220.

Biber, Douglas / Conrad, Susan / Reppen, Randi 1998. *Corpus linguistics: Investigating language structure and use*. Cambridge: Cambridge University Press.

Biber, Douglas / Johansson, Stig / Leech, Geoffrey / Conrad, Susan / Finegan, Edward 1999. *Longman grammar of spoken and written English*. Harlow: Longman.

Carroll, John B. / Davies, Peter / Richman, Barry 1971. *The American Heritage word frequency book*. New York: American Heritage Publishing Co.

Chafe, Wallace 1982. Integration and involvement in speaking, writing, and oral literature. In Tannen, Deborah (ed.) *Spoken and written language: Exploring orality and literacy*. Norwood, N.J.: Ablex, 35-53.

Chafe, Wallace 1992. The importance of corpus linguistics to understanding the nature of language. In Svartvik, Jan (ed.) *Directions in corpus linguistics. Proceedings of Nobel Symposium 82, 4–8 August 1991*. Berlin: Mouton de Gruyter, 79-103.

Chambers, J. K. / Trudgill, Peter / Schilling-Estes, Natalie (eds) 2002. *The Handbook of Language Variation and Change*. Oxford: Blackwell.

Cheshire, Jenny 2005. Syntactic variation and beyond: Gender and social class variation in the use of discourse-new markers. *Journal of Sociolinguistics* 9/4, 479-508.

Collins, Peter 1991. *Cleft and pseudo-cleft constructions in English*. London and New York: Routledge.

Collins, Peter / Peters, Pam 2004. Australian English: Morphology and syntax. In Kortmann, Bernd / Burridge, Kate / Mesthrie, Rajend / Schneider, Edgar W. / Upton, Clive 2004. *A handbook of varie-*

ties of English. Vol. 2: *Morphology and syntax*. Berlin and New York: Mouton de Gruyter, 593-610.

Deutschmann, Mats 2006. Social variation in the use of apology formulae in the BNC. In Renouf, Antoinette / Kehoe, Andrew (eds), 205-221.

Ellegård, Alvar 1978. *The syntactic structure of English texts. A computer-based study of four kinds of text in the Brown University Corpus*. Gothenburg Studies in English 43. Göteborg: Acta Universitatis Gothoburgensis.

Esser, Jürgen 1993. *English linguistic stylistics*. Tübingen: Niemeyer.

Francis, W. Nelson / Kučera, Henry (with the assistance of Mackie, Andrew W.) 1982. *Frequency analysis of English usage: Lexicon and grammar*. Boston: Houghton Mifflin.

Granger, Sylviane (ed.) 1998. *Learner English on computer*. London and New York: Longman.

Greenbaum, Sidney 1991. The development of the International Corpus of English. In Aijmer, Karin / Altenberg, Bengt (eds), 83-91.

Greenbaum, Sidney / Svartvik, Jan 1990. The London-Lund Corpus of Spoken English. In Svartvik, Jan (ed.), 11-59.

Hermerén, Lars 1986. Modalities in spoken and written English: An inventory of forms. In: Tottie, Gunnel / Bäcklund, Ingegerd (eds), 57-91.

Hofland, Knut / Johansson, Stig 1982. *Word frequencies in British and American English*. Bergen: Norwegian Computing Centre for the Humanities and London: Longman.

Holmes, Janet / Sigley, Robert 2002. What's a word like *girl* doing in a place like this? Occupational labels, sexist usages and corpus research. In Peters, Pam / Collins, Peter / Smith, Adam (eds) *New frontiers of corpus research. Papers from the Twenty First International Conference on English Language Research on Computerized Corpora*. Amsterdam and New York: Rodopi, 247–263.

Hudson-Ettle, Diana M. / Josef, Schmied 1999. *Manual to accompany the East African Component of the International Corpus of English*. Department of English, Chemnitz University of Technology. [Available online at URL <http://www.tu-chemnitz.de/phil/english/chairs/linguist/real/independent/eafrica/index.html>.]

Hundt, Marianne 1997. Has BrE been catching up with AmE over the past thirty years? In Ljung, Magnus (ed.), 135-151.

Hundt, Marianne 1998. *New Zealand English Grammar: Fact or Fiction?* Amsterdam: Benjamins.

Hundt, Marianne / Hay, Jennifer / Gordon, Elizabeth 2004. New Zealand English. In Kortmann, Bernd / Burridge, Kate / Mesthrie, Rajend / Schneider, Edgar W. / Upton, Clive 2004. *A handbook of varieties of English*. Vol. 2: *Morphology and syntax*. Berlin and New York: Mouton de Gruyter, 560-592.

Johansson, Stig (in collaboration with Leech, Geoffrey / Goodluck, Helen) 1978. *Manual of information to accompany the Lancaster-Oslo/Bergen corpus of British English, for use with digital computers*. Department of English, University of Oslo.

Johansson, Stig / Hofland, Knut 1989. *Frequency analysis of English vocabulary and grammar*. Vol. 1–2. Oxford: Clarendon Press.

Johansson, Stig / Stenström, Anna-Brita (eds) 1991. *English computer corpora: Selected papers and research guide*. Berlin: Mouton de Gruyter.

Jones, Susan / Sinclair, John M. 1974. English lexical collocations. *Cahiers de Lexicologie* 24, 15-61.

Kilgarriff, Adam 2001a. Comparing corpora. *International Journal of Corpus Linguistics* 6/1, 1-37.

Kilgarriff, Adam 2001b. Web as corpus. In Rayson, Paul / Wilson, Andrew / McEnery, Tony / Hardie, Andrew / Khoja, Shereen (eds) *Proceedings of the Corpus Linguistics 2001 conference*. Lancaster: UCREL, 342-344.

Kortmann, Bernd / Burridge, Kate / Mesthrie, Rajend / Schneider, Edgar W. / Upton, Clive 2004. *A handbook of varieties of English*. Vol. 2: *Morphology and syntax*. Berlin and New York: Mouton de Gruyter.

Krogvig, Inger / Johansson, Stig 1984. *Shall* and *will* in British and American English: A frequency study. *Studia Linguistica* 38/1, 70-87.

Kučera, Henry / Francis, W. Nelson 1967. *Computational analysis of present-day American English*. Providence, R.I.: Brown University Press.

Labov, William 1966. *The social stratification of English in New York City*. Washington, D.C.: Center for Applied Linguistics.

Labov, William 1972. *Sociolinguistic patterns*. Philadelphia: University of Pennsylvania Press.

Lee, David Y. W. 2005. *Modelling variation in spoken and written language: the multi-dimensional approach revisited.* London: Routledge.

Leech, Geoffrey 2003. Modality on the move: The English modal auxiliaries 1961-1992. In Facchinetti, Roberta / Krug, Manfred / Palmer, Frank (eds) *Modality in contemporary English.* Berlin and New York: Mouton de Gruyter, 223-240.

Leech, Geoffrey. 2004. Recent grammatical change in English: Data, description, theory. In Aijmer, Karin / Altenberg, Bengt (eds) *Advances in corpus linguistics. Papers from the 23rd International Conference on English Language Research on Computerized Corpora (ICAME 23), Göteborg 22-26 May 2002.* Amsterdam and New York: Rodopi, 61-81.

Leech, Geoffrey / Fallon, Roger 1992. Computer corpora – what do they tell us about culture? *ICAME Journal* 16, 29-50.

Leech, Geoffrey / Smith, Nicholas 2005. Extending the possibilities of corpus-based research on English in the twentieth century: A prequel to LOB and FLOB. *ICAME Journal* 29, 83-98.

Leitner, Gerhard 1991. The Kolhapur Corpus of Indian English. Intra-varietal description and/or inter-varietal comparison. In Johansson, Stig / Stenström, Anna-Brita (eds), 215-232.

Ljung, Magnus (ed.) 1997. *Corpus-based studies in English. Papers from the Seventeenth International Conference on English Language Research on Computerized Corpora (ICAME 17).* Amsterdam and Atlanta: Rodopi.

Lyons, John 1968. *Introduction to theoretical linguistics.* London: Cambridge University Press.

Macaulay, Ronald. 2002. Discourse variation. In: Chambers, J. K. / Trudgill, Peter / Schilling-Estes, Natalie (eds), 283-305.

Mair, Christian 1997. Parallel corpora: A real-time approach to the study of language change in progress. In: Ljung, Magnus (ed.), 195-209.

Mair, Christian. 1998. Corpora and the study of the major varieties of English: Issues and results. In Lindquist, Hans / Klintborg, Staffan / Levin, Magnus / Estling, Maria (eds) *The major varieties of English. Papers from MAVEN 97, Växjö 20-22 November 1997.* Acta Wexionensia Humaniora. No. 1.Växjö: Växjö University, 139-157.

Mair, Christian 2006. Tracking ongoing change and recent diversification in present-day standard English: The complementary role of small and large corpora. In Renouf, Antoinette / Kehoe, Andrew (eds), 355-376.

Mair, Christian / Hundt, Marianne 2002. Short term diachronic shifts in part-of-speech frequencies: A comparison of the tagged LOB and F-LOB corpora. *International Journal of Corpus Linguistics* 7/2, 245-264.

Meyer, Charles F. 2004. Can you really study linguistic variation in linguistic corpora? *American Speech* 79/4, 339-355.

Nakamura, Junsaku 1993. Quantitative comparison of modals in the Brown and LOB corpora. *ICAME Journal* 17, 29-48.

Nelson, Gerald 1996. The design of the corpus. In Greenbaum, Sidney (ed.) *Comparing English worldwide: The International Corpus of English.* Oxford: Clarendon, 27-35.

Nelson, Gerald / Wallis, Sean / Aarts, Bas 2002. Exploring natural language. *Working with the British component of the International Corpus of English.* Amsterdam and Philadelphia: Benjamins.

Oostdijk, Nelleke 1988. A corpus linguistic approach to linguistic variation. *Literary and Linguistic Computing* 3/1, 12-25.

Pintzuk, Susan 2003. Variationist approaches to syntactic change. In Joseph, Brian D. / Janda, Richard D. (eds) *Handbook of historical linguistics.* Oxford: Blackwell, 506-528.

Quirk, Randolph 1960. Towards a description of English usage. *Transactions of the Philological Society, 1960.* Oxford: Blackwell, 40-61.

Renouf, Antoinette 2003. WebCorp: Providing a renewable data source for corpus linguists. *Language and Computers* 48, 39-58.

Renouf, Antoinette / Kehoe, Andrew (eds) 2006. *The changing face of corpus linguistics.* Amsterdam and New York: Rodopi.

Reppen, Randi / Fitzmaurice, Susan M. / Biber, Douglas 2002. *Using corpora to explore linguistic variation.* Amsterdam and Philadelphia: Benjamins.

Rissanen, Matti 1989. Three problems in connection with the use of diachronic corpora. *ICAME Journal* 13, 16-19.

Sand, Andrea / Siemund, Rainer 1992. LOB – 30 years on … , *ICAME Journal* 16, 119-122.

Shastri, S. V. 1988. The Kolhapur Corpus of Indian English and work done on its basis so far. *ICAME Journal* 12, 15-26.

Sigley, Robert 1997. The influence of formality and channel on relative pronoun choice in New Zealand English. *English Language and Linguistics* 1/2, 207-232.

Sigley, Robert 2006. Corpora in studies of variation. In Keith, Brown (ed.) *Encyclopedia of Language & Linguistics*, vol 3. Oxford: Elsevier, 220-226.

Svartvik, Jan (ed.) 1990. *The London-Lund Corpus of Spoken English: Description and research.* Lund Studies in English 82. Lund: Lund University Press.

Svartvik, Jan / Quirk, Randolph (eds) 1980. *A corpus of English conversation.* Lund Studies in English 56. Lund: CWK Gleerup.

Tottie, Gunnel 1986. The importance of being adverbial. Adverbials of focusing and contingency in spoken and written English. In Tottie, Gunnel / Bäcklund, Ingegerd (eds), 93-118.

Tottie, Gunnel 1991. *Negation in English speech and writing.* San Diego, etc.: Academic Press.

Tottie, Gunnel / Bäcklund, Ingegerd (eds) 1986. *English in speech and writing: A symposium.* Studia Anglistica Upsaliensia 60. Uppsala: Almqvist & Wiksell.

Wilson, Andrew 2005. Modal verbs in written Indian English: A quantitative and comparative analysis of the Kolhapur Corpus using correspondence analysis. *ICAME Journal* 29, 151-169.

ROBERT SIGLEY

Assessing Corpus Comparability Using a Formality Index: The Case of the Brown/LOB Clones

1. Introduction[1]

For a variety of reasons, corpus linguists often want to make comparisons between different corpora. For example, we may want to check that our results are reproducible in other samples; to compare different varieties of a language; or to look at how language changes across time by comparing samples from different time periods.

The Brown/LOB clones listed in Table 1 are a set of corpora which were designed specifically to let researchers make such comparisons. Each is a 1-million-word sample of edited written English, consisting of 500 2000-word text samples, based on the sampling frame used for the Brown corpus of American English (Francis 1964) and the LOB corpus of British English (Johansson 1978). Both Brown and LOB represent texts published in 1961. Christian Mair's team at Freiburg, Germany, constructed the parallel Frown and FLOB corpora using American and British texts published between 1990 and 1992 (Hundt/Sand/Siemund 1998; Hundt/Sand/Skandera 1998). The Wellington Corpus of Written New Zealand English (Bauer 1993; henceforth WWC) is a parallel corpus of New Zealand writings from 1986-90. Thus we can compare American, British and New Zealand writings using Frown, FLOB, and WWC; and we can study change between 1961 and 1991 by comparing Brown with Frown, or LOB with FLOB (see for

1 The author would like to thank Bernadette Vine, Mark Chadwick, Laurie Bauer, and Andrea Sand for assistance in accessing the various corpora. Previous versions of this research were presented at ICAME 19 in Freiburg, May 1999, and the JAECS conference in Nara, April 2001; the present version has greatly benefitted from audience comments, from feedback by anonymous reviewers for the *Journal of English Linguistics*, and from email correspondence with Nicholas Smith. Any remaining errors are of course the author's responsibility.

example Yamazaki, this volume). All of these corpora are available on the ICAME CD-ROM (Hofland/Lindebjerg/Thunestvedt 1999), together with two other parallel corpora not analysed here: the Kolhapur corpus of Indian English (with a base year of 1978), and the Australian Corpus of English (with a base year of 1986). More recently, further parallel corpora of British English have also been constructed to represent the 1900s and the 1930s (Leech/Hundt/Mair/Smith 2009).

Time: / Variety:	1960s	1980s/90s
American English	Brown (1961 AmE)	Frown (1991-92 AmE)
British English	LOB (1961 BrE)	FLOB (1991 BrE)
New Zealand English		WWC (1986-90 NZE)
Australian English		ACE (1986 AusE)
Indian English	Kolhapur (1978 Indian English)	

Table 1. The parallel corpora of edited writing based on Brown/LOB.

1.1. The problem of interpreting observed linguistic differences between corpora

Corpus comparisons involve a serious interpretative problem. Suppose we do see a significant difference between two corpora in some specific variable. Such an observation might indicate a real linguistic difference between the varieties and/or time periods represented by those corpora. However, to confirm that interpretation, at least five types of alternative explanation would first need to be eliminated.

First, there could be some more general difference in stylistic norms between varieties, as suggested by Biber's (1987) comparison of Brown and LOB, which characterises the LOB data as slightly but systematically "more edited", "less interactive" and "less abstract" than American English as represented by Brown. Such general stylistic differences could potentially account for observed differences in variant frequency, if our variants of interest have different stylistic values.

Second, there could be some relevant differences or changes in institutional norms or rules enforced during editing, which would produce certain usage differences specific to particular genres, or specific to texts from a particular (institutional) source. For example, Leech *et al.* (2009) identify several variables that appear to be systematically prescribed against by American but not British editors in formal writings, including restrictive relative *which*, and the use of passives in academic writing.

Third, there might be some less consciously directed stylistic "drift" in what is normal practice for a particular genre (as demonstrated by Biber/Finegan 1989, 1992).

Alternatively, there could be some variation or change in the social distribution of contributors to a genre, which might be expected to reflect wider trends or differences in society. For example, Sigley/Holmes (2002) note that less than a third of the fiction texts in Brown have female authors, compared with over half in WWC. Such differences in social representation could potentially influence the overall stylistic norms observed in the genre(s) thus affected.

Finally, the observed difference might be attributable to a more purely methodological source: the sampling procedures used in compiling the corpora could produce either accidental or systematic mismatches in what kind of language event (or what kind of language producer) is included in the corpora (or in some subsets thereof). It is thus of considerable importance to be able to establish whether corpora are sufficiently similar to permit us to interpret such comparisons, both across the corpus as a whole, and across each defined subset that we wish to compare.

One important type of evidence that may be used to choose among these competing explanations is the textual distribution of the observed linguistic features, in terms of the text types, and the number of texts within each type, in which the feature is evident. Any truly systematic dialect difference should be found in texts from many different sources (though we may expect such features to be more strongly marked in genres with a more localised readership and less strongly enforced norms, such as fiction, or hobby magazines). By contrast, differences in enforced norms may be quite narrowly limited to texts from one text type, and possibly even from one sampled institutional source.

A second type of evidence is the linguistic generality of the difference: differences seen in one isolated variable tend to suggest the influence of an institutional norm, whereas more general patterns of variation support some wider linguistic trend. Biber (1987) is a pioneering example of this approach to interpretation (see also the survey of

Biber's research in Johansson, this volume); more recently, Leech *et al.* (2009), after surveying grammatical variation among the LOB/Brown and FLOB/Frown corpora in more linguistic detail, have noted several potentially meaningful clusters of differences, which they describe as indicating (partially opposed) trends over time of "colloquialisation" (in which some features typical of informal speech, especially the use of personal pronouns, and avoidance of passive voice, are becoming more widespread in edited writing) and "densification" (in which information is becoming more concentrated within noun phrases).

On the specific topic of evaluating corpus comparability, Kilgarriff (2001: 118) provides a typology of possible differences between corpora, including not only systematic differences in language use (e.g. as a result of some real difference in the varieties targetted), but also differences in degree of homogeneity (differences in the range of variation contained within each corpus). When, as in the case of the LOB/Brown clones, each corpus is itself a parallel stratified sample comprised of subsamples of many different registers of language, we should expect the corpora to show very similar ranges of variation overall; but there could still be differences in range within certain of the text category subsamples, and so it will be necessary to conduct comparisons not only of the corpora as a whole, but also of each distinct text category.

1.2. Differences in contents of "matched" corpora

Sampling differences are possible even in supposedly "matched" corpora because (as also noted by Johansson, this volume) there is an unavoidable conflict between the requirements of comparability (i.e., that all of our corpora should have parallel content as far as possible) and representativeness (i.e., that each corpus should accurately reflect the variety it is intended to sample). These two goals come into conflict because any particular language variety may not be used for exactly the same range of functions in every society, by all social groups, or in all historical periods. For example, if we want to compare American fiction with British or New Zealand fiction, we need to note that the American genre of Western novels may find no exact parallel in other varieties. If we include Westerns, then the American fiction sample will be less directly comparable with fiction samples from other varieties. Yet if we were to exclude Westerns from comparison, our American sample would be less representative of American fiction as a whole. Corpus compilers (and subsequently, also investigators selecting texts from corpora for comparative purposes) are thus forced to seek a compromise between the two objectives.

The primary objective in collecting FLOB was to create the closest possible match to LOB, even to the extent of sampling the same newspapers and periodicals where this was possible (Mair 1997: 196; Hundt/Sand/Siemund 1998). But otherwise, the Brown/LOB clones in practice had to sample what was available in each variety, within the limit of the overall sampling frame, and this has resulted in a number of minor differences in corpus content, as summarised in Table 2.

Firstly, within Reportage (Category A), Brown and LOB include subcategories of "society" and "cultural" articles, which roughly correspond to "feature articles" in WWC. Secondly, there are slight differences in the total numbers of texts representing categories E (Hobbies), F (Popular Lore), and G (Biography and essays). Thirdly, as a direct result of differences in national political systems, there are differences in the institutions that are represented in category H (Miscellaneous/official documents), especially as regards texts recording court proceedings and parliamentary debates. Fourthly, in category J (Academic writings), there are minor differences in the number and order of texts representing some subcategories; but also, within each general topic field included, it was not possible to match the exact topics of research across different countries and time periods. (For example, the "natural science" subcategory for WWC consists exclusively of biology articles, as might be expected of a small country in which scientific research is mainly government-funded and largely directed towards either understanding and preserving native species, or improving agricultural yields.) Finally, and most importantly, insufficient special-genre fiction was published in New Zealand in the mid-1980s to allow the WWC compilers to follow that part of the Brown/LOB sampling frame. As a result, WWC contains only one general "Fiction" category. WWC fiction texts are split into two groups, K and L, but only as an artefact of the text numbering system; the division does not signal any meaningful distinction.[2]

1.3. Differences in organisation of material in "matched" corpora

One other serious problem affecting more detailed comparisons of subcategories in the Brown/LOB clones is that the corpora differ considerably in ordering of texts between subcategories. As a result, it is not possible simply to match up texts with the same text number across different corpora and trust that they are of the same type. The problem is compounded by the fact that the corpus manuals for FLOB and Frown (and also, except for press materials, Brown) do not explicitly indicate which subcategory a text is intended to represent (though the organisation of FLOB at least mostly appears to follow LOB). In press material and academic writing, the subcategory can usually be inferred from the list of sources for each text; but for some categories (particularly for category G in Brown and Frown, and for Fiction texts in WWC), it is necessary to read through each text to determine its subcategory membership. The subcategory assignments used for comparison, resulting from such work, are listed in Tables 3-8.

2 WWC does contain some texts identifiable as Adventure, Romance, and Humour, and even a few that may be classified as representing Mystery and Science Fiction, as listed in Table 8 – but this was possible only after the collection period for fiction texts was extended from the base year of 1986 up to 1990. For example, only two science fiction novels were published in New Zealand in 1986, and both were written by British expatriates (Philip Mann, Craig Harrison), hence ineligible for inclusion. Conversely, several highly successful and prolific New Zealand authors of romantic novels (e.g. Robyn Donald and Susan Napier) could not be included because their works were edited and published overseas.

Category	Texts	Subcategories	Known differences
A. Reportage	44	• politics; • sports; • briefs; • financial; • features (≈society, culture)	• Brown, LOB, Frown and FLOB contain 'society' and 'culture' articles, corresponding to 'features' in WWC. • The corpora differ in ordering of texts by subcategory; cf. Table 3.
B. Editorial	27	• institutional editorials; • commissioned opinion; • letters to editor	• Brown, LOB and WWC differ in ordering of texts between subcategories; cf. Table 4.
C. Reviews	17		
D. Religion	17		
E. Hobbies	38 (36 in Brown)		• Brown and LOB have slightly different numbers of texts in categories E, F, & G. (WWC and FLOB follow LOB; Frown follows Brown.)
F. Popular lore	44 (48 in Brown)		
G. Biography, belles lettres, essays	77 (75 in Brown)	• biography; • arts and literature; • general essays	• Brown and Frown do not separate the subcategories of category G structurally; cf. Table 5.
H. Official documents	30	• government reports; • parliamentary or legal debates or proceedings; • industry reports	• Different institutions are sampled (necessitated by differences in systems of government); cf. Table 6.
J. Academic writings	80	• natural sciences; • medicine; • maths/computing; • behavioural sciences; • humanities; • technology and engineering.	• There are minor differences in number and order of texts representing each subject field; cf. Table 7. The ranges of topics represented within each field in each corpus also differ.
K.–R. Fiction	126		• WWC contains only one (general) fiction category. The other corpora have the category structure shown; cf. Table 8. • Brown explicitly includes "Western" fiction within Adventure.
K. General	29		
L. Mystery/detective	24		
M. Science fiction	6		
N. Adventure (and Western)	29		
P. Romance	29		
R. Humour	9		

Table 2. Differences in text category composition for Brown/LOB clones.

FLOB closely follows LOB in category A (Reportage) as shown in Table 3; but none of the other corpora are exactly matched to each other at the same level of detail. In category B (Editorial; Table 4) FLOB again follows LOB, while Frown follows WWC (rather than Brown). Categories C (Reviews), D (Religion), E (Hobbies) and F (Popular Lore) do not contain structural subcategories. For category G (Table 5),

LOB, FLOB and WWC all share the same structure, but the texts in Brown and Frown are distributed among the subtypes of Biography, Essay, and Literary Criticism seemingly without any order. For category H (Miscellaneous/official documents; Table 6), Frown follows Brown, whereas WWC and FLOB (mostly) follow LOB. In category J (Academic writing; Table 7), the order of texts matches up for the subcategories of natural sciences, mathematics, and technology, but there are differences in the order and number of texts representing subjects in the social sciences and humanities (Frown follows Brown, whereas LOB is the model for WWC and, slightly less exactly, FLOB). Finally, Table 8 lists the texts within the WWC Fiction category that can be assigned to one of the more specific genre categories used in the other corpora.

Corpus: / Subcategory:	Brown (1961 AmE)	LOB (1961 BrE)	WWC (1986 NZE)	Frown (1991 AmE)	FLOB (1991 BrE)
Politics	A01–10, 34–37	A01–06, 20–21, 27–31	A01–14	A01–14	A01–06, 20–21, 27–31
Sports	A11–15, 38–39	A07–08, 22–23, 32–33, 41	A15–21	A15–21	A07–08, 22–23, 32–33, 41
Briefs	A19–25, 41–42	A11–14, 24, 34–37, 43	A22–30	A25–33	A11–14, 24, 34–37, 43
Financial	A26–28, 43	A15–16, 25, 38	A31–34	A34–37	A15–16, 25, 38
Features			A35–44		
Society	A16–18	A09–10, 42		A22–24	A09–10, 42
Culture	A29–33, 40, 44	A17–19, 26, 39–40, 44		A38–44	A17–19, 26, 39–40, 44

Table 3. Differences in text subcategory organisation between Brown/LOB clones, for Reportage texts (Category A).

Corpus: / Subcategory:	Brown (1961 AmE)	LOB (1961 BrE)	WWC (1986 NZE)	Frown (1991 AmE)	FLOB (1991 BrE)
Institutional editorials	B01–07, 20–22	B01–04, 12–13, 17–19, 25	B01–10	B01–10	B01–04, 12–13, 17–19, 25
Commissioned opinion	B08–14, 23–25	B05–08, 14–15, 20–22, 26	B11–20	B11–20	B05–08, 14–15, 20–22, 26
Letters to editor	B15–19, 26–27	B09–11, 16, 23–24, 27	B21–27	B21–27	B09–11, 16, 23–24, 27

Table 4. Differences in text subcategory organisation between Brown/LOB clones, for Editorial texts (Category B).

Subcategory \ Corpus:	LOB/ FLOB/ WWC	Brown (1961 AmE)	Frown (1991 AmE)
Biography	G01–35	G06–07, 14, 31–34, 36–41, 45, 47–55, 58–60, 64, 66–68, 75	G01, 04, 08, 13, 31, 34–42, 45, 47–49, 51–55, 58–60, 62, 67, 68, 74
Arts and literature	G36–50	G08–09, 12, 13, 15, 16, 18, 19, 26–28, 46, 63, 69, 71, 73, 74	G05, 12, 14, 16, 19, 21, 24, 26, 27, 29, 32, 33, 43, 46, 64, 66, 73
General essays	G51–77	G01–05, 10–11, 17, 20–25, 29, 30, 35, 42–44, 56, 57, 61, 62, 65, 70, 72	G02, 03, 06, 07, 09–11, 15, 17, 18, 20, 22, 23, 25, 28, 30, 44, 50, 56, 57, 61, 63, 65, 69–72, 75

Table 5. Differences in text subcategory organisation for Biography and belles lettres texts (Category G).

Subcategory \ Corpus:	Brown (1961 AmE)	LOB (1961 BrE)	WWC (1986 NZE)	Frown (1991 AmE)	FLOB (1991 BrE)
Government reports	H01–02, 04–08, 10, 11, 14, 15, 18–21, 23, 24	H01–12, 20–24	H01–12, 20–24	H01–02, 04–08, 10, 11, 14, 15, 18–21, 23, 24	H01–12, 20–24
Legal proceedings	H03, 09, 16–17	H18–19	H18–19	H03, 09, 16–17	H19
Acts	H12, 22	H13–14	H13–14	H12, 22	H13–14
Debates	H13	H15–17	H15–17	H13	H15–18
Industry/ miscellaneous	H25–30	H25–30	H25–30	H25–30	H25–30

Table 6. Differences in text subcategory organisation for Official documents (Category H).

Subcategory \ Corpus:	Brown (1961 AmE)	LOB (1961 BrE)	WWC (1986 NZE)	Frown (1991 AmE)	FLOB (1991 BrE)
Natural sci	J01–12	J01–12	J01–12	J01–12	J01–12
Medicine	J13–17	J13–17	J13–17	J13–17	J13–17
Mathematics	J18–21	J18–21	J18–21	J18–21	J18–21
Sociology	J22–27	J26–31	J26–31	J22–27	J22–27
Psychology	J28–31	J22–25	J22–25	J28–31	J28–31
Linguistics	J32–35	J32–35	J32–35	J32–35	J32–35
Political sci	J36–41	J40–47	J40–47	J36–41	J36–41
Law	J42–46	J48–50	J48–50	J42–46	J42–46
Education	J47–49	J36–39	J36–39	J47–50	J47–49
Philosophy	J50–53	J51–54	J51–54	J51–54	J50–53
History	J54–58	J55–59	J55–59	J55–58	J54–58
Literature/arts	J59–68	J60–68	J60–68	J59–68	J59–68
Technology	J69–80	J69–80	J69–80	J69–80	J69–80

Table 7. Differences in text subcategory organisation for Academic writing (Category J).

Category: \ Corpus:	Brown/LOB/ Frown/FLOB	WWC (1986 NZE)
K. General	K01–29	All of K01–99 and L01–27. *However, for the present study, the following texts are separated out as representing more specialised genres:*
L. Mystery/detective	L01–24	K33, K38, K64, L20
M. Science fiction	M01–06	K66, K76, K80
N. Adventure/Western	N01–29	K01, K05, K17, K25, K30, K65, K67, K86, K93, K94, K96, L16
P. Romance	P01–29	K06, K07, K16, K19, K22, K37, K47, K70, K73, K74, K89, L03, L12
R. Humour	R01–09	K59, K68, K84, K98, L13, L18, L21, L23, L27

Table 8. Differences in text subcategory organisation for Fiction texts (Categories K–R).

1.4. Approaches to linguistic comparisons of corpora

Previous general comparisons of corpora (e.g. Hofland/Johansson 1982; Leech/Fallon 1992; Kilgarriff 2001) have focussed almost exclusively on wordform frequencies, as being something relatively easy to count. Such studies attempt to identify the vocabulary items that are most differentiated in distribution between varieties, or most characteristic of one particular variety. These comparisons are interesting in their own right; however, to the extent that they are based on specific content words, they may be greatly influenced by differences in text topic, and so may not be especially useful as more general predictors of behaviour on any other linguistic variable.

An alternative approach is to employ a careful triangulation using a number of different linguistic variables (e.g. Hundt 1998, Lindquist/Levin 2001, and especially, Leech *et al.* 2009). While this is certainly effective in the long run, conducting a large number of detailed analyses within a consistent analytical framework can be extremely time-consuming. Moreover, it may be difficult to interpret the frequency differences found for many of the individual variables used until after some critically large body of evidence has been amassed.

In an attempt to find a short-cut to interpreting inter-corpus differences, the present research instead uses general stylistic comparisons as an initial baseline, which can then help interpret the distribution of specific linguistic variables investigated in subsequent research. In this approach, each general stylistic dimension is constructed as an index score based on counts of many different language features associated with the relevant style contrast. However, it should be recognised that broad stylistic measures themselves require some functional interpretation. In particular, it is necessary to confirm that any significant differences in index score do indeed reflect general stylistic differences based on broad patterns of co-occurrence of features, rather than resulting from a highly significant difference on only one contributing linguistic variable. (As part of the present research, follow-up checks of all apparently significant differences in index score were conducted by removing each of the counts in turn from the index score to confirm that differences were not dependent on any one count, and each count was also separately evaluated for significance of inter-corpus differences; see Section 3.2.) It should be stressed that this broad stylistic approach is not intended to replace more detailed functional analyses, but to inform them. It should also be acknowledged that accumulated evidence from more detailed functional analyses of variables may eventually necessitate some reinterpretation of the broad stylistic differences initially identified.

One especially important stylistic dimension is that of "formality" (indeed, within sociolinguistics, the terms "style" and "formality" are often used interchangeably). The "formality" of a language event may be broadly defined as the extent to which the participants feel socially constrained in their behaviour (including language); "formality" in this psychological sense is closely associated with the tension between social cohesion (conformity) and individual freedom, and is expected to be salient in all human interaction. It also follows that this dimension should be linked to almost any socially salient linguistic variable (i.e., any variable for which the variants are subject to social judgements or prescriptions), and so is expected to be relevant to much of the linguistic variation that we may be interested in describing. As it happens, research within the "multi-feature/multidimensional" paradigm has identified one very similar dimension with potentially universal relevance. Of all of the functional dimensions defined for English by Biber (1988), the dimension contrasting "informational versus interactional focus" remained consistently prominent in models for other languages (Biber 1995), and also in subsequent reanalyses of English using differently-weighted samples, different definitions of linguistic counts, or different mathematical assumptions about factor models (Lee 2005). It is therefore especially important that corpora be comparable on this functional dimension. For these reasons, I set out to construct a general measure of formality to compare the five parallel corpora of written English. Section 2 defines the formality measure to be used; Section 3 presents the results of the inter-corpus comparison, broken down further by category in Section 4, and by subcategory in Section 5.

2. Defining the formality index

The general measure of "formality" used in the present research is a slightly simplified version of the wordform-based index reported in Sigley (1997a). In outline, it is derived as follows. First, a test corpus is chosen for the purpose of defining the measure (Section 2.1). Second, a range of different linguistic feature counts are defined (in practice, mostly in terms of a list of functionally-related wordforms), each associated with some linguistic function(s) expected to be correlated either with a "formal" or an "informal" style of language (Section 2.2). These counts are normalised for text length and then converted to standard normal variates (with an average of 0 and a variance of 1). Third, the variation shared between the normalised counts is extracted as a small number of summary dimensions using principal component analysis (PCA; Section 2.3). The pattern of the count loadings on these dimensions forms one way of interpreting the dimensions. Finally, index scores are calculated on each principal component retained, as a weighted sum of the standard normal variates for each count in each text (Section 2.4). At this stage, the interpretation of the principal components used can be checked by investigating the distribution of text categories (Section 2.5) or alternatively, the linguistic characteristics of the texts occupying the most extreme positions on each dimension (Section 2.6). The index defined on the test corpus can then also be applied to the texts in each of the corpora to be compared.

Before obtaining the feature counts, one necessary preliminary task, more time-consuming than all of the subsequent data processing, was to convert all of the corpora to the same coding scheme to ensure comparability of concordancer output. In practice, WSC, FLOB and

Frown were edited to make them compatible with the markup used in LOB and WWC. (By comparison, coding differences in Brown were relatively minor, and it was possible to create a parallel command file which produced equivalent output without editing that corpus.)

2.1. The test corpus (WSC+WWC)

The formality index needs to be defined using texts representing as full a stylistic range as possible. In particular, the possibility of "colloquialisation" raised by Leech *et al.* (2009) requires the inclusion of colloquial speech as a reference point. Of the available written corpora, only WWC has a companion spoken corpus from the same regional variety in approximately the same time frame (the million-word Wellington Corpus of Spoken New Zealand English, described in Holmes/Vine/Johnson 1998; henceforth WSC). Thus the index was defined on the New Zealand English corpora (WWC+WSC), and subsequently applied to the remaining written corpora. The text composition of WWC has already been described in Table 2 above; the text category composition of WSC is summarised in Table 9.

Text category	Texts	Words
DGB (Talkback radio)	37	84,321
DGI (Broadcast interviews)	40	96,775
DGU (Parliamentary debates)	14	22,446
DGZ (Transactions and meetings)	80	102,332
DPC (Face-to-face conversations)	226	500,363
DPF (Telephone conversations)	46	70,156
DPH (Oral history interviews)	10	21,972
DPP (Porirua social dialect survey interviews)	11	31,058
MSN (Broadcast news)	36	28,929
MST (Broadcast monologues)	6	11,205
MSW (Broadcast weather reports)	12	3,641
MUC (Sports commentary)	10	26,010
MUJ (Judge's summation)	2	4,489
MUL (Lectures)	14	30,406
MUS (Teacher monologues)	8	12,496
Total	551	1,046,599

Table 9. Text category composition of the Wellington Corpus of Spoken NZ English (WSC); after Holmes/Vine/Johnson (1998: 15).

The text categories used were originally classified into four main groups as “scripted monologues” (MS*), “unscripted monologues” (MU*), “general-domain dialogues” (DG*), and “private dialogues” (DP*), with the main focus of collection being natural conversation (DPC). However, these broad labels do not necessarily accurately reflect the contents of individual texts: e.g. some of the sports commentaries are dialogues, and some parliamentary debates are at least partly scripted. As a result of differences in extent of the different language events sampled (for example, the fact that weather reports are typically only a few minutes long), the texts are not all of constant length. Longer events (such as the conversations) were sampled in extracts of approximately 2000 words, extending to the end of the next turn.

2.2. Selecting counts to index formality

For the formality index constructed in Sigley (1997a), 29 different counts were used, capturing such aspects of informality as involvement (indexed by a count collecting feedback and agreement markers; also one reason for including counts for 1st/2nd-person pronouns), freedom to express personal stance (indexed by a count collecting emphatics or amplifiers, though also expected to correlate with 1st-person pronoun use), and a high degree of shared knowledge, favouring relatively inexplicit reference, including pro-forms (1st/2nd-person pronouns; 3rd-person pronouns; *it*; pro-form *do*; demonstrative pronouns/determiners; and *there*, occurring more often as an “empty” subject than as the locative pronoun) and other forms with low intrinsic meaning, which may also be favoured by on-line processing limits on vocabulary retrieval (generic or superordinate nouns; core verbs), and reduced forms (contractions), as opposed to forms with relatively high intrinsic meaning, such as complex noun phrases (indexed by counting *the*, indefinite articles, nominal suffixes, and the predominantly abstract case-marking prepositions *of*, *in*, and *by*) and some other items providing descriptive detail or grounding (e.g. adjectives, place/time adverbs, adverbial *as*, and spatial prepositions), which may be expected to be more ambivalent in terms of formality *per se*, but are still worth exploring in light of Biber’s characterisation of his most relevant dimension as “informational vs. interactive focus”. Other counts used in the original analysis were the verbal lexemes *be*, *have*, *will*, and other auxiliaries (mostly *can/could*) indicating, amongst other things, direct questions; *to* (as an infinitive particle or locative preposition); non-relative subordinator *that*; verbs associated with reported speech; and hedges/downtoners.

One practical problem with Sigley's (1997a) index was its requirement for manual disambiguation of certain wordforms (*her* as possessive versus object pronoun; *'s* as possessive versus verbal contraction; *that* as non-relative subordinator versus relativiser versus demonstrative). This would have been impracticable to carry out on the extended dataset under consideration here, and so for the present research, the problem was avoided by: dropping the subordinator and demonstrative counts (which the earlier study had in any case identified as not consistently correlated with formality across spoken and written texts); including all pronominal possessives within the personal pronoun counts; and estimating the contraction *'s* from a limited set of recurring two-word phrases (bigrams) identified as relatively unambiguous (i.e., not attested with possessive function in the NZE corpora). Several other counts yielding inconsistent loadings between speech and writing (verbs of reported speech, and *will*) were also dropped from the current analysis. A final modification was the introduction of several sets of *wh*-pronouns (e.g. indexing *wh*-questions as one measure of involvement), which had been excluded from the original index only because that was to be used in studying the distribution of relativisers including *which* (Sigley 1997b).

In total, 25 counts were used. These were mostly based on sets of high-frequency wordforms, with no manual tagging, and no grammatical pattern searches. The final wordform sets used are listed in Table 10. It will be noted that some of these sets (most obviously, the "hedges") include several somewhat multifunctional wordforms. Wordforms were assigned to their most common functional category as identified by inspection of random 1% concordances for all counts across WSC and WWC, but there may still be considerable "noise" in some counts. (The subsequent steps involved in using PCA to derive overall index scores have the effect of minimising the contributions of the least interpretable counts.)

(1) **1st/2nd-person pronouns** = {I me my you your we us our},
(2) **3rd-person pronouns** = {he him his she her they them their},
(3) **adjectives** = {bad big black bright close dark early first free full good hard high large last late light like little long nice old open other small tall real round same white wide far short strong young weak},
(4) **adverbs** = {after again already before during here then while often later since today yesterday yet until soon well somehow sometime* once now usually},
(5) **be** = {am are is was were be being been aren isn wasn weren m re s},
(6) **core verbs** = {come comes coming came feel feels felt feeling find finds found get got getting gets give given gives gave giving go goes going gone went keep keeps kept keeping know knew knowing known knows let lets letting look looking looked looks make made making makes put putting puts see sees saw seeing seen start starts started starting begin begins began begun beginning take taking taken takes took think thinks thinking thought use used using want wants wanted},
(7) **do** = {do did doing don didn does doesn done},
(8) **emphatics** = {just very so such too all both must right never always course every really ever whole simply even sure nothing still best no only any finally everyone},
(9) **generic nouns** = {thing* time* place* something someone somewhere somebody group others people way* lot bit sort kind ones anything everything anyone},
(10) **have** = {have has had having haven hasn hadn d ve},
(11) **hedges** = {about almost around may might maybe perhaps rather quite several somewhat},
(12) **feedback** = {er erm um umm oh mm mhm yeah yes},
(13) **nominal suffixes** = {*ion *ions *ment *ments *ness *nesses *ity *ities},
(14) **other auxiliaries** = {can could cannot should shouldn couldn need needs needn needed needing ought oughtn},
(15) **(spatial) prepositions** = {for on with at from up into over through down between under off against away next past behind along round upon towards among above across back out},
(16) **impersonal *wh*-pronouns** = {which what},
(17) ***wh*-adverbs** = {where when why how},
(18) **as**, (19) **by**, (20) **in**, (21) **it**, (22) **of**, (23) **the**, (24) **there**,
(25) **contractions** – defined in a separate command file including relatively unambiguous bigrams for *'s*: {*n't it's that's he's she's there's what's who's where's how's let's here's when's something's name's mine's them's why's everything's stuff's time's nothing's think's *'d *'ve *'ll *in' *'m *'re}.[3]

Table 10. Wordform-based counts used for the formality index.

The Oxford Concordance Program (OCP) was used to obtain counts for each of the 25 sets in each text of each corpus (approximately

3 The list of bigrams indicating contracted forms in *'s* was derived from a full concordance for *'s* in WWC+WSC: every bigram occurring at least twice without any possessive tokens was retained. For example, *think's* is a recurring unambiguously contracted form, e.g. "that [...] works out at ten dollars a day which I think's a bit steep" (WSC DPC308 0820). By contrast, *thing's*, although more common as a contraction, also occurred as a possessive, so is not included in the count.

6x500x25=75,000 data points). Each count, x_{ij} (the raw score for count i in text j) was divided by text length, yielding a corrected count per thousand words, X_{ij}, and then scaled to a standard normal variate $z_{ij} = (X_{ij}-\mu_i)/\sigma_i$ (using the means and standard deviations from WWC+WSC, as listed in Table 11) before applying PCA.

2.3. Principal component analysis (PCA)

PCA is similar to common factor analysis (CFA) as used by Biber (1988, 1995), in that both give a reduced number of dimensions for quantitative textual description and classification. Mathematically, their factor solutions differ primarily in that PCA assumes random error to be negligible (which is generally true for the first few factors), and only allows orthogonal factors (whereas CFA provides options for correlated factors). In fact, unrotated orthogonal factor models from the two methods are often very similar. However, they differ considerably in focus: PCA creates factors to summarise variation in the counts, whereas CFA constructs variation in the counts in terms of contributions from underlying factors and error terms. The present task seeks one particular target dimension psychologically relevant to actual speakers, rather than a multidimensional space of descriptive linguistic or functional contrasts; the counts have been selected to correlate with (aspects of) that dimension, rather than reflecting all possible dimensions of variation; and the aim of the factor analysis is primarily to summarise this shared variation, rather than to explore separate underlying descriptive dimensions. These differences require that the present index uses PCA rather than CFA. PCA will usually give one main interpretable dimension (or at most a very small number of dimensions) so will tend to result in a multi-feature unidimensional analysis. In the present analysis, PCA was performed using Systat 5.2.1 for the Macintosh.

PCA applied to z_{ij} (the set of standard normal variates for each count in each text) yields a set of w_{ik} (factor weights of count i on factor k), in which the weights are determined roughly by how closely the counts correlate with each other. PCA produces as many output dimensions as the number of input counts, but most can be ignored as capturing only negligible quantities of the original variance. Of the 25 principal components obtained from the present analysis, only the first two (PC1 and PC2) were potentially useful summary dimensions. Subsequent principal components each accounted for less than 5% of the total variance, and had at most one component loading with absolute magnitude over 0.5, and so were discarded as being uninterpretable.

PC1, accounting for 46.8% of the overall variance, and strongly associated with text category (squared multiple R = .879) is the desired formality index. PC2, comprising 8.5% of the variance, and moderately associated with text category (squared multiple R = .530), probably reflects a dimension contrasting concrete description with abstract argument, though that interpretation must remain tentative, since in this analysis PC2 has very few counts with high-magnitude weights, and the counts that make the largest contributions to PC2 (such as prepositions) are notoriously multifunctional. The weights or loadings of the counts on these dimensions are listed in Table 11 and plotted in Figure 1.

The distribution of count loadings on PC1 is consistent with this factor operating as a general formality measure. Positive weights on PC1 are obtained for counts corresponding to "informality" (especially 1st/2nd-person pronouns, contracted forms, and "core" verbs), and negative weights for counts indexing "formality" (mostly consisting of counts associated with complex noun phrases). By contrast, count loadings on PC2 do not allow as consistent an interpretation: negative weights on PC2 are obtained for counts presenting spatial and temporal information (prepositions, and adjectives), but also by 3rd-person pronouns (other than *it*); and there are few counts with strong positive loadings (impersonal *wh*-pronouns, and nominal suffixes).

Count	Mean text frequency/1000w for WSC+WWC	Standard deviation for WSC+WWC	Loading on PC1	Loading on PC2
(01) 1st/2nd-person pronouns	46.147	36.627	+0.899	+0.045
(02) 3rd-person pronouns	29.478	19.921	+0.324	–0.503
(03) adjectives	17.703	6.685	+0.389	–0.390
(04) adverbs	15.559	6.348	+0.614	–0.192
(05) *BE*	54.261	12.964	+0.644	+0.396
(06) core verbs	35.220	18.781	+0.902	–0.075
(07) *DO*	9.678	7.968	+0.860	+0.121
(08) emphatics	32.652	16.454	+0.867	+0.099
(09) generic nouns	13.753	7.561	+0.673	+0.182
(10) *HAVE*	15.909	6.378	+0.580	+0.044
(11) hedges	7.091	3.566	+0.446	+0.153
(12) feedback	25.826	31.133	+0.817	+0.135
(13) nominal suffixes	18.394	17.274	–0.762	+0.461
(14) other auxiliaries	6.719	4.235	+0.401	+0.294
(15) (spatial) prepositions	47.082	12.554	–0.278	–0.753
(16) impersonal *wh*-pronouns	6.288	3.738	+0.405	+0.504
(17) *wh*-adverbs	5.766	3.416	+0.561	–0.022
(18) *as*	4.948	3.369	–0.541	+0.246
(19) *by*	3.253	2.922	–0.779	+0.191
(20) *in*	15.901	7.318	–0.736	+0.179
(21) *it*	16.105	10.494	+0.791	+0.160
(22) *of*	23.310	12.478	–0.818	+0.355
(23) *the*	50.665	21.310	–0.868	–0.027
(24) *there*	4.925	3.713	+0.495	+0.041
(25) contractions	25.601	23.273	+0.934	+0.057

Table 11. Summary statistics and loadings for wordform counts in the NZE corpora (WSC+WWC).

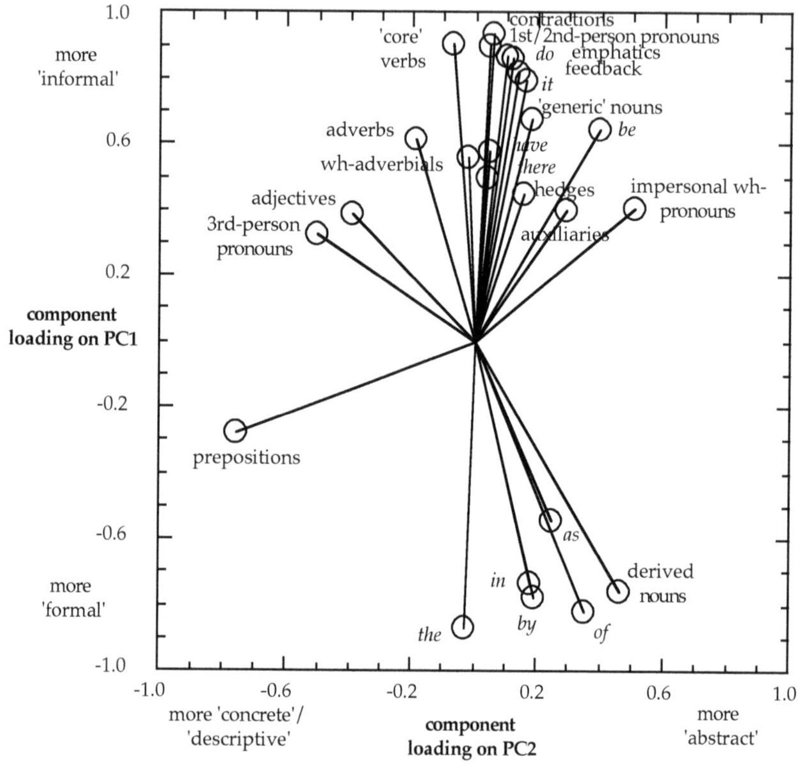

Figure 1. Count loadings on the first two principal components.

2.4. *Calculating factor scores*

Using the weights listed in Table 11, factor scores were calculated for each text in each of the written corpora as the weighted sum of all the text's normalised counts. The factor score of text *j* on principal component *k* is therefore given by:

$$FS_{jk} = \sum_{i=1}^{25} w_{ik} z_{ij}$$

2.5. Text category distribution for WSC+WWC

The overall distribution of mean scores for the WWC/WSC text categories (Table 12; Figure 2) is much as expected: private dialogues are at the most "informal" end of PC1, and academic, legal and governmental reports at the most "formal" end. Mean category PC1 scores cover a range of 30, from +14 to –16; individual text scores range from +22 to –20. A large proportion of the variation in factor scores for individual texts is linked to text category membership. (However, the standard deviations listed for PC1 in Table 12 are close to 3 for most text categories, showing that there is still variation within each category.) Meanwhile, the distribution of text categories on PC2 spans the range between "concrete" weather and sports reporting, and "abstract" legal arguments. Figure 2 also shows that, even though the factor scores are by definition not correlated over the entire test corpus, within the written text categories "formality" is significantly correlated with "abstractness" (Pearson $r = -0.603$ for text index scores on PC1 and PC2 in WWC, $p < 0.001$); hence PC2 probably should be retained for comparison of written corpora by "formality", despite its lesser importance and more tentative interpretation.

Text category	Texts	PC1 mean	PC1 (s.d.)	PC2 mean	PC2 (s.d.)
WSC DGB (Talkback radio)	37	+7.74	(2.85)	+0.93	(0.89)
WSC DGI (Broadcast interviews)	40	+4.03	(3.49)	+1.25	(1.78)
WSC DGU (Parliamentary debates)	14	−7.13	(4.88)	+1.60	(1.52)
WSC DGZ (Transactions/meetings)	80	+10.94	(3.88)	+0.93	(1.52)
WSC DPC (Conversations)	226	+11.42	(2.72)	+0.00	(1.33)
WSC DPF (Phone calls)	46	+13.25	(2.84)	+0.52	(1.14)
WSC DPH (Oral history)	10	+5.74	(4.41)	−0.38	(1.04)
WSC DPP (Dialect survey)	11	+12.45	(2.08)	−0.03	(1.16)
WSC MSN (News broadcasts)	36	−9.31	(3.22)	−1.21	(1.50)
WSC MST (Broadcast talks)	6	−9.12	(2.97)	+1.24	(1.52)
WSC MSW (Weather reports)	12	−11.38	(2.56)	−6.09	(2.28)
WSC MUC (Commentary)	10	−1.52	(2.37)	−3.79	(1.14)
WSC MUJ (Judicial speech)	2	−2.63	(1.96)	+3.37	(1.99)
WSC MUL (Lecture)	14	+0.02	(5.74)	+2.26	(1.13)
WSC MUS (Classroom monologues)	8	+10.16	(6.08)	+1.77	(1.32)
WWC A (Reportage)	44	−9.61	(3.05)	−0.50	(1.09)
WWC B (Editorials)	27	−8.57	(2.77)	+0.55	(1.13)
WWC C (Review)	17	−10.13	(2.12)	−0.06	(0.95)
WWC D (Religion)	17	−11.23	(3.73)	+1.58	(1.76)
WWC E (Hobbies)	38	−8.81	(2.87)	−0.89	(1.68)
WWC F (Popular lore)	44	−9.10	(4.92)	+0.13	(1.61)
WWC G01–35 (Biography)	35	−7.10	(4.58)	−1.07	(1.19)
WWC G36–50 (Arts and literature)	15	−11.15	(3.51)	+1.81	(1.69)
WWC G51–77 (Essays)	27	−9.66	(4.88)	+1.79	(1.76)
WWC H (Official documents)	30	−15.33	(2.81)	+2.18	(1.21)
WWC J (Academic)	80	−12.92	(3.84)	+1.86	(1.57)
WWC K/L (Fiction)	126	−1.75	(4.92)	−2.78	(1.41)

Table 12. Summary statistics for factor scores on PC1 and PC2 for each text category in the NZE corpora.

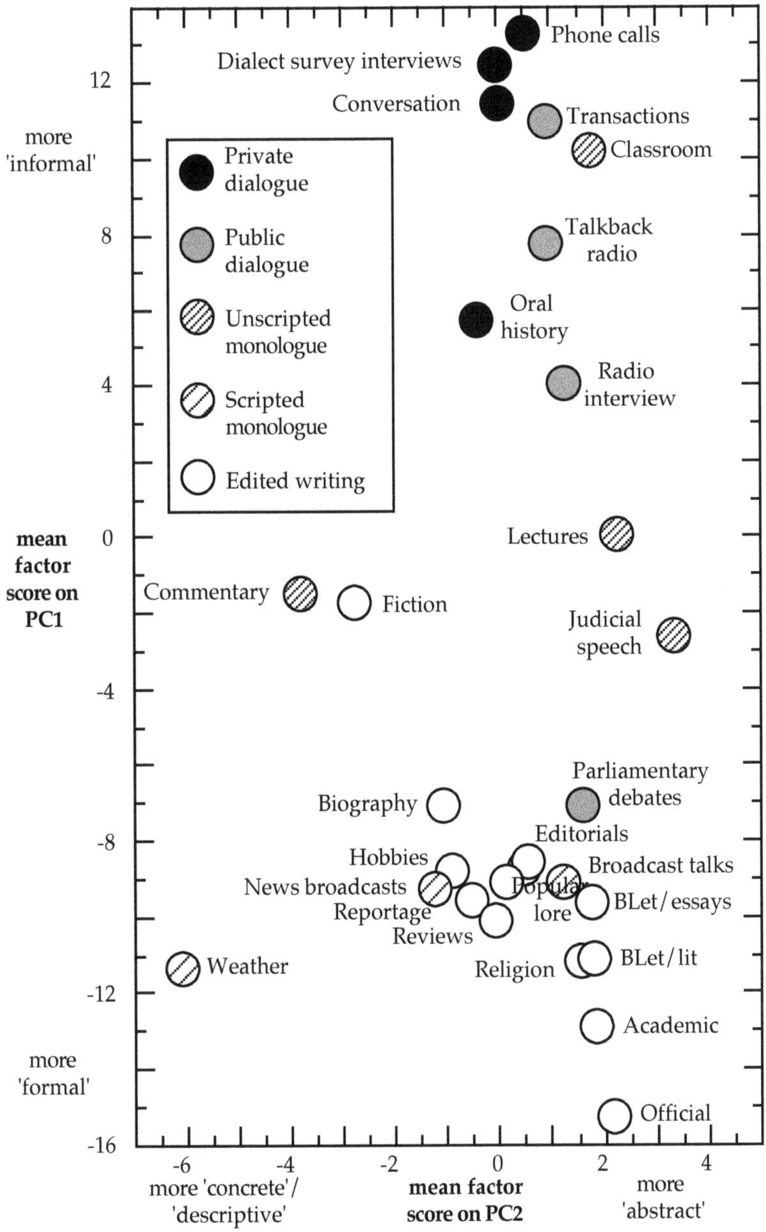

Figure 2. Mean factor scores for WSC/WWC text categories.

2.6. Sample text extracts

Within the New Zealand English data, the texts representing the extremes of formality are H14 (PC1= –22.2) and DPF049 (PC1= +20.5). Short extracts of each of these texts are contrasted in Figure 3. For ease of reading, all WWC corpus formatting codes have been removed, and original italics have been reconstructed where necessary. Some WSC codes have been retained, e.g. for emphasis, overlapping speech, and latching; see Stubbe (this volume) for details. Items with strongly negative loadings (< –0.5) on PC1 are marked by underlining, and items with strongly positive loadings (> +0.5) in boldface.

As already noted, some tokens are used in ways inconsistent with the function assigned to the wordform count: for example, in H14, *let* is used as a full lexical verb, and *such* is used for specification of identity, not as an emphatic. Conversely, some clear markers of formality in the text (*hereby; said* marking coreference, as in *said land*) cannot be included in the index, as they have vanishingly low frequency outside the most formal texts. The items included in the index, being for practical reasons mostly limited to high-frequency wordforms, are probably not themselves the most salient markers of "formality". Nevertheless, they tend to occur within and alongside constructions that are more obvious indicators of formality level (e.g. the counts for *in* and *of* capture the phrase "in respect of" in H14, whereas the counts for *be*, *do*, and 2nd-person pronouns capture the direct questions in DPF049). The overall stylistic contrast between these extracts is very clear, and is satisfactorily (if perhaps indirectly) captured by the items indexed. The items with the largest contributions to the index are also the items with the least potential for error. Moreover, with approximately half of all word tokens in the test corpus contributing in some way to the index score, enough items are included in each text's index score as to render the few errors inconsequential.

Extract (a) from WWC text H14 (Official documents), PC1= –22.2

43. *Old Synagogue building and curtilage* – (1) Section 4 of the principal Act **is** hereby amended by repealing subsection (6), and substituting the following subsections:
"(6) **Until** the Council passes a resolution under subsection (5) of this section in respect of the land thirdly described in the First Schedule to this Act (old Synagogue site), or in respect of **any** part of **it**, the Council may **let** or lease the same or **any** remaining part to **which such** a resolution **has** not **been** applied, for **such** professional, commercial, cultural, or community purposes as the Council considers will **be** likely to require minimum interference with the external appearance of the old Synagogue building, **yet** will ensure that the building **is kept** in constant **use**.
"(6A) **Any such letting** or leasing may permit the tenant or lessee, subject to the Council's supervision, to **make** alterations or additions to that building, within the foregoing limitations, but the Council may nevertheless permit the demolition or replacement of **any** other building on the said land if, in the Council's opinion, **such** demolition or replacement would enhance the appearance or impact of the old Synagogue building and will assist with the financial viability of the **use** to **which** the property **is** to **be put**.

(WWC text H14 014–033)

Extract (b) from WSC text DPF049 (Phone call), PC1 = +20.5

BD:	**Yes, good** afternoon.
AA:	[*tut*] **Oh good, are you** sitting //down **having** cups of tea? \
BD:	/[*exhales*]\\ No <?>mum</?> **we've just done** that, **we're just about** to **start it.**
AA:	**You haven't even started yet** /=
BD:	=/Anyway, **so what's** the story, **are you** finished?
AA:	**YOU HAVEN'T EVEN STARTED** GARDENING **YET**/=
BD:	=/**We have started** gardening.
AA:	**You have done** some.
BD:	**Yes.**
AA:	**Oh good. Oh well that's good.**
BD:	Not much.

(WSC text DPF049 0005–0080)

Figure 3. Text extracts representing extreme scores on PC1.

Extract (a) from WWC text J51 (Academic writing), PC2= +6.3

2. PLATO'S THEORY OF PREDICATION

The naming view of predication makes no distinction between proper names, like 'Socrates' and common nouns, like 'leucodendron'. Likewise the explicit discussion of naming that we find in Plato's *Cratylus* moves to and fro from one kind of word to the other. The *Cratylus* is concerned with the question of whether names merely reflect convention, or whether there is a notion of their correct application. The dialogue begins using as examples 'Cratylus' and 'Hermogenes', but then, at 385a, switches immediately to the question of whether it is correct to call a horse a man, with no hint that any different question is at issue; and the same switching occurs throughout the dialogue. In English the distinction would be marked by the indefinite article. One would speak of calling Cratylus 'Cratylus' but of calling a man 'a man'. In Greek this is not possible, and the passage in question simply speaks of calling ιπον, 'ανθροπον.

(WWC text J51 025–040)

Extract (b) from WSC text MSW007 (Weather report), PC2= –10.0

SR: Good afternoon. Here is the five day forecast until midnight Saturday the eleventh of May. Situation: a shallow low is moving slowly away from the North Island followed by a ridge of high pressure; a cold front should move northwards over the country on Thursday and Friday followed by a disturbed west to southwest flow. Here are the district forecasts up to midnight on Saturday; Northland, Auckland, Waikato, Waitomo, Taumarunui, and Taranaki: dry through Friday with southwesterlies easing; a period of rain on Saturday. Bay of Plenty, Rotorua, Taupo, Taihape: brief rain at first; from tomorrow onwards fine with not much wind; some rain on Saturday. Wanganui, Manawatu: becoming fine everywhere tomorrow; northwesterlies developing on Thursday; a period of rain on Friday becoming fine again on Saturday. Gisborne: showers and southerlies dying out by Thursday; fine after that, however some rain on Saturday.

(WSC text MSW007 0005–0090)

Figure 4. Text extracts representing extreme scores on PC2.

Figure 4 presents short extracts from the texts forming the extremes on PC2. Again, items with strong negative loadings (corresponding to "concrete description") are underlined; there are no items in these extracts with strong positive loadings. The texts differ most clearly in concentration of place/time information: the text with the most positive PC2 score (J51) contains relatively little such information, whereas the text with the most negative PC2 score (MSW007) contains a high concentration of place/time information.

3. Results of overall corpus formality comparisons

For display purposes, in the following sections the mean factor scores are plotted for each text category; however, it should be noted at the outset that the means were not used as the basis for statistical comparisons. Differences between corpora were instead evaluated using Kruskal-Wallis nonparametric ANOVA, based on the rank order of index scores for texts from the five corpora, within a given text (sub)category. The Kruskal-Wallis test result tends to reflect the consistency rather than the size of any observed difference; but it has the advantage that it is not much affected by individual outlier values (which may be expected to influence the results of tests on means for smaller subcategories).

3.1. Overall comparison of corpora on mean scores for PC1 and PC2

On comparing the overall mean index scores for the written corpora (Table 13; Figure 5), the first point to note is that the differences are very small: all corpus means are within a range of the order of 1 index unit, or less than 5% of the total range found in the NZE test corpus. The differences are also small relative to the amount of variation present in each written corpus. (As expected, all of the written corpora show essentially equivalent overall ranges of variation: all have standard deviations of approximately 6.1±0.2 scale units on PC1, and 2.3±0.2 scale units on PC2.) Nevertheless, the rank differences in scores across all texts are marginally significant ($p<0.05$ by Kruskal-Wallis nonparametric ANOVA) on PC1, and indicative ($p<0.06$) on PC2, justifying closer inspection. Subsequent pairwise tests using Mann-Whitney *U* suggest that WWC is less "abstract" than either LOB ($p=0.019$) or FLOB ($p=0.011$), while Brown is more "formal" than either WWC ($p=0.004$) or LOB ($p=0.019$). The differences observed here between LOB and Brown largely corroborate the findings of Biber (1987). On the other hand, FLOB is a close match to LOB ($p=0.661$ on PC1, $p=0.853$ on PC2), and Frown is an acceptable match to Brown ($p=0.204$ on PC1, $p=0.426$ on PC2).

Corpus:	Brown (1961 AmE)	LOB (1961 BrE)	WWC (1986 NZE)	Frown (c1991 AmE)	FLOB (c1991 BrE)	*p*-value (Kruskal-Wallis *H*)
PC1 mean (s.d.)	–9.44 (6.04)	–8.46 (6.14)	–8.29 (5.89)	–8.84 (6.32)	–8.60 (6.12)	*p*=0.047 *
PC2 mean (s.d.)	–0.03 (2.42)	+0.12 (2.26)	–0.22 (2.31)	–0.10 (2.13)	+0.20 (2.31)	*p*=0.058

Table 13. Overall mean factor scores for the five written corpora.

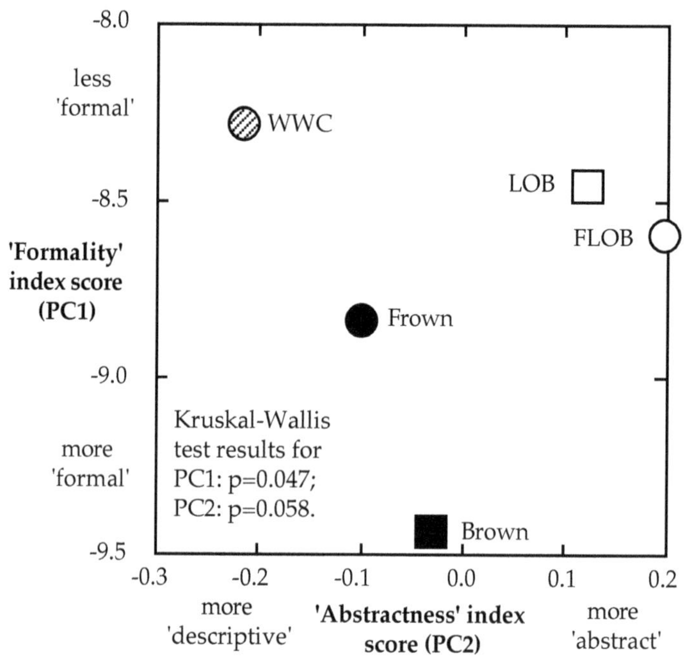

Figure 5. Mean factor scores for written corpora.

The fact that inter-corpus differences are identified as (marginally) significant justifies a more detailed investigation of individual differences between corpora, to check whether these differences apply across the entire corpus, or are instead limited to particular (sub)categories. However, first it is necessary to confirm whether the differences observed for index scores reflect general stylistic differences, or instead only reflect specific linguistic differences on some individual contribution to the score.

3.2. A check on linguistic generality of principal component scores

Followup checks were conducted, firstly by comparing the corpora on each linguistic count in isolation, and secondly by recalculating the PC1 and PC2 index scores without the contribution of each linguistic count in turn. Many of the individual counts did yield significant inter-corpus differences. Some differences were consistent with a trend of colloquialisation, some opposed to it, and some unrelated to such a trend.

Differences consistent with colloquialisation were that: contractions were more frequent in Frown, FLOB and WWC than in LOB and Brown (Frown Reportage showing an especially large difference in this direction); *the* was more frequent in Brown, and least frequent in Frown and FLOB (suggesting a decrease in complex noun phrases in AmE, and to a lesser degree also in BrE, but also at least partly explained by an increase in determiner deletion within Reportage); *of* was more frequent in LOB and Brown than in FLOB and Frown (also consistent with a decrease in complex noun phrases: but possibly also reflecting an increased preference for possessives using *'s*).

Opposed to any overall "colloquialisation" trend, though, were the following patterns: an apparent increase in frequency of derived nouns (in line with Leech *et al.*'s "densification" trend; these were also consistently more frequent in the AmE corpora than in BrE/NZE, as noted by Biber 1987); an apparent decrease in impersonal *wh*-pronouns; and an apparent decrease in frequency of emphatics (one highly speculative interpretation is that expression of personal opinion might be now more often regarded as usual, so less often explicitly marked by such signals).

Other apparently significant differences were not necessarily related to change over time, but may instead indicate differences in regional varieties. For example, *there* was less frequent (and decreasing) in AmE; *it* was relatively more frequent in the BrE corpora; *by* was more frequent in the BrE corpora; *have* was more frequent, and *be* less frequent, in AmE than in BrE/NZE; adverbs were less frequent in AmE (especially Frown) than in the BrE corpora; and generic nouns were more frequent in WWC than in the other corpora. Several of these differences may be indirectly related to the higher frequencies of passive constructions noted by Leech *et al.* for some genres of BrE.

Nevertheless, findings for the overall index score on PC1 proved fairly robust. The significance of overall differences between corpora on PC1 remained close to p=0.05 on removing most individual counts. The extreme cases were that significance for PC1 increased to p=0.009 on removing *by*, and conversely, decreased to conventionally nonsignificant levels on removing *have* (p=0.096) or *be* (p=0.198). Significant pairwise differences between corpora also mostly remained significant, and corpora maintained the same rank order of scores, on removing any individual count (the only minor exception being that removing *of* reversed the order of WWC and LOB). Furthermore, significant differences between corpora within Reportage (A) and Academic (J) categories remained significant on removing any single count.

Results for PC2, however, were much less consistent – which is only to be expected, as fewer counts make any strong contribution to PC2 index scores, and so those counts have more influence on the overall score differences. (Somewhat surprisingly, removing the preposition count *increased* the significance of observed inter-corpus differences on PC2.)

4. Results of corpus comparisons across text categories

4.1. Corpus comparisons across text categories on PC1

Comparing mean category scores on PC1 (Table 14; Figure 6) shows, again, that the variation between corpora is small relative to the amount of variation between text categories, with the differences between categories being similar for all five corpora; the standard deviations listed in Table 14 also confirm the presence of a similar range of variation for each corpus within most text categories. However, there is a tendency for Brown to be on the more "formal" side of most text categories, with this difference being clearest for Reportage (p=0.001) and Editorials (p=0.040). There is also a significant difference among Academic texts (p<0.010), where the scores for FLOB/WWC vs. LOB suggest that British or New Zealand academic articles may be becoming slightly less "formal" on this scale (but there is little evidence of any overall change in

American academic writings). Finally, there is a marginally significant difference (p=0.043) between corpora for category G (Belles Lettres).[4] All of these categories contain stylistically different subcategories; accordingly, each of these apparently significant differences will be followed up in more detail in Section 5.

Text category:	Corpus:	Brown (1961 AmE)	LOB (1961 BrE)	WWC (1986 NZE)	Frown (c1991 AmE)	FLOB (c1991 BrE)	*p*-value (Kruskal-Wallis *H*)
A (Reportage)	mean	–12.03	–9.89	–9.61	–9.08	–9.34	p<0.001
	(s.d.)	(2.78)	(3.36)	(3.05)	(3.32)	(3.20)	***
B (Editorial)	mean	–10.13	–8.81	–8.57	–8.64	–8.64	p=0.040
	(s.d.)	(3.47)	(2.43)	(2.77)	(2.45)	(2.90)	*
C (Reviews)	mean	–10.29	–10.99	–10.13	–10.21	–9.67	p=0.547
	(s.d.)	(1.99)	(2.31)	(2.12)	(2.51)	(2.56)	
D (Religion)	mean	–10.74	–9.78	–11.23	–13.68	–12.44	p=0.077
	(s.d.)	(4.25)	(5.29)	(3.73)	(4.00)	(4.28)	
E (Hobbies)	mean	–9.78	–8.91	–8.81	–8.13	–9.12	p=0.529
	(s.d.)	(3.45)	(3.86)	(2.87)	(3.43)	(3.92)	
F (Popular lore)	mean	–10.60	–9.28	–9.10	–10.98	–10.33	p=0.438
	(s.d.)	(4.50)	(5.38)	(4.92)	(3.88)	(4.95)	
G (Biography /	mean	–10.53	–9.98	–8.78	–10.53	–11.09	p=0.043
belles lettres)	(s.d.)	(4.17)	(3.78)	(4.74)	(4.36)	(4.04)	*
H (Official	mean	–15.98	–13.65	–15.33	–15.51	–14.16	p=0.203
documents)	(s.d.)	(4.26)	(5.04)	(2.81)	(4.85)	(4.39)	
J (Academic)	mean	–14.43	–14.44	–12.92	–14.63	–13.16	p=0.010
	(s.d.)	(4.24)	(3.39)	(3.84)	(3.42)	(3.91)	**
K–R (Fiction)	mean	–2.19	–0.98	–1.75	–1.08	–1.14	p=0.065
	(s.d.)	(4.18)	(3.97)	(4.92)	(4.28)	(4.43)	

Table 14. Text category scores for PC1, by corpus.

4 A conventionally "significant" result of p<0.05 has somewhat less meaning when we are simultaneously considering many different test results, as in the comparisons of corpus (sub)categories. Strictly speaking, the critical significance level should be adjusted for the number of tests conducted, e.g. by applying a (modified) Bonferroni correction. Hence, p-values of 0.01-0.05 among a *set* of five independent tests should be regarded as merely indicative.

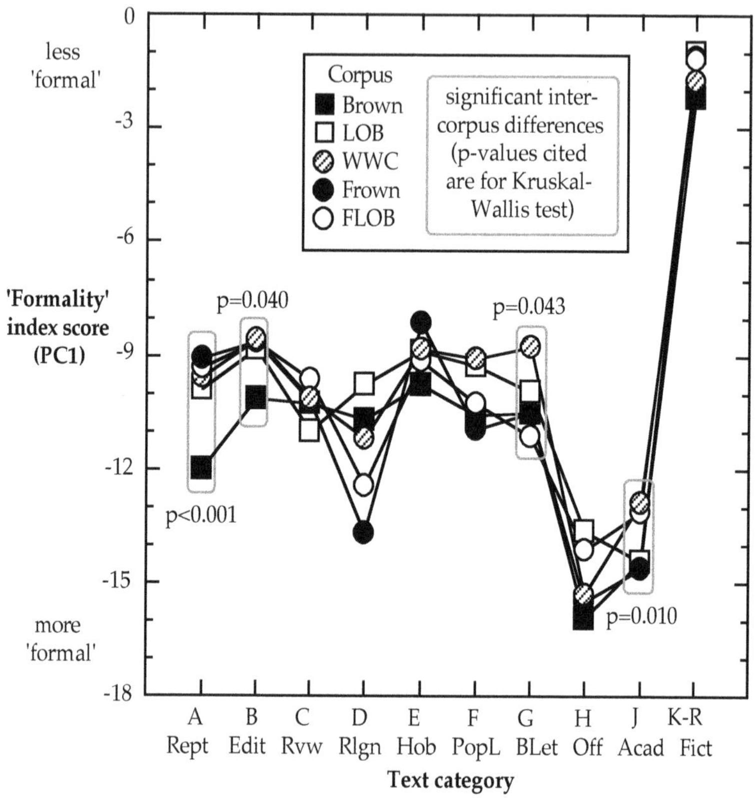

Figure 6. Mean text category scores for PC1, by corpus.

4.2. Corpus comparisons across text categories on PC2

There are also some significant differences on PC2 (Table 15; Figure 7) for the text categories E (Hobbies), F (Popular Lore), and K–R (Fiction). However, it is not easy to interpret these differences, not only because of the greater uncertainty in interpreting PC2, but also because guidelines for collecting texts for these categories were rather loose, and (for Hobbies and Popular Lore) governed by topic rather than style. The tendency towards more "abstract" scores for Popular Lore in the more recent corpora might reflect an increased specialisation in leisure publications, or shifts in relevant topics, for example towards personal computing; but the Hobbies samples show exactly the opposite stylistic trend, so that it is not clear that any meaningful generalisations are possible. In the case of Fiction, at least, there are potentially meaningful subcategories (albeit not officially used in WWC) that can be explored further in Section 5.

Text category:	Corpus:	Brown (1961 AmE)	LOB (1961 BrE)	WWC (1986 NZE)	Frown (c1991 AmE)	FLOB (c1991 BrE)	*p*-value (Kruskal-Wallis *H*)
A (Reportage)	mean	–0.64	–0.89	–0.50	–0.70	–1.19	p=0.250
	(s.d.)	(1.71)	(1.39)	(1.09)	(1.23)	(1.43)	
B (Editorial)	mean	+0.87	+1.25	+0.55	+0.67	+0.93	p=0.123
	(s.d.)	(1.23)	(0.90)	(1.13)	(0.97)	(1.04)	
C (Reviews)	mean	+0.26	+0.50	–0.06	–0.54	+0.16	p=0.053
	(s.d.)	(1.09)	(1.47)	(0.95)	(0.70)	(1.16)	
D (Religion)	mean	+2.00	+2.28	+1.58	+2.47	+2.37	p=0.347
	(s.d.)	(1.57)	(1.29)	(1.76)	(1.24)	(1.91)	
E (Hobbies)	mean	+0.04	+0.22	–0.89	–1.11	–0.43	p<0.001
	(s.d.)	(1.80)	(1.29)	(1.68)	(1.25)	(1.49)	***
F (Popular lore)	mean	+0.02	–0.10	+0.13	+0.88	+0.84	p=0.007
	(s.d.)	(1.93)	(1.60)	(1.61)	(1.51)	(1.65)	**
G (Biography / belles lettres)	mean	+0.84	+0.94	+0.49	+0.29	+0.76	p=0.297
	(s.d.)	(2.13)	(2.03)	(2.07)	(1.87)	(2.19)	
H (Official documents)	mean	+2.02	+1.97	+2.18	+1.44	+2.19	p=0.091
	(s.d.)	(0.95)	(1.23)	(1.21)	(0.96)	(1.53)	
J (Academic)	mean	+2.09	+2.23	+1.86	+2.01	+2.40	p=0.164
	(s.d.)	(1.47)	(1.33)	(1.57)	(1.22)	(1.53)	
K–R (Fiction)	mean	–2.71	–2.34	–2.78	–2.37	–2.03	p<0.001
	(s.d.)	(1.58)	(1.49)	(1.41)	(1.41)	(1.47)	***

Table 15. Text category scores for PC2, by corpus.

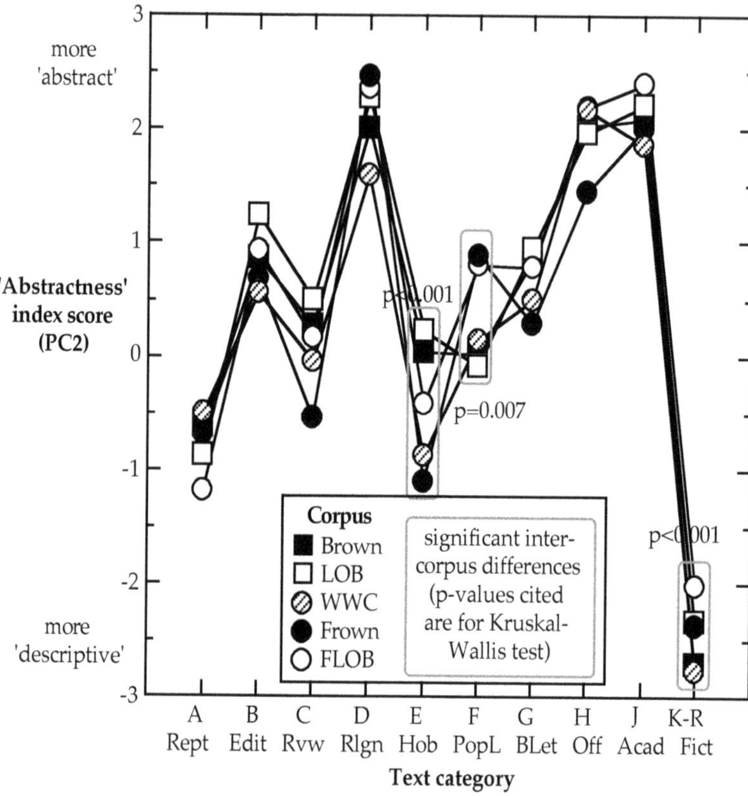

Figure 7. Mean text category scores for PC2, by corpus.

5. Results of corpus comparisons across subcategories

The present section provides a more detailed breakdown of inter-corpus differences within the text categories for which significant overall stylistic differences have been identified and for which relevant subcategories can be defined: namely, Reportage; Editorials; Biography and Belles Lettres; Academic writing; and Fiction. (However, for the Academic subcategories, comparisons will be limited to PC1, partly because, as seen in Figure 7, the Academic samples do not differ greatly on PC2 overall, and partly because the large number of subcategories makes a two-dimensional plot too crowded for legibility.)

5.1. Corpus comparisons across subcategories for Reportage and Editorials (Categories A and B)

In press reportage, the Brown corpus data is consistently the most "formal" in every subcategory (Table 16; Figure 8).[5] Brown is also most "formal" for institutional editorials and letters to the editor (Table 17; Figure 9). The inter-corpus differences on PC1 are most significant for political reporting and institutional editorials ($p<0.001$ in both cases: hence these test results remain significant at $p<0.05$ even after a Bonferroni correction for the number of tests performed). Conversely, differences are negligible in both personal opinion articles and reviews, in which there is minimal editorial influence. The most likely explanation for such a pattern is that the stylistic differences reflect changes in editorial or institutional norms for newspaper style: specifically, that American journalism (and especially, political reporting) became less "formal" on average between 1961 and 1991.

Several potentially relevant institutional changes in American journalism took place over this period. First, a less deferential approach to political reporting emerged from late-1960s counterculture. The reporting of the Watergate scandal was a symptom of this trend, but also a catalyst for its extension, as the scandal helped to (re)establish the questioning of government as a central role of the national press (a position explicitly adopted by several editorials sampled in WWC and FLOB). Second, the "Fairness Doctrine" (which had required American newspapers to allocate space to all sides of a story) was repealed in 1987: hence Brown reportage was under more severe constraints on treatment of (especially, political) topics than the reportage sampled in Frown. A third institutional change was the entry of British-style tabloids (and also, a large number of British tabloid editors and journalists) into the American market during the 1970s, under the control of Rupert Murdoch (*Star*) and Generoso Pope (*National Enquirer*), as documented by Taylor (1991: 81). The last of these changes had no direct impact on the data sampled for Frown, in that no texts were sourced from the British-influenced tabloids; but there may have been some

---

5 The ellipses in these graphs have no statistical function: they are merely a visual device for collecting together the points representing the mean index scores for each subcategory.

more generalised drift towards a tabloid style in other newspapers in response to this invasion.

Text subcategory:	Corpus:	Brown (1961 AmE)	LOB (1961 BrE)	WWC (1986 NZE)	Frown (c1991 AmE)	FLOB (c1991 BrE)	*p*-value (Kruskal-Wallis *H*)
Politics	PC1 mean	−14.00	−12.22	−9.85	−10.24	−11.74	$p<0.001$
	(s.d.)	(2.16)	(1.48)	(2.60)	(2.09)	(2.06)	***
Sports	PC1 mean	−9.27	−7.09	−8.52	−7.20	−6.36	$p=0.415$
	(s.d.)	(2.83)	(1.52)	(2.76)	(4.71)	(1.95)	
Briefs	PC1 mean	−12.46	−9.90	−11.06	−9.59	−9.81	$p=0.092$
	(s.d.)	(1.57)	(3.72)	(1.58)	(3.49)	(1.60)	
Financial	PC1 mean	−13.66	−11.11	−12.23	−9.59	−12.24	$p=0.307$
	(s.d.)	(2.09)	(4.16)	(2.32)	(2.21)	(1.35)	
Society and Culture /Features	PC1 mean	−10.18	−8.35	−7.66	−8.08	−6.67	$p=0.155$
	(s.d.)	(2.01)	(3.58)	(3.90)	(3.57)	(3.21)	
Politics	PC2 mean	+0.72	−0.33	−0.13	−0.32	−0.28	$p=0.206$
	(s.d.)	(1.51)	(1.01)	(0.98)	(1.01)	(0.67)	
Sports	PC2 mean	−2.75	−2.79	−1.50	−1.89	−3.41	$p=0.319$
	(s.d.)	(0.73)	(0.81)	(0.94)	(1.64)	(0.79)	
Briefs	PC2 mean	−0.77	−0.80	−1.38	−0.74	−1.36	$p=0.301$
	(s.d.)	(1.16)	(1.39)	(0.80)	(0.67)	(1.03)	
Financial	PC2 mean	+0.01	−0.20	+0.06	−0.23	−0.16	$p=0.981$
	(s.d.)	(0.96)	(0.70)	(0.70)	(0.57)	(0.44)	
Society and Culture /Features	PC2 mean	−1.20	−0.64	+0.26	−0.54	−1.05	$p=0.042$
	(s.d.)	(1.39)	(1.32)	(0.66)	(1.42)	(1.46)	*

Table 16. Text subcategory scores by corpus for Reportage (Category A).

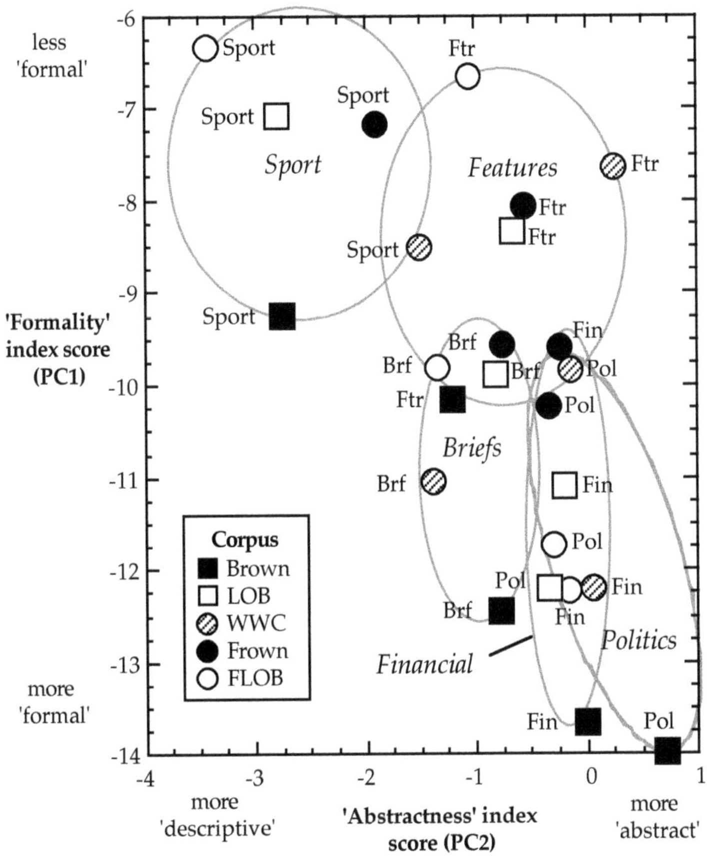

Figure 8. Mean subcategory scores for Reportage (A) on PC1*PC2.

Text subcategory:	Corpus:	Brown (1961 AmE)	LOB (1961 BrE)	WWC (1986 NZE)	Frown (c1991 AmE)	FLOB (c1991 BrE)	*p*-value (Kruskal-Wallis *H*)
Institutional editorials	PC1 mean	−12.10	−8.15	−10.38	−8.85	−10.43	$p<0.001$
	(s.d.)	(1.39)	(1.88)	(0.88)	(1.50)	(1.47)	***
Commissioned personal opinion	PC1 mean	−7.91	−9.24	−6.53	−7.68	−6.41	$p=0.200$
	(s.d.)	(4.65)	(2.45)	(3.28)	(3.33)	(2.63)	
Letters to editor	PC1 mean	−10.47	−9.17	−8.91	−9.73	−9.26	$p=0.614$
	(s.d.)	(1.40)	(3.18)	(1.82)	(1.76)	(2.93)	
Institutional editorials	PC2 mean	+1.40	+1.34	+1.10	+0.17	+1.16	$p=0.015$
	(s.d.)	(0.80)	(1.00)	(1.03)	(0.69)	(0.63)	*
Commissioned personal opinion	PC2 mean	−0.25	+0.87	−0.35	+0.75	+0.30	$p=0.055$
	(s.d.)	(1.07)	(0.86)	(0.97)	(1.09)	(1.17)	
Letters to editor	PC2 mean	+1.72	+1.65	+1.05	+1.28	+1.48	$p=0.363$
	(s.d.)	(0.69)	(0.67)	(0.60)	(0.83)	(0.95)	

Table 17. Text subcategory scores by corpus for Editorial (Category B).

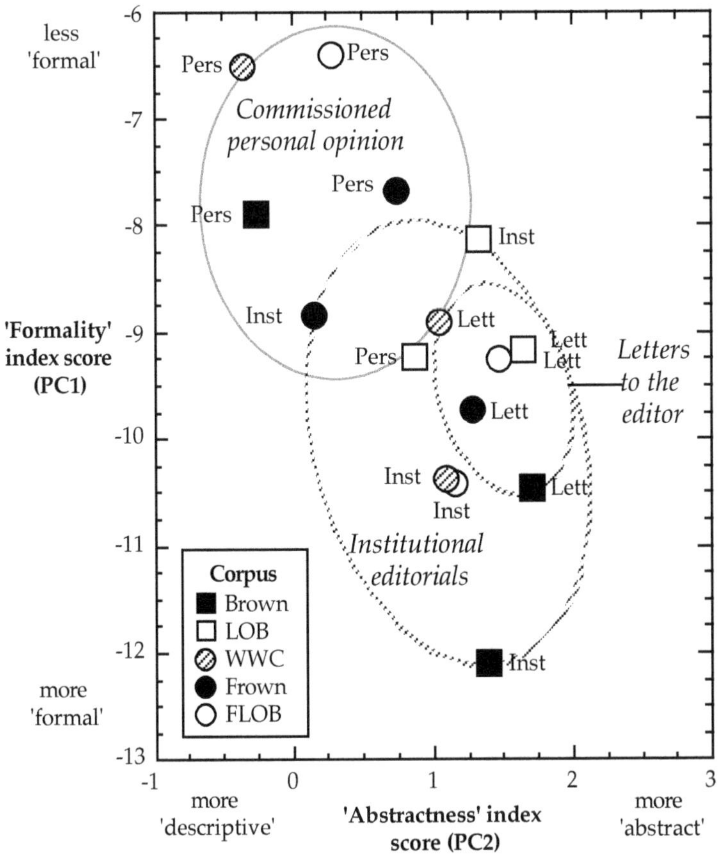

Figure 9. Mean subcategory scores for Editorials (B) on PC1*PC2.

5.2. Corpus comparisons across subcategories for Biography and belles lettres (Category G)

One important point to make about "Biography and Belles Lettres" is that it is not in fact a single stylistic category in any of the corpora, and should not be treated as such. "General essays" show no consistent stylistic distinction from essays on arts and literature (which are, in turn, stylistically indistinguishable from the Arts texts collected for the Academic category); but all corpora show an extremely large and consistent difference in index scores between both of these subcategories and the "Biography" texts (Table 18; Figure 10). Given this stylistic (and also institutional) divide between subcategories, it is surprising that all three subcategories show the same opposition between FLOB (most "formal") and WWC (least "formal", with the exception of LOB art and literature essays); however, the differences between corpora within each of the subcategories on PC1 are small enough to be due to chance (and indeed, the overall significance for corpus differences across the category as a whole was marginal for PC1, at p=0.043, and nonsignificant for PC2, at p=0.297). General essays do show an apparently significant inter-corpus difference on PC2, but even this becomes marginal after applying a Bonferroni correction.

Text subcategory:	Corpus:	Brown (1961 AmE)	LOB (1961 BrE)	WWC (1986 NZE)	Frown (c1991 AmE)	FLOB (c1991 BrE)	p-value (Kruskal-Wallis H)
Biography	PC1 mean	–8.11	–8.33	–0.41	–7.99	–8.75	p=0.838
	(s.d.)	(3.70)	(3.67)	(1.48)	(4.15)	(3.32)	
Arts and literature	PC1 mean	–12.56	–10.96	–11.15	–13.03	–14.00	p=0.056
	(s.d.)	(3.50)	(3.01)	(3.50)	(3.02)	(2.54)	
General essays	PC1 mean	–12.03	–11.56	–9.66	–11.75	–12.50	p=0.195
	(s.d.)	(3.77)	(3.53)	(4.88)	(3.94)	(3.96)	
Biography	PC2 mean	–0.89	–7.10	–1.07	–1.01	–1.09	p=0.473
	(s.d.)	(1.48)	(4.58)	(1.19)	(1.32)	(1.19)	
Arts and literature	PC2 mean	+1.39	+1.30	+1.81	+1.23	+2.07	p=0.446
	(s.d.)	(1.63)	(1.28)	(1.69)	(1.72)	(1.49)	
General essays	PC2 mean	+2.48	+2.49	+1.79	+1.13	+2.42	p=0.009
	(s.d.)	(1.46)	(1.82)	(1.76)	(1.66)	(1.57)	**

Table 18. Text subcategory scores by corpus for Biography and belles lettres (Category G).

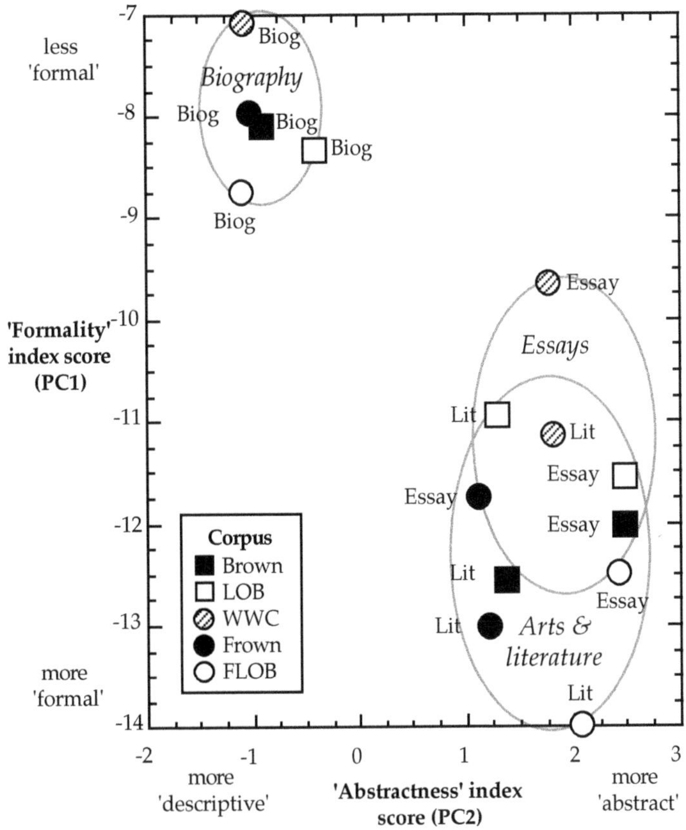

Figure 10. Mean subcategory scores for Category G on PC1*PC2.

5.3. Corpus comparisons across subcategories for Academic writings (Category J)

There is a tendency for WWC and FLOB to appear less "formal" on PC1 than the other corpora over most Academic subcategories (Table 19; Figure 11), suggesting a slight trend towards a less formal academic style, at least outside the USA. However, partly because there are few texts in each subcategory, corpus differences within subcategories reach significance only for Technology (p=0.012) and Medicine (p=0.005). Most of the difference in the Technology subsection lies in FLOB, whose texts score as slightly, but consistently, less formal than those in the other corpora. For Medicine, the WWC sample is not only more informal on average, but also shows a larger standard deviation, than those in the other corpora. Much of the inter-corpus difference for the Medicine subcategory can be attributed to the WWC texts covering a wider range of topics and audiences, including not only detailed papers for specialists, but also more general articles on preventative healthcare for GPs and patients.

Text subcategory:	Corpus:	Brown (1961 AmE)	LOB (1961 BrE)	WWC (1986 NZE)	Frown (c1991 AmE)	FLOB (c1991 BrE)	*p*-value (Kruskal-Wallis *H*)
Natural sci	PC1 mean	−16.04	−15.90	−14.03	−17.09	−15.06	*p*=0.070
	(s.d.)	(4.30)	(2.99)	(2.32)	(2.29)	(2.11)	
Medicine	PC1 mean	−17.91	−12.95	−8.37	−16.64	−12.04	*p*=0.005
	(s.d.)	(2.60)	(2.73)	(4.18)	(2.17)	(3.29)	**
Mathematics	PC1 mean	−12.73	−11.85	−11.78	−10.33	−11.91	*p*=0.829
	(s.d.)	(3.24)	(2.56)	(2.27)	(3.75)	(2.77)	
Sociology	PC1 mean	−15.25	−13.69	−13.22	−15.29	−12.08	*p*=0.611
	(s.d.)	(5.43)	(4.57)	(4.99)	(3.17)	(3.62)	
Psychology	PC1 mean	−10.59	−13.28	−12.12	−12.56	−14.62	*p*=0.383
	(s.d.)	(4.87)	(1.22)	(6.07)	(0.68)	(2.70)	
Linguistics	PC1 mean	−12.13	−16.18	−11.32	−12.40	−10.01	*p*=0.201
	(s.d.)	(6.07)	(3.04)	(4.41)	(3.52)	(3.99)	
Political sci	PC1 mean	−14.42	−14.21	−13.09	−13.88	−16.31	*p*=0.466
	(s.d.)	(3.78)	(2.92)	(4.02)	(3.04)	(2.70)	
Law	PC1 mean	−17.65	−15.73	−16.06	−16.92	−14.94	*p*=0.791
	(s.d.)	(1.70)	(5.18)	(2.73)	(2.59)	(2.78)	
Education	PC1 mean	−12.76	−15.67	−9.69	−14.82	−9.82	*p*=0.162
	(s.d.)	(1.84)	(3.16)	(4.33)	(2.32)	(5.52)	
Philosophy	PC1 mean	−11.52	−12.64	−9.60	−11.19	−4.96	*p*=0.112
	(s.d.)	(7.82)	(4.70)	(1.22)	(2.00)	(4.87)	
History	PC1 mean	−13.36	−13.63	−14.50	−15.51	−14.06	*p*=0.796
	(s.d.)	(2.01)	(2.56)	(2.54)	(2.58)	(4.41)	
Literature/arts	PC1 mean	−11.50	−13.60	−13.07	−12.98	−14.30	*p*=0.396
	(s.d.)	(2.53)	(3.96)	(3.46)	(4.95)	(3.68)	
Technology	PC1 mean	−16.50	−15.62	−15.27	−15.46	−13.31	*p*=0.012
	(s.d.)	(2.23)	(3.38)	(2.78)	(2.24)	(1.55)	*

Table 19. Text subcategory scores on PC1 by corpus for Academic writings (Category J).

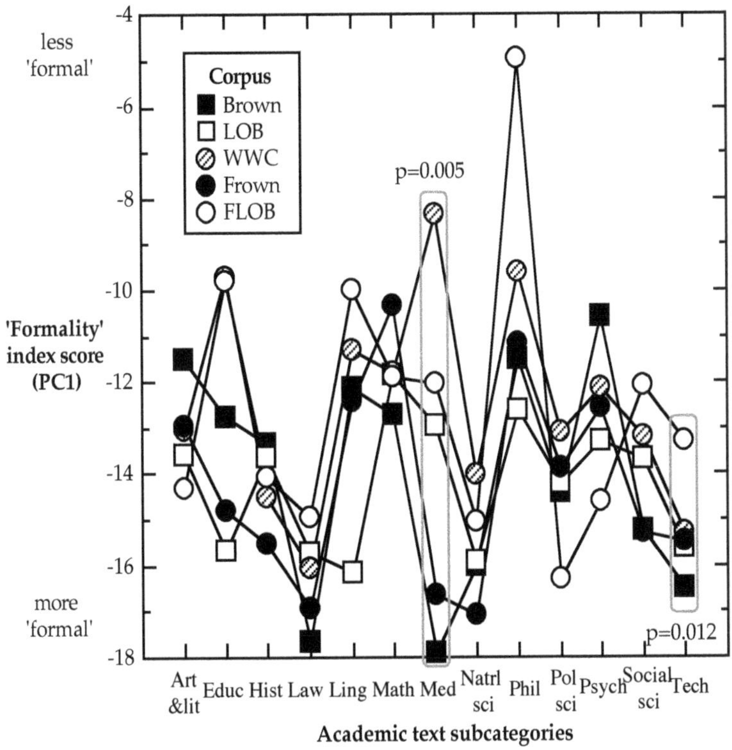

Figure 11. Mean subcategory scores on PC1 for academic writing (J).

5.4. Corpus comparisons across subcategories for Fiction (Categories K–R)

Corpus differences within fiction subcategories (Table 20; Figure 12) are mostly negligible, with the exception of Humour. The apparent trend towards increased informality in that subcategory (with LOB and Brown being the two most formal samples, then WWC, then FLOB, and finally Frown at the most informal end) might suggest that erudite humour is being replaced by the merely rude; but this would be to overinterpret the available data. Much humour derives from deliberate play with and mismatching of formality levels, so that humour is especially ill-defined as a stylistic category, and we should expect larger variation between and within texts than is usual even for other fiction categories. In such small samples as these (9 texts, for those corpora with a separate Humour category), large differences between sample means might easily result from the inclusion of only a handful of atypical texts. The Frown humour sample is clearly distanced from those of the other corpora; and closer inspection of its constituent texts suggests it may be a rather unrepresentative sample of American humorous fiction, as it contains one text (R02) actually by a British author,[6] and one instructional text for writers (R05) which seems intended primarily as nonfiction.[7] Nevertheless, these problematic texts are not clearly the reason for the Frown sample's more "informal" average score: R05 is the most formal text included in the section (scoring –4.1 on PC1).

Regarding PC2, the significant overall tendency for FLOB and Frown fiction texts to score as (slightly) less "descriptive" and more "abstract" than fiction in the other corpora (as seen in Table 15) seems to be genre-specific, being largely limited to the categories of Mystery/detective and Adventure.

---

6 The work in question is Douglas Adams' novel *Mostly Harmless*. The misunderstanding may have arisen because it was published simultaneously in Britain and the United States, and the compilers happened to sample the one chapter that is set in New York.

7 The advice contained (e.g. on avoiding writer's block) is sufficiently practical that the work sampled seems much more likely to be an actual "self-help" book than a parody of the genre. Nevertheless, for marketing purposes, the publishers have classified the book as "Humor", and realistically, corpus compilers have little choice but to trust such labels.

Text category:	Corpus:	Brown (1961 AmE)	LOB (1961 BrE)	WWC (1986 NZE)	Frown (c1991 AmE)	FLOB (c1991 BrE)	*p*-value (Kruskal-Wallis *H*)
K. General	PC1 mean	–3.35	–1.42	–1.58	–2.33	–0.40	p=0.050
	(s.d.)	(4.25)	(4.10)	(4.71)	(4.70)	(3.48)	
L. Mystery/ detective	PC1 mean	–0.82	–0.52	+0.71	–0.14	+1.52	p=0.340
	(s.d.)	(4.19)	(4.65)	(4.90)	(3.93)	(3.55)	
M. Science Fiction	PC1 mean	–2.86	–3.83	–5.06	–1.18	–4.33	p=0.484
	(s.d.)	(3.63)	(1.59)	(9.31)	(2.63)	(4.96)	
N. Adventure/ Western	PC1 mean	–3.30	–1.58	–2.58	–3.18	–3.52	p=0.379
	(s.d.)	(3.42)	(3.26)	(4.95)	(4.19)	(4.90)	
P. Romance	PC1 mean	+0.05	+1.66	–0.21	+1.06	–0.31	p=0.109
	(s.d.)	(3.28)	(2.54)	(5.41)	(3.54)	(3.89)	
R. Humour	PC1 mean	–5.32	–5.45	–4.49	+0.45	–3.51	p=0.025
	(s.d.)	(5.29)	(2.60)	(4.15)	(3.33)	(3.96)	*
K. General	PC2 mean	–2.79	–2.08	–2.80	–2.41	–2.14	p=0.049
	(s.d.)	(1.29)	(1.15)	(1.41)	(1.43)	(1.43)	*
L. Mystery/ detective	PC2 mean	–3.04	–2.03	–2.74	–1.55	–1.62	p=0.002
	(s.d.)	(1.48)	(1.58)	(0.61)	(1.04)	(1.15)	**
M. Science Fiction	PC2 mean	–1.03	–1.62	–0.32	–2.00	–2.37	p=0.201
	(s.d.)	(1.17)	(1.46)	(1.13)	(1.18)	(1.65)	
N. Adventure/ Western	PC2 mean	–3.37	–3.12	–3.52	–2.47	–1.90	p<0.001
	(s.d.)	(1.40)	(1.45)	(1.10)	(1.31)	(1.35)	***
P. Romance	PC2 mean	–2.73	–2.60	–3.09	–3.00	–2.68	p=0.784
	(s.d.)	(1.57)	(1.50)	(1.39)	(1.42)	(1.32)	
R. Humour	PC2 mean	–0.57	–1.10	–2.03	–2.31	–0.90	p=0.032
	(s.d.)	(1.17)	(1.04)	(1.09)	(1.84)	(1.43)	*

Table 20. Text subcategory scores by corpus for Fiction (Categories K–R).

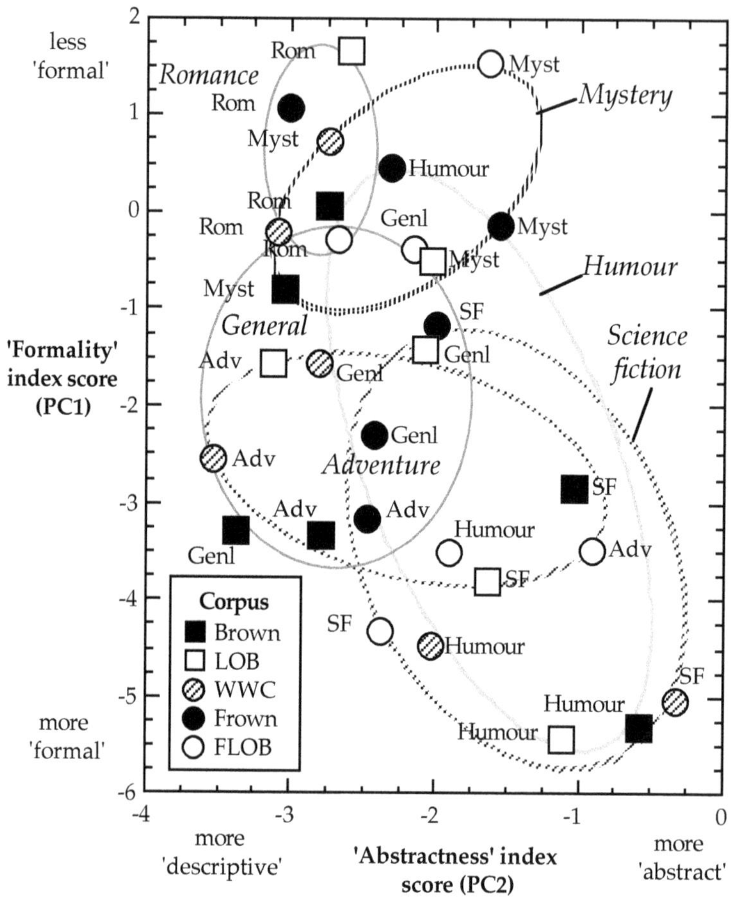

Figure 12. Mean subcategory scores for Fiction on PC1*PC2.

6. Conclusions

This paper has demonstrated the use of factor analysis for a general preliminary evaluation of corpus comparability. A general index of "formality" has been defined using PCA on selected sets of high-frequency wordforms. Comparisons of text category means confirm that the index correlates reliably with situational factors of the communication event; and checks on linguistic generality by removing individual counts suggest that the PC1 index score is a sufficiently robust measure for general use.

The results of using the PC1 score as a formality index for a stylistic comparison of the members of the Brown/LOB family of corpora indicate, firstly, that diachronic comparisons of LOB with FLOB, or of Brown with Frown, are entirely justified, with the possible exception of US Reportage, where there is some evidence of change in institutional norms, away from a noticeably more "formal" style in Brown to a more "informal" style in Frown.

Secondly, comparisons of individual variables between national regional varieties using these same corpora are more problematic, but are still justifiable, provided that several known differences are taken into account. One general difference is that, in many text categories, WWC appears to be slightly less "formal" than the other corpora in this set (so that higher frequencies of nonstandard variants observed in WWC may not necessarily indicate any separate specific linguistic change in progress compared to LOB or Brown). Another difference is that Brown appears slightly more "formal" than the other corpora overall; however, this difference is especially marked for Reportage and Editorials (categories A and B) – again, probably reflecting differences in institutional norms – so that comparisons of those text categories need to be interpreted with particular caution.

References

Bauer, Laurie 1993. *Manual of information to accompany the Wellington Corpus of Written New Zealand English.* Wellington: Department of Linguistics, Victoria University of Wellington.

Biber, Douglas 1985. Investigating macroscopic textual variation through multifeature/multidimensional analyses. *Linguistics* 23, 337-360.

Biber, Douglas 1986. Spoken and written textual dimensions in English: resolving the contradictory findings. *Language* 62, 384-414.

Biber, Douglas 1987. A textual comparison of British and American writing. *American Speech* 62, 99-119.

Biber, Douglas 1988. *Variation across speech and writing*. Cambridge: Cambridge University Press.

Biber, Douglas 1995. *Dimensions of register variation: A cross-linguistic comparison*. Cambridge: Cambridge University Press.

Biber, Douglas / Finegan, Edward 1989. Drift and the evolution of English style: a history of three genres. *Language* 65, 487-517.

Biber, Douglas / Finegan, Edward 1992. The linguistic evolution of five written and speech-based English genres from the seventeenth to the twentieth centuries. In Rissanen, M. / Ihalainen, O. / Nevalainen, T. / Taavitsainen, I. (eds) *History of Englishes: new methods and interpretations in historical linguistics*. Berlin: Mouton, 688-704.

Francis, W. Nelson 1964. *Manual of information to accompany a standard sample of present-day edited American English, for use with digital computers*. Providence, R.I.: Department of Linguistics, Brown University.

Hofland, Knut / Johansson, Stig 1982. *Word frequencies in British and American English*. Bergen: Norwegian Computing Centre for the Humanities.

Hofland, Knut / Lindebjerg, Anne / Thunestvedt, Jørn 1999. *ICAME Collection of English Language Corpora.* [CD-ROM. ISBN 82-7283-091-4.]

Holmes, Janet / Vine, Bernadette / Johnson, Gary 1998. *Guide to the Wellington Corpus of Spoken New Zealand English.* Wellington: Victoria University of Wellington.

Hundt, Marianne 1998. *New Zealand English Grammar: Fact or Fiction?* Amsterdam: Benjamins.

Hundt, Marianne / Sand, Andrea / Siemund, Rainer 1998. *Manual of information to accompany the Freiburg–LOB Corpus of British English ('FLOB').* Freiburg: Englisches Seminar, Albert-Ludwigs-Universität Freiburg.

Hundt, Marianne / Sand, Andrea / Skandera, Paul 1999. *Manual of information to accompany the Freiburg–Brown Corpus of American English ('Frown').* Freiburg: Englisches Seminar, Albert-Ludwigs-Universität Freiburg.

Johansson, Stig 1978. *Manual of information to accompany the Lancaster-Oslo/Bergen Corpus of British English, for use with digital computers*. Oslo: Department of English, University of Oslo.

Kilgarriff, Adam 2001. Comparing corpora. *International Journal of Corpus Linguistics* 6, 97-133.

Lee, David Y. W. 2005. *Modelling variation in spoken and written language: the multi-dimensional approach revisited.* London: Routledge.

Leech, Geoffrey / Fallon, Roger 1992. Computer corpora – what do they tell us about culture? *ICAME Journal* 16, 29-50.

Leech, Geoffrey / Hundt, Marianne / Mair, Christian / Smith, Nicholas 2009. *Change in contemporary English.* Cambridge: Cambridge University Press.

Lindquist, Hans / Levin, Magnus 2001. Apples and oranges: on comparing data from different corpora. In Mair, Christian / Hundt, Marianne (eds) *Corpus linguistics and linguistic theory.* Amsterdam: Rodopi, 201-213.

Mair, Christian 1997. Parallel corpora: a real-time approach to language change in progress. In Magnus Ljung (ed.) *Corpus-based studies in English: Papers from the Seventeenth International Conference on English-Language Research Based on Computerized Corpora (ICAME 17).* Amsterdam: Rodopi, 195-209.

Sigley, Robert 1997a. Text categories and where you can stick them: a crude formality index. *International Journal of Corpus Linguistics* 2, 199-237.

Sigley, Robert 1997b. The influence of formality and channel on relative pronoun choice in New Zealand English. *English Language and Linguistics* 1, 207-232.

Sigley, Robert / Holmes, Janet 2002. Looking at *girls* in corpora of English. *Journal of English Linguistics* 30: 138-157.

Taylor, S. J. 1991. *Shock! Horror! The tabloids in action.* London: Black Swan.

SEBASTIAN HOFFMANN / ROBERT SIGLEY

Approaching a Linguistic Variable: *That*-Omission in Mandative Sentences

1. A framework for analysing linguistic variables

The present chapter aims to introduce some important issues in description and explanation of linguistically-conditioned variation, using as a case study an investigation of the variable presence vs. absence of the complementiser *that* introducing mandative subjunctive clauses. To begin with, however, we need to step back a little and consider what is involved in any scientific study of language. Science progresses by systematically testing a set of starting hypotheses to establish whether there are conditions under which certain hypotheses are observed to fail (see e.g. Kitcher's (1995) extension of Popper's falsificationalist framework to cases where hypotheses are tested in sets or "bundles"). This process strictly allows only qualified conclusions regarding the conditions under which each hypothesis *might* be valid. Within linguistics, the procedure of variable-rule analysis is a powerful means of conducting such a scientific research programme. However, it is also true that research following this process is by definition always a work in progress: our state of knowledge is incomplete and conditional, and there are always further hypotheses remaining to be tested. As such, all research reports (including the research reported here) are necessarily incomplete. Where we choose to pause and publish our results depends on choosing some appropriate practical balance point regarding which assumptions are to be accepted conditionally, and which to be explicitly tested, for our specific objectives. We should not necessarily expect research to yield any final definite conclusions. We should expect, however, that research reports should be as explicit as possible about the assumptions that remain to be tested, and the conditions that attach to the conclusions made.

The investigation of a linguistic variable can be divided into a number of ordered steps, in the service of three broad research aims, namely description, confirmation, and exploration, as presented in the schematic outline in Figure 1.

1.1. Comparative description

Any comparative study of variation must involve at least the four following steps:

(a) *Delimiting the scope of the variable to be investigated* (i.e. defining the object of study, in terms of several defined variants, occurring in a certain defined functional environment).

(b) *Extracting tokens of the variable from the corpus* to create a dataset for description and statistical analysis.

(c) *Describing each token in the dataset* in terms of a number of categorical dimensions or "factor groups", each consisting of several mutually-exclusive category labels for environmental "factors" that are hypothesised to partially influence (or at least, to be associated with) certain realisations of the variable. (This step itself may constitute an iterative, qualitative, exploration of the data; however, such analysis will not be the main focus of the present paper.)

(d) *Describing the distribution of variants,* by counting the raw frequencies and percentages of each variant associated with each factor (and/or, by constructing crosstabulations, percentages of variants associated with certain combinations of factors).

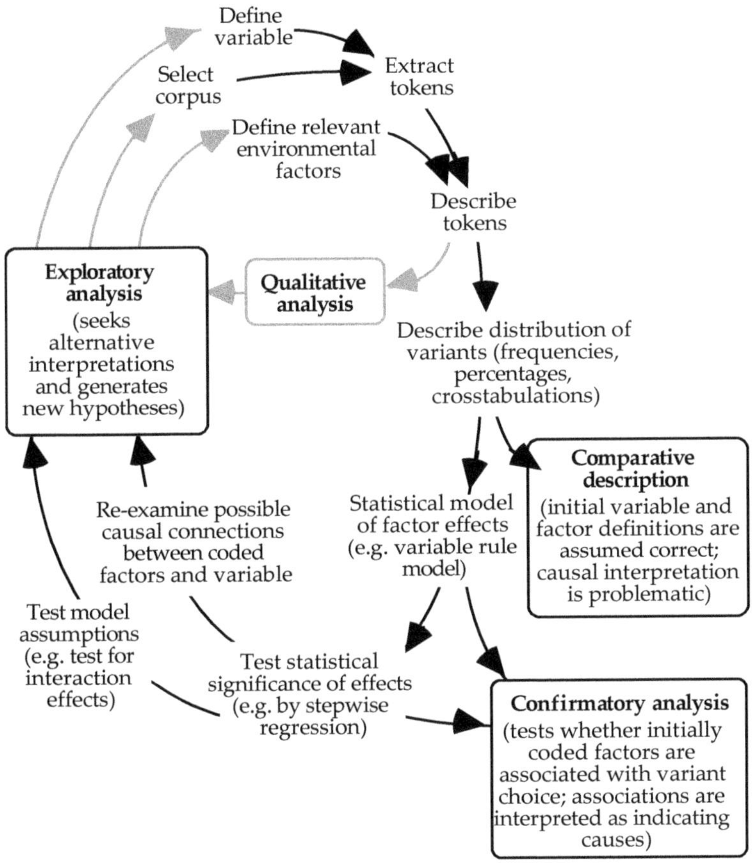

Figure 1. Stages in analysing a linguistic variable.

If we are working with a clearly-defined variable and a previously-agreed set of descriptive factors, and the main purpose of our research is to check or extend previous findings by comparing them with observations from a new or different dataset, then we could pause here, and publish an account of the distribution of variants under differing sets of conditions. Comparisons with past studies often necessitate such a stopping point: many existing reports provide only tables of frequencies or percentages, in which case such figures are all we can use to conduct comparisons with our present findings. Such comparisons can help establish the generalisability of findings based on the new data, and to check against gross methodological differences in the definition and description of the dataset.

However, the variant distribution may not be directly interpretable in any causal sense, because the different descriptive factors that have been used to categorise each token usually are not independently distributed across the dataset: certain combinations of factors are more likely than others. As a result, linguistic data is full of distributional confounds, and so we cannot immediately tell whether an observed difference in variant frequency is directly associated with the tabulated descriptive dimension(s), or is instead causally linked to some other confounding factor whose distribution is associated with some of the factors tabulated. One way of correcting for the association of factors on different factor groups would be to construct a full cross-tabulation of cells; but for most datasets, such a table would be unmanageably large (e.g., even a relatively small codeset of 5 factor groups, each with 3 factors, could produce as many as $3^5 = 243$ occupied cells), with most cells too sparsely inhabited to allow any reliable comparison. Thus, in most cases, any attempt at confirming proposed causal connections requires more sophisticated statistical analysis.

1.2. Confirmatory analysis

(e) Statistical modelling allows us to correct for the distribution of tokens across all other coded factor groups, in order to identify whether factors have a direct association (and so, possibly, a direct causal connection) with particular variants. This step involves constructing some statistical model of the data, such as a "variable-rule model" (a form of logistic regression analysis; see Paulillo 2002 for a comprehensive description), which uses the variant distribution in each cell of the dataset to estimate overall effect terms for each coded factor.

A logistic regression model relates the log odds of the variant frequency in each cell to an overall tendency for occurrence, plus a sum of effects from each factor (on each of *k* defined factor groups) present in the cell. The model is fitted by maximising the model's likelihood (the probability that the observed data could be produced by the model). Variable-rule programs (such as VARBRUL 2000 or GoldVarb X) report these effects on a logit scale: the overall tendency is reported as an "input probability" (p_0), and factor effects are reported as "factor weights" ranging from p_i=0 (categorically disfavouring the modelled variant) through p_i=0.5 (representing no effect) to p_i=1 (categorically favouring the modelled variant).

Variable rule model: $$\ln\left(\frac{p_{cell}}{1-p_{cell}}\right)=\ln\left(\frac{p_0}{1-p_0}\right)+\sum_{i=1}^{k}\ln\left(\frac{p_i}{1-p_i}\right)X_i$$

Note, however, that any environment producing truly categorical behaviour (a so-called "knockout" environment) must be excluded from the model, because if p=0 or p=1, then the expression ln ($p/(1-p)$) is undefined. One other important limitation is that, by default, this model assumes that each of the coded factors affects the variable independently. Each factor is assumed to have one constant effect across the entire dataset, and interaction effects (extra effects associated with certain combinations of factors) are assumed to be negligible. (These assumptions can be tested, and interaction effects can be added to the model; but in practice this is not often done.)

(f) Evaluating the significance of each factor group's contribution to the model. This is performed within variable-rule analysis by comparing the likelihoods of two related models (e.g. one containing the relevant factor group, and an otherwise identical model lacking that factor group). The likelihood ratio (or equivalently, the difference in log-likelihood) is the basis of a statistical test for the significance of the contribution of the extra modelled effects in the more complex model, compared to the number of extra parameters needed to model those effects (Paulillo 2002: 137-151). Variable-rule programs perform an automated series of model comparisons, known as "stepwise regression", to establish which factor groups should be retained in the model (Paulillo 2002: 85f).

Such work lets us confirm more directly whether or not the particular factors we have decided to include in our model have any significant overall connection to our variable. These apparent effects might be tentatively interpreted as indicating causal links – if we have not overlooked any other important factors. This is typically the endpoint for most published accounts of variable-rule analyses. It is also the endpoint for the most easily accessible guides to analysis, such as

Tagliamonte (2006), although the more technical statistical treatment in Paulillo (2002) does include a description of some techniques for extending models to include interaction effects.[1]

1.3. Exploratory analysis

Nevertheless, it is possible (and desirable) for research to go further, by systematically testing the assumptions of independent factor effects (as in Sigley 2003), and by carefully re-evaluating what different causal connections might underlie the influences identified as significant for (combinations of) factors coded in the dataset. Thus a fully exploratory analysis of linguistic variation that may question the definitions used in research, and generate further hypotheses for investigation, should involve the following extra steps:
(g) Checking the assumptions of the model (i.e., whether all factor groups actually do influence the variable independently, with separate causal connections). If such checks identify significant "interaction effects" (combinations of factors that have effects not predictable from combining the factors' overall "main" effects), it may be necessary either to add those combinations as new factors, or to re-examine the data to look for new, as-yet-identified causal factors associated with those combinations. Interaction effects may also indicate problems with the original definition of the variable, and/or of the descriptive factor labels applied (i.e., they may reflect the presence of several different processes, following different rules, underlying the observed choices, and/or they may indicate that some factor labels have different meanings, and so different effects, under different conditions).
(h) Constructing and testing causal interpretations for the factors identified as having significant effects. The general method for testing proposed causes is to go back to the dataset, reclassify tokens according to whether or not the proposed cause applies, and then add that new

1 Tagliamonte (2006) does offer valuable suggestions for exploratory research, but mostly from the perspective of the initial definition of the variable and selection of descriptive factors, as would be necessary in cases without extensive pre-existing literature.

factor group to the model to test whether it has any effect beyond those influences already identified.

Using variable-rule analysis to explore linguistic variation is ideally an iterative process, in that steps (e)-(h) usually lead to further recoding and remodelling of the data; thus a thorough investigation aiming at a robust explanatory account will often need several cycles of analysis. Such use of variable-rule analysis may best be described as a heuristic approach, leading to an evolving discovery of the linguistic conditions constraining the variable. Under this approach, the definitions of the variable and the coded factors are regarded as conditional working hypotheses, potentially subject to falsification by the results of later steps in the process. However, there is an obvious practical problem in reporting the results of such work: it is difficult if not impossible to do full descriptive justice to all of these stages within the length of a typical article. The account below follows a research project only through the phases of comparative description and initial statistical modelling; detailed explicit suggestions are offered for the steps necessary to continue the investigation, but implementation of the exploratory phase will be left for future research.

2. Defining the linguistic variable

2.1. An observed alternation of forms

The process of defining a linguistic variable starts with the observation that alternation is possible between two or more linguistic forms. For example, it is a well-documented fact that there is variation between *that* and zero linkage in sentences with finite object clauses, as in example (1):

(1) He said (that) there was no need to look for help.

Furthermore, omitting the complementiser in (1) does not result in any change in denotative meaning. This alternation meets all the criteria for treatment as a linguistic variable: several distinct linguistic forms are possible, and they are mutually exclusive (only one may be chosen at a time); the forms fulfill exactly the same linguistic function (introducing a subordinate clause); and a "potential environment of use" can be easily defined by identifying all instances of that broad function. However, it is possible that the alternation might be subject to different conditions in different types of clause, and so it may be necessary to define the variable more narrowly, by identifying a particular set of clauses for investigation.

2.2. Previous research

The general topic of *that*-omission in object clauses has been comparatively well-studied. The alternation between *that* and Ø has been the subject of much previous research, which has clearly established that it is not a case of entirely unconstrained "free variation". Various factors have been identified as being associated with (so, possibly influencing) the choice of linkage (as summarised in Biber *et al.* 1999: 680ff).

Both synchronic and diachronic studies support the general view that register/genre plays an important role in *that*-omission. Jespersen (1928: 33) writes that the unmarked clause "is preferred in conversation, in easy literary prose, also in easy poetry", whereas "in scientific prose, authors [...] prefer the express indication by means of *that*." This is amply confirmed by comparing the results from Finegan/Biber's (1995) study of the registers of Sermons and Medicine (showing a very strong preference for *that*, at 83-89%), with Thompson/Mulac's (1991) study of college student conversations (showing an equally strong preference for zero linkage, at 86%). Finegan/Biber (1995: 247-249) also cite results for Letters, a rather heterogeneous text type which "represent[s] more variability among writers and periods, highly dependent as well on topic and other parameters"; these were found to lie between those extremes, with a slight preference for *that* overall (53%).

Storms (1966) suggests that the stylistic distribution of Ø vs. *that* may reflect a subtle functional difference between those forms. He claims that Ø more closely reflects the subjective state of the speaker or writer, conveying a more private, familiar and friendly impression, and as such "carries an emotive load" (1966: 262), whereas the use of *that* places more emphasis on the actual content conveyed by the utterance, and so is preferred when that information is the focus of attention, as in scientific and scholarly texts. Commenting on the sentence *It appears that the northern part of the reverse hemisphere is covered by uplands, with many large craters*, he notes that "omission of *that* would introduce an element of subjectivity or emotiveness" and "would suggest a certain amount of surprise" (1966: 265). In practice, however, it is not possible for a corpus linguist, as an outside observer, to directly apply Storms' subjective semantic distinction; instead, we must use objectively verifiable criteria such as the presence of personal and/or pronominal subjects, and semantic features of the verb such as referring to an "interior" vs "exterior" event.

Another much-cited conditioning factor is the need to use *that* in more complex sentences in order to avoid ambiguity or to ease understanding. For example, an adverb occurring between the matrix verb and the subject of the subordinate clause could potentially be read as belonging to either clause; the insertion of *that* resolves this ambiguity (Elsness 1984: 523ff; Finegan/Biber 1995: 253).

The type of matrix verb has also been described as highly influential. For example, Rissanen (1991: 288) writes that "differences between individual verbs are of major importance", noting that *think* generally favours Ø, whereas more variation is observed with *say*. Rissanen suggests that until they are naturalised, "Newly borrowed verbs probably favour the explicit link" (1991: 288), and also notes that "verbs with low frequency (with object clauses), or with a more specific meaning, favour *that*" (1991: 285).

Other factors that have been identified as having a significant influence over the choice between *that* and Ø include the following:

- Pronominal subjects of the subordinate clause are consistently found to favour omission: cf. Elsness (1984), Rissanen (1991), Thompson/Mulac (1991). The same factor has also been shown to promote Ø-marking of object relative clauses, cf. Quirk *et al.* (1985: 1252); Sigley (1997: 408-412) demonstrates that its effect remains highly significant when corrected for correlations with text style, antecedent specificity, and relative clause length.
- Additionally, even within pronominal subjects, a tendency has been observed for 1st and 2nd person subjects to favour Ø (cf. Finegan/Biber 1995).

- Coreferentiality of the subjects in the matrix and subordinate clauses may favour Ø (cf. Elsness 1984). However, this feature must itself be significantly associated with cases in which one or both subjects are pronominal, and so its effect cannot be easily separated from those of the two preceding factors.
- Matrix verbs expressing epistemicity, such as *think* and *guess*, are most likely to be used without *that*. Thompson/Mulac (1991: 237) suggest that this reflects an erosion of the distinction between 'main' and 'complement' clauses in such sentences. Alternatively, such cases might be characterised as demonstrating a direct effect from style, or from a functional correlate of style such as Storms' semantic criterion.

One problem with these reported findings is that these proposed causal factors are highly intercorrelated. As a result, overall figures leave it unclear whether, or to what extent, these factors may independently influence the occurrence of *that*. Thompson/Mulac (1991) attempted to address this question by creating a "modified data base consisting of those utterances which contained only one of the variables" discussed in their paper. The results were disappointing: only 20% of their data could be used for such matched comparisons and, although the observed tendencies pointed "in the predicted direction", the reduced sample size entailed that very few differences could be confirmed as statistically significant. They write:

> This exercise raises an intriguing methodological question: do we learn more about a phenomenon we are investigating if we report findings from a greatly diminished data base in which variables are considered strictly independently, or do we learn more if we report findings from a full database with variables confounded such that it is indeterminate which one is responsible for the occurrence of *that*? (1991: 249f)

However, as has already been noted, this dilemma can largely be resolved by constructing a variable-rule model (which, in modelling the outcome in each occupied cell, makes use of every matched comparison possible in a dataset).

A second serious problem is that almost all previous findings are based on the behaviour of a limited set of very frequent verbs, such as *know, think, say, tell, hope, guess,* and *believe* – none of which are suasive. As a result, there may be a systematic gap in our knowledge. In some cases, data extraction was explicitly limited to frequent verbs (e.g. to allow more efficient retrieval of tokens of Ø); but the problem remains even in more inclusive studies such as Ellinger (1933) and Storms (1964), because naturally-occurring datasets are overwhelmingly swamped by constructions with the few most frequent verbs, with which Ø-marking is generally preferred (at least in informal text); hence any overall description of the occurrence of Ø from such data is effectively a description only of those common cases. Neither Ellinger nor Storms has enough data to comment specifically on the suasive verbs that they do include, such as *propose* or *recommend*. We might suspect that rarer constructions, with less frequently-occurring verbs, might potentially show differences in behaviour (e.g. along the lines signalled by Rissanen); but such cases have so far generally escaped scholarly attention, partly because the corpora used (such as the 1-million-word "standard" LOB or Brown corpora) do not provide sufficient relevant data.

2.3. A refined object of study: object clause marking in mandative subjunctive clauses

One specific type of rarer construction that seems worth investigating to compare with the results available for more common object clause constructions is that of a mandative sentence containing an object clause of a suasive matrix verb, as in (2).

(2) The inquiry recommended Ø 10 officials should be disciplined. (CEM:1831)[2]

As far as we are aware, there has as yet been no study of *that*-omission in mandative sentences, no doubt due to the extremely low frequency of the phenomenon in question (at roughly one instance per 50,000 words). Consequently, there has been little reference to *that*-omission in existing studies of the mandative subjunctive and its periphrastic and indicative variants. For example, among the examples cited by Övergaard (1995), a small number exhibit zero linkage, but this feature is not explicitly com-

2 References given are always to the corresponding texts in the BNC and contain the name of the text as well as the line number. Relevant parts of each example have been italicised.

mented on. Quirk *et al.* (1985: 156) similarly indicate the omissibility of *that* in their examples of the mandative subjunctive, but do not elaborate any further on the factors influencing this choice. The low frequency of Ø also means that in a small sample, the choice of *that* may appear categorical; thus Elsness (1984: 521), surveying *that* vs. Ø in object clauses, writes that tokens "with subjunctive verbs are in my material invariably THATs", and so "less interesting with respect to the THAT/ZERO distribution". Some authors even go so far as to question the stylistic acceptability of *that*-omission in such instances; McCawley (1988: 142), for example, describes Ø with subjunctives as "mildly odd".

The only explicit reference to *that*-omission in mandative sentences in the works consulted for the present paper occurs in Thyberg (1996: 14f), who comments only that no conclusive difference could be found in types of mandative subjunctive associated with *that* vs. Ø, and provides no figures either for the relative frequency of *that*-omission or its distribution among the different genres found in his corpus. Again, the problem appears to be a lack of relevant data.

Fortunately, the availability of much larger corpora such as the 100-million-word British National Corpus (henceforth BNC) has now greatly increased the possibilities for quantitative studies of lower-frequency linguistic features. For the present paper, the variation between *that* and zero linkage will be investigated in mandative sentences containing object clauses; specifically, in the subclass of mandative sentences containing a suasive matrix verb.[3] It will thus be possible to compare our findings with those of earlier studies based on a much more frequent set of verbs.

In analysing *that*-omission in mandative sentences, we hope to achieve the following goals. By limiting our focus to a semantically and functionally rather narrowly defined subset of verbs that allow object complementation with *that*, we control for the influence of some factors that may determine the use of *that* or Ø (e.g. verb epistemicity and subject coreferentiality). On the other hand, this set of verbs is in some ways radically different from those most commonly studied (e.g. in range of

3 Mandative sentences in which the suasive item is instead a noun (e.g. "The *requirement* that analysis be objective [...]", ALB:284) or adjective ("It is *imperative* […] that a burial site be purchased", ACG: 426) are not discussed in this paper, as this would impede comparison of data with other studies.

subject type, and in text category distribution). In comparing our findings with those of previous work on *that*-complementation (Section 4), we will thus be able to determine more clearly which of the proposed factors influencing the use of *that* or Ø can be regarded as applying generally, i.e. without dependence on a particular context or type of sentence. In doing so, we offer a partial solution to the problem mentioned by Thompson/Mulac (1991): if factors are found to have a clear influence in contexts where conditions apply that are very different from those described in their paper, this can be regarded as tentative evidence for the independent status of these factors. A fuller solution is then presented in the form of a variable-rule analysis (Section 5) showing which of the factors considered have independent and statistically significant effects on the choice of linkage employed. Subsequently, we discuss some alternative possible causal explanations for the effects thus identified, and on that basis suggest some refinements for further exploration (Section 6).

3. Method

3.1. Data extraction

Tokens of mandatives with object clauses were retrieved from the British National Corpus using two different, though overlapping, search patterns designed to ensure meaningful coverage of Ø (which of course cannot be searched for directly). The first was a relatively simple search over the whole BNC for instances of *be* not preceded by any modal verb, followed by manual postediting to retain only mandative examples; this yielded a database (Dataset A) of 3254 sentences containing a mandative subjunctive with *be,* as in (3):

(3) (September 6) I *suggest that* the Tory logo of a flaming torch *be replaced* by either a cuckoo or an oozelum bird. (HAE:4420)

The tokens in Dataset A thus mostly represent passive constructions, but also include some active sentences with the full verb *be*. Within those limits, Dataset A contains virtually all such examples in the BNC.

The second database (Dataset B) was obtained by retrieving all tokens of the seven lexical verbs that had been observed most commonly in Dataset A (*demand*, *insist*, *order*, *propose*, *recommend*, *request*, and *suggest*, collectively covering about half the tokens), from a restricted subcorpus of 20 million words, consisting of 5 million words from each of the text types of "imaginative prose", "applied science", "world affairs" and "arts".

It is important to note that the two databases intersect: all the instances of passive mandative subjunctives as well as active constructions with *be* in Dataset B are also in Dataset A. This allows an immediate check against methodological error: any striking differences between the results obtained from the two databases for the overlapping tokens would clearly point to an inconsistency in coding. (The overall figures for the two databases, however, may differ considerably, either because of the difference in text category coverage, or because of the skewed textual distribution of passive constructions.)

Another important point to make is that the BNC as a whole, and the sample used for Dataset B, differ from the data used in other studies such as Thompson/Mulac (1991) or Rissanen (1991) not only in size but also in composition. As such, unqualified direct comparisons of our findings with those of other scholars are problematic, and differences encountered in our results will have to be approached with particular care in order not to jump to premature conclusions. For this reason, a much smaller third dataset (Dataset C) was also created, by randomly selecting 1000 sentences from the same 20-million-word subset of BNC as was used for Dataset B, and coding up the tokens of object clauses contained therein with the four verbs studied by Rissanen (*know, think, tell, say*), specifically to provide a variable-rule model for comparison.

Certain constructions were excluded from analysis because they preclude any choice between *that* and Ø. For example, coordination of the object clause with a preceding NP, as in (4), makes the omission of *that* impossible.

(4) It also *recommended* the appointment of a Chief Inspector of Constabulary answerable to the Home Secretary, and *that the post be filled* without delay. (EEC:1411)

Similarly, sentences containing parenthetic use of suasive verbs, as in (5), were excluded:

(5) The old building, *we proposed*, should be adapted to create a mixture of shopping and fast food establishments, with restaurants and pubs in the corner pavilions on the river. (AR9:1794)

Finally, in cases where one suasive verb was followed by several dependent clauses, only the first instance was counted, and the others discarded, on the basis that, unless *that* is in fact chosen, it is impossible to tell whether subsequent clauses are potential sites for independent subordination, or instead form a conjoined subordinated item.

Out of the 3254 instances of mandative subjunctives with *be* (Dataset A), 2324 sentences (71.4%) have a verb as the suasive item. After eliminating multiple subordination as well as those instances where syntactic constraints made a choice between *that* and Ø impossible, 2147 sentences remained for further study. Applying similar restrictions left 1729 tokens of mandative sentences with *that*-complement clauses for analysis in Dataset B, and 279 object clauses in Dataset C.

3.2. Data description

Tokens were coded for nine features, largely following the factors already identified in previous research (as described in Section 2.2):

(i) the realisation of the variable as *that* vs. Ø;
(ii) the identity of the matrix verb;
(iii) the person of the matrix verb (1st/2nd/3rd/unclear/passive);
(iv) the type of subordinate clause subject (pronominal or non-pronominal);
(v) the person of the subordinate-clause verb;
(vi) the voice of the subordinate-clause verb (active/passive);
(vii) the mood of the subordinate-clause verb (indicative, subjunctive, ambiguous, or modal);
(viii) the presence of an intervening item between the verb and the object clause; and
(ix) the BNC text type.

4. Comparative results for distribution of *that* vs. Ø

4.1. Overall frequency of that*-omission*

Compared to previous results for other types of object clauses, the overall figures for Dataset A (Table 1) show a surprisingly low frequency of Ø (at only 6.6% of tokens). From this figure alone, however, we cannot yet claim to have shown any special feature of mandative subjunctives. To some extent, the preference for *that* might reflect the fact that 90% of texts in the BNC are from writing. (The potential impact of this stylistic effect can indirectly be shown by considering only the tokens from spoken texts: in that subset, the rate of omission rises to 17 out of 112 tokens, or 15%.) Furthermore, the bulk of Dataset A consists of passive subordinate clauses, which could favour *that* in their own right, and are also almost certainly drawn preferentially from the most formal writings. The 183 active clauses with *be* also contained in Dataset A do show a slightly (though not significantly) higher frequency of Ø, at 8.7%; but these clauses are not strictly comparable with the passives.

	Ø		*that*		Total
	n	%	n	%	n
Mandative subjunctive + passive	125	*6.4%*	1839	*93.6%*	1964
Mandative subjunctive + full verb *be*	16	*8.7%*	167	*91.3%*	183
Overall	141	*6.6%*	2006	*93.4%*	2147

Table 1. Distribution of *that* and zero linkage for passive constructions and sentences containing the full verb *be* over the whole BNC (based on Dataset A).

To check whether the low frequency of Ø is general to mandative subjunctives or is more accurately associated with passive tokens, it is necessary to use Dataset B (Table 2). The overall level of Ø in Dataset B is still comparatively low (16.2%), but the breakdown by verb voice confirms a clear difference in the use of *that*-omission between active and passive object clauses: Ø is more than five times more likely in active constructions than in passives (at 23.3% vs. 4.2% Ø, respectively). Meanwhile, the rate of Ø in passive tokens is similarly low in both datasets, but not exactly the same. It is not clear whether the slightly lower rate in Dataset B is due to the difference in text category distribution (e.g., that Dataset B excludes spoken data), and/or the specific verbs included, and/or differences in the typical subjects of those verbs.

This overall comparison points to two important consequences. Firstly, the overall low frequency of Ø may not preclude the possibility of much higher rates of use within some subset of this data (especially within Dataset B: hence this will be the main focus of our description below). Secondly, comparisons of overall figures are not especially helpful, and so we will need instead to break the data down further to examine the range of possibilities within specific environments of use.

	Ø		*that*		Total
Voice:	n	%	n	%	n
Active	253	*23.3%*	834	*76.7%*	1087
Passive	27	*4.2%*	615	*97.8%*	642
Overall	280	*16.2%*	1449	*83.8%*	1729

X^2 (1*df*) = 108.15, $p << 0.001$[4]

Table 2. Distribution of *that* and zero linkage in mandative sentences, by voice in the subordinate clause, for selected verbs, in selected BNC text categories (Dataset B).

4.2. Association of that *vs Ø with other environmental features*

The results from Table 2 are broken down further by verb mood in Table 3, which shows that *that*-omission in active constructions is especially likely in subordinate clauses containing either indicatives (30% Ø), as in (6), or ambiguous forms that could be either subjunctive or indicative (39% Ø), as in (7).

(6) If a certain course appears particularly relevant to an individual, then the County Librarian may *suggest* he or she *attends*. (BNM:428)

(7) During a recent TV interview in France she *demanded* the cameras *have* special filters to hide her wrinkles. (CEK:7067)

4 Because each table in Section 4 presents results for only one or two factor groups, which generally show highly significant distributional confounds with other coded factors, chi-squared test results should be taken as indicative only. Factor group significance should strictly be measured by model likelihood comparisons, as reported in Section 5.

Conversely, Ø is least likely overall in subordinate clauses containing modal constructions, though it remains more frequent with actives than with passives (12% vs. 4%, respectively). The figures for mandative subjunctive forms lie somewhere in the middle, with 21% Ø in active constructions such as (8), vs. 4% in passives such as (9).

(8) The natives *insisted he burn* the book or they would attack him. (HH4:976)

(9) I *suggest* this iniquity *be removed* as soon as possible. (AHU:902)

Table 3 also shows that mandative subjunctive forms are disproportionately associated with passive complements: 264/ 470 (=56%) of the subjunctive forms retrieved in Dataset B occur with passives, whereas the indicative and modal forms both occur more often with active complementation. Given that passive constructions are a typical feature of more formal texts, this association is consistent with the claim that mandative subjunctive forms are predominantly used in formal contexts.

	Ø		*that*		Total
Voice and mood:	n	%	n	%	n
Active verb forms:					
mandative subjunctive	40	*20.5%*	156	*79.5%*	195
modal	58	*12.4%*	413	*87.6%*	469
indicative	29	*29.9%*	68	*70.1%*	97
ambiguous	126	*39.0%*	197	*61.0%*	323
Passive verb forms:					
mandative subjunctive	12	*4.4%*	264	*95.6%*	275
modal	13	*3.9%*	321	*96.1%*	332
indicative	2	*6.3%*	30	*93.8%*	32
Total	280	*16.2%*	1449	*83.8%*	1729

X^2 (6*df*) = 213.21, $p \ll 0.001$

Table 3. Distribution of *that* and zero linkage in mandative sentences by voice and mood of the subordinate clause (Dataset B).

At 16%, the overall frequency of *that*-omission in Dataset B is low compared to results cited for other studies of object clauses. One reason why this set of mandative sentences might appear to show greater preference for *that* than other object clauses may lie in the kinds of subjects found in mandative sentences. Elsness (1984: 532) observes that "zero connective is particularly frequent if the matrix and/or OBCL subjects are in either the 1st or the 2nd person"; the large majority of the matrix-clause subjects (1320 out of 1729, or 74%) in the sentences of Dataset B are instead third-person forms, which tend to favour *that* (Table 4). In part, this may reflect the relative formality of the writings analysed here: by contrast, in their conversational data, Thompson/ Mulac (1991: 243) report only 12% of matrix subjects as third person.

Table 4 clearly shows that, as observed for other object clauses, omission of *that* in mandatives is much more frequent after first or second person subjects in the matrix clause (33% and 54% Ø respectively), as opposed to third person subjects (only 13% Ø). Finally, the very low frequency of *that*-omission after passive constructions in the matrix clause confirms that the voice of the verb in both the object clause and in the matrix clause is highly correlated with the kind of linkage employed (cf. Table 2 above).[5]

	Ø		*that*		Total
Matrix-clause subject:	n	%	n	%	n
1st person	88	*33.5%*	175	*66.5%*	263
2nd person	15	*53.6%*	13	*46.4%*	28
3rd person	172	*13.0%*	1148	*87.0%*	1320
passive	2	*2.0%*	98	*98.0%*	100
unclear	3	*16.7%*	15	*83.3%*	18
Total	280	*16.2%*	1449	*83.8%*	1729

X^2 (4*df*) = 111.18, $p < 0.001$

Table 4. Occurrence of *that* vs. Ø, by matrix clause subject type (Dataset B).

A very similar pattern emerges when we consider the subject of the subordinate clause (Table 5): firstly, the majority of all subjects are in the third person (1429 out of 1729 instances); and secondly, sentences with first or second person subjects again exhibit a much higher frequency of *that*-omission (with 39% and 49% Ø respectively, as against 11% Ø across all third-person subjects). However, as all of the first or second person subjects are pronominal, we also need to separate out the pronominal third-person subjects from non-pronominal examples in order to make a direct comparison isolating the effect of pronoun form from that of person itself.

5 Passive matrix constructions are treated separately in Table 4 because in mandative sentences they can only occur in the third person. In the case of first and second person passive constructions, a non-finite clause would have to be substituted, e.g. "You were ordered *to stay and help our friends*" (G0L:1299).

Subordinate clause subject:	Ø n	Ø %	*that* n	*that* %	Total n
1st person pronoun	72	*39.3%*	111	*60.7%*	183
2nd person pronoun	49	*49.5%*	50	*50.5%*	99
3rd person pronoun	87	*26.6%*	240	*73.4%*	327
other 3rd person	69	*6.3%*	1033	*93.7%*	1102
unclear	3	*16.7%*	15	*83.3%*	18
Total	280	*16.2%*	1449	*83.8%*	1729

Table 5. Occurrence of *that* vs. Ø, by subordinate clause subject type (Dataset B).

The data in Table 5 confirms a general tendency for pronominal subordinate clause subjects to favour Ø (for pronominal vs. other, X^2 (1*df*) = 223.45, $p \ll 0.001$), which remains clear even within the third-person subjects alone (X^2 (1*df*) = 107.32, $p \ll 0.001$); nevertheless, the third-person pronoun subjects are still associated with significantly lower use of Ø than first or second person pronouns (for person within pronoun subjects only, $X^2 = 20.84$ (2*df*), $p < 0.001$). Hence the hypothesis that subject person may influence the form of clause linkage seems to be supported by these raw figures; but there also appears to be a much stronger influence from pronominal subjects in favouring Ø, as in (10), in contrast to longer noun phrases as subjects, as in (11), which overwhelmingly favour *that* (with only around 6% Ø observed in Dataset B).

(10) He'd thrown the receiver off the hook, but she was haranguing the empty line, *demanding he reply.* (CRE:2213)

(11) The seasonal nature of the industry's work *demanded that the timing of training courses be carefully selected.* (ALC:941)

The same effect has also been noted for pronominal subjects of other object clauses (Elsness 1984, Thompson/Mulac 1991), and a parallel effect has also been conclusively established for pronominal subjects of relative clauses (e.g. Cofer 1975, Olofsson 1981, Sigley 1997). Elsness suggests that the two clauses may be psychologically more closely linked because pronouns are (formally or semantically) "lighter"; but the most commonly advanced explanation is that the distinction between (personal) pronoun case forms helps to eliminate ambiguity and facilitate sentence processing. Therefore, in example (10), the grammatical function of the pronoun *he* is clearly defined and there is no risk of local ambiguity. By contrast, in (11), omission of *that* could have resulted in an initial misinterpretation of *the timing* as an object of *demand*.

Nevertheless, however plausible such a proposed causal mechanism may be, the comparison of overall percentages in Table 5 does not immediately exclude other interpretations in terms of distributional associations. Firstly, given the correlation of pronouns (and especially, first and second person pronouns) with informal, interactive text styles, it may be expected that the distributions shown in Tables 4 and 5 are not independent. If personal pronouns are more likely as the subject of the matrix clause, then they should also be more likely as the subjects of subordinate clauses in the same text; thus there may be considerable overlap in the source texts for the subsets with pronominal subjects identified in both tables. There may also be more direct correlation between the occurrence of pronominal subjects in both clauses in the same sentence (so that the "first/second person" or "subject pronoun" subsets in both tables could largely consist of the same tokens). Secondly, because pronouns express coreference, they must be associated with a further proposed causal factor promoting zero linkage, i.e. coreference between the subjects of the matrix and subordinate clauses (Elsness, 1984: 526). One point of difference between mandatives and other object clause environments is that the volition expressed in the main clause is usually directed at some other entity than that of the subject of the matrix clause, so that the object clause subject usually has a different referent (except in passive constructions such as *I demand I be allowed to speak*); the resulting overall lower incidence of subject coreference could contribute towards the overall lower incidence of Ø in mandatives.

An overall comparison of figures for each text category (Table 6) confirms that, just as with other object clauses (cf. Storms 1966: 264), text type appears to be an important factor influencing *that*-omission in mandative sentences: Ø is preferentially associated with less formal text categories. However, it is likely that this pattern reflects in part the differential occurrence of pronominal subjects across these text categories; hence the overall figures in Tables 4, 5, and 6 are not easily interpretable in isolation, and a more reliable interpretation will require a variable-rule model.

	Ø linkage		*that*		Total
Text category:	n	%	n	%	n
imaginative prose	134	*40.6%*	196	*59.4%*	330
arts	67	*20.9%*	253	*79.1%*	320
applied science	46	*10.9%*	376	*89.1%*	422
world affairs	33	*5.0%*	624	*95.0%*	657
Total	280	*16.2%*	1449	*83.8%*	1729

$X^2\ (3df) = 219.34,\ p << 0.001$

Table 6. The distribution of *that* and zero linkage in mandative sentences across four selected text types from the BNC (Dataset B).

Of the four text categories compared in Table 6, "imaginative prose" shows the highest frequency of zero linkage (at over 40%), whereas more formal text categories show much lower rates of *that*-omission. The low rate of Ø in "applied science" is consistent with an editorial drive towards clarity in academic writing (cf. Ellinger 1933: 107). A slightly surprising result is the even lower rate in "world affairs" (at only 5% Ø), which suggests that press material is even more systematically edited to avoid ambiguity. Such an interpretation is consistent with the observation that news editing attempts to present clear, unambiguous stories – even at the cost of introducing factual errors (as demonstrated by Bell 1991: 217ff).

Most previous studies of variation in object clause marking have identified considerable differences in preference for Ø vs. *that* with different verbs. Some scholars posit stylistic reasons (e.g. Ellinger 1933; Elsness 1984); others point to semantic features such as the degree of epistemicity expressed by the verb (e.g. Thompson/Mulac 1991). Semantically, the verbs analysed in the present study form a unified group, in that they all express various degrees of volition; any significant differences must therefore be explained by reasons other than meaning or function. Nevertheless, as shown in Table 7 below, the distribution of *that* and zero still varies significantly with respect to the suasive verb in the matrix clause.

Verb:	Ø n	Ø %	*that* n	*that* %	Total n
order	1	*1.5%*	67	*98.5%*	68
request	2	*4.0%*	48	*96.0%*	50
propose	8	*4.5%*	171	*95.5%*	177
recommend	13	*5.5%*	229	*94.5%*	238
demand	21	*10.8%*	179	*89.2%*	195
insist	50	*16.6%*	252	*83.4%*	302
suggest	185	*26.9%*	503	*73.1%*	688
Total	280	*16.2%*	1449	*83.8%*	1729

X^2 (6*df*) = 116.11, $p < 0.001$

Table 7. Distribution of *that* and Ø in complement clauses after seven suasive verbs in a subset of the BNC (Dataset B).

One trend immediately apparent in Table 7 is that there is a strong correlation (Spearman $\rho = +0.93$, $p < 0.005$ for one-tailed test) between the frequency of each verb in this function (as measured by the number of tokens extracted in this dataset), and the observed level of preference for Ø in its object clauses. *Order*, *propose*, and *request* exhibit very low frequencies of Ø (below 5%), whereas *that*-omission occurs most frequently with the most frequent suasive verb, *suggest*. This result largely corroborates Rissanen's (1991: 285) observation that verb frequency influences the choice of linkage. Nevertheless, we cannot yet conclude that verb frequency is a direct causal factor. Type/token ratio (i.e., average vocabulary frequency) is a well-known correlate of text style; thus we also need to consider the distribution of these verbs across text types. Unsurprisingly, it turns out that the verbs with a low frequency of *that*-omission are largely restricted to "world affairs" and "applied science", whereas the verbs with the highest incidence of Ø are also very common in "imaginative prose" and "arts". For example, "world affairs" accounts for 52/68 (76%) of the tokens of *order,* 104/179 (58%) of *propose*, and 23/50 (46%) of *request*, as against only 98/302 (32%) for *insist* and 205/688 (30%) for *suggest*. As such, separating the effects of verb type from text category (and, given our comments on Tables 4–6, also from other correlates such as pronominal subjects) will require variable-rule analysis.

There may also be a more direct causal connection between verb type and choice of clause marker, as a way of reducing the potential for ambiguity. Thus an alternative explanation for the differences evident in Table 7 is that some constructions with certain of these suasive verbs could be more difficult to interpret correctly without *that*. The relative ease of reaching the correct interpretation of a mandative sentence with a particular verb form could perhaps be estimated by examining the conditional probabilities (given the preceding context) that the word-form is a verb; that it has a suasive function; and that it takes an object clause. However, given the processing effects already suggested above, we would also need to consider whether the clause has a pronominal subject. *Order*, which has the lowest frequency of *that*-omission, can have various meanings (both suasive and non-suasive), leading to a potential for (at least temporary) structural ambiguity with Ø, and thus a preference for *that*. In (12), for example, omission of *that* would produce transient ambiguity, resulting in a garden-path sentence; the reading "order margin notes to be made..." could not be eliminated until the reader reaches *would remain secret*. (Other readings, such as "order the notes alphabetically", or "place an order for delivery" are also possible, but less likely given the courtroom context invoked by the subject *judges*.)

(12) However the judges did *order that margin notes* made by the so-called nymphomaniac on their genital size, sexual skills and bedroom fantasies *would remain secret*. (CEM:2503)

A survey of the examples with *order* in Dataset B revealed that more than half of all sentences would confront the reader with similar transient ambiguity if *that* were left out – in large part because very few finite object clauses following *order* had personal pronouns as subjects, as shown in Table 8.[6]

---

6 Instead, personal pronouns after *order* take the form of direct objects followed by non-finite clauses, so fall outside the scope of the variable under investigation.

Verb:	pronoun				other subject				% pronouns as subjects
	Ø	%	*that*	%	Ø	%	*that*	%	
suggest	148	*44%*	187	*56%*	37	*10%*	316	*90%*	48.7%
insist	38	*29%*	91	*71%*	12	*7%*	161	*93%*	42.7%
demand	13	*20%*	52	*80%*	8	*6%*	127	*94%*	32.5%
propose	4	*20%*	16	*80%*	4	*3%*	155	*97%*	11.2%
request	1	*9%*	10	*91%*	1	*3%*	38	*97%*	22.0%
recommend	4	*9%*	39	*91%*	9	*5%*	190	*95%*	17.8%
order	0	*0%*	4	*100%*	1	*2%*	63	*98%*	6.0%
Total	208	*34%*	399	*66%*	72	*6%*	1050	*94%*	35.1%

Table 8. Distribution of *that* and Ø in complement clauses by suasive verb and subordinate clause subject type (Dataset B).

By contrast, just under half of all subjects in subordinate clauses after *suggest* are personal pronouns, which greatly reduces the potential for structural ambiguity (and these tokens account for 148/185=80% of the Ø-linkage observed after this verb). The verb *insist*, showing the second highest association with Ø, has the lowest inherent structural ambiguity of any of these verbs, as it cannot take a noun as direct object; but even so, most of the Ø-linked subordinate clauses after *insist* have pronominal subjects. This result indicates that the contribution of the verb to processing is probably less important than the contribution of the subject as a clause marker.

One final contribution to processing difficulty potentially favouring the choice of *that* is the presence of some intervening item (usually an adverb or adverbial phrase) between the matrix verb and the subordinate clause subject, as in (13). In such instances, the adverb could possibly be interpreted as modifying either clause, and the ambiguity would then only be resolved if *that* is present; hence Elsness (1984: 519) claims *that* will be retained "to avoid ambiguity".

(13) MPs *demanded yesterday that* the Jordan Government free all political detainees. (A9M:359)

However, in practice very few of the sentences attested with intervening items between the two clauses would actually result in any unresolvable ambiguity. Example (14) shows one of these rare cases: here, in the absence of *that*, the adverbial *inside the Administration block* could potentially describe either the Major's location when making the demand, or (as is intended) a locative condition within the demand.

(14) A Captain in KGB he might be, [...] feared by the superior in rank and the inferior in fortune, but *the Major had demanded that inside the Administration block in the mornings he should wear his uniform.* (CJT:441)

Even local ambiguity, as in (15), where the adverbial *henceforth* would eventually resolve any ambiguity in scope of *on April 22* even in the absence of *that*, is only rarely encountered.

(15) The delegates had, however, gone further than the Premier by *demanding on April 22 that the country's President should henceforth be elected* by popular vote, rather than by the two Houses of the Sejm, as at present. (HKT:1084)

Nevertheless, Table 9 shows that an overt connective appears to be highly favoured when there is an intervening item. Ø-linkage occurred in only 5/248 (2%) of the instances where an intervening item was found between the matrix verb and the subject of the subordinate clause. Due to the scarcity of sentences actually containing potential ambiguity, it seems highly unlikely that avoidance of ambiguity *per se* is the main influence on this preference for *that*. Rather, the overall observed tendency must reflect a more general response to sentence complexity: an overt *that* helps in the processing of information in longer and more complex sentences, and is therefore less likely to be omitted than in simpler sentences.

	Ø linkage		*that*		Total
	n	%	n	%	n
intervening item	5	*2.0%*	243	*98.0%*	248
no intervening item	275	*18.6%*	1206	*81.4%*	1481
Total	280	*16.2%*	1449	*83.8%*	1729

X^2 (1*df*) = 42.88, $p < 0.001$

Table 9. The distribution of *that* and Ø with respect to the presence or absence of an intervening item between the matrix verb and the subject of the object clause.

Despite the plausibility of this explanation, the same caveat applies here as to the preceding tables: the comparison in Table 9 may need to be corrected for potential confounds. In particular, we should expect a significant association between sentence complexity and text category. Hence, to allow a more conclusive interpretation of these factors' influence on the choice between Ø and *that*, we must now turn to the results of variable-rule modelling.

5. Variable rule model results

5.1. The variable-rule model for Dataset B

Stepwise regression on Dataset B produces a best-fit model including modelled effects for all factor groups with significant contributions to the model, with factor weights ranging from 0 (highly disfavouring Ø) through 0.5 (neutral) to 1.0 (highly favouring Ø). Additionally, an estimate of the statistical significance for each factor group's contribution relative to that model can be obtained from the log-likelihood comparisons reported during stepwise regression (either on adding nonsignificant contributions to the model, or removing significant contributions from it). These results are summarised in Table 10.

The first point to note is that the input weight is very low (0.073), indicating the overwhelming preference for *that* rather than Ø among these mandative tokens. Secondly, the *p*-values reported for hierarchical model comparisons confirm that most of the factor groups describing Dataset B actually do have independently significant effects[7] – except for the mood of the subordinate clause verb, and the person of the subordinate clause subject. In the latter case, the apparently significant difference indicated by a simple chi-squared test (on Table 5) has turned out to be entirely explicable in terms of confounds with the other factor groups, including person of the matrix clause, text category, and matrix verb. Thirdly, the modelled effects generally follow the same rank order as the raw percentages, and so the model largely confirms as significant the tendencies observed in the previous section. Moreover, we are now in a position to rank these effects in order of decreasing significance.

---

7 Chi-squared tests for goodness of fit were conducted on all 28 possible models containing only two factor groups. After applying the Bonferroni correction to adjust the critical level of significance for the number of tests performed, no single pairwise interaction effect could be confirmed as significant by this means; hence, as a first-order approximation, the modelled factor effects can be treated as independent. Nevertheless, the fit for the overall model was very poor, indicating that some significant variation in the dataset, possibly including higher-order interaction effects, remains unaccounted for.

The single most important influence on choice of Ø in this dataset is whether or not the subordinate clause subject is a pronoun. Pronominal subjects are confirmed to highly favour Ø (weight=0.693); nonpronominal subjects disfavour Ø (weight=0.392).

The second most important influence comes from text category. Independently of the distribution of pronominal subjects across the four text categories sampled, Ø is favoured in imaginative fiction (weight=0.720), and least favoured in world affairs (weight=0.343).

The third-ranked constraint is whether or not there is some element intervening between the verb and its object clause: intervening items greatly disfavour Ø (weight=0.088).

Factor group (with significance relative to this model)	Ø / total	% Ø	Factor weight (over 0.5 favours Ø)
1) Subject in subordinate clause			($p<0.001$)
personal pronoun	208 / 607	*34.3%*	0.693
other	72 / 1122	*6.4%*	0.392
2) Text type			($p<0.001$)
imaginative prose	134 / 330	*40.6%*	0.720
arts	67 / 320	*20.9%*	0.588
applied science	46 / 422	*10.9%*	0.501
world affairs	33 / 657	*5.0%*	0.343
3) Intervening item			($p<0.001$)
no	275 / 1481	*18.6%*	0.596
yes	5 / 248	*2.0%*	0.088
4) Verb lexeme			($p<0.001$)
suggest	185 / 688	*26.9%*	0.659
insist	50 / 302	*16.6%*	0.454
demand	21 / 200	*10.8%*	0.437
propose	8 / 179	*4.5%*	0.398
recommend	13 / 242	*5.5%*	0.358
request	2 / 50	*4.0%*	0.257
order	1 / 68	*1.5%*	0.243
5) Voice of subordinate clause verb			($p=0.003$)
active	253 / 1087	*23.3%*	0.567
passive	27 / 642	*4.2%*	0.389
6) Person of matrix clause verb			($p=0.020$)
2nd person	15 / 28	*53.6%*	0.796
1st person	88 / 263	*33.5%*	0.537
3rd person	172 / 1320	*13.0%*	0.507
unclear	3 / 18	*16.7%*	0.440
passive	2 / 100	*2.0%*	0.250
7) Mood of subordinate clause verb (non-significant)			($p=0.057$)
8) Person of subordinate clause verb (non-significant)			($p=0.118$)
Overall (input weight)	280 / 1729	*16.2%*	0.073

Table 10. Best-fit variable-rule model for factors affecting Ø-marking of object clauses in mandative constructions (Dataset B).

The fourth most important influence is the identity of the matrix verb, which therefore seems confirmed to have an effect beyond that predictable from the verbs' textual distribution and/or association with pronominal subjects. Ø is most favoured after *suggest* (weight=0.659), and least favoured after *order* (weight=0.243). As with the raw percentages of Ø in Table 7, the factor weights roughly follow the observed rank order of verb frequency in this function (Spearman ρ = +0.86, $p < 0.01$), suggesting that – at least when verb function is controlled, as in this dataset – relative frequency may be an important contribution to each verb's tendency to (dis)favour Ø.

The voice of the subordinate clause, and the person and voice of the matrix clause, are also identified as being significantly associated with the Ø/*that* choice, in ways not entirely predictable from the known association of these features with text category. Passives in the subordinate clause moderately disfavour Ø (weight=0.389), as do passives in the matrix clause (weight=0.250); conversely, second-person matrix subjects appear to favour Ø (weight=0.796). However, there is reason for caution in interpreting these apparent effects. The only extreme weights for matrix person are obtained for very low-frequency environments; by contrast, the more frequent first-person and third-person environments both show neutral weights (close to 0.50). Moreover, the majority of the second-person tokens are questions, as in (16), which may not be entirely comparable with examples in declarative sentences. Almost all such questions have a zero link, and in several of these examples an overt connective would sound quite unidiomatic.

(16) "So *how*, then, *do you propose we get to know each other*?" he asked in the same soft tone. (JXU:0179)

Finally, the features producing these significant effects for person and/or voice are strongly associated with textual style (passives mark a formal and impersonal style, whereas second person pronouns indicate an informal, interactive style), and so the modelled effects in each case could easily be a proxy for effects arising from stylistic variation between texts from the same category.

5.2. Comparing models for different sets of object clauses

As a way of testing the generality of these effects, two further models were also constructed. Of the verbs included in Dataset B, *suggest* is the only one to show roughly even distribution across all four text categories; hence a model was constructed for the 688 tokens of *suggest* alone, in order to confirm whether the effects of text category are truly independent from those of verb lexeme. Finally, to examine whether the effects observed for Dataset B are unique to mandative constructions, or shared more generally by other object clauses, a model was constructed for Dataset C, a small sample of 279 tokens of object clauses with the verbs *know*, *think*, *tell* and *say*. The resulting factor weights for all three models are compared in Table 11.

The three models differ considerably in input weight: Ø is generally more likely with *suggest* (27%; input weight=0.162) than in Dataset B as a whole, and much more likely overall (60%; input weight=0.637) in the non-mandative object clauses of Dataset C. There are also some differences in the factor groups that can be included (obviously, the model for *suggest* cannot include variation by verb lexeme; and verb mood is irrelevant for describing Dataset C).

Nevertheless, there are several striking commonalities between the three models. The subordinate clause subject is consistently identified as having a highly significant effect: pronouns favour Ø (with approximately the same modelled weights) in all cases. (The impact of a pronominal subject appears slightly reduced with *suggest*; but this is probably only because it is a more typical environment for that verb than the others.) The effect of intervening items in favouring *that* is also significant across all three models (though it is relatively less important in Dataset C, possibly because of the smaller sample size). These two processing constraints therefore seem to hold quite generally for all object clause marking; this result should come as no surprise, given that parallel effects for both factors have also been observed in object relative clauses.

Significant differences by text category are also confirmed for all three models. The model for *suggest* shows essentially the same text-category effects as observed for Dataset B as a whole. The effects modelled in Dataset C, too, show Ø to be consistently disfavoured in texts from "applied science" (weight=0.399) and especially "world affairs" (weight=0.209), and relatively favoured in both "arts" and "imaginative prose"; however, "imaginative prose" does not have as extreme an effect in Dataset C as in the mandative datasets (possibly because a higher proportion of the tokens in Dataset C are from that text category, and possibly because the verbs in Dataset C have a range of different functions, which may be distributed differentially across text categories).

Factor group (with *p*-values giving significance of contribution relative to best-fit model, from stepwise regression log-likelihood comparisons)	1. All mandative constructions (Dataset B; *n*=1729)	2. Tokens of *suggest* only (Dataset B; *n*=688)	3. Non-mandatives (Dataset C; *n*=279)
	Factor weight (weights above 0.5 favour Ø)		
1) Subject of subordinate clause	($p<0.001$)	($p<0.001$)	($p<0.001$)
pronominal	0.693	0.632	0.615
non-pronominal	0.392	0.374	0.340
2) Text type	($p<0.001$)	($p<0.001$)	($p<0.001$)
imaginative prose	0.720	0.703	0.633
arts	0.588	0.604	0.639
applied science	0.501	0.435	0.399
world affairs	0.343	0.313	0.209
3) Intervening item	($p<0.001$)	($p<0.001$)	($p=0.037$)
no	0.596	0.617	0.550
yes	0.088	0.095	0.248
4) Verb lexeme	($p<0.001$)	(inapplicable)	($p=0.009$)
suggest	0.659	——	*think* 0.605
insist	0.454	——	*say* 0.539
demand	0.437	——	*tell* 0.504
propose	0.398	——	*know* 0.241
recommend	0.358	——	
request	0.257	——	
order	0.243	——	
5) Voice of subordinate clause verb	($p=0.003$)	($p=0.003$)	($p=0.496$)
active	0.567	0.572	——
passive	0.389	0.283	——
6) Person of matrix clause verb	($p=0.020$)	($p=0.257$)	($p=0.014$)
2nd person	0.796	——	0.716
1st person	0.537	——	0.615
3rd person	0.507	——	0.457
unclear	0.440	——	0.327
passive	0.250	——	0.062
7) Mood of subordinate clause verb	($p=0.057$)	($p=0.010$)	(inapplicable)
indicative	——	0.644	——
mandative subjunctive	——	0.589	——
ambiguous	——	0.588	——
modal	——	0.409	——
8) Person of subord. clause verb	($p=0.118$)	($p=0.117$)	($p=0.391$)
(not significant in any model)	——	——	——
Overall (input weight)	0.073	0.162	0.637

Table 11. Best-fit variable-rule models for factors affecting Ø linkage in object clauses.

The identity of the lexical verb is selected as a significant influence on Ø-marking in Dataset C, and as in Dataset B, the factor weights can be partially linked to verb frequency – though with one important exception in this case. The dataset contains 118 tokens of *say* (57% Ø), 79 of *think* (82% Ø), 46 of *know* (50% Ø) and 36 of *tell* (36% Ø). The verb most strongly favouring Ø is *think* (weight=0.605), which indicates that its particular function of expressing an "internal" event may outweigh its lower frequency relative to *say*; however, the remaining three (more functionally similar) verbs do show a rank order of factor weights consistent with their observed frequency in the dataset.

Slightly less expected is the closely parallel set of effects for the factor group of matrix person (or, perhaps more accurately, matrix voice, as the strongest single effect included therein is that of matrix passives disfavouring Ø) in Datasets B and C. However, the same factor group has no significant influence in the model for *suggest*, which seems to support the idea that the modelled effects reflect individual text style rather than any direct causal connection to voice itself. Meanwhile, the factor group of subordinate-clause voice has as significant a contribution (and much the same modelled effects) for *suggest* as for Dataset B as a whole; but it is not identified as having any effect for Dataset C, possibly because the stylistic effects linked to passive constructions have been captured by the matrix clause person/voice factor group instead (yielding a factor weight for matrix passives of 0.062, highly disfavouring Ø).

A final, somewhat odd, result is that the factor group describing verb mood in the subordinate clause is selected as significant for sentences containing *suggest*, with indicative forms favouring Ø (0.644) and modal constructions somewhat disfavouring Ø (0.409); however, this factor group was not found to be significant in the overall dataset. It can be noted that there is a significant association between mood and text category (modal constructions are commonest in "world affairs", whereas ambiguous forms are commonest in "imaginative prose" – and are mostly associated with the verb *suggest*); hence it is possible that this factor group might, like verb voice, capture some aspect of individual text style. However, considerably more data, for a wider range of verbs, would be needed to test this hypothesis.

6. Discussion

At this point, we have successfully confirmed that several proposed causal influences on object clause marking identified for common verbs such as *say*, *think*, or *tell* also apply to rarer verbs in mandative constructions. Mandative sentences show an overall lower probability of zero-marking, which may partly result from the lower verb frequency, partly from the distribution of these constructions in texts favouring more formal, explicit styles, and partly from an association with less easily processed syntactic environments. However, they still show significant effects in common with other object clauses: from pronominal subjects of the object clause; from intervening material; and from the observed frequency of the particular verb introducing the construction. They also show a similar pattern of variation with text category. To a good approximation, then, it appears that these different types of object clause constructions can be considered aspects of one linguistic variable; the few differences that are observed are limited to less significant model contributions, with less certain interpretations.

However (as always in scientific research), there are also some areas of remaining uncertainty. Our statistical models can only be as good as the distinctions that have been identified and coded for inclusion, and so we need to examine whether any explanatory factors may have been overlooked, and to consider exactly what causal connections may underlie the observed significant associations with our variable. One detail showing the need for such work is that all of the "best-fit" models reported above are nevertheless very poor fits to the observed data (with $p<0.0001$ that the data could be produced by the model). This is generally true of most complex variable-rule models, and should not be a cause for alarm – it does not mean that the effects so far identified are necessarily incorrect – but it does indicate that some other important sources of variation have not yet been accounted for. A particular aspect of our findings requiring some further explanation is the apparent inconsistency in significance of effects associated with passive constructions in the matrix and/or subordinate clauses favouring *that*, and second-person constructions favouring Ø.

Even the most important influence identified, that of pronominal object clause subjects favouring Ø, versus nonpronominal object clause subjects favouring *that*, is open to re-examination. Thus far the effect has been attributed mostly to the fact that pronouns are overtly case-marked; but that explanation must be at best partial, given that the most favourable environment of all for Ø occurs when the object clause has the subject *you*, which does not unambiguously mark subject case. Hence case-marking probably should be considered as merely one (albeit an important one) of many different ways in which pronominal subjects might contribute to easier processing of an object clause. Accordingly, we may predict a range of subtler influences, with a large difference between most pronouns and most other noun phrases, but also some variation within both sets, depending on how easily the subject can be identified as a subject (and so operate as a clause-initial marker in its own right, favouring Ø).

The effect of *you* can perhaps be explained by noting that second-person reference implies that the addressee (typically also the reader) is assumed to have privileged access to contextual knowledge that could aid processing. First-person pronouns, by contrast, mark personal stance, and imply that the author or narrator has contextual knowledge, but not necessarily that a reader or listener shares it. Pronouns are also semantically definite in context (i.e., they usually have a previously-assigned specific referent). Further, most personal pronouns (except *it* and *they*) explicitly signal animacy. Both definiteness and animacy are typical of (and so may contribute to easing the identification and processing of) grammatical subjects. Pronouns are also typically shorter than most other noun phrases, which may further aid rapid recognition (cf. the explanation in terms of "lightness" given by Elsness 1984). Finally, pronouns are typically unmodified, which limits the range of constructions they occur in (e.g., subject pronouns are typically immediately followed by their finite verb), further contributing to processing ease.

Several of these properties are also shared by some subsets of nonpronominal subject noun phrases: e.g. proper names also mark animacy, may generally be assumed to be semantically definite, and are also typically unmodified. As a result, we should expect to find some differences in influence among different types of nonpronominal subject noun as well. Overall, the proposed effects from these various properties would predict a general rank order of influence on Ø similar to that presented in Table 12. Some of these individual effects have already been indicated for subjects of relative clauses (cf. Sigley 1997: 317); their potential influence on object clause marking can and should be tested in future research by conducting a more detailed multivariate description of the subjects of object clauses.

Feature: / Subject NP type:	Context assumed known to reader/ addressee	Subject case explicitly marked	Short	Limited syntactic contexts (e.g., no modifiers)	Animate	Definite (referent assumed known in context)
I / we	–	+	+	+	+	+
you	+	–	+	+	+	+
he / she	–	+	+	+	+	+
they	–	+	+	+	–	+
it	–	–	+	+	–	+
proper name, with given referent	–	–	–	+	+	+
definite animate (*the girl*)	–	–	–	–	+	+
indefinite animate (*a man*)	–	–	–	–	+	–
definite inanimate (*the ball*)	–	–	–	–	–	+
indefinite inanimate (*a book*)	–	–	–	–	–	–

Table 12. Possible contributions of subject features to object clause processing.

The influence of the verb lexeme may also need to be divided into several separate causal dimensions, especially if this description is to be extended to a wider range of matrix verbs. The models constructed for Datasets B and C suggest that the relative frequency with which a verb occurs with an object clause may contribute to processing ease, and so to the preference for Ø-marking; but it also seems that certain features of verb functions such as reference to an "internal" event (*think*) versus an "external" one (*say*) need to be distinguished in order to allow useful generalisations. We might also need to consider the relative likelihood of other competing structures after each verb, e.g. the probability that the verb occurs instead with a noun phrase as a direct object; however, the limited comparisons possible in the present data (e.g. of *insist* vs. *order*) suggest that such effects may have relatively little additional impact.

Finally, the influence of text category and/or "formality" of style also could, and probably should, be decomposed into several separate explanatory dimensions, especially if data is to be investigated from a wider stylistic range (e.g. including conversation). The text category label may capture such information as: the generally acceptable style level for a particular genre; a range of typical language functions performed in that genre; and possibly also some institution-based differences in the extent and focus of editing (e.g. for factual accuracy, or linguistic correctness, or avoidance of ambiguity). However, Biber (1988, 1995) has conclusively demonstrated that there can be considerable stylistic variation between texts within a given register; and this stylistic variation is not captured by the text category label itself. If the variable under investigation is in fact directly linked to formality, then some measure of formality level for each individual text (such as that used by Sigley, this volume) also needs to be included in the model. Otherwise, the effect of text style will be forced onto the modelled effects for any other factor(s) coded that happen to be strongly associated with style. This is potentially a serious limitation of the models constructed here; such indirect style effects seem the most likely explanation of the various apparent effects observed in the present data for passive constructions in the matrix and/or subordinate clauses, and also for the apparent influence of person in the matrix clause. Testing this hypothesis would require calculating and including in the model some more direct measure of style level for each individual text, which, for the quantity of data analysed here, would be a far from trivial task.

7. Conclusions

Overall, mandative sentences containing finite object clauses show a much lower preference for Ø-linking than the more common object clause constructions that have been studied to date. Nevertheless, our findings confirm that clause-marking in mandative sentences largely follows the same constraints already reported in previous research on other types of object clause, and so may be regarded as part of the same variable. Despite the presence of significant associations between the proposed causal factors, variable-rule modelling has identified highly significant independent influences from the presence of a pronominal subject in the object clause (favouring Ø-linking) and the presence of intervening material between the verb and the object clause (favouring the overt marker *that*).

The comparisons of variable rule models for different sets of object clauses offer more direct confirmation that mandative sentences behave in many ways similarly to other sentences containing finite object clauses: for both mandative and non-mandative sentences, parallel effects are observed not only for the aforementioned processing constraints, but also for verb and text category/style. The matrix verb shows significant effects mostly consistent with the claim that verbs occurring less often with finite object clauses are also more likely to favour *that* (but also suggesting some differences in overall preference for Ø resulting from functional differences between verbs). Further, the models show broadly similar effects for the overall style level and institutional editing behaviour characterising major text categories (e.g. news articles, which may be more consistently edited to avoid ambiguity, overwhelmingly favour *that*, whereas less formal texts such as in fiction show a higher preference for Ø). Other more direct effects from the style levels of individual texts seem to underlie parallel effects modelled for voice and person in the matrix clause.

Nevertheless, the topic of *that* vs. zero linkage has certainly not yet been exhausted. More comprehensive coverage of the variable is desirable (with treatment extended to other sets of verbs, and to a wider range of different texts), and more detailed study is necessary to arrive at more accurate accounts of the actual causal connections in the data. Several promising directions for such investigation have been identified in our discussion (unpacking the effects of clause subjects as subsidiary markers, the effects of the matrix verb, and the effects of text style and register). Given the size of the BNC, the existence of other large corpora, and the progress made in accessing the data contained in the corpus, we can confidently expect some resolution of these issues in the not too distant future.

References

Bell, Allan 1991. *The Language of News Media.* Oxford: Blackwell.

Biber, Douglas 1988. *Variation across Speech and Writing.* Cambridge: Cambridge University Press.

Biber, Douglas 1995. *Dimensions of Register Variation: a Cross-Linguistic Comparison.* Cambridge: Cambridge University Press.

Biber, Douglas / Johansson, Stig / Leech, Geoffrey / Conrad, Susan / Finegan, Edward 1999. *Longman Grammar of Spoken and Written English.* London and New York: Longman.

Cofer, Thomas M. 1975. Performance constraints on relative pronoun deletion. *Linguistics* 157, 13-32.

Ellinger, J. 1933. Substantivsätze mit oder ohne *that* in der neueren englischen Literatur. *Anglia* 57, 78-109.

Elsness, Johan 1984. *That* or zero? a look at the choice of object clause connective in a corpus of American English. *English Studies* 65, 519-533.

Finegan, Edward / Biber, Douglas 1995. *That* and zero complementisers in Late Modern English: Exploring ARCHER from 1650–1990. In Aarts, Bas / Meyer, Charles F. (eds) *The Verb in Contemporary English. Theory and Description.* Cambridge: Cambridge University Press, 241-257.

Jespersen, Otto 1928. *A Modern English Grammar on Historical Principles.* Volume III. London: George Allen & Unwin / Copenhagen: Ejnar Munksgaard.

Kitcher, Philip 1995. *The Advancement of Science: Science without Legend, Objectivity without Illusions.* Oxford: Oxford University Press.

Mair, Christian 1995. Changing patterns of complementation, and concomitant grammaticalisation, of the verb *help* in present-day British English. In: Aarts, Bas / Meyer, Charles F. (eds) *The Verb in Contemporary English. Theory and Description.* Cambridge: Cambridge University Press, 258-272.

McCawley, James D. 1988. *The Syntactic Phenomena of English.* Volume 1. Chicago and London: The University of Chicago Press.

Olofsson, Arne 1981. *Relative Junctions in Written American English.* Goteburg: Acta Universitatis Gothoburgensis; Gothenburg Studies in English 50.

Övergaard, Gerd 1995. *The Mandative Subjunctive in American and British English in the 20th Century.* Upsalla: Acta Universalis Upsaliensis; *Studia Anglistica Upsaliensia* 94.

Paulillo, John C. 2002. *Analyzing Linguistic Variation: Statistical Models and Methods.* Stanford, CA: CSLI Publications.

Quirk, Randolph / Greenbaum, Sidney / Leech, Geoffrey / Svartvik, Jan 1985. *A Comprehensive Grammar of the English Language.* London and New York: Longman.

Rand, David / Sankoff, David 1990. *GoldVarb version 2. A variable rule application for the Macintosh™.* Montréal: Centre de recherches mathématiques, Université de Montréal.

Rissanen, Matti 1991. On the history of *that*/zero as object clause links in English. In Aijmer, Karin / Altenberg, Bengt (eds) *English Corpus Linguistics.* London: Longman, 272-289.

Sigley, Robert 1997. *Choosing Your Relatives: Relative Clauses in New Zealand English.* PhD thesis, Victoria University of Wellington, New Zealand.

Sigley, Robert 2003. The importance of interaction effects. *Language Variation and Change* 15, 227-263.

Storms, G. 1966. *That*-clauses in modern English. *English Studies* 47, 249-270.

Tagliamonte, Sali A. 2006. *Analysing Sociolinguistic Variation.* New York: Cambridge University Press.

Thompson, Sandra A. / Mulac, Anthony 1991. The discourse conditions for the use of the complementizer *that* in conversational English. *Journal of Pragmatics* 15, 237-251.

Thyberg, E. 1996. The mandative subjunctive in British and American English: A corpus study. Unpublished term paper. Växjö University.

Section 2
Descriptions of Synchronic Linguistic Variation

GRAEME KENNEDY

Semantic Preference of High-Frequency Mental Verbs in the British National Corpus

1. Introduction

1.1. The uses of variation

In *Discoveries* (1640), the English playwright, Ben Jonson wrote:

> Language most shews a man. Speak, that I may see thee. It springs out of the most retired and inmost parts of us, and is the image of the parent of it, the mind. No glass renders a man's form or likeness so true as his speech.

Consistent with Jonson's views, systematic variation in the use of words and grammatical patterns has continued to be used to categorise linguistic behaviour. The focus of research has included interest in the behaviour of individual speakers, or that of groups, as defined by such variables as geographical location, social class, gender, genre, or linguistic change over time.

Most recently, corpus-based research has also revealed that systematic linguistic variation can be seen in the way in which words that might seem to be semantically related (e.g. *stop, end, finish*) can be associated with quite different sets of collocates. Analysis of the British National Corpus (BNC) suggests that whereas *stop* tends to be strongly associated with verbs marking unpleasant, irritating or negative behaviours or processes (e.g. *fussing, crying, interrupting, whingeing*), *end* tends to precede nouns marking big or unpleasant processes or events (e.g. *war, conflict, siege, chaos, suffering, disaster*), and *finish* tends to be associated with words marking small-scale activities or events (e.g. *meals, washing, games* or *unpacking*). Stubbs (2001: 65) described the collocational relationship between a type or lemma and a set or group of semantically-related words as one of 'semantic preference'. As an example, the word *large* shows semantic preference for 'quantity words' such as *size, amount, part,* or *proportion.*

Verb class	Frequency per million tags	% of corpus	% of verbs
lexical verbs	109,383	10.9	54.2
be	48,404	4.8	24.0
do	10,396	1.0	5.1
have	15,956	1.6	7.9
modals	17,830	1.8	8.8
Total	201,969	20.2	100

Table 1. Verb distribution in the BNC.

Collocational relationships are thus seen not as occurring between two or more words which occur repeatedly in each other's company, but rather between a word or a number of semantic sets associated with that word. As a further example, Stubbs (2001: 89) suggests that the verb *undergo* has semantic preference for words associated with medicine, change, testing, and involuntariness (e.g. being *forced* to *undergo* a process).

1.2. Scope of the present research

The present paper describes variation in the semantic preferences associated with ten high frequency lexical verbs occurring in the BNC, using frequency of occurrence as collocations, and strength of collocational bonding (as measured by the Mutual Information (MI) value), as the basis of the analysis. The purpose of the study was to explore whether the collocates which associate with each of the ten lexical verbs have any systematic semantic characteristics. A corpus-based analysis was undertaken to see if it is possible to identify what it is that speakers of English are most likely to *want, enjoy, remember,* and so on, and whether there are any common semantic categories to which the predicates of the ten words each belong. That is, whereas Biber *et al.* (1999) focused on the semantic category to which the lexical verb keywords belong, the present analysis focuses on the semantic and grammatical characteristics of what follows the keyword. As shown in Table 1, lexical verbs typically account for almost eleven percent of all the words in a corpus and over 54 percent of the verbs. Table 2 summarises the analysis of Biber *et al.* (1999: 360), who have suggested that lexical verbs can be classified into seven major semantic domains.

Semantic domain	% of lexical verbs
activity verbs	49
mental verbs	19
communication verbs	12
existence verbs	8
occurrence verbs	5
causative verbs	4
aspectual verbs	3
Total	100

Table 2. Major semantic domains of lexical verbs.

Although many lexical verbs have more than one sense and can occur in more than one semantic domain, most verbs, according to Biber *et al.* (1999: 361), have a 'core meaning'. The ten verbs selected for analysis in the present study are listed in Table 3. They are all 'mental verbs', a subset of lexical verbs, and were selected mainly because they are of high enough frequency so as to produce enough tokens for reliable analysis.

Mental verbs	Rank of verbs in the BNC	Frequency per million words
want	23	945
follow	43	460
like	46	424
consider	71	289
remember	82	268
understand	91	238
love	150	150
enjoy	156	146
prefer	305	68
hate	404	50

Table 3. Mental verbs in the BNC.

According to Biber *et al.* (1999: 362), mental verbs "denote a wide range of activities and states experienced by humans", including meanings associated with cognition (e.g. *think, feel, decide, calculate, assume*), and meanings expressing attitudes or desires (e.g. *want, like, love, doubt*). *Want*, the most frequent mental verb used in this study, is ranked 23rd most frequent in the BNC, occurring 945 times per million words. As shown in Table 3, only *prefer* and *hate* among the ten verbs analysed fall outside the 156 most frequent lexical verbs in the corpus.

1.3. Methodology

The methodology used in this analysis is similar to the one adopted for a description of amplifier collocations (Kennedy 2003). The software BNCWeb (Lehrmann *et al.* 2002) was used to identify and retrieve the collocates of the ten mental verbs. For each of these verbs, two separate analyses were undertaken. First, the eighty most frequently occurring collocates of each of the ten mental verbs were identified, and then the eighty most strongly bonded collocates were identified using the Mutual Information (MI) value formula as given by Church/Hanks (1990). The results of both analyses are listed in Tables 4 to 13. The frequency and MI value of each collocate is calculated automatically by the BNCWeb software, and although the MI value tends to highlight collocations containing low frequency words, it nevertheless is a useful way of indicating the relative strength of the collocational bond between words in phrases. For both frequency and MI values, only those collocations which occurred in eight or more different texts in the corpus were included in the analysis. This requirement that a collocation had to occur in at least eight texts in the corpus was intended to reduce the likelihood of the analysis being distorted by very rare, strongly-bonded collocations occurring in very few texts. A further limitation undertaken to prevent the analysis being overwhelmed by large numbers of collocations of limited interest, was to include only content word collocates of the ten mental verbs. Thus, collocations such as *like a, want his, remember the, enjoy in,* were deliberately excluded. The main categories of function words omitted from the analysis included personal and possessive pronouns, determiners, prepositions, adverbial particles, modals, negatives, numerals, conjunctions, comparatives, and interrogative pronouns. An obvious consequence of omitting collocations containing function words, however, was that high frequency multiword units such as phrasal verbs were not included in the analysis.

In retrieving the collocates of the ten mental verbs, the lemma of each verb was used. That is, for *like*, the types *like, liked, likes,* and *liking* were all treated as part of a single lemma. Only the collocates occurring to the right of the headword, within a space of 4 words (i.e., the window size was +1 to +4), were considered. A pilot analysis had shown that this window size was appropriate because predicates to the right of the keyword were the main focus of the analysis, and because Sinclair *et al.* (1970: 8) had demonstrated that frequently-occurring words predict more reliably to the right of the keyword than to the left. It should be kept in mind, however, that the collocates associated with each keyword can have positive or negative polarity. That is, the software identifies *gardening* as a collocate which follows *enjoy* whether it occurs in the phrase *She enjoys gardening* or *She doesn't enjoy gardening*.

2. Results for individual high-frequency mental verbs

2.1. Like

As shown in Table 3, *like* is the 46th most frequent verb in the BNC, occurring about 424 times per million words. Table 4(a) shows that the most frequent collocate associated with *like* is *see* (occurring 1266 times in the corpus), while Table 4(b) shows that *congratulate* is the most strongly bonded collocate of *like*. By frequency, *like* is often followed by collocates which are the infinitive form of other very high frequency verbs (e.g. *see, know, go, think, say*). On the other hand, the MI values in Table 4(b) show that *like* is strongly associated with words that are part of 'communicative formulae', e.g. *I'd like to (congratulate, apologise, propose, thank, remind, emphasise, invite, toast, quote, clarify, (pay) tribute, assure, express, introduce, comment, speak, mention, suggest, recommend, (express) appreciation*). At least twenty-eight of the 80 strongest collocations associated with *like* are part of such communicative formulae. Table 4 also reveals the kinds of things or activities that speakers of English in the BNC *liked* (or *did not like*) at the end of the 20th century when the corpus was compiled. These include *gardening, cooking, swimming, movies, cats,* and *gossip*. Food items which occur in the BNC as collocates of *like* include the following (some of which are of lower frequency or MI value than is shown in Table 4, or which occur in fewer than eight texts). They give an interesting insight into the culinary tastes or food items with which the British were familiar at the end of the 20th century. They include *cuppa, almonds, buns, sherry, custard, strawberry, bananas, yoghurt, mince, crisps, brandy, tuna, rum, pie, coffee, biscuits, ginger, grapes, garlic, sausages, tea, steak, chocolate, peas, cheese, bacon, mushroom, nuts, cake, chicken, pudding, cream, sweets, tomato, whisky, beer, potatoes, lamb, sandwiches, soup* and *egg*. Perhaps surprisingly, we do not find *bread, fish and chips, noodles, pizza, wine,* or *sushi* strongly associated with *like* (or *not like*) in the BNC.

1	*see*	1266	21	*work*	194	41	*sound*	121	61	*music*	86
2	*know*	805	22	*now*	185	42	*other*	118	62	*another*	86
3	*go*	598	23	*best*	182	43	*play*	117	63	*please*	85
4	*think*	557	24	*put*	179	44	*own*	116	64	*speak*	85
5	*say*	422	25	*talk*	176	45	*stay*	105	65	*children*	84
6	*get*	368	26	*just*	175	46	*information*	102	66	*really*	82
7	*make*	365	27	*doing*	172	47	*women*	101	67	*buy*	81
8	*people*	353	28	*something*	171	48	*meet*	100	68	*change*	80
9	*take*	341	29	*keep*	165	49	*read*	99	69	*further*	80
10	*come*	323	30	*then*	158	50	*good*	98	70	*show*	80
11	*very*	313	31	*give*	152	51	*feel*	97	71	*leave*	78
12	*hear*	302	32	*tell*	150	52	*have*	96	72	*add*	77
13	*look*	299	33	*try*	147	53	*well*	95	73	*home*	76
14	*way*	296	34	*help*	142	54	*man*	91	74	*eat*	75
15	*idea*	294	35	*new*	135	55	*able*	90	75	*nice*	75
16	*thank*	253	36	*call*	135	56	*point*	90	76	*old*	74
17	*ask*	246	37	*drink*	132	57	*write*	87	77	*myself*	74
18	*things*	235	38	*use*	124	58	*coffee*	87	78	*time*	73
19	*better*	202	39	*bit*	124	59	*tea*	87	79	*men*	72
20	*here*	200	40	*going*	122	60	*find*	87	80	*nothing*	72

Table 4. Collocates of *like* in the BNC, (a) sorted by frequency.

1 *congratulate*	5.8	21 *coffee*	3.2	41 *comment*	2.9	61 *sound*	2.6
2 *donate*	4.6	22 *hats*	3.2	42 *express*	2.9	62 *privacy*	2.6
3 *apologise*	4.2	23 *emphasise*	3.2	43 *borrow*	2.9	63 *taste*	2.5
4 *hear*	4.0	24 *chat*	3.2	44 *chocolate*	2.8	64 *explore*	2.5
5 *sherry*	4.0	25 *admire*	3.2	45 *dancing*	2.8	65 *sit*	2.5
6 *propose*	3.9	26 *ask*	3.2	46 *eat*	2.8	66 *spend*	2.5
7 *thank*	3.9	27 *clarify*	3.2	47 *accompany*	2.8	67 *discuss*	2.5
8 *dislike*	3.8	28 *cats*	3.1	48 *outfit*	2.8	68 *write*	2.5
9 *remind*	3.8	29 *tribute*	3.0	49 *introduce*	2.8	69 *gossip*	2.5
10 *emphasize*	3.8	30 *biscuits*	3.0	50 *quote*	2.7	70 *recommend*	2.4
11 *donation*	3.6	31 *garlic*	3.0	51 *cheese*	2.7	71 *swimming*	2.4
12 *respected*	3.6	32 *kissing*	3.0	52 *add*	2.7	72 *movies*	2.4
13 *invite*	3.6	33 *pretend*	3.0	53 *speak*	2.7	73 *cooking*	2.4
14 *sincere*	3.6	34 *sing*	2.9	54 *join*	2.7	74 *cake*	2.4
15 *drink*	3.6	35 *see*	2.9	55 *bacon*	2.7	75 *appreciation*	2.4
16 *gardening*	3.4	36 *talk*	2.9	56 *highlight*	2.7	76 *reminded*	2.4
17 *brandy*	3.4	37 *assure*	2.9	57 *ride*	2.7	77 *joke*	2.4
18 *toast*	3.3	38 *tea*	2.9	58 *admired*	2.6	78 *touching*	2.4
19 *pie*	3.3	39 *volunteer*	2.9	59 *mention*	2.6	79 *admit*	2.4
20 *idea*	3.3	40 *smell*	2.9	60 *stay*	2.6	80 *suggest*	2.3

Table 4. Collocates of *like* in the BNC, (b) sorted by MI values.

2.2. Love

We have seen that the verb *like* tends to be followed particularly by the infinitive forms of verbs, collocates functioning as part of 'communicative formulae', and by food nouns. We might expect the verb *love* to have similar collocates. Analysis of the BNC, however, presents a different picture. As shown in Table 5, only about 18 percent of the collocates which follow *love* are verbs, while about 57 percent are nouns, or indefinite or reflexive pronouns. Table 5(a) shows that on grounds of frequency of occurrence speakers or writers of English in the BNC tend to *love* nouns denoting personal entities, including *children, each other, people, God, man, someone, anyone, one another, woman, neighbour, father, mother, husband, wife, myself, women, yourself, himself, daughter, ourselves*.

The MI values showing the strength of bonding between *love* and its collocates in the BNC are shown in Table 5(b). Again, personal or domestic nouns or reflexive pronouns are strongly bonded with *love*. They include *neighbour, one another, each other, enemies, ourselves, mummy, darling, kids, husband, anybody, daughter, yourself, Mum, myself, brother, children, wife, child*. Somewhat incongruously, Table

5(b) shows *love* to be also a reasonably strong collocate of *hate, hated, and enemies*. Apart from *humans* and *animals,* Table 5(a) shows that the British ***love*** (the) *way, life, things, work, music, country, job, everything* and *playing*, while Table 5(b) shows that they also *love dancing, cooking, countryside, cake, chocolate, songs, poetry, swimming, singing, music, cricket, flowers, stories, letters, walking, painting, clothes, colours, driving, challenges, sports* and *theatre*. Adverbials associated with *love* include *dearly, deeply, never, always, passionately,* and *forever*.

1 *see*	120	21 *anyone*	50	41 *woman*	37	61 *myself*	28
2 *very*	107	22 *then*	49	42 *doing*	36	62 *take*	28
3 *way*	91	23 *work*	49	43 *neighbour*	35	63 *women*	28
4 *children*	90	24 *music*	48	44 *best*	35	64 *yourself*	28
5 *each other*	85	25 *now*	48	45 *father*	35	65 *wanted*	28
6 *people*	81	26 *one another*	48	46 *little*	34	66 *still*	27
7 *God*	80	27 *play*	47	47 *mother*	34	67 *well*	27
8 *dearly*	73	28 *come*	45	48 *nothing*	34	68 *everything*	27
9 *man*	66	29 *again*	44	49 *only*	34	69 *own*	26
10 *hate*	66	30 *new*	44	50 *never*	33	70 *anything*	26
11 *life*	64	31 *place*	43	51 *enough*	33	71 *himself*	26
12 *go*	64	32 *country*	43	52 *wanted*	32	72 *better*	25
13 *hear*	63	33 *ones*	42	53 *job*	32	73 *daughter*	25
14 *just*	62	34 *child*	42	54 *old*	32	74 *feel*	25
15 *know*	59	35 *even*	41	55 *always*	32	75 *another*	24
16 *world*	57	36 *other*	40	56 *minute*	31	76 *ourselves*	24
17 *someone*	55	37 *get*	40	57 *husband*	30	77 *thought*	24
18 *here*	54	38 *really*	39	58 *wife*	30	78 *animals*	24
19 *said*	53	39 *going*	38	59 *else*	30	79 *playing*	24
20 *things*	50	40 *first*	38	60 *time*	29	80 *deeply*	24

Table 5. Collocates of *love* in the BNC, (a) sorted by frequency.

1 *dearly*	8.7	21 *cooking*	3.3	41 *someone*	2.6	61 *beautiful*	2.2
2 *cherish*	7.2	22 *sing*	3.2	42 *animals*	2.5	62 *myself*	2.2
3 *passionately*	6.7	23 *hear*	3.2	43 *die*	2.5	63 *dance*	2.2
4 *loathe*	6.5	24 *mummy*	3.2	44 *husband*	2.5	64 *clothes*	2.2
5 *hate*	5.4	25 *darling*	3.2	45 *cricket*	2.4	65 *song*	2.2
6 *neighbour*	5.3	26 *kids*	3.1	46 *anybody*	2.4	66 *brother*	2.2
7 *one another*	5.1	27 *countryside*	3.0	47 *daughter*	2.4	67 *somebody*	2.2
8 *hated*	4.8	28 *cake*	3.0	48 *yourself*	2.4	68 *colours*	2.2
9 *cared*	4.2	29 *chocolate*	3.0	49 *sight*	2.4	69 *playing*	2.2
10 *each other*	4.0	30 *dogs*	2.8	50 *flowers*	2.4	70 *play*	2.1
11 *respected*	4.0	31 *minute*	2.8	51 *stories*	2.3	71 *listen*	2.1
12 *dressing*	3.9	32 *songs*	2.8	52 *letters*	2.3	72 *watch*	2.1
13 *admired*	3.8	33 *God*	2.8	53 *mum*	2.3	73 *driving*	2.0
14 *dancing*	3.8	34 *anyone*	2.8	54 *walking*	2.3	74 *sports*	2.0
15 *deeply*	3.7	35 *poetry*	2.7	55 *dress*	2.3	75 *children*	1.9
16 *enemies*	3.6	36 *swimming*	2.7	56 *bits*	2.3	76 *missed*	1.9
17 *forever*	3.6	37 *singing*	2.7	57 *watching*	2.2	77 *challenge*	1.9
18 *honour*	3.5	38 *music*	2.7	58 *fly*	2.2	78 *theatre*	1.9
19 *ourselves*	3.4	39 *horses*	2.6	59 *painting*	2.2	79 *wife*	1.8
20 *tender*	3.4	40 *smell*	2.6	60 *Jesus*	2.2	80 *child*	1.8

Table 5. Collocates of *love* in the BNC, (b) sorted by MI values.

2.3. Enjoy

The 156th most frequent lexical verb in the BNC is *enjoy*. It occurs 146 times per million words. Table 6(a) shows that *enjoy* collocates most frequently with *life* (occurring 244 times) and that the participants recorded in the BNC also frequently associate *enjoy* with reflexive pronouns (including *themselves, himself, yourself, myself, herself, ourselves*), and also with *people, together, sex, company, meeting,* and *relationships*.

The MI values in Table 6(b) similarly show that *enjoy* is strongly bonded with reflexive pronouns (including *yourselves, yourself, oneself, ourselves, myself, themselves,* and *herself*), and with a variety of pleasurable sensations. These include *comforts, pleasures, popularity, delights, privileges, hospitality, scenery, sunshine, prestige, fame, freedom, luxury, prosperity, holidays, jokes, warmth, success, trips, retirement, countryside, sex, entertainment, leisure, performances,* and *friendship.*

Table 6 also shows that a large number of the collocates of *enjoy*, whether identified by frequency of occurrence or MI values, are words ending in *-ing*. According to the BNC the British enjoy (by frequency) *working, playing, reading, having, going, watching, making, meeting, seeing,* and *looking*. By MI they enjoy *gardening, skiing, relaxing,* *watching, dancing, cooking, playing, reading,* and *singing*. Many of these activities are enjoyed *immensely, hugely,* or *enormously*. Not surprisingly, the objects of *enjoy* are typically positive things.

1 *life*	244	21 *freedom*	78	41 *going*	53	61 *popularity*	42
2 *themselves*	204	22 *holiday*	76	42 *here*	52	62 *views*	42
3 *himself*	168	23 *experience*	73	43 *meal*	50	63 *then*	42
4 *good*	160	24 *time*	68	44 *ourselves*	50	64 *power*	42
5 *so*	157	25 *such*	68	45 *watching*	49	65 *long*	42
6 *yourself*	154	26 *status*	66	46 *minute*	49	66 *part*	39
7 *company*	149	27 *too*	66	47 *music*	49	67 *now*	39
8 *myself*	128	28 *people*	65	48 *making*	48	68 *immensely*	38
9 *success*	101	29 *new*	65	49 *great*	48	69 *better*	38
10 *very*	100	30 *own*	62	50 *meeting*	48	70 *seeing*	37
11 *herself*	99	31 *evening*	61	51 *best*	47	71 *position*	37
12 *work*	98	32 *same*	60	52 *other*	47	72 *Christmas*	37
13 *working*	97	33 *high*	59	53 *only*	47	73 *special*	37
14 *support*	94	34 *food*	57	54 *view*	47	74 *reputation*	37
15 *day*	84	35 *game*	57	55 *last*	45	75 *looking*	36
16 *full*	83	36 *first*	55	56 *relationship*	44	76 *way*	36
17 *playing*	81	37 *years*	55	57 *considerable*	44	77 *fruits*	36
18 *reading*	81	38 *together*	55	58 *job*	44	78 *protection*	35
19 *having*	81	39 *sex*	54	59 *things*	43	79 *moment*	35
20 *benefits*	78	40 *little*	54	60 *drink*	43	80 *even*	35

Table 6. Collocates of *enjoy* in the BNC, (a) sorted by frequency.

1 *immensely*	6.9	21 *lifestyle*	5.0	41 *benefits*	4.3	61 *trips*	3.9
2 *yourselves*	6.6	22 *skiing*	4.9	42 *reputation*	4.3	62 *holidays*	3.9
3 *comforts*	6.5	23 *revival*	4.9	43 *delicious*	4.3	63 *colourful*	3.8
4 *hugely*	6.4	24 *yourself*	4.9	44 *holiday*	4.3	64 *status*	3.8
5 *pleasures*	6.2	25 *relaxing*	4.9	45 *monopoly*	4.3	65 *retirement*	3.8
6 *fruits*	6.2	26 *sensation*	4.8	46 *joke*	4.2	66 *spell*	3.8
7 *vogue*	6.0	27 *fame*	4.7	47 *autonomy*	4.2	67 *taste*	3.8
8 *leisurely*	6.0	28 *freedom*	4.7	48 *themselves*	4.1	68 *lively*	3.8
9 *popularity*	6.0	29 *sights*	4.7	49 *boom*	4.1	69 *countryside*	3.8
10 *delights*	5.6	30 *outdoor*	4.6	50 *warmth*	4.1	70 *trip*	3.8
11 *privileges*	5.6	31 *meal*	4.6	51 *ride*	4.1	71 *superb*	3.7
12 *spectacle*	5.6	32 *luxury*	4.6	52 *privilege*	4.0	72 *singing*	3.7
13 *hospitality*	5.5	33 *prosperity*	4.5	53 *renaissance*	4.0	73 *sex*	3.7
14 *scenery*	5.3	34 *patronage*	4.5	54 *watching*	4.0	74 *entertainment*	3.7
15 *prestige*	5.2	35 *oneself*	4.5	55 *chat*	3.9	75 *surroundings*	3.7
16 *sunshine*	5.2	36 *ourselves*	4.5	56 *dancing*	3.9	76 *finest*	3.6
17 *immunity*	5.2	37 *advantages*	4.4	57 *cooking*	3.9	77 *leisure*	3.6
18 *thrill*	5.2	38 *myself*	4.4	58 *playing*	3.9	78 *herself*	3.6
19 *enormously*	5.2	39 *rewards*	4.3	59 *success*	3.9	79 *performances*	3.6
20 *gardening*	5.0	40 *privileged*	4.3	60 *reading*	3.9	80 *friendship*	3.6

Table 6. Collocates of *enjoy* in the BNC, (b) sorted by MI values.

2.4. *Want*

Table 7(a) shows that the mental verb *want* most frequently precedes another verb, as, for example, in *I (don't) want to go*. In fact, on grounds of frequency of occurrence, over 58 percent of the collocates of *want* are the infinitive forms of other high frequency English verbs. In Table 7(b) over 85 percent of the collocates of *want* are infinitives.

Table 7(b) however, also shows that in terms of strength of bonding 34 percent of the collocates of *(not) want* tend to have a negative, or even punitive dimension. These include *embarrass, weep, vomit, rid, intrude, offend, spoil, prolong, disappoint, frighten, disturb, kill, scream, hassle, smack, shout, punish, die, hurt, interrupt, revenge, divorce, cry, confess, destroy, flee, pursue*. Further, Table 7(b) shows that *want* is associated with personal behaviour, significant life events or milestones including *marry, kiss, cuddle, weep, divorce*. In passing, we might note that the few food nouns strongly bonded to *want* are not normally considered to be prominent in a healthy diet. They include *biscuits, crisps* and *pudding*.

1 *know*	3162	21 *stay*	553	41 *again*	328	61 *someone*	222
2 *go*	3144	22 *keep*	525	42 *change*	327	62 *good*	211
3 *see*	2289	23 *people*	516	43 *live*	327	63 *life*	207
4 *get*	2187	24 *help*	482	44 *another*	326	64 *sell*	207
5 *make*	1349	25 *use*	477	45 *try*	306	65 *anyone*	205
6 *some*	1222	26 *play*	467	46 *move*	296	66 *bring*	197
7 *have*	1147	27 *now*	466	47 *new*	292	67 *part*	195
8 *any*	1116	28 *work*	464	48 *things*	281	68 *children*	195
9 *something*	966	29 *here*	456	49 *time*	264	69 *join*	195
10 *talk*	945	30 *find*	448	50 *show*	262	70 *other*	194
11 *take*	935	31 *leave*	444	51 *speak*	239	71 *read*	193
12 *say*	918	32 *tell*	444	52 *sure*	239	72 *pay*	189
13 *come*	902	33 *buy*	438	53 *spend*	232	73 *kill*	189
14 *back*	883	34 *ask*	405	54 *run*	228	74 *nothing*	186
15 *all*	840	35 *money*	405	55 *write*	227	75 *else*	185
16 *hear*	738	36 *then*	393	56 *own*	226	76 *everything*	183
17 *put*	628	37 *home*	377	57 *meet*	224	77 *become*	182
18 *give*	586	38 *too*	359	58 *stop*	224	78 *job*	181
19 *look*	581	39 *think*	355	59 *start*	224	79 *learn*	179
20 *anything*	580	40 *just*	341	60 *marry*	223	80 *feel*	178

Table 7. Collocates of *want* in the BNC, (a) sorted by frequency.

1	*pry*	5.1	21	*stay*	3.9	41	*curl*	3.3	61	*get*	2.8
2	*marry*	4.8	22	*dwell*	3.8	42	*kiss*	3.2	62	*retain*	2.8
3	*cuddle*	4.7	23	*borrow*	3.8	43	*hurt*	3.2	63	*confess*	2.8
4	*embarrass*	4.5	24	*kill*	3.7	44	*interrupt*	3.2	64	*preserve*	2.8
5	*weep*	4.4	25	*scream*	3.7	45	*sell*	3.1	65	*destroy*	2.8
6	*savour*	4.3	26	*impress*	3.7	46	*join*	3.1	66	*flee*	2.8
7	*vomit*	4.3	27	*hassle*	3.6	47	*know*	3.1	67	*pudding*	2.8
8	*rid*	4.3	28	*swap*	3.6	48	*speak*	3.1	68	*leave*	2.8
9	*biscuit*	4.2	29	*go*	3.5	49	*emphasise*	3.1	69	*play*	2.8
10	*intrude*	4.2	30	*buy*	3.5	50	*invest*	3.0	70	*learn*	2.8
11	*talk*	4.2	31	*smack*	3.5	51	*revenge*	3.0	71	*throw*	2.8
12	*hear*	4.2	32	*crisps*	3.4	52	*hug*	3.0	72	*listen*	2.8
13	*offend*	4.1	33	*shout*	3.4	53	*tougher*	3.0	73	*ask*	2.8
14	*spoil*	4.0	34	*anymore*	3.4	54	*divorce*	3.0	74	*inherit*	2.8
15	*pee*	4.0	35	*retire*	3.4	55	*cry*	3.0	75	*tea*	2.8
16	*prolong*	4.0	36	*punish*	3.3	56	*lose*	2.9	76	*build*	2.8
17	*confide*	4.0	37	*spend*	3.3	57	*abolish*	2.9	77	*wee*	2.8
18	*disappoint*	4.0	38	*apologise*	3.3	58	*explore*	2.9	78	*write*	2.8
19	*frighten*	3.9	39	*die*	3.3	59	*drink*	2.9	79	*convey*	2.7
20	*disturb*	3.9	40	*toast*	3.3	60	*emphasize*	2.9	80	*pursue*	2.7

Table 7. Collocates of *want* in the BNC, (b) sorted by MI values.

2.5. Prefer

Table 8 suggests that speakers of British English tend to *prefer* positive things or activities. There is no overwhelming semantic or grammatical preference, although it can be noted that some of the collocates of *prefer* tend to be associated with 'choice' or 'alternatives' (e.g. *instead, different, new, option, other, version, alternative*) or 'maintaining the status quo' (e.g. *keep, remain, stick to, stay, retain, maintain, leave, traditional, hold, focus, concentrate*).

1	*use*	100	21	*give*	35	41	*men*	22	61	*let*	17
2	*see*	86	22	*play*	32	42	*spend*	22	62	*come*	17
3	*keep*	86	23	*approach*	30	43	*eat*	21	63	*others*	17
4	*work*	81	24	*company*	30	44	*buy*	21	64	*word*	17
5	*own*	68	25	*leave*	29	45	*alone*	21	65	*anonymous*	17
6	*call*	66	26	*like*	28	46	*new*	21	66	*know*	16
7	*stay*	62	27	*talk*	28	47	*different*	20	67	*stick*	16
8	*do*	61	28	*look*	28	48	*say*	20	68	*put*	16
9	*take*	56	29	*things*	27	49	*working*	20	69	*longer*	16
10	*go*	56	30	*home*	26	50	*women*	19	70	*someone*	16
11	*remain*	52	31	*people*	24	51	*system*	19	71	*called*	16
12	*think*	51	32	*concentrate*	24	52	*get*	19	72	*discuss*	16
13	*instead*	50	33	*old*	23	53	*money*	19	73	*rely*	15
14	*live*	46	34	*avoid*	23	54	*forget*	19	74	*only*	15
15	*other*	45	35	*believe*	23	55	*deal*	19	75	*then*	15
16	*make*	42	36	*pay*	23	56	*term*	19	76	*food*	15
17	*all*	40	37	*wait*	22	57	*themselves*	19	77	*speak*	15
18	*some*	39	38	*such*	22	58	*life*	18	78	*here*	15
19	*way*	36	39	*quiet*	22	59	*light*	17	79	*version*	15
20	*something*	36	40	*water*	22	60	*care*	17	80	*walk*	15

Table 8. Collocates of *prefer* in the BNC, (a) sorted by frequency.

1	*anonymity*	7.0	21	*describe*	3.4	41	*watch*	2.6	61	*longer*	2.0
2	*anonymous*	6.0	22	*option*	3.2	42	*cash*	2.6	62	*own*	2.0
3	*concentrate*	5.1	23	*soft*	3.1	43	*send*	2.6	63	*simple*	2.0
4	*remain*	4.6	24	*rich*	3.0	44	*travel*	2.6	64	*risk*	2.0
5	*rely*	4.6	25	*focus*	3.0	45	*methods*	2.5	65	*alternative*	2.0
6	*stay*	4.4	26	*approach*	3.0	46	*sell*	2.5	66	*drive*	1.9
7	*stick*	4.0	27	*version*	3.0	47	*formal*	2.4	67	*word*	1.9
8	*quiet*	3.9	28	*talk*	2.9	48	*build*	2.4	68	*work*	1.9
9	*call*	3.9	29	*buy*	2.8	49	*follow*	2.4	69	*someone*	1.9
10	*instead*	3.9	30	*die*	2.8	50	*sit*	2.3	70	*direct*	1.8
11	*ignore*	3.8	31	*speak*	2.8	51	*myself*	2.3	71	*independent*	1.8
12	*forget*	3.8	32	*use*	2.8	52	*style*	2.3	72	*themselves*	1.8
13	*keep*	3.7	33	*alone*	2.7	53	*believe*	2.2	73	*take*	1.8
14	*retain*	3.7	34	*term*	2.7	54	*deal*	2.2	74	*food*	1.7
15	*spend*	3.7	35	*play*	2.7	55	*pay*	2.1	75	*give*	1.7
16	*avoid*	3.6	36	*walk*	2.6	56	*hold*	2.1	76	*greater*	1.7
17	*discuss*	3.6	37	*maintain*	2.6	57	*accept*	2.1	77	*hear*	1.7
18	*eat*	3.6	38	*leave*	2.6	58	*method*	2.1	78	*company*	1.7
19	*live*	3.5	39	*traditional*	2.6	59	*tea*	2.1	79	*light*	1.7
20	*wait*	3.5	40	*drink*	2.6	60	*separate*	2.1	80	*simply*	1.7

Table 8. Collocates of *prefer* in the BNC, (b) sorted by MI values.

2.6. Hate

Even with the exclusion of personal pronouns from the analysis, for the reasons noted earlier, the collocates of *hate* seem overwhelmingly to have personal associations. In terms of frequency Table 9(a) suggests that people *hate* other *people, myself, herself, women, each other, anyone, himself, men, man, everyone, someone, father, husband, woman*. The words *body, hair*, and *guts* can also have personal associations. On grounds of strength of bonding in Table 9(b) we find that *hate* is associated with *myself, each other, herself, anyone, everyone, husband, women, himself, someone, men, people, father, woman, man, mother, parents*. Closer analysis shows that whereas we find *He hates my guts*, or *I hate his guts* (and also, indicating a similar strength of feeling, *I hate the sight of him*), we are less likely to find *I hate his* (or *her*) *hair*, although *I hate my hair* is not so uncommon. Other frequent or strongly-bonded collocates of *hate* in the corpus include *cold, school, life, place, job, music, dress, sight, name, working, shopping, lying, being, going, making, seeing,* and *knowing*. Twenty-five of the 160 collocates of *hate* listed in Table 9 are verbs ending in *-ing*, and many of the collocates excluded from the analysis because they occurred in fewer than eight texts, were also verbs ending in *-ing*.

1 *so*	98	21 *men*	24	41 *anything*	14	61 *feeling*	11
2 *all*	83	22 *things*	23	42 *anyway*	14	62 *shopping*	11
3 *think*	71	23 *every*	22	43 *sight*	13	63 *stuff*	11
4 *people*	64	24 *just*	22	44 *sound*	12	64 *such*	11
5 *see*	57	25 *man*	22	45 *coming*	12	65 *father*	11
6 *way*	53	26 *now*	20	46 *then*	12	66 *seeing*	11
7 *hate*	48	27 *school*	20	47 *very*	12	67 *husband*	10
8 *like*	48	28 *too*	20	48 *lose*	12	68 *old*	10
9 *myself*	48	29 *here*	20	49 *other*	12	69 *playing*	10
10 *herself*	38	30 *guts*	19	50 *enough*	12	70 *fear*	10
11 *women*	35	31 *word*	18	51 *someone*	12	71 *tell*	10
12 *each other*	34	32 *love*	18	52 *job*	11	72 *time*	10
13 *idea*	33	33 *said*	17	53 *called*	11	73 *lying*	10
14 *doing*	30	34 *making*	16	54 *name*	11	74 *cold*	10
15 *going*	30	35 *place*	16	55 *everything*	11	75 *hair*	10
16 *thought*	29	36 *go*	15	56 *sitting*	11	76 *never*	10
17 *say*	27	37 *admit*	15	57 *music*	11	77 *own*	10
18 *anyone*	26	38 *body*	15	58 *really*	11	78 *told*	9
19 *himself*	25	39 *life*	15	59 *made*	11	79 *water*	9
20 *even*	25	40 *everyone*	15	60 *work*	11	80 *woman*	9

Table 9. Collocates of *hate* in the BNC, (a) sorted by frequency.

1 *disappoint*	8.0	21 *having*	2.9	41 *talking*	1.9	61 *man*	1.1
2 *guts*	7.9	22 *anyway*	2.8	42 *coming*	1.9	62 *tell*	1.0
3 *hate*	6.6	23 *everyone*	2.8	43 *body*	1.8	63 *called*	1.0
4 *hated*	5.8	24 *fear*	2.7	44 *making*	1.8	64 *place*	1.0
5 *admit*	4.6	25 *doing*	2.7	45 *every*	1.7	65 *mother*	1.0
6 *myself*	4.6	26 *word*	2.5	46 *things*	1.7	66 *like*	1.0
7 *each other*	4.3	27 *playing*	2.5	47 *way*	1.7	67 *parents*	1.0
8 *shopping*	4.1	28 *husband*	2.5	48 *school*	1.7	68 *ever*	1.0
9 *herself*	3.8	29 *women*	2.4	49 *thought*	1.7	69 *all*	1.0
10 *lying*	3.7	30 *feeling*	2.4	50 *people*	1.6	70 *too*	1.0
11 *sight*	3.6	31 *sound*	2.4	51 *anything*	1.6	71 *here*	1.0
12 *lose*	3.5	32 *himself*	2.3	52 *job*	1.5	72 *even*	1.0
13 *anyone*	3.4	33 *cold*	2.3	53 *see*	1.5	73 *life*	1.0
14 *knowing*	3.3	34 *love*	2.3	54 *father*	1.5	74 *water*	1.0
15 *seeing*	3.3	35 *think*	2.2	55 *going*	1.5	75 *told*	1.0
16 *dress*	3.3	36 *music*	2.1	56 *name*	1.4	76 *big*	1.0
17 *stuff*	3.2	37 *hair*	2.1	57 *so*	1.3	77 *really*	0.4
18 *idea*	3.2	38 *someone*	2.0	58 *woman*	1.3	78 *war*	0.4
19 *sitting*	2.9	39 *men*	1.9	59 *say*	1.2	79 *fact*	0.4
20 *being*	2.9	40 *everything*	1.9	60 *enough*	1.2	80 *working*	0.3

Table 9. Collocates of *hate* in the BNC, (b) sorted by MI values.

2.7. Understand

Table 10 shows that the mental verb *understand* is associated, as might be expected, with words relating to language, cognition or knowledge. Language-related collocates in Table 10, as identified by frequency of occurrence or MI values, include *meaning, mean, means, meant, language, word(s), sentences, message, spoken, linguistic, say, said, saying, terms,* and *English.*

Understand occurs most frequently with abstract nominal notions marked by such words as *terms, processes, feelings, position, system, importance, role, everything, point, anything, reason(s) significance, life, business, nothing,* and *implications.* In terms of their MI values, the most strongly bonded collocates of *understand* similarly tend to be associated with abstract notions denoting cognitive concepts and processes. These include *workings, complexities, dynamics, rationale, feelings, motives, processes, mechanisms, nature, significance, implications, reasoning, logic, concepts, context, origins, phenomena, complexities, evolution, principles, motivation, importance, causes, universe, underlying, limitations, each other, one another, reasons, situation,* and *responsibilities.*

1	*people*	220	21	*things*	82	41	*use*	59	61	*clearly*	46
2	*said*	215	22	*other*	81	42	*want*	58	62	*anything*	45
3	*nature*	174	23	*meant*	77	43	*processes*	58	63	*know*	45
4	*better*	158	24	*saying*	72	44	*just*	58	64	*means*	45
5	*so*	148	25	*like*	72	45	*feelings*	57	65	*exactly*	44
6	*well*	145	26	*own*	71	46	*too*	53	66	*reason*	44
7	*only*	139	27	*needs*	70	47	*position*	53	67	*significance*	44
8	*way*	116	28	*social*	70	48	*even*	52	68	*happened*	44
9	*going*	113	29	*happening*	70	49	*involved*	51	69	*life*	44
10	*meaning*	111	30	*world*	68	50	*new*	51	70	*reasons*	43
11	*something*	108	31	*context*	67	51	*system*	51	71	*women*	43
12	*language*	106	32	*fully*	66	52	*time*	50	72	*nothing*	43
13	*each other*	105	33	*behaviour*	63	53	*importance*	50	73	*different*	43
14	*very*	104	34	*work*	63	54	*role*	49	74	*feel*	42
15	*mean*	103	35	*situation*	62	55	*everything*	47	75	*business*	42
16	*now*	100	36	*process*	60	56	*point*	47	76	*say*	41
17	*word*	100	37	*words*	60	57	*human*	47	77	*local*	41
18	*such*	99	38	*English*	60	58	*felt*	46	78	*implications*	41
19	*then*	94	39	*man*	60	59	*first*	46	79	*basic*	39
20	*problems*	86	40	*terms*	59	60	*government*	46	80	*part*	39

Table 10. Collocates of *understand* in the BNC, (a) sorted by frequency.

1	*workings*	4.6	21	*logic*	3.4	41	*language*	2.8	61	*depth*	2.4
2	*complexities*	4.6	22	*perfectly*	3.4	42	*word*	2.7	62	*exactly*	2.4
3	*dynamics*	4.6	23	*commands*	3.4	43	*sentences*	2.7	63	*accepted*	2.3
4	*happening*	4.3	24	*concepts*	3.3	44	*importance*	2.7	64	*roles*	2.3
5	*correctly*	4.2	25	*context*	3.3	45	*respond*	2.7	65	*saying*	2.3
6	*interpret*	4.1	26	*one another*	3.3	46	*behaviour*	2.6	66	*reasons*	2.3
7	*rationale*	4.1	27	*fully*	3.2	47	*referring*	2.6	67	*situation*	2.3
8	*meaning*	4.1	28	*import*	3.1	48	*relationships*	2.6	68	*stake*	2.2
9	*instinctively*	4.0	29	*origins*	3.1	49	*biological*	2.6	69	*instructions*	2.2
10	*reluctance*	4.0	30	*meant*	3.1	50	*causes*	2.5	70	*linguistic*	2.1
11	*feelings*	3.7	31	*phenomena*	3.1	51	*universe*	2.5	71	*historical*	2.1
12	*motives*	3.7	32	*complexity*	3.1	52	*message*	2.5	72	*psychological*	2.1
13	*processes*	3.7	33	*evolution*	3.1	53	*better*	2.5	73	*responsibilities*	2.1
14	*mechanisms*	3.7	34	*principles*	2.9	54	*spoken*	2.5	74	*basic*	2.1
15	*each other*	3.6	35	*psychology*	2.9	55	*underlying*	2.5	75	*politics*	2.1
16	*nature*	3.6	36	*concept*	2.9	56	*subtle*	2.4	76	*needs*	2.1
17	*appreciate*	3.6	37	*motivation*	2.9	57	*limitations*	2.4	77	*relate*	2.1
18	*significance*	3.5	38	*thoroughly*	2.8	58	*mechanism*	2.4	78	*origin*	2.1
19	*implications*	3.5	39	*risks*	2.8	59	*distinction*	2.4	79	*deeply*	2.0
20	*reasoning*	3.5	40	*broader*	2.8	60	*reference*	2.4	80	*happened*	2.0

Table 10. Collocates of *understand* in the BNC, (b) sorted by MI values.

2.8. *Follow*

Whereas *understand* tends to be associated especially with certain language-related concepts, and with a wide-ranging number of abstract notions associated with cognition, the mental verb sense of *follow* (meaning *understand*, as in *I couldn't follow what he was saying*) might be expected to have similar associations. However, Table 11 suggests that this is not the case. In addition to being associated with words relating to a physical route (e.g. *path, course, line, footsteps, road, route, track, trail, contours, suit, heels, wake*), or obedience to instructions or a model (e.g. *instructions, rules, advice, policy, guidelines, syllabus, recommendations, dictates, pattern, example, procedure, way, tradition*), the most striking semantic preference group associated with *follow* in the BNC, seems to be 'notable events as points of reference'. These include *death, war, election, defeat, accident, incident, collapse, resignation, debacle, assassination, coup, massacre, invasion, outbreak, collision, break up, riots, earthquake, break down, announcement, clashes, raids, demise, arrest, termination, abolition, seizure, overthrow, abandonment, dissolution*. About 40 percent of the MI collocates of *follow* in Table 11 have the sense of 'notable events as points of reference'. What may be surprising is that *follow* does not seem to be used very much in the sense of *understand* in the top 80 collocates, whether defined by frequency of occurrence or strength of bonding. Possibly, *follow* either is not often used in this sense, or it may be used in contexts not providing content words as collocates, as when checking comprehension (*You following this?*), or admitting incomprehension (*I'm not following*).

1 *suit*	310	21 *period*	149	41 *war*	99	61 *collapse*	79
2 *pattern*	292	22 *route*	147	42 *work*	99	62 *discussion*	78
3 *example*	291	23 *closely*	146	43 *so*	98	63 *lines*	77
4 *path*	281	24 *years*	143	44 *election*	96	64 *way*	75
5 *same*	268	25 *rules*	142	45 *publication*	95	65 *guidelines*	74
6 *death*	228	26 *success*	139	46 *defeat*	95	66 *home*	73
7 *instructions*	198	27 *advice*	138	47 *such*	93	67 *resignation*	71
8 *course*	195	28 *general*	133	48 *next*	92	68 *page*	69
9 *line*	194	29 *report*	125	49 *track*	91	69 *procedures*	69
10 *first*	189	30 *visit*	118	50 *practice*	85	70 *made*	68
11 *later*	187	31 *new*	118	51 *day*	83	71 *end*	68
12 *last*	179	32 *then*	117	52 *number*	82	72 *week*	68
13 *other*	176	33 *successful*	113	53 *immediately*	81	73 *different*	67
14 *decision*	166	34 *government*	111	54 *incident*	81	74 *case*	65
15 *meeting*	161	35 *series*	110	55 *accident*	81	75 *tradition*	65
16 *recent*	156	36 *set*	107	56 *months*	80	76 *introduction*	65
17 *footsteps*	156	37 *very*	104	57 *agreement*	80	77 *wake*	65
18 *similar*	154	38 *earlier*	101	58 *father*	80	78 *talks*	64
19 *road*	149	39 *announcement*	101	59 *procedure*	80	79 *major*	64
20 *year*	149	40 *long*	99	60 *policy*	79	80 *reports*	63

Table 11. Collocates of *follow* in the BNC, (a) sorted by frequency.

1 *footsteps*	6.8	21 *guidelines*	4.3	41 *outbreak*	3.8	61 *dissolution*	3.5
2 *step-by-step*	5.4	22 *collapse*	4.3	42 *seizure*	3.7	62 *recommendation*	3.5
3 *contours*	5.4	23 *instincts*	4.2	43 *departure*	3.7	63 *clashes*	3.5
4 *suit*	5.3	24 *consultations*	4.2	44 *overthrow*	3.7	64 *raids*	3.5
5 *debacle*	5.2	25 *paths*	4.2	45 *collision*	3.7	65 *recommendations*	3.5
6 *instructions*	5.1	26 *ratification*	4.2	46 *completion*	3.7	66 *demise*	3.4
7 *spate*	5.1	27 *coup*	4.0	47 *allegations*	3.7	67 *signing*	3.4
8 *obediently*	4.9	28 *closely*	4.0	48 *leisurely*	3.6	68 *arrest*	3.4
9 *path*	4.8	29 *faithfully*	4.0	49 *logically*	3.6	69 *discovery*	3.4
10 *dictates*	4.8	30 *defeat*	4.0	50 *fortunes*	3.6	70 *termination*	3.4
11 *announcement*	4.7	31 *pursuits*	4.0	51 *gaze*	3.6	71 *directions*	3.4
12 *trail*	4.7	32 *publication*	4.0	52 *break-up*	3.6	72 *disclosure*	3.4
13 *revelations*	4.7	33 *precedent*	4.0	53 *riots*	3.5	73 *abolition*	3.3
14 *disclosures*	4.6	34 *wake*	4.0	54 *withdrawal*	3.5	74 *succession*	3.3
15 *blindly*	4.5	35 *route*	3.9	55 *disagreements*	3.5	75 *protests*	3.3
16 *heels*	4.5	36 *massacre*	3.9	56 *earthquake*	3.5	76 *logic*	3.3
17 *stint*	4.4	37 *lobbying*	3.9	57 *breakdown*	3.5	77 *arrests*	3.2
18 *resignation*	4.3	38 *lengthy*	3.8	58 *syllabus*	3.5	78 *reasoning*	3.2
19 *pattern*	4.3	39 *invasion*	3.8	59 *procession*	3.5	79 *adventures*	3.2
20 *assassination*	4.3	40 *incident*	3.8	60 *abandonment*	3.5	80 *track*	3.2

Table 11. Collocates of *follow* in the BNC, (b) sorted by MI values.

2.9. Remember

The most frequent and strongly bonded collocates of *remember* tend to be characterised by childhood, domesticity, and unsurprisingly, events in the past. The domestic collocates in Table 12 include *mother, father, night, school, birthdays, childhood, dreams, excitement, kid, aunt, crying, daddy, visiting, dad, singing, riding, lessons, wedding, uncle, kiss.* Collocates associated with the past include *last, used to, once, then, back, ago, afterwards, past, still, went, happened*, and words with past tense endings. Some of the collocates of *remember* as identified by the MI values suggest that speakers of English place some value on accuracy of recall, e.g. *exactly, clearly, vividly, rightly, distinctly, correctly.*

One notable characteristic of the collocates of *remember* is that they are often lexical verb forms ending in *-ing*. In terms of frequency they include *saying, seeing, going, thinking, coming, telling, doing, feeling, reading, talking*, whereas in terms of MI value, the *-ing* endings include *seeing, waking, mentioning, telling, saying, thinking, hearing, feeling, reading, picking, wondering, walking, discussing, arriving, watching, coming, asking, crying, visiting, sitting, singing, riding, talking, buying.* It is worth noting also in Table 12 that *remember* tends to be associated with 'communication' words, including *said, saying, told, telling, hearing, discussing, asking, talking, mentioning, called, promise, words, conversations, names.*

1	*time*	348	21	*anything*	134	41	*telling*	80	61	*here*	61
2	*said*	346	22	*so*	130	42	*always*	80	62	*past*	61
3	*now*	242	23	*days*	115	43	*man*	80	63	*times*	59
4	*first*	230	24	*people*	114	44	*names*	76	64	*called*	59
5	*name*	223	25	*got*	105	45	*exactly*	74	65	*great*	58
6	*last*	223	26	*mother*	103	46	*nothing*	74	66	*thing*	58
7	*well*	208	27	*told*	99	47	*clearly*	74	67	*take*	57
8	*saying*	192	28	*little*	99	48	*happened*	73	68	*reading*	56
9	*seeing*	185	29	*years*	98	49	*doing*	73	69	*details*	55
10	*very*	183	30	*ever*	91	50	*also*	71	70	*know*	55
11	*too*	167	31	*just*	89	51	*everything*	71	71	*such*	54
12	*day*	162	32	*went*	89	52	*feeling*	68	72	*good*	51
13	*something*	159	33	*thinking*	87	53	*back*	67	73	*school*	50
14	*only*	150	34	*other*	87	54	*own*	67	74	*use*	49
15	*things*	149	35	*night*	86	55	*quite*	66	75	*even*	49
16	*used*	146	36	*coming*	85	56	*year*	66	76	*vividly*	48
17	*once*	143	37	*father*	85	57	*came*	65	77	*talking*	47
18	*words*	141	38	*way*	83	58	*ago*	63	78	*word*	46
19	*going*	140	39	*long*	83	59	*rightly*	62	79	*never*	46
20	*old*	138	40	*then*	80	60	*put*	62	80	*still*	46

Table 12. Collocates of *remember* in the BNC, (a) sorted by frequency.

1 *vividly*	6.8	21 *name*	3.2	41 *wondering*	2.4	61 *father*	2.0
2 *fondly*	6.0	22 *occasion*	3.1	42 *aunt*	2.4	62 *smell*	2.0
3 *birthdays*	5.7	23 *exactly*	3.0	43 *walking*	2.4	63 *singing*	2.0
4 *rightly*	5.5	24 *remark*	2.9	44 *details*	2.4	64 *facts*	2.0
5 *seeing*	4.9	25 *forever*	2.9	45 *afterwards*	2.4	65 *riding*	2.0
6 *waking*	4.9	26 *thinking*	2.9	46 *discussing*	2.3	66 *talking*	2.0
7 *affection*	4.6	27 *hearing*	2.8	47 *arriving*	2.3	67 *things*	2.0
8 *mentioning*	4.5	28 *dreams*	2.7	48 *watching*	2.2	68 *days*	2.0
9 *correctly*	4.2	29 *excitement*	2.7	49 *coming*	2.2	69 *buying*	1.9
10 *distinctly*	4.2	30 *birthday*	2.7	50 *asking*	2.2	70 *lessons*	1.9
11 *telling*	3.9	31 *words*	2.7	51 *crying*	2.2	71 *ever*	1.9
12 *childhood*	3.8	32 *happened*	2.6	52 *bits*	2.2	72 *detail*	1.9
13 *gratitude*	3.7	33 *feeling*	2.6	53 *daddy*	2.2	73 *wedding*	1.9
14 *exact*	3.7	34 *reading*	2.5	54 *mother*	2.2	74 *occasions*	1.9
15 *conversations*	3.6	35 *picking*	2.4	55 *visiting*	2.2	75 *promise*	1.9
16 *saying*	3.5	36 *clearly*	2.4	56 *everything*	2.1	76 *lady*	1.9
17 *names*	3.4	37 *anything*	2.4	57 *sitting*	2.1	77 *uncle*	1.8
18 *clarity*	3.4	38 *kid*	2.4	58 *dad*	2.1	78 *lock*	1.8
19 *prayers*	3.3	39 *conversation*	2.4	59 *once*	2.1	79 *ago*	1.8
20 *incident*	3.3	40 *encounter*	2.4	60 *dream*	2.0	80 *kiss*	1.8

Table 12. Collocates of *remember* in the BNC, (b) sorted by MI values.

2.10. Consider

Most of the collocates of *consider* in Table 13 are nouns or adjectives. In Table 13(b) alone about 40 percent of the collocates identified by MI values are adjectives. Analysis of the collocates in the table suggests that users of English tend to associate *consider* with parts, options, alternatives and possible outcomes, e.g. *example, question, chapter, implications, application, effect, problems, evidence, use, issues, aspects, options, proposals, merits, alternatives, feasibility, possibility, inclusion, verdict, proposition, consequences, impact.* The ways in which speakers of English *consider* phenomena include *carefully, (in) detail, separately, together, seriously* (rather than *frivolously*). They also *consider* matters as *appropriate, inappropriate, significant, prudent, undesirable, unsafe, suitable, unnecessary, unacceptable, feasible.*

1 *all*	269	21 *so*	134	41 *problem*	89	61 *example*	70
2 *any*	236	22 *best*	130	42 *time*	89	62 *various*	70
3 *following*	235	23 *many*	129	43 *just*	87	63 *separately*	70
4 *only*	222	24 *new*	125	44 *far*	86	64 *then*	70
5 *such*	207	25 *part*	124	45 *taking*	84	65 *options*	69
6 *important*	199	26 *question*	122	46 *evidence*	83	66 *changes*	69
7 *case*	192	27 *matter*	121	47 *use*	83	67 *problems*	68
8 *other*	181	28 *implications*	119	48 *issues*	81	68 *issue*	68
9 *first*	166	29 *here*	110	49 *number*	81	69 *section*	68
10 *possibility*	166	30 *good*	104	50 *aspects*	81	70 *general*	67
11 *necessary*	161	31 *application*	101	51 *alternative*	80	71 *again*	66
12 *appropriate*	160	32 *effect*	100	52 *future*	79	72 *whole*	66
13 *very*	158	33 *essential*	100	53 *way*	78	73 *using*	65
14 *chapter*	157	34 *both*	100	54 *context*	78	74 *proposals*	64
15 *too*	155	35 *himself*	98	55 *significant*	77	75 *report*	62
16 *detail*	155	36 *next*	97	56 *own*	77	76 *relevant*	62
17 *carefully*	149	37 *position*	97	57 *now*	76	77 *impact*	61
18 *further*	138	38 *ways*	96	58 *work*	74	78 *need*	61
19 *possible*	138	39 *different*	91	59 *needs*	71	79 *information*	61
20 *themselves*	136	40 *action*	90	60 *later*	71	80 *people*	61

Table 13. Collocates of *consider* in the BNC, (a) sorted by frequency.

1 *expedient*	5.7	21 *withdrawing*	4.4	41 *harmful*	3.6	61 *proposal*	3.2
2 *resigning*	5.7	22 *undesirable*	4.4	42 *briefly*	3.6	62 *merit*	3.2
3 *merits*	5.6	23 *prudent*	4.3	43 *individually*	3.5	63 *proposals*	3.2
4 *separately*	5.3	24 *unsafe*	4.3	44 *issuing*	3.5	64 *extending*	3.2
5 *unsuitable*	5.2	25 *inappropriate*	4.2	45 *essential*	3.5	65 *buying*	3.2
6 *delicacy*	4.9	26 *inferior*	4.2	46 *viable*	3.5	66 *alternative*	3.2
7 *appointing*	4.9	27 *options*	4.2	47 *trivial*	3.5	67 *superior*	3.2
8 *alternatives*	4.8	28 *bids*	4.2	48 *objections*	3.5	68 *context*	3.2
9 *desirable*	4.8	29 *submissions*	4.1	49 *aspects*	3.4	69 *consequences*	3.1
10 *feasibility*	4.8	30 *possibilities*	4.0	50 *proposition*	3.4	70 *necessary*	3.1
11 *implications*	4.7	31 *unreasonable*	3.9	51 *seriously*	3.4	71 *competent*	3.1
12 *unfit*	4.6	32 *marrying*	3.8	52 *chapter*	3.4	72 *explanations*	3.1
13 *detail*	4.6	33 *appropriate*	3.8	53 *applying*	3.4	73 *following*	3.0
14 *possibility*	4.5	34 *chapters*	3.7	54 *suitable*	3.3	74 *legitimate*	3.0
15 *worthy*	4.5	35 *abnormal*	3.7	55 *unnecessary*	3.3	75 *objection*	3.0
16 *installing*	4.5	36 *acceptable*	3.7	56 *application*	3.3	76 *submission*	3.0
17 *favourably*	4.5	37 *isolation*	3.7	57 *unacceptable*	3.3	77 *impact*	3.0
18 *inclusion*	4.4	38 *verdict*	3.6	58 *feasible*	3.2	78 *recommendations*	3.0
19 *unlucky*	4.4	39 *fortunate*	3.6	59 *worthwhile*	3.2	79 *adequate*	2.9
20 *carefully*	4.4	40 *adopting*	3.6	60 *sufficiently*	3.2	80 *sacred*	2.9

Table 13. Collocates of *consider* in the BNC, (b) sorted by MI values.

3. Conclusion

This paper set out to demonstrate how a corpus can be used to gain insights into the nature of collocations, and in particular, into systematic variation in the semantic characteristics of the predicates of lexical verbs. The value of a large corpus such as the BNC can be to provide a rich enough picture of language in use to demonstrate patterns of variation which in turn can reveal aspects of semantic preferences and semantic concerns within a speech community. All ten lexical verbs considered in this analysis are mental verbs. Some might seem, superficially at least, to be roughly synonymous with each other. Yet they display considerable variation in the semantic preferences which speakers of the language associate them with.

Corpus-based description can provide an enhanced empirical basis for exploring the nature of language, and in particular, the semantic aspect of phraseology which appears to lie at the heart of language. In addition to exploring the nature of language and contributing to linguistic theory, phraseological research seems to be well-placed to make a greater contribution to second language acquisition theory, curriculum design and teaching materials development, by demonstrating what it is that language learners have to acquire when they set out to learn a language.

References

Biber, Douglas / Johansson, Stig / Leech, Geoffrey / Conrad, Susan / Finegan, Edward 1999. *Longman grammar of spoken and written English*. Harlow: Longman.

Church, Kenneth / Hanks, Patrick 1990. Word association norms, mutual information, and lexicography. *Computational Linguistics* 16, 22-29.

Kennedy, Graeme 2003. Amplifier collocations in the British National Corpus: Implications for English language teaching. *TESOL Quarterly* 37, 467-487.

Lehrmann, Hans-Martin / Schneider, Peter / Hoffmann, Sebastian 2002. *BNCWeb*. Zurich: University of Zurich.

Sinclair, John / Jones, Susan / Daley, Robert 1970. *English Collocation Studies: The OSTI Report*. (Edited by Ramesh Krishnamurthy 2004) London: Continuum.

Stubbs, Michael 2001. *Words and Phrases*. Oxford: Blackwell.

TERUHIKO FUKAYA

Functional Variation in Use of *Though* and *When* Clauses

1. Introduction[1]

It is well-known (e.g. Carter/McCarthy 2006: 557-559) that there are two classes of conjunctions in English: coordinating conjunctions or coordinators (e.g. *and*, *but*, *or*) and subordinating conjunctions or subordinators (e.g. *because*, *if*, *though*). Coordinators conjoin units of equal status and function, while a subordinator connects a subordinate clause to its main clause. For instance, compare the following two examples:

(1) I had a word with her about it **but** she wasn't very sympathetic.

(2) **Although** I had a word with her about it she wasn't very sympathetic.

(Thompson 2004: 197)

Both sentences illustrate the logico-semantic relation of concession (i.e. the situation in which one clause is unexpected in view of the other clause) but they are distinct in the relative semantic prominence of the two clauses. In (1), the two constituent clauses (i.e. "I had a word with her about it" and "she wasn't very sympathetic") are of equal status. In (2), however, the subordinate clause "I had a word with her about it" is dependent upon the main clause "she wasn't very sympathetic."

Although the grammatical categories of coordinating and subordinating conjunctions are well-established in general use, some linguists have noted the existence of marginal cases, and have suggested that the boundary between the two functional labels may be more accurately regarded as gradient rather than strictly categorical. For in-

1 I would like to express my deep gratitude to Phillip R. Morrow and to the editors of this volume for stimulating comments and stylistic suggestions. Needless to say, all remaining inadequacies are my own responsibility.

stance, Quirk *et al.* (1985: 928) note that "linking words which are not coordinators nevertheless resemble coordinators," referring to the fact that *though* can replace *but* in a construction like "The weather will be warm **but** windy." Similarly, Thompson (2004: 202) mentions that "When certain dependent clauses are in final position in a complex, they can often feel more like paratactic clauses." He has in mind especially the following pair of sentences:

(3) a. You make many good points, **but** the line of argument is not always clear.

b. You make many good points, **although** the line of argument is not always clear.

Although is normally categorized as a subordinating conjunction, but in example (3b), the relationship between the two clauses before and after the conjunction seems coordinate rather than subordinate/superordinate.

The aim of the present study is to broaden our understanding of this overlap between coordinators and subordinators by contrasting lexically as well as syntactically the extent to which the two English subordinating conjunctions *when* and *though* play the role of coordinators in English corpora. Since an important distinguishing feature of coordinators is to link elements that are parts of clauses, rather than whole clauses, particular attention is given to constructions in which *when* and *though* are used in front of nouns, participles, adjectives, and adverbials, e.g. "The admiral walked clumsily, though with dignity" (Quirk *et al.* 1985: 929). The wider the range of conjoined items attested other than complete clauses, and the higher the proportions of such uses, the closer a word such as *when* or *though* comes to functioning like a prototypical coordinator.

The attested behaviour of *when* and *though* will subsequently be given a functional interpretation within the framework of Halliday's systemic functional grammar, in which subordinators are regarded as having an "enhancing" function, placing the circumstantial information introduced in a relation to the main clause, and coordinators as having an "extending" function, introducing a more independent piece of information. Possible explanations for observed functional differences between *though* and *when* will be suggested.

While the present analysis will concentrate on comparison of *when* and *though*, the slightly more explicit but functionally interchangeable form *although* will also be considered where necessary.

Though and *although* are interchangeable in many instances; however, *although* tends to be favoured in more formal contexts.

Before moving on to an analysis of *when* and *though* on the functional gradient between subordinators and coordinators, it remains to describe the corpora used in this research and the reason for using these. In the first stage the complements of these conjunctions will be syntactically and functionally compared using the British component of the International Corpus of English (ICE-GB). Since this representative corpus consists of one million words of contemporary British English, 60% spoken and 40% written, it will be linguistically feasible to gain an overall picture of conjunction use in English. By contrast, the subsequent more detailed analysis of complementation patterns requires considerably more data, and so is based on the 100-million-word British National Corpus (BNC). The two corpora are best suited to complementary functions: ICE-GB is appropriate for the study of English syntax whereas BNC is an excellent resource for the study of English lexis.

2. Existing Standard Descriptions

Current English dictionaries such as the *Oxford Advanced Learner's Dictionary* (OALD), the *Cambridge Advanced Learner's Dictionary* (CALD), and the *Longman Dictionary of Contemporary English* (LDOCE), all identify two separate meanings for the conjunctions *though/ although*: the first being roughly equivalent to "despite the fact that" (OALD, 2005: 1598); and the second "used to add a fact or an opinion that makes the previous statement less strong or less important" (*loc. cit.*). LDOCE and CALD both note that the second of these uses is "like 'but'" (LDOCE, 2005: 1727). The wording of the OALD entry ("previous statement") also suggests that in this usage the clause introduced by *though* follows the main clause, as would be expected for a coordinator like *but*. A similar point is also made by Carter/McCarthy (2006: 45).

The example sentences listed in English dictionaries indicate considerable differences in the range of possible complements that may be introduced by the conjunctions *when* and *though*. *When* may introduce finite clauses, or non-finite clauses involving *-ed* or *-ing* participles, as illustrated by the examples in (4) below:

(4) a. **When the family came here from Russia**, they were penniless. [finite clause]

b. **When mixed with water** the powder forms a smooth paste. [*-ed* clause] (LDOCE 2005: 1727)

c. **When eating a whole cooked fish**, you should never turn it over to get at the flesh on the other side … [*-ing* clause] (COBUILD 2006: 1657)

LDOCE (2005: 1879) describes the occurrences of non-finite complement clauses such as in (4b) and (4c) by being "used to mention a type of event or situation when talking about what happens on occasions of that type." This condition restricts the tense of (4b) and (4c) to the present tense. By contrast, both *though* and *although* allow a wider range of complement types, as illustrated in (5), including clauses, adjectives, adverbs, and prepositional phrases.

(5) a. **Though she's almost 40**, she still plans to compete. [finite clause]

b. The rooms, **though small**, were pleasant and airy. [adjective]

c. The offenders were dealt with firmly **though fairly**. [adverb]

d. **Although in poor health**, she continued to carry out her duties. [prepositional phrase]

(LDOCE 2005: 42, 1727)

It might be objected that the complement types of (5b) to (5d) are rather exceptional; but direct evidence from complementation frequencies in corpus data will be presented in the following section (especially Table 5 below) to confirm the representativeness of such complement types.

As a starting point for corpus analysis, it is useful to check the descriptions of possible types of non-finite complements of *when* and *though* provided by comprehensive descriptive English grammars. Quirk *et al.* (1985: 1004-1006), discussing the complement types possible for different subordinators, classify both *when* and *(al)though* as being subordinators that (i) may take finite clauses, (ii) may take *-ed* clauses and verbless clauses, as shown by examples (6a) and (6b), and (iii) may take *-ing* clauses, as shown by (6c) and (6d) below.

(6) a. **When taken according to the directions**, the drug has no side effects. [*-ed* clause]

b. **Although not yet six months old**, she was able to walk without support. [verbless clause]

c. **When returning merchandise**, be sure to bring your receipt. [*-ing* clause]

d. **Though understanding no Spanish**, she was able to communicate with the other students. [*-ing* clause]

(Quirk *et al.* 1985: 1005)

Therefore Quirk *et al.*'s description does not immediately distinguish the subordinators *when* and *though* in terms of their complement clause types.

However, Sinclair's *Collins COBUILD English Grammar* makes further observations concerning the clauses introduced by *when* and (*al*)*though*. These conjunctions have in common the property that they can be used in front of finite and non-finite clauses. However, they show rather different preferences of use in terms of the types of subordinate clause they tend to occur with. The subordinate conjunction *when* can occur with *-ing* and *-ed* clauses, as in (6a, c), and also a prepositional phrase and an adjective.

(7) a. Man acquires great technological mastery of the world but, **when under threat**, reverts with terrifying ease to his primitive past. [prepositional phrase]

b. She had previously spoken seldom and then only **when necessary**. [adjective] (Sinclair 2005: 348)

Sinclair (2005) points out one further syntactic difference, in that *(al)though*, unlike *when*, can be followed by a noun phrase, as in (8).

(8) It was an unequal marriage, **although a stable and long-lasting one**. [noun phrase] (Sinclair 2005: 360)

This construction is taken up also by Carter/McCarthy (2006) as part of the usage description of *although* and *though*.

In systemic functional grammar, Halliday/Matthiessen (2004) deal with subordinate conjunctions in the analysis of the clause complex. *When* and *though* are both analyzed as hypotactic (i.e. subordinate) markers for finite and non-finite clauses. Their function is that of enhancing the main clause by qualifying it in terms of time and concessive conditions, respectively.

Furthermore, they note that the conjunctions *when* and *though*, which are normally subordinate, "often occur in what seems closer to a paratactic function" (Halliday/Matthiessen 2004: 415) when their subordinate clause follows the main clause; for example,

(9) Did you read that column eight article the other day about the woman who was driving along somewhere on the this country road **when hail just suddenly started pouring down**. So she got really scared, and she stopped and she pulled over to the side of the road. (Halliday/Matthiessen 2004: 416)

In (9), the clause introduced by *when* adds an important development in the narrative, and does not function as a purely circumstantial qualification. Instead, it appears that the *when*-clause and the main clause (i.e. "who was driving […] this country road") are given equal status.

These descriptions of the usage of *when* and *though* suggest that these conjunctions can introduce syntactically similar sorts of finite and non-finite clausal complements, but with some differences in detail of distribution, in that examples provided for complements of *when* are most often *-ing* and *-ed* clauses. Examples cited for complements of *though* additionally include noun, adjective and prepositional phrases. However, such descriptions leave it unclear whether the differences are qualitative or quantitative; and the descriptions given in reference grammars and dictionaries do not provide any detailed description of possible lexical differences in the complements typically introduced. For such information, it is necessary to turn to corpus evidence. Accordingly, the following section will confirm the extent to which such differences in use are evident in a corpus, and that evidence will be used as the basis for determining the positions of these conjunctions on the functional continuum between prototypical coordinators and prototypical subordinators. Subsequently, a more detailed lexical description of the subordinate clauses introduced by *when* and *though* will be presented.

3. Corpus analysis

This section presents the results of an investigation of *when* and *though* in ICE-GB, focussing on (i) the position of the introduced clause relative to the main clause (Section 3.1); (ii) the types of syntactic elements introduced, with particular attention to the potential for non-finite and verbless clauses (Section 3.2); and (iii) the lexical characteristics of the elements introduced, based on data from the larger BNC corpus (Section 3.3).

3.1. Positions of when/though *clauses*

Clauses headed by subordinating conjunctions can be placed in two main positions with reference to the main clause: initial or final. They can also occur between the subject and the beginning of the verb phrase.

(10) a. **Subordinator** + Subordinate Clause, Main Clause [initial position]

b. Main Clause + **Subordinator** + Subordinate Clause [final position]

c. Subject + **Subordinator** + Subordinate Clause + Verb Phrase [medial position]

By contrast, when two clauses are linked by coordinating conjunctions, there is no choice regarding the relative positions of the clauses and the connector.

(11) Clause 1 + **Coordinator** + Clause 2

(11) is clearly more closely equivalent to (10b) than to (10a) or (10c). As such, it can be argued that a subordinator used in order (10b) is thereby closer in function to a coordinator than a subordinator used in order (10a) or (10c). As pointed out in Section 2, most commentators regard the order (10b) as closer semantically as well as structurally to coordinator use, typically paraphrasing *though* in (10b) in terms of the coordinator *but*.

The three conjunctions *when*, *though* and *although* are all capable of appearing both in initial and final positions, but the question is how frequently they take either position in a corpus. Table 1 presents data from ICE-GB for the choice between initial and final positions of clauses introduced by *when*, *though*, and *although*.

	Initial		Final	
when	688	(43%)	912	(57%)
though	49	(33%)	100	(67%)
although	190	(53%)	171	(47%)

Table 1. Positional distribution of clauses introduced by *when*, *though* and *although* in ICE-GB.

If the introduction of clauses in final position is to be equated to coordinator-like usage, then of the three forms, *though* has the highest proportion of use introducing clauses in final position (at 67%), and so can be regarded as the form closest in function to a coordinator. Conversely, *although* has the most consistent use introducing clauses in initial position (53%), and so seems to have considerably less functional overlap with coordinators than do the other two forms.

Two other linguistic factors can be noted as influencing the distribution of the three conjunctions in Table 1. The first is that the distribution of *though* and *although* is largely predictable from the difference in the forms' explicitness: the fuller form *although* tends to occur in more prominent positions, and so is favoured in initial position (e.g. Peters 1995, Berube 2005). However, this is by no means categorical. The second factor potentially affecting the use of these words is the degree of semantic overlap with common coordinators. *Though* is semantically close to the rather more frequent coordinating conjunction *but* (which occurs 2533 times in ICE-GB), which might be expected to form a basis for analogous use of *though* in coordinator-like ways. On the other hand, *when* signals a specific meaning (a time relationship) that is not entailed by any coordinator; thus for *when*, there is no coordinator in English as closely related in meaning, and so there is no clear basis for any analogous use in ways similar to a coordinator.

Nevertheless there is one highly relevant use of *when* worth mentioning, in which *when* connects two antithetic situations, and implies concession as well as indicating a time relationship (i.e. "... at a time when, otherwise, ..."), as in (12) below.

(12) His saves then enabled Liverpool to force a 1–1 draw **when** they might well have been beaten. <ICE-GB:W2C-004 #37:2>

In this sentence, the conjunction *when* expresses the concessive relationship of the two clauses: the situation in the main clause (i.e. the clause preceding *when*) is contrary to expectation in light of the situation in the subordinate clause (i.e. the clause following *when*). Although the prototypical use of *when* is to qualify a main clause in terms of time, (12) shows *when* functioning more like a coordinator. In this use, the *when* clause is in final position. As might be expected, this more coordinator-like use of *when* is overwhelmingly associated with clauses in final position. The written texts from ICE-GB contain 12 instances of clauses introduced by concessive *when*, of which 11 are placed clause-finally.

3.2. Non-finite when/though *clauses*

A second aspect of the use of such conjunctions as *when* and *though* that may create some functional overlap with coordinators is that, as shown in (13) below, they have some potential to connect constituents other than finite clauses.

(13) a. Our friendship in Paris was **a short one, though a good one**, I think. <ICE-GB:W1B-001 #113:3>

b. If Beckett makes few value judgements in his text, it is because his whole position is one of **assertive though ungrounded** evaluation. <ICE-GB: W2A-004 #30:1>

In (13a), the conjunction *though* seems to connect two noun phrases (*a short one* and *a good one*) that function as predicates in their respective clauses. In (13b), *though* is used to connect two adjectives. Thus in both cases the elements connected are clause constituents, rather than complete clauses. As such usage appears similar to the use of coordinators to connect clause constituents, it should be possible to use the extent to which a conjunction is observed to introduce constituents smaller than clauses as a measure of how closely it approaches the usage of a coordinator.

Two issues immediately arise for investigation. The first is the range and distribution of the elements other than finite clauses that can be introduced by these conjunctions. The second is the extent to which the occurrence of such elements correlates with the position of the conjunction in relation to the main clause. It might be expected that if the two features (of introduction of elements other than finite clauses, and final position) mutually define a more coordinator-like function for a conjunction, they should be more likely to co-occur.

The first concern is with the ratio between finite and non-finite clauses introduced by *when, though* and *although* in the corpus. Table 2 compares the three conjunctions in terms of frequency of complement type.

	Finite		Non-finite / verbless		Total	
when	1629	(93%)	118	(7%)	1747	(100%)
though	154	(75%)	52	(25%)	206	(100%)
although	362	(93%)	26	(7%)	388	(100%)

Table 2. Distribution of finite and nonfinite *when/though/although* clauses.

(Note that Table 2 includes the complements of *when, though* and *although* in medial position.) This table shows that the non-finite or verbless *though* clauses greatly outnumber those of *when* and *although*, implying that *though* is more coordinator-like than *when* and *although.*

The next question is whether nonfinite and verbless complements with *when, though,* and *although* are in initial position or in final position.

	Initial		Final	
when	36	(33%)	72	(67%)
though	6	(13%)	41	(87%)
although	7	(39%)	11	(61%)

Table 3. Positions of *when/though/although* in non-finite and verbless clauses in ICE-GB.

Final position is unmarked for non-finite and verbless clauses, as has been more generally observed by Biber *et al.* (1999: 831).

A further question arises from Table 3: What types of non-finite and verbless clauses occur, and with what frequencies? Table 4 provides a more detailed syntactic classification of elements other than finite clauses in ICE-GB.

	when		*though*		*although*	
+Noun or Noun phrase	0	(0%)	6	(12%)	4	(15%)
+Verb phrase (*-ing* / *-ed* clauses)	105	(89%)	5	(10%)	8	(31%)
+Adjective or Adjective phrase	8	(7%)	11	(21%)	8	(31%)
+Adverb or Adverb phrase	0	(0%)	7	(13%)	2	(8%)
+Prepositional phrase	5	(4%)	22	(42%)	4	(15%)
+*though* + *only* + *if* + clause	0	(0%)	1	(2%)	0	(0%)

Table 4. Classification of non-finite *when/though/although* clauses in ICE-GB.

Frequencies for many of these constructions are too low to allow definitive conclusions. However, it can still be noted that the predominant use of *when* (89% of these tokens) is to introduce nonfinite clauses with *-ing* and *-ed* participles. By contrast, *though* and *although* occur with a wider variety of non-finite and verbless complements.

To confirm these general statements, more extensive data for *when* and *though* from a larger corpus is needed. To this end, 3000 tokens of each were sampled at random from the 100-million-word BNC. The non-finite complements occurring in this sample were found to be distributed as shown in Table 5. The focus of corpus analysis is on the contrast in frequency between the non-finite *when* and *though* clauses.

	when		*though*	
+Noun phrase	0	(0%)	84	(12.9%)
+Verb phrase (*-ing* / *-ed* clauses)	293	(88.5%)	132	(20.3%)
+Adjective phrase	23	(7%)	230	(35.4%)
+Adverbial phrase	1	(0.3%)	46	(7.1%)
+ Prepositional phrase	14	(4.2%)	157	(24.2%)
+*though* + *only* + *if* + clause	0	(0%)	1	(0.1%)
Total	331	(100%)	650	(100%)

Table 5. Classification of non-finite *when/though* clauses in BNC.

Though there are differences in the quantitative detail, the qualitative differences observed for Table 4 also hold true of Table 5. Almost 90% of the non-finite complements introduced by *when* consist of verb phrases including *-ed* or *-ing* participles. By contrast, the non-finite complements introduced by *though* are more evenly distributed across all of the categories identified in Table 5. A functional interpretation of the observations made here will be given in the next section.

We have already seen above that (unlike *when*, but like coordinators) *though* readily allows linking of a wide range of phrase types other than finite clauses. It is therefore not too surprising that *though* also behaves like a coordinator in permitting word-level linking, in sequences of [adjective + *though* + (*not*) adjective] or [adverb + *though* + (*not*) adverb], as illustrated in (14).

(14) a. Even her brothers were **kind, though embarrassed** ... (EFP 38)

b. Public sector higher education (such as polytechnics) have a **similar, though not identical** hierarchy of posts ... (H8D 1359)

c. He clicked his heels and bowed to Lexandro **briefly, though ceremoniously**. (CJJ 1034)

Out of the adjective phrases in the BNC sample introduced by *though*, 73/230 examples follow variations on the pattern of (14). Similarly, 19 of the 46 adverbial clauses introduced by *though* occur in a sequence of two adverbs linked by *though*. Such examples clearly demonstrate that the conjunction *though* can link clause constituents.

3.3. Lexical patterns of when/though *clauses*

A further way of comparing conjunction usage is to consider the lexical range possible for the various types of complement clauses, as an indicator of how well established each grammatical construction is. The more generally acceptable (or, the less marked) a construction is, the wider should be the range of lexical items attested in that construction. Hence if a conjunction introduces non-finite clausal complements with a wider range of verb forms, this may be taken as evidence that such complements are more generally acceptable, and so, as evidence that the conjunction is more readily able to be used in such coordinator-like functions.

Lexical analysis of complement clauses introduced by *when* and *though* was performed as follows. For each of the three conjunctions *when*, *though*, and *but*, the 100 words in the BNC immediately following each conjunction, and most highly ranked (by *t*-scores) as collocates of that conjunction, were identified. Then, two pairwise comparisons of these lists were performed: (i) the list for *when* was compared with that for *though*; and (ii) the list for *though* was compared with that for *but*. Table 6 shows the top twenty right-hand first collocates of *when*, *though* and *but*.

Collocate rank by *t*-score	*when*	*though*	*but*
1	*you*	*it*	*it*
2	*he*	*he*	*I*
3	*I*	*not*	*he*
4	*they*	*they*	*they*
5	*we*	*I*	*there*
6	*it*	*she*	*also*
7	*she*	*the*	*she*
8	*the*	*there*	*not*
9	*there*	*this*	*we*
10	*asked*	*some*	*if*
11	*one*	*we*	*you*
12	*compared*	*his*	*this*
13	*his*	*still*	*the*
14	*considering*	*perhaps*	*then*
15	*my*	*these*	*when*
16	*her*	*of course*	*what*
17	*dealing*	*most*	*that*
18	*people*	*many*	*now*
19	*your*	*its*	*er*
20	*someone*	*only*	*only*

Table 6. The 20 strongest collocates of *when*, *though* and *but*.

Other than the pronouns and noun phrases that would be expected as clause subjects, collocates of *when* are almost entirely limited to *-ing* and *-ed* participles. There are only two exceptions, namely the adjectives *necessary* and *appropriate*. The phrases *when necessary* and *when appropriate* behave as fixed phrases, positioned either at the beginning or the end of clauses, as shown in (15).

(15) a. Where wives were active they often provided cover **when necessary**. (ALC 1023)

b. These schemata are stored away, and produced **when appropriate**. (EV4 575)

These phrases usually occur without any modifiers in the corpus, but their concordance lines indicate also that they allow collocational development such as coordination of the closely synonymous phrases (e.g. *as and when necessary/appropriate*, *if and when necessary*) and the adverbial modification of *when necessary/appropriate* (e.g. *only when necessary/appropriate*, *when absolutely necessary*).

The other outstanding set of collocates for *when* are *-ing* and *-ed* forms of verbs. The most frequent participial verb forms collocating with *when* are listed in (16), along with their frequencies in parentheses.

(16) a. *considering* (312), *using* (254), *dealing* (241), *making* (227), *working* (151), *choosing* (113), *buying* (110), *deciding* (96), *discussing* (98), *assessing* (93)

b. *asked* (525), *compared* (361), *used* (231), *faced* (181), *required* (148), *applied* (130), *confronted* (116), *viewed* (96), *pressed* (79), *combined* (78)

These verbs share a general meaning of "(physically or mentally) processing something". In context, such processing is often used to introduce a topic change (or, a change in focus within the same general topic) into the discourse. For example, in (17) below, the sequence *when considering* shifts the focus to the application of Oakeshott's concept of knowledge to science.

(17) **When considering** science, Oakeshott's aim is slightly different. The idea that science is a product of thought, a world of experience rather than pure fact, is not really controversial. The key issue which Oakeshott addresses in relation to science is the belief that science is experience; that is, the belief that the methods of science are fitted to a reality which exists outside scientific thought. (EAJ 60)

In this passage, the first sequence *when considering* brings up a new topic of *science*, which is gradually developed by the following sentences. A typical example of the *when* + passive participle clause construction is presented in (18).

(18) One night he went to her house, poured paraffin through the letter-box and on to the front door, and set it alight. One of the woman's children died in the ensuing fire. **When asked** why he did it, D replied: "Just to wake her up and frighten her." (ACJ 92)

In (18), the preceding text describes a sequence of events between a man [D] and a woman. The clause introduced by *When asked* then serves to introduce the stated intent of the man's actions, which is highly relevant information in the context of a criminal trial (e.g. in deciding whether to prosecute for murder or for manslaughter). Thus, both the *-ing* participle in (17) and the passive participle in (18) are tightly connected to *when*, forming a unit with similar topic-introducing functions in both cases.

By contrast, the complements of *though* are more similar in range to those of *but*, including adjectives (or adjective phrases) as in (19), prepositional phrases as in (20), adverbs as in (21), non-finite (participial) clauses as in (22), and finite clauses as in (23).

(19) a. Many utterances can be parsed in a number of ways which are phonemically similar **though** lexically different. <adjective phrase> (HX9 2034)

b. It was cruel **but** effective. <adjective> (AC3 144)

(20) a. In the first place, there are universal factors which contribute powerfully, in almost all cases, **though in** different measure (see Brubaker, 1992), to the formation of a sense of nationality … <prepositional phrase> (H9F 686)

b. "I Should Be So Lucky" shot to number one, not just in Britain and Australia **but in** 16 other countries besides. <prepositional phrase> (ADR 434)

(21) a. The presentation appearance of the horizontal moon, for instance, can properly, **though** falsely, be said to be larger than the presentation appearance of the meridian moon. <adverb> (CK1 207)

b. I have used my vote in the General Election once or twice, **but** not recently. <adverb> (G39 1658)

(22) a. […] words describing parts of the body, **though** having a particular anatomical reference, do not necessarily have that reference for lay people, even intelligent lay people. <non-finite clause> (B14 1565)

b. By not eating I was going back to the security of needing my family, not being relied upon **but** having someone to rely on instead. <non-finite clause> (CAP 1045)

(23) a. Its bottom octave is too weak for ordinary use, **though** it is attractive when extremely lightly accompanied. <full clause> (GVS 226)

b. Gossip may not be a female prerogative, **but** it certainly is so in the social stereotype of women. <full clause> (EBR 235)

Another trait shared by clauses introduced by *though* and *but* is that they favour negative collocates. The negator *not* has one of the highest *t*-scores (association strengths) among the most frequent collocates for each of these conjunctions: respectively, *though not* (1212 tokens in

BNC, *t*=31.67) has the 3rd highest *t*-score out of collocations involving *though*, and *but not* (8959 tokens, *t*=73.11) has the 8th highest *t*-score from collocations involving *but* (see Table 6). Other negative collocates of both conjunctions include *by no means*, *never*, *hardly*, and *far from*. Moreover, the phrases (*though not* and *but not*) also appear functionally similar in that both are frequently followed by non-finite and verbless clauses.

Nevertheless, there are still several notable differences in the collocation patterns of *though* and *but*. The 100 most frequent collocates of *but* include simple and complex conjunctions with very high *t*-scores, such as *if*, *when*, *because*, *after*, *once*, *while*, *even if*, *although*, *as soon as*, *now that*, and *before*, as in (24).

(24) a. You can use a side kick still, **but if** the attack is really effective the opponent will be on top of you before you can launch it. (A0M 594)

b. He saw them to the door **but when** they rode past a minute later, it was already shut. (A0N 1766)

By contrast, the collocate list for *though* includes only three conjunctions (*if*, *when* and *since*), and these occur with somewhat lower *t*-scores. A further difference between these collocation patterns is that, unlike *though*, the high-frequency collocates of *but* include *wh*-words, as in (25). Parallel clauses involving *though* seem to be impossible.

(25) a. You could add extra vitamins and minerals **but how** much should you give? (A17 972)

b. I have also heard it said that the lemon reduced the foam to manageable proportions, **but why** would anyone want to flatten a naturally sparkling drink? (A14 331)

The usage differences between *but* and *though* may be explained as follows. The basic function of *but* is to coordinate two clauses that are of equal status; for this reason, the two clauses conjoined by *but* are related but more independent from each other than those connected by *though*. Due to their common semantics, the syntactic behaviours of *though* and *but* are parallel, but their lexical collocates show differences consistent with the fact that the two clauses connected by *but* have an equal and independent status, rather than being in a subordinate/superordinate relationship. In (25), the second conjunct is not subordinate to the first conjunct, so it can be syntactically and lexically more independent. The two clauses of (25a) deal with "vitamins and minerals", but the second conjunct does not rest on the first, so a *wh*-question clause may be used.

4. Functional interpretation of *when/though*

A functional explanation of these findings is possible within the systemic functional framework of M.A.K. Halliday. Halliday/Matthiessen (2004: 373f), discussing how one clause may be used in a construction with another clause, introduce a notion of "expansion", which refers to the horizontal development of the text by linking the clauses that make up the clause complex. They further distinguish three types of expansion of a clause's content: namely, "elaboration", in which one clause elaborates on another by giving more information about it (e.g. *i.e., for example*); "extension", in which one clause extends beyond another by addition, contrast or replacement (i.e. *and*, *but*, *or*); and "enhancement", in which one clause embellishes around another by specifying the time, place, cause or condition (e.g. *when*, *because*, *if*). Under this classification, a clause followed by *but* is typically expanded through paratactic extension, while clauses introduced by *when* or *though* (whether finite or nonfinite) expand the main clause through hypotactic enhancement.

In the discussion of extension and enhancement, Halliday and other functionalists sometimes add a caveat: distinctions such as 'paratactic versus hypotactic' and 'extension versus enhancement' should be determined not by the words themselves but by which function they fulfill in discourse. For instance, Halliday/Matthiessen (2004: 406) note that "When the sense [of *and*] is 'and then', and 'and so' and the hypotactic version is an enhancing dependent clause, we can interpret the paratactic nexus as one of enhancement instead of one of extension." They reiterate the point by saying that "Certain conjunctions that are normally hypotactic [...] often occur in what seems closer to a paratactic function when the enhancing clause follows the primary one." (2004: 415).

Returning to the conjunction *though* and its concessive clauses, it is time now to reconsider what functional relation the main and subordinate clauses create in connection with the semantics of *though*. The first issue is where the *though* clause occurs in a sentence: initial position (I) or medial position (M) or end position (E).

(26) (I), main clause Subject, (M), main clause Predicator, main clause Complements, (E)

When the *though* clause occupies the initial or medial positions, it is usually interpreted as a circumstantial element, meaning something like 'in spite of the fact …'. There are two reasons why it is a circumstantial adjunct. One is that the *though* clause in the initial and medial positions and the main clause do not bear a relation of two like elements of equal status but a relation between a subordinate and a superordinate. The other is that the conjunction *though* is used to qualify the main clause with a circumstantial feature of concession instead of further specifying (viz. elaborating) or adding something to (viz. extending) it. Therefore, the function of the *though* clause in initial and medial positions should be hypotactic enhancement.

The third possible location of a clause introduced by *though* is in end-position. Such use may be represented schematically as in (27a), which seems closely parallel to use of *but* as in (27b).

(27) a. Clause 1 (main clause) + *though* + Clause 2 (subordinate clause).
b. Clause 1 + *but* + Clause 2.

Because of obvious strong correspondences between (27a) and (27b), systemic functional grammarians feel (27a) to be more like a paratactic clause than a hypotactic one. So this *though* signals a paratactic enhancing relation, whose function is reflected in the meaning of *though* in (27a): 'but it is also true that …'. In other words, (27a) is a case of coordination with a circumstantial aspect. This functional reading can be applied equally to non-finite *-ing* clauses and *-ed* clauses introduced by *though*, as shown by the fact that (28a) can be paraphrased as (28b).

(28) a. Thirteen persons (21 percent) showed some signs of ethical and moral sense, **though** accepting much of the Nazi claim that the Jews had caused Germany harm. (ADD 1022)

b. Thirteen persons (21 percent) showed some signs of ethical and moral sense, **though** they accepted much of the Nazi claim that the Jews had caused Germany harm.

We can regard (28a) as a case of paratactic enhancement, because of the apparent similarity between (28a) and (28b).

Here it is important to keep in mind the big picture of functional relationship between the *when/though* clause and the main clause. As shown in Table 7, the systems of paratactic/hypotactic and elaboration/extension/enhancement intersect to define the basic types of clause complex. Furthermore, the table shows that the *when/though* clause and the main clause can function as paratactic enhancement as well as hypotactic enhancement. Examples are given for the types relevant for the present discussion.

		(i) **paratactic**	(ii) **hypotactic**
expansion	(a) elaboration		
	(b) extension	*It's an old car,* ***but*** *it's very reliable.* *The offenders were dealt with firmly* ***though*** *fairly.*	
	(c) enhancement	*Leonard was nine* ***when*** *his father died.* *I enjoyed the movie,* ***though*** *I thought it was too long.*	***When*** *he was in the air force he flew Tornado jets.* ***Though*** *she is retired, she's still very active.*

Table 7. Basic types of clause complex (excluding projection), adapted from Halliday/Matthiessen (2004: 380), with examples from LDOCE.

Significantly, *though* can also perform a function of paratactic extension parallel to *but* when connecting adjectives or adverbs, as already seen in example (14), repeated below as (29).

(29) a. Even her brothers were **kind, though embarrassed** … (EFP 38)

b. Public sector higher education (such as polytechnics) have a **similar, though not identical** hierarchy of posts … (H8D 1359)

c. He clicked his heels and bowed to Lexandro **briefly, though ceremoniously**. (CJJ 1034)

The meaning that *though* carries in (29) is not 'in spite of the fact that …', but rather "used like *but* to add a fact or opinion that makes what you have just said seem less definite, less important" (LDOCE 2005: 1727). Functionally speaking, it is not appropriate to say that the verbless clauses in (29) qualify the preceding clauses in terms of concession. They just add another adjective or adverb in a contrastive manner. Therefore (29) establishes the relation of extension rather than enhancement. Moreover, because the adjective or adverb phrases in (29) can be said to form the contrastive linking of adjectives or adverbs of equal status, the relationship is paratactic, but not hypotactic.

5. Conclusion

This paper has investigated the observed use of the subordinators *when* and *though* in terms of a functional gradient between features more characteristic of subordinators, and features more characteristic of coordinators. Two main features have been proposed to define this scale. The first is the potential for variation in position of the element introduced: most subordinators allow variation between clause-final and clause-initial position, whereas elements introduced by coordinators must be placed in final position. The second is the possible range of types of element introduced: for many subordinators this is limited to (finite) clauses, whereas coordinators can be used more generally to connect any two phrases of the same type. Based on the corpus evidence analysed here from ICE-GB and the BNC, *though* tends to favour final position more than does *when*; and *though* is attested to introduce a range of non-clausal elements that are either impossible or much less likely with *when*. Hence, on both criteria, *though* is found to be used in ways further from the core subordinator behaviours, and closer to coordinator behaviours, than is *when*. A more detailed functional analysis of *when* and *though* based on their strongest and most frequent collocates is consistent with *when* having (in Hallidayan terms) functions of hypotactic and paratactic enhancement, whereas *though* has functions ranging from hypotactic enhancement, through paratactic enhancement, to paratactic extension.

The different syntactic and functional behavior of the two subordinators may be explained by the fact that, for the subordinator *though*, there is a very common coordinator parallel in meaning (*but*), which may serve as a model for functional expansion of *though*. By comparison, there is no analogous temporal coordinator available for *when*.

References

Berube, M.S. 2005. *The American Heritage Guide to Contemporary Usage and Style*. Boston: Houghton Mifflin.

Biber, Douglas / Johansson, Stig / Leech, Geoffrey / Conrad, Susan / Finegan, Edward 1999. *Longman Grammar of Spoken and Written English*. Harlow: Longman.

Carter, R. / McCarthy, M. 2006. *Cambridge Grammar of English*. Cambridge: Cambridge University Press.

Halliday, M.A.K. / Matthiessen, M.I.M. 2004. *An Introduction to Functional Grammar*. 3rd edition. London: Arnold.

Peters, Pam 1995. *The Cambridge Australian English Style Guide*. Cambridge: Cambridge University Press.

Quirk, Randolph / Greenbaum, Sidney / Leech, Geoffrey / Svartvik, Jan 1985. *A Comprehensive Grammar of the English Language*. Harlow : Longman.

Sinclair, John 2005. *Collins COBUILD English Grammar*. 2nd edition. Glasgow: HarperCollins.

Thompson, G. 2004. *Introducing Functional Grammar*. 2nd edition. London: Arnold.

Dictionaries

Sinclair, John 2006. *Collins COBUILD Advanced Learner's English Dictionary*. 5th edition. Glasgow: HarperCollins. [COBUILD]

Summers, D. 2005. *Longman Dictionary of Contemporary English*. 4th edition. Harlow: Pearson Education. [LDOCE]
Walter, E. 2005. *Cambridge Advanced Learner's Dictionary*. 2nd edition. Cambridge: Cambridge University Press. [CALD]
Wehmeier, S. 2005. *Oxford Advanced Learner's Dictionary*. 7th edition. Oxford: Oxford University Press. [OALD]

SHUNJI YAMAZAKI

Comparing Adjective Comparison across Genre and Time in Standard Varieties of Modern English

1. Introduction[1]

The comparison of adjectives has attracted the attention of both grammarians and historians of the English language. Numerous studies in this area have attempted to determine rules or tendencies in the choice of inflectional or periphrastic comparison, and also to identify the factors that may affect the choice of either comparison. However, many of these studies have lacked precise numerical information and descriptive adequacy.

Only recently have corpus-based studies begun to improve this situation, and a number of hypotheses have been put forward concerning what factors determine the choice of inflectional *-er* comparison versus periphrastic *more* + Adj. comparison. A quantitative analysis of adjective comparison in English language from a historical perspective suggests that periphrastic comparison marked the comparative and superlative forms of adjectives in Old English, and after the periphrastic forms first appeared in the 13th century, by the start of the 16th century they had become as frequent as they are now (Kytö 1996, Kytö/Romaine 2000). Previous findings suggest that disyllabic adjectives in the 18th century were not as clear-cut as monosyllable or multi-syllable adjectives, though disyllabic adjectives preferred periphrastic comparison (Kytö/ Romaine 2000, Suematsu 2004). Bauer's (1994) corpus-based survey of differences between current American and British English provided one starting point; quantitative analyses were subsequently performed to

1 I would like to express my gratitude for audience feedback, and especially for detailed comments from Geoffrey Leech, at the initial presentation of this research at ICAME 26 in Ann Arbor. The present version has additionally benefited from comments and suggestions by Robert Sigley, who also assisted with the statistical tests.

determine the factors that decide the choice of comparison in Modern British English using the core written BNC and the LOB.

Previous studies (Sweet 1891, Jespersen 1909-49, and Quirk/Greenbaum/Leech/Svartvik 1985) have explicitly demonstrated that the main factors to determine the comparative forms of adjectives are: (i) the number of syllables in the adjective, (ii) whether the final syllable is stressed, and (iii) the kind of suffix the adjective has. Leech/Culpeper (1997) confirm that the number of syllables and the kind of suffix are the major factors (with predominant use of inflectional comparison on bases of one syllable, and periphrastic comparison on bases of three or more syllables), and also conclude more tentatively that a number of disyllabic adjectives show some degree of shift towards periphrastic comparison, and that inflectional comparatives are more likely to have an attributive function, and periphrastic comparatives a predicative function. However, they also note (1997: 371) that the influence of text type or text genre has yet to be investigated:

> Quantitative evidence is still lacking for the definitive investigation of diachronic trends in the use of the two forms of comparison. Existing corpora need to be investigated further both regarding the choice of comparison with individual words and word types, and the extent to which medium and text type influence the choice (an important area of investigation we have omitted).

It is therefore important to re-examine previous findings using similarly constructed one-million-word corpora and regional varieties of corpora (American vs. British) to answer the following research questions:

(i) Does the number of syllables in the adjective, specifically disyllabic adjectives, differentiate inflectional comparison from periphrastic comparison?
(ii) Is there any additional effect from stylistic preferences?
(iii) Does the suffix of the adjective decide the choice of inflectional or periphrastic comparison?
(iv) Are there any similar effects observed for superlative forms?

Although corpora of considerable size are necessary to establish conclusive results, the current paper uses four one-million-word corpora (the Brown, LOB, Frown, and FLOB corpora) mainly because they are similarly constructed one-million-word corpora allowing parallel comparisons across both time (1960s vs. 1990s) and regional variety (American vs. British), and also because they are of a manageable size for a comparative study. Each corpus consists of 15 different text categories, which for the purpose of the current paper have been grouped into four sets: (i) Press (text categories from A to C, 17.6%); (ii) General nonfiction (text categories from D to H, 41.2%); (iii) Academic writing (text category J, 16.0%); (iv) Fiction (text categories from K to R, 25.2%).

In order to allow a more precisely controlled comparison, the following forms of adjectives in this paper are excluded because there are irregular forms or no directly corresponding inflectional forms: (i) comparison of defective adjectives (e.g. *better, best, worse, worst*), (ii) negative adjective comparison (e.g. *less, least*), (iii) umlaut comparison (e.g. *elder, eldest*).

Not only comparative forms but superlative forms are included in this paper, in order to investigate whether similar effects can be seen in superlative forms.

2. Formal features of comparison

2.1. Comparative and superlative forms

Table 1 below displays the overall frequencies of inflectional and periphrastic comparison in the four corpora. Nearly two thirds of comparative forms are inflectional (65.5%); by contrast, superlatives favour inflectional forms less strongly, with 45.4% being periphrastic forms as against 34.5% in comparative forms.

	comparatives		superlatives	
	inflectional	periphrastic	inflectional	periphrastic
Overall	6,291 *65.5%*	3,317 *34.5%*	2,763 *54.6%*	2,302 *45.4%*

Table 1. Overall frequencies of inflectional and periphrastic comparison (across all four parallel corpora).

A breakdown of inflectional and periphrastic comparison figures by corpus (Table 2) shows similar frequencies of both adjective forms within each corpus; i.e. in each of the four corpora examined, there is a stronger tendency for comparatives to occur as inflectional forms (approximately 65% of cases overall) and a weaker tendency for superlatives to be inflectional forms (approximately 55%). However, the table below also illustrates a slight increase of periphrastic comparative forms in both American English (comparing the Brown and Frown corpora, 1961 vs. 1991) and British English (comparing the LOB and FLOB corpora, 1961 vs. 1991): 34.4% to 35.6%, and 32.9% to 35.2% respectively, and an increase of inflectional superlative forms in both American and British English: 53.3% to 54.4%, and 54.0% to 56.4% respectively. Comparisons of the overall figures for each corpus suggest a slight leveling of this difference over time: i.e. the two 1991 corpora show slightly lower proportions of inflectional forms for comparatives (64.4%, 64.8% respectively), but slightly higher proportions for superlatives (54.4%, 56.4% respectively) than the 1961 data.

		comparatives		superlatives	
		inflectional	periphrastic	inflectional	periphrastic
American English	Brown (1961)	1,593 *65.6%*	834 *34.4%*	665 *53.3%*	583 *46.7%*
	Frown (1991)	1,487 *64.4%*	822 *35.6%*	703 *54.4%*	590 *45.6%*
British English	LOB (1961)	1,581 *67.1%*	776 *32.9%*	650 *54.0%*	554 *46.0%*
	FLOB (1991)	1,630 *64.8%*	885 *35.2%*	745 *56.4%*	575 *43.6%*

Table 2. Frequencies of inflectional and periphrastic comparison in each of the four LOB/Brown parallel corpora.

2.2. Number of syllables and comparison

As many previous research papers (Sweet 1891, Jespersen 1909-49, and Quirk *et al.* 1985) have suggested, the number of syllables in the adjective is one of the most important factors determining the choice of comparison. Table 3 below is a table of overall frequencies of comparative forms according to the length of adjective base for comparative affixation. As Table 3 shows, there is almost categorical inflectional comparison in one-syllable adjectives and categorical periphrastic comparison on adjectives of three or more syllables (97.9% and 100% respectively), whereas disyllabic adjectives show an apparently evenly divided variation between inflectional and periphrastic comparatives (42.8% against 57.2%)[2] : e.g. disyllabic inflectional and periphrastic comparatives – *earlier* 308, *easier* 188, *simpler* 51 and *more likely* 97, *more complex* 42, *more recent* 30.

One syllable		Two syllables		Three or more syllables	
inflectional	periphrastic	inflectional	periphrastic	inflectional	periphrastic
5,435 *97.9%*	118 *2.1%*	856 *42.8%*	1,145 *57.2%*	0 *0.0%*	2,054 *100.0%*

Table 3. Overall distribution of comparative forms by adjective (base) length.

Though the tendencies in bases of one syllable and of three or more syllables are similar in superlatives (97.6% inflectional comparison with one-syllable bases and 99.6% periphrastic comparison in bases of three or more syllables) as Table 4 (overall frequencies of superlative forms by the length of adjective base) displays, there are predominantly more periphrastic superlatives in two syllables (62.0%). Disyllabic superlatives have a higher tendency to take periphrastic comparison than disyllabic comparatives (62.0% against 57.2%): e.g. periphrastic superlatives – *most likely* 43, *most famous* 37, *most common* 32.

One syllable		Two syllables		Three or more syllables	
inflectional	periphrastic	inflectional	periphrastic	inflectional	periphrastic
2,361 *97.6%*	59 *2.4%*	396 *38.0%*	646 *62.0%*	6 *0.4%*	1,597 *99.6%*

Table 4. Overall distribution of superlative forms by adjective (base) length.

The overall categorical preferences for inflected forms with monosyllabic adjectives, and periphrastic forms with adjectives of three or more syllables, are also evident in each of the four corpora (Tables 5 and 6). However, the corpora show noticeable differences in disyllabic adjectives – as expected, because this is the environment of greatest po-

2 Figures for disyllabic periphrastic comparatives in the LOB corpus given by Leech and Culpeper (1997) differ from those in the present paper, mainly because the present study excludes some comparative forms such as defective adjectives, negative adjectives and umlaut adjectives.

tential variation. Periphrastic comparison seems to have increased both for comparatives and superlatives, and in both American and British English; periphrastic comparatives increase from 53.2% to 61.8% in American English, and from 50.7% to 62.8% in British English, whereas periphrastic superlatives increase from 63.9% to 67.7% in American English, and from 55.7% to 60.4% in British English. The observed tendency of a shift to periphrastic comparison in disyllabic adjective comparison in British English corroborates previous findings by Leech/Culpeper (1997) using the core written BNC and the LOB; however, the current paper shows that the same shift to periphrastic comparison in disyllabic comparative and superlative forms is also observed in American English.

	One syllable		Two syllables		Three or more syllables	
Corpus	inflectional	periphrastic	inflectional	periphrastic	inflectional	periphrastic
Brown	1,358 *97.5%*	35 *2.5%*	235 *46.8%*	267 *53.2%*	0 *0.0%*	532 *100.0%*
Frown	1,300 *98.0%*	26 *2.0%*	187 *38.2%*	302 *61.8%*	0 *0.0%*	494 *100.0%*
LOB	1,343 *98.0%*	28 *2.0%*	238 *49.3%*	245 *50.7%*	0 *0.0%*	503 *100.0%*
FLOB	1,434 *98.0%*	29 *2.0%*	196 *37.2%*	331 *62.8%*	0 *0.0%*	525 *100.0%*

Table 5. Distribution of comparative forms, by adjective (base) length and corpus.

	One syllable		Two syllables		Three or more syllables	
	inflectional	periphrastic	inflectional	periphrastic	inflectional	periphrastic
Brown	569 *97.4%*	15 *2.6%*	95 *36.1%*	168 *63.9%*	1 *0.2%*	400 *99.8%*
Frown	619 *97.8%*	14 *2.2%*	83 *32.3%*	174 *67.7%*	1 *0.2%*	402 *99.8%*
LOB	541 *97.5%*	14 *2.5%*	108 *44.3%*	136 *55.7%*	1 *0.2%*	404 *99.8%*
FLOB	632 *97.5%*	16 *2.5%*	110 *39.6%*	168 *60.4%*	3 *0.8%*	391 *99.2%*

Table 6. Distribution of superlative forms, by adjective (base) length and corpus.

Because variation is largely limited to cases involving disyllabic adjectives, the remaining discussion will be limited to just those cases.

2.3. Text genres and comparison

In order to investigate some intrinsic differences in markedness between inflectional and periphrastic markers that might be expected to correlate with more general stylistic choices, the 15 text genres are collected into four groups: Press (Text categories A to C), General (Text categories D to H), Academic (Text category J), and Fiction (Text categories K to R). The groups of 'Press', 'Academic', and 'Fiction' texts represent particularly interesting extremes of formality level and degree of institutional control of language forms; the 'General' group comprising the remainder of the corpus is strictly uninterpretable as it contains texts representing a wide range of formality levels, from the least formal nonfiction writings of Biography, to parts of Sections H and G (Official documents and Belles Lettres) that are stylistically similar to Academic writings (Section J).[3] The following table shows the percentage of texts making up each group in each of these corpora. These percentage figures need to be kept in mind when considering the actual frequencies of comparison below.

Major text category	Press	General	Academic	Fiction
Percentage	17.6%	41.2%	16.0%	25.2%

Table 7. Genre composition (as % of texts) in each million-word corpus.

As Table 8 shows, all four genre groups show similar proportions of inflectional comparatives, ranging from 63.5% to 69.7%. However, the frequency of comparison varies significantly by text formality; comparative forms occur proportionally more in the General and Academic material (50.6% vs. 41.2%, and 22.8% vs. 16.0%) and proportionally less in Fiction (11.4% vs. 25.2%).

3 The Essay/Literary criticism subcategories of text category G, and certain of the government/official reports within category H, are similar to the Academic texts of text category J, both institutionally and stylistically (see Sigley, this volume).

Category:	Press		General		Academic		Fiction	
Form:	inflect-ional	peri-phrastic	inflect-ional	peri-phrastic	inflect-ional	peri-phrastic	inflect-ional	peri-phrastic
Tokens	933 *63.5%*	537 *36.5%*	3,148 *64.8%*	1,712 *35.2%*	1,451 *66.3%*	738 *33.7%*	759 *69.7%*	330 *30.3%*
Total	1,470 (15.2%)		4,860 (50.6%)		2,189 (22.8%)		1,089 (11.4%)	

Table 8. Overall distribution of comparative forms by major text category (across all four corpora).

By contrast, there is more variation in choice of form by genre for superlatives (Table 9). Academic writing is the only genre group which includes more periphrastic superlative forms than inflectional (53.2% vs. 46.8%) (Biber 1988). Academic texts appear to relatively favour comparatives and disfavour use of superlative functions (as might be expected in a genre characterised by more cautious, or more hedged statements). Superlatives occur in General texts and Fiction in about the same relative proportions as comparatives (thus, 51.9% and 10.2% of superlatives respectively). By contrast, there is higher than expected use of superlative forms in Press. This is implied by Bell's (1991) listing of 'superlativeness' as an important news value: it is to be expected that journalists will use superlative forms wherever possible to maximize the apparent news value of the events covered; e.g. *greatest* news, *saddest* moment, *most difficult* target.

Category:	Press		General		Academic		Fiction	
Form:	inflect-ional	peri-phrastic	inflect-ional	peri-phrastic	inflect-ional	peri-phrastic	inflect-ional	peri-phrastic
Tokens	688 *58.9%*	480 *41.1%*	1,370 *52.1%*	1,259 *47.9%*	352 *46.8%*	400 *53.2%*	353 *68.4%*	163 *31.6%*
Total	1,168 (23.1%)		2,629 (51.9%)		752 (14.8%)		516 (10.2%)	

Table 9. Overall distribution of superlative forms by major text category (across all four corpora).

The overall figures for comparative and superlative forms by genre will now be divided by corpus to check for systematic regional differences and for diachronic shifts in usage.

Category:	Press		General		Academic		Fiction	
Corpus:	inflect-ional	peri-phrastic	inflect-ional	peri-phrastic	inflect-ional	peri-phrastic	inflect-ional	peri-phrastic
Brown	247 *63.3%*	143 *36.7%*	747 *64.1%*	418 *35.9%*	388 *67.6%*	186 *32.4%*	211 *70.8%*	87 *29.2%*
Frown	250 *63.8%*	142 *36.2%*	692 *63.2%*	403 *36.8%*	337 *61.7%*	209 *38.3%*	208 *75.4%*	68 *24.6%*
LOB	254 *64.8%*	138 *35.2%*	834 *66.7%*	416 *33.3%*	338 *70.6%*	141 *29.4%*	155 *65.7%*	81 *34.3%*
FLOB	182 *61.5%*	114 *38.5%*	875 *64.8%*	475 *35.2%*	388 *65.8%*	202 *34.2%*	185 *66.3%*	94 *33.7%*

Table 10. Distribution of comparative forms, by corpus and major text category.

Table 10 indicates a slight tendency towards an increased preference for periphrastic comparative forms in General and Academic writings in both American and British English; however, the reverse is true of Fiction, and there is no consistent trend apparent for Press material. Overall, there is no significant change in preference for inflectional vs. periphrastic forms evident either for American English ($X^2(1df)=0.796$, $p=0.373$) or for British English ($X^2(1df)=2.78$, $p=0.096$).

The only comparison reaching the conventional 5% level of significance is for American Academic writing (X^2(1*df*, with Yates' correction)=3.976, $p=0.046$); but given the number of tests performed, this result cannot be regarded as conclusive.

Further confirmation that we should be cautious of interpreting even the apparently consistent differences as evidence of systematic change comes from examining the same choice in superlative forms, for which the opposite overall trend is seen: i.e. a slight increase in preference for inflection.

Category:	Press		General		Academic		Fiction	
Corpus:	inflect-ional	peri-phrastic	inflect-ional	peri-phrastic	inflect-ional	peri-phrastic	inflect-ional	peri-phrastic
Brown	153 *59.3%*	105 *40.7%*	341 *51.0%*	328 *49.0%*	85 *44.0%*	108 *56.0%*	86 *67.2%*	42 *32.8%*
Frown	188 *61.6%*	117 *38.4%*	350 *51.7%*	327 *48.3%*	78 *41.5%*	110 *58.5%*	87 *70.7%*	36 *29.3%*
LOB	155 *55.2%*	126 *44.8%*	331 *51.6%*	310 *48.4%*	77 *48.1%*	83 *51.9%*	87 *71.3%*	35 *28.7%*
FLOB	192 *59.3%*	132 *40.7%*	348 *54.2%*	294 *45.8%*	112 *53.1%*	99 *46.9%*	93 *65.0%*	50 *35.0%*

Table 11. Distribution of superlative forms, by corpus and major text category.

Differences between the corpora in choice of superlative form fail to reach statistical significance, either for the corpora as a whole (for Brown vs. Frown, $X^2(1df)=0.30$, $p=0.584$, and for LOB vs FLOB, $X^2(1df)=1.532$, $p=0.216$) or for any single major text category ($p>0.50$ in all cases). However, there are some indications of an apparent increase in overall frequency of use of superlatives in British English ($X^2(3df)=11.732$, $p=0.008$), and a slight tendency for an increase in overall use of superlatives in Press material from both varieties ($p<0.10$ after Yates' correction in both cases).

2.4. Number of syllables and text genres

This section conducts a more detailed comparison of text categories and genres controlling for the known categorical effects of adjective length, because there is essentially no variation in frequency by genre of corpus except for disyllabic bases. Therefore, from this point on, this study will focus only on disyllabic adjectives. Disyllabic comparatives in all four genres favour periphrastic comparatives. The frequency of periphrastic comparison appears correlated to text formality, ranging from 51.8% in the least formal category (Fiction) through 53.7% in Press and 57.0% in General writings, to 63.3% in the most formal major category (Academic writings).

The overall frequency of disyllabic comparison is similarly correlated to formality, and disyllabic comparatives are relatively more common in Academic and General texts, and underrepresented in Press and Fiction.

Category:	Press		General		Academic		Fiction	
Construction:	inflect-ional	peri-phrastic	inflect-ional	peri-phrastic	inflect-ional	peri-phrastic	inflect-ional	peri-phrastic
Frequency of two-syllable bases	149 *46.3%*	173 *53.7%*	427 *43.0%*	567 *57.0%*	158 *36.7%*	272 *63.3%*	122 *48.2%*	131 *51.8%*
	322 (16.1%)		994 (49.7%)		430 (21.5%)		253 (12.7%)	
Relative freq. per 10,000 words	18.3		24.1		26.9		10.0	

Table 12. Distribution of disyllabic comparative constructions by major text category (across all four corpora).

Table 13 below shows that nearly two-thirds of disyllabic superlatives in three genres (Press, General and Academic) are periphrastic superlatives, with the highest proportion of periphrastic superlatives in the Press material section (64.7%); by contrast, these are relatively disfavoured in Fiction (42.0%). This may be accounted for in terms of Bell's (1991) proposed news value of 'superlativeness', from which it can be predicted that news stories should tend to favour superlative constructions wherever possible in order to maximize the total news value of the story. (However, it is important to note that Bell's analysis predicts only a higher frequency of superlative function, and does not specify any particular preference in form.)

Category:	Press		General		Academic		Fiction	
Construction:	inflect-ional	peri-phrastic	inflect-ional	peri-phrastic	inflect-ional	peri-phrastic	inflect-ional	peri-phrastic
Frequency of two-syllable bases	77	141	199	360	62	103	58	42
	35.3%	*64.7%*	*35.6%*	*64.4%*	*37.6%*	*62.4%*	*58.0%*	*42.0%*
	218 (20.9%)		559 (53.6%)		165 (15.8%)		100 (9.7%)	

Table 13. Overall distribution of disyllabic superlative constructions by genre (across all four corpora).

Generally speaking, disyllabic comparatives favour periphrastic comparative forms in all four genres in each corpus (Table 14). However, there are noticeable increases of periphrastic comparative forms apparent in Academic writings both in American and British English (52.5% to 75.2%, and 50.0% to 70.6%), though disyllabic periphrastic comparatives in all four genres in each corpus show a slight increase both in American and British English.

Compared to disyllabic comparatives, disyllabic superlatives (Table 15) show a slightly greater preference for periphrastic forms in all genres except Fiction, with the highest proportion of disyllabic periphrastic superlatives occurring in Academic texts (76.3%).

Category:	Press		General		Academic		Fiction	
Corpus:	inflect-ional	peri-phrastic	inflect-ional	peri-phrastic	inflect-ional	peri-phrastic	inflect-ional	peri-phrastic
Brown	45 *48.4%*	48 *51.6%*	111 *45.3%*	134 *54.7%*	47 *47.5%*	52 *52.5%*	32 *49.2%*	33 *50.8%*
Frown	34 *46.6%*	39 *53.4%*	95 *40.1%*	142 *59.9%*	29 *24.8%*	88 *75.2%*	29 *46.8%*	33 *53.2%*
LOB	40 *44.9%*	49 *55.1%*	121 *49.8%*	122 *50.2%*	45 *50.0%*	45 *50.0%*	32 *52.5%*	29 *47.5%*
FLOB	30 *44.8%*	37 *55.2%*	100 *37.2%*	169 *62.8%*	37 *29.4%*	89 *70.6%*	29 *44.6%*	36 *55.4%*

Table 14. Distribution of disyllabic comparative forms, by corpus and major text category.

Category:	Press		General		Academic		Fiction	
Corpus:	inflect-ional	peri-phrastic	inflect-ional	peri-phrastic	inflect-ional	peri-phrastic	inflect-ional	peri-phrastic
Brown	13 *29.5%*	31 *70.5%*	54 *35.8%*	97 *64.2%*	9 *23.7%*	29 *76.3%*	19 *63.3%*	11 *36.7%*
Frown	18 *32.1%*	38 *67.9%*	41 *30.8%*	92 *69.2%*	13 *27.7%*	34 *72.3%*	11 *52.4%*	10 *47.6%*
LOB	22 *40.7%*	32 *59.3%*	58 *43.3%*	76 *56.7%*	18 *56.3%*	14 *43.7%*	10 *41.7%*	14 *58.3%*
FLOB	24 *37.5%*	40 *62.5%*	46 *32.6%*	95 *67.4%*	22 *45.8%*	26 *54.2%*	18 *72.0%*	7 *28.0%*

Table 15. Distribution of disyllabic superlative forms, by corpus and major text category.

3. Constructions observed with selected adjective suffixes

The present section will investigate the distribution of comparative construction type found with individual suffixes, in light of the comments made by Quirk *et al.* (1985): i.e. that the kind of suffix affects the choice of comparison and the word endings *-y, -ow, -le* are predominantly associated with inflectional comparison. Table 16 below lists frequencies of inflectional or periphrastic comparison for selected types with these word endings which are clearly consistent with Quirk *et al.*'s description.

	easy	*early*	*happy*	*pretty*	*narrow*	*able*	*gentle*	*noble*	*simple*
-er	188	308	27	11	26	2	11	4	51
-est	19	81	21	10	2	5	2	7	64
more	3	0	0	1	2	0	2	1	2
most	0	0	0	0	0	5	2	2	0

Table 16. Frequencies of inflectional and periphrastic comparison for bases ending in *-y, -ow, -le.*

The data in Table 17 tests Quirk *et al.*'s suggestion that comparison on bases using the negative prefix *un-* is mainly inflectional. Though there are very few tokens of the items listed by Quirk *et al.*, some variation is still evident, with the base *unlikely*, at least, seemingly preferring periphrastic comparison.

	unfriendly	*unhappy*	*unlikely*
er/est	0	1 (*unhappiest*)	2 (*unlikeliest*)
more	0	1	2
most	2	0	14

Table 17. Frequencies of inflectional and periphrastic comparison for bases with the negative prefix *un-*.

Quirk *et al.*'s description of *-ing, -ed* participial forms as favouring periphrastic comparison is overwhelmingly confirmed in these corpora, as shown in Table 18.

	-ing	*-ed*
-er/-est	0	0
more	224	384
most	220	159

Table 18. Frequencies of inflectional and periphrastic comparison with participle forms.

	likely	*friendly*	*lively*	*costly*
-er	2	4	5	4
-est	1	1	1	1
more	97	4	4	4
most	43	2	1	2

Table 19. Frequencies of inflectional and periphrastic comparison for bases with suffix *-ly*.

Quirk *et al.* comment that *-ly* may favour periphrastic forms. However, though the most common base of this type, *likely*, is indeed most often found in periphrastic constructions, other *-ly* bases exhibit greater variation between inflectional and periphrastic forms (Table 19).

Next we examine Quirk *et al.*'s list of adjectives which take both inflectional and periphrastic forms. Table 20 below shows that the types *cruel, polite, pleasant, handsome* are attested in both inflectional and periphrastic comparison, but *common* seems to favour periphrastic forms, whereas *quiet* is only attested in inflectional forms in these corpora.

	common	*quiet*	*solid*	*cruel*	*polite*	*pleasant*	*handsome*
er	4	14	0	1	0	3	2
est	7	2	0	2	1	1	3
more	16	0	2	1	2	6	1
most	32	0	0	0	0	0	3

Table 20. Frequencies of inflectional and periphrastic comparison for adjective bases cited as allowing variation.

To investigate a possible shift in American and British English in a maximally controlled environment, the following two tables list the commonly recurring types, *likely* and *common.* Tokens of *likely* in periphrastic comparison show an apparent increase in frequency both in American and British English over the thirty year period between Brown/LOB and Frown/FLOB.

	Brown	Frown	LOB	FLOB	Total
more	13	32	10	42	97
most	10	15	5	13	43

Table 21. Distribution of periphrastic comparison of *likely* by corpus.

The adjective type *common* shows an increase in use of periphrastic forms both in American and British English, other than for superlatives in the British data.

	Brown	Frown	LOB	FLOB	Total
more	3	6	1	6	16
most	7	10	8	7	32

Table 22. Distribution of periphrastic comparison of *common* by corpus.

4. Conclusions

This investigation has reexamined previous findings using four similarly constructed one-million-word corpora representing several different types of writings in order to identify the main factors to determine the comparative forms of adjectives, especially the number of syllables in the adjective, and the kind of suffix the adjective has. The following conclusions seem supported by the present research. Firstly, bases of one syllable, and of three or more syllables, show almost no variation, and disyllabic adjectives are evenly divided. Secondly, a shift to periphrastic comparison in both disyllabic comparative and superlative forms is observable in both American and British English. Thirdly, there is some formality dependence both in frequency of comparison use and preference in form of comparison used with disyllabic adjectives. For example, the least formal category of Fiction uses proportional few comparative and superlative forms. Fourthly, higher use of superlatives is observed in the Press section, which is consistent with Bell's (1991) proposed news value of 'superlativeness'. Fifthly, the type of suffix affects comparison, largely as described by Quirk *et al.* (1985), with the exception of *-ly* bases, which do not entirely behave as expected. Finally, the adjectives *likely* and *common* show a greater increase in periphrastic use over the thirty year period under investigation, both in American and British English.

References

Bauer, Laurie 1994. *Watching English Change: An Introduction to the Study of Linguistic Change in Standard Englishes in the Twentieth Century*. London: Longman.

Biber, Douglas 1988. *Variation across Speech and Writing*. Cambridge: Cambridge University Press.

Jespersen, Otto 1909-49. *A Modern English Grammar on Historical Principles*. London: Allen & Unwin.

Kytö, Merja 1996. 'The Best and Most Excellent Way': The Rivalling Forms of Adjective Comparison in Late Middle and Early Modern English. In Svartvik, Jan (ed.) *Words: Proceedings of an International Symposium: Lund, 25-26 August 1995*. Stockholm: Almqvist and Wiksell, 123-41.

Kytö, Merja / Romaine, Suzanne 2000. Adjective Comparison and Standardisation Processes in American and British English from 1620 to the Present. In Wright, Laura (ed.) *The Development of Standard English 1300 to 1800*. Cambridge: Cambridge University Press, 171-94.

Leech, Geoffrey / Culpeper, Jonathan 1997. The Comparison of Adjectives in Recent British English. In Nevalainen, Terttu / Kahlas-Tarkka, Leena (eds) *To Explain the Present: Studies in the Changing English Language in Honour of Matti Rissanen*. Helsinki: Societe Neophilologique, 353-73.

Leech, Geoffrey / Hundt, Marianne / Mair, Christian / Smith, Nicholas 2009. *Changes in Contemporary English: A Grammatical Study*. Cambridge: Cambridge University Press.

Quirk, Randolph / Greenbaum, Sidney / Leech, Geoffrey / Svartvik, Jan 1985. *A Comprehensive Grammar of the English Language*. London: Longman.

Suematsu, Nobuko 2004. The Comparison of Adjectives in 18th Century English. *North-Western European Language Evolution* 45, 33-50.

Sweet, Henry 1891. *A New English Grammar: Logical and Historical*. Oxford: Clarendon Press.

Section 3
Descriptions of Diachronic Linguistic Variation

MATTI RISSANEN

On the Occurrence and Variation of the Adverbial Subordination Markers *Þe* and *Þæt* in Old English Texts

1. Introduction[1]

The rise and development of adverbial subordinators is related to one of the basic questions in English historical syntax or morpho-syntax: how to connect the elements of the sentence. These questions relate to even more general aspects of text and discourse: how to indicate relations between ideas, propositions and utterances in a logical and coherent way.

The topic of this paper represents a very minor part in the development of adverbial subordinate linking, i.e. the use of overt markers of adverbial subordination, *þæt* and *þe*, in the Old English period. It is obvious, however, that the appearance and increasing frequency of these two grammatical words, especially *þe*, play an important role in the history of the earliest stages of the development of subordination in English. Furthermore, the early use and later loss of these markers are of interest in tracing the steps of the grammaticalisation of English adverbial subordinators.

As the term suggests, adverbial subordinators mark the relation between the main clause and an adverbial subordinate clause. This relation can be local, temporal, causal, conditional, concessive, final, consecutive or comparative (for Old English, see e.g. Mitchell 1985; Kortmann 1997, 1998). This survey focuses mainly on the variation in the use of *þæt* and *þe* with adverbial subordinators, although attention will also be given to the variation of these two particles with zero

1 The research reported here was supported in part by the Academy of Finland Centre of Excellence funding for the Research Unit for Variation, Contacts and Change in English at the Department of English, University of Helsinki.

marker, i.e. the subordinator used without *þæt* or *þe*.[2] Examples are taken from and figures of frequencies based on the Old English part of the *Helsinki Corpus* (see Kytö 1996), and on the *Dictionary of Old English Corpus in Electronic Form* compiled in Toronto.[3]

The earliest history of English adverbial subordinators, including the use of the particles *þæt* and *þe*, has been the subject of a fairly large number of studies. Mitchell (1985) is indispensable for this topic as for all studies of Old English syntax. Kortmann's (1997) survey of adverbial subordinators in various periods of English is also most valuable, although he mainly calls attention to the typological aspects of the development and taxonomy of these connectives. There are also a number of articles and monographs which consist of detailed descriptions of the occurrence of individual subordinators, such as: Adams (1907); Shearin (1903; 1909); Jäger (1923); van Dam (1957); Rissanen (1997; 1998). Less attention has been given to the comparison of the occurrences of *þæt* and *þe* with reference to a larger number of adverbial subordinators and to the differing frequencies in various Old English sub-periods. In the following, some observations focussing on these issues are presented, in the hope that they may contribute to our understanding of the earliest development of the hierarchical arrangement of the clauses in a sentence and of the emergence of overt markers of this hierarchy. They may also illuminate some points related to Kortmann's (1997: 291) questions concerning "the major changes in the morphological make-up of adverbial subordinators" and "the preferred sources of adverbial subordinators in the older periods of English".

---

2 *þæt* and *þe* also have important functions as independent subordinators in Old English, introducing noun clauses and relative clauses, as in:
þa cwæð he: Forðy ic hit þe secge eft, þy ic nolde **þæt** ðu wende **þæt** se God **þe** fæder is and fruma eallra gesceafta, **þæt** him ahwonan utan come his sio hea goodnes **þe** he full is. (Boethius BOETHAL 84)
'Then he said, "Therefore I said it to you because I did not wish **that** you would think **that** God, **who** is the father and beginning of all created things, **that** the high goodness **that** he is full of would come to him from anywhere outside."'

3 The capitalized abbreviated titles in the reference line of the *Helsinki Corpus* examples refer to the text list in Kytö (1996: 169-230). The examples taken from the *Dictionary of Old English Corpus* are marked by DOEC at the end of the reference line.

2. Variation between zero, *þæt* and *þe* in Old English

Examples (1) to (3) illustrate the three types of adverbial subordinator marking in Old English.

(1) oft ryhtwise menn mid ðys hwilendlican anwealde weorðað upahæfene, **oð** hie ðurh ðone anwald weorðað mid synnum gefangne, (Past Care 391 CP)

'Righteous men are often exalted by this transitory authority, **until** they are caught by sins through this authority.'

(2) hiene þa Cynewulf on Andred adræfde, & he þær wunade **oþ þæt** hiene an swan ofstang æt Pryfetes flodan; (A-S Chronicle 46 CHRONA2)

'Cynewulf then drove him into Andred, and there he lived **until** a swineherd stabbed him by the River Privett.'

(3) Alecgað hit ðonne forhwæga on anre mile þone mæstan dæl fram þæm tune, þonne oðerne, ðonne þæne þriddan, **oþ þe** hyt eall aled bið on þære anre mile (Ohthere 20 OHTHR3)

'They place it [the money] then at the distance of about one mile from the village, the largest part, then the second, then the third, **until** it has all been placed within that one mile.'

In (1), the subordinator *oþ* 'until' is used without *þæt* or *þe*; this can be called the use with zero marker. In (2) *oþ* is used with the overt marker *þæt* and in (3) with *þe*. The function of the subordinator is obviously the same in all the three instances; thus the addition of *þæt* or *þe* seems to be motivated merely by the wish to distinguish the form of the subordinator from that of the preposition. It can be assumed that this overt marking stands as evidence of the increasing consciousness of the hierarchical order of the clauses of the sentence.

The following questions are of primary importance in tracing the appearance and frequency of *þæt* and *þe* with adverbial subordinators:

1. Why do the markers of adverbial subordination, *þæt* and *þe*, appear in Old English?
2. What kind of factors affect the use of zero, *þæt* or *þe* with adverbial subordinators?

3. Was the path of grammaticalisation of the adverbial subordinator always subordinator + zero → subordinator + *þæt* → subordinator + *þe*?

The answer to the first question of course pertains to the development of subordination in Old English. It is generally agreed that coordination is older than subordination in English (see Mitchell 1985, I: 696, and the bibliographical references he gives). This is of course difficult to prove but it is obvious that the other alternatives, coordination developing from subordination or both emerging simultaneously and independently, are less likely. If this starting-point is accepted, it is only to be expected that most adverbial subordinators develop from adverbs, prepositions or prepositional noun phrases. The most natural explanation is that the main task of the overt marker (*þe* or *þæt*) is to indicate the subordinator function of the preceding element. Thus, *oþ* in example (1) could theoretically speaking be either a preposition or a subordinator, although the context, of course, makes the correct analysis easy. In examples (2) and (3), *þæt* and *þe* efficiently mark *oþ* as a subordinator.

Table 1 shows the subordinators discussed in this paper. They are listed on the basis of whether they occur mainly with zero marker, *þæt* or *þe*.[4]

Mainly with zero	Mainly with *þæt* or zero	Mainly with *þe* or zero
gif	*butan*	*ær* + dem. pron. (*þam/þon/þy*)
siþþan	*oþ*	*æfter* + dem. pron.
ær	*forþ*	*for* + dem. pron.
	nu	*mid* + dem. pron.
	to + dem. pron. (*þam/þon/þy*)	*wiþ* + dem. pron.
		þa hwile
		þeah

Table 1. Use of subordination marker with Old English adverbial subordinators.

This list does not comprise all the adverbial subordinators found in Old English texts but with its fifteen items (out of the total of thirty or so),[5] it should be representative of the various types and illustrate the points raised in this paper.

4 The original function of *þæt* and *þe* is discussed in Mitchell (1985, II: 243-245).

5 Kortmann (1997: 292) lists forty Old English items, but some of them are phrasal and can hardly be taken as subordinators showing a considerable

2.1. Adverbial subordinators used mainly with zero marker

The most basic of the Old English adverbial subordinators is without a doubt *gif* 'if' (see Braunmüller 1978: 104; cf., however, Kortmann 1997: 310). There is no evidence of its use as a preposition or adverb in Old English. There is only one unambiguous instance of its use with *þæt* (Mitchell 1985, II: 845):

(4) **gyf þæt** þonne hwylc mon sy þæt him on his mode to earfoðe þince, þæt he on ælce tid swa forwernedlice lyfige, tylige he þonne huru þæt he þis fæsten selost afæste (HomU 44. 284.9 DOEC)

'**If** there is any man to whom it seems too difficult to live so abstemiously, he should at least most carefully observe this fasting.'

This example is late and may foreshadow the early Middle English rapid increase in the use of *þæt* with adverbial subordinators (see Section 3, below). It is also possible, although less likely, that the *þæt* following *gif* is a cataphoric demonstrative pronoun 'that'.

The consistent use of *gif* with zero marker supports the hypothesis that the original function of the overt adverbial subordination markers was to distinguish the subordinator from the adverb or the preposition: with *gif* this kind of need did not exist.

The subordinators *siþþan* and *ær* are used with zero marker in practically all extant examples despite the fact that both are also used as adverbs and *ær* also appears as a preposition. *Siþþan* 'since', 'after' goes back to a prepositional phrase formed with the preposition *siþ* and the instrumental form of the demonstrative pronoun *þan/þon* (OED, s.v. *sithen, adv., conj.*, and *prep.*; cf. Mitchell 1985, II: 349-350). Thus, it can be regarded as "less basic" than *gif*, but the grammaticalisation of this form must have occurred very early, much earlier than that of the combinations listed in the right-hand column of Table 1. It is also significant that *siþþan* is not used as a preposition.[6] There are no clear

degree of grammaticalisation. As to the problem of deciding whether an adverbial connective is an adverb or a subordinator, see Mitchell (1985, II: 250-255; 291-308). This uncertainty does not, however, decisively affect the overall view of the appearance or frequencies of the individual subordinators.

6 Mitchell (1985, II: 930) gives one possible example of the prepositional use.

instances of *siþþan þæt*, while the subordinator occurs several hundred times without the overt marker, as in (5):

(5) Her Danihel forþferde, þa was xliii wintra agan **siþþan** he onfeng biscepdome. (A-S Chronicle 46 CHRONA2)

'In this year Daniel died, at that time 43 years had passed **since** he became bishop.'

Ær can be used both as an adverb and as a preposition in addition to its subordinator use. When it is used as a preposition with the demonstrative pronoun, the subordinator is frequently followed by the marker *þe* (see Section 2.3., below), but, significantly, when it is used as a subordinator by itself, as in example (6), it is used with the zero marker.

(6) se cyning ælfred æfter þam gehorsudan here mid fierde rad oþ Exanceaster & hie hindan ofridan ne meahte **ær** hie on þam fæstene wæron, þær him mon to ne meahte; (A-S Chronicle 74 CHRONA2)

'King Alfred rode with his army after the mounted heathen army as far as Exeter and he could not overtake them **before** they were in the fortress, where they could not be reached.'

The only instances of *ær þæt* occur in interlinear glosses, in which the combination renders the Latin *prius quam* or *ante quam* (7). The marker *þe* occurs three times in Old English texts in the phrase *þon(ne) ær þe* 'as soon as', as in example (8) (see Mitchell 1985, II: 373)

(7) [In diebus illis factum est uerbum domini ad me dicens **prius quam** te formarem in utero noui te et **ante quam** exires de uulua sanctificate et prophetam in gentibus dedi te] on dagvm ðæm aworden væs word drihtnes to me cvoeðende **aer þæt** ðec ic gisceope in hrife ic wiste ðec & **ær þæt** gieadest of vombe ic gihalgade & witge in cynnvm ic gisalde ðe. (Durham Ritual 55.1. DOEC)

'In those days God said to me, "**before** I created you in the womb I knew you and **before** you were delivered from the womb I hallowed you and gave you as a prophet to nations." '

(8) Ðu cuist nu ðæt þu wille geswican **ðon ær ðe** ðu genoh hæbbe. (Pastoral Care 331.3 DOEC)

'Now you say that you will cease **as soon as** you have enough.'

Thus, a tentative conclusion can be drawn that when single-word adverbs developed subordinator function, the most natural form was without a subordination marker. Whether they had originally had one, most likely *þæt*, is a question that must remain unanswered.[7]

2.2. Adverbial subordinators used with zero marker or þæt

As can be seen in Table 1, the most common Old English subordinators with which the marker *þæt* occurs fairly frequently are *butan, oþ*, and, somewhat surprisingly, *to* + dem. pron. The subordinator *butan* goes back to a local prepositional adverb *be utan* 'on the outside' (OED s.v. *but, prep., conj., adv.*). The grammaticalisation of this form certainly took place at a very early date, in pre-historic Old English (cf. *siþþan*, above). The variation between the use of zero marker and *þæt* with this subordinator is interesting, as it illustrates the role of semantics in the choice of the marker. This is shown by examples (9) and (10):

(9) Soð ic eow secge, þæt ge sylfe ne becumað into heofonan rice, **buton** eower rihtwisnys beo eallunga mare ætforan minum Fæder þonne þæra bocera is and ðæra Sunderhalgena. (Ælfric Homilies 533 AELFR15)

'I tell you truly that you will not come to the Kingdom of Heaven **unless** your righteousness be altogether greater before my Father than that of the Scribes or Pharisees.'

(10) Hwæt wille we eow swiðor secgan be ðisum symbeldæge. **buton þæt** maria cristes modor wearð on ðisum dæge of ðisum geswincfullum middanearde genumen up to heofenan rice. (Ælfric Homilies 259 AELFR2/29)

'What will we say more to you about this feast-day **except that** Mary the Mother of Christ was on this day taken to the Kingdom of Heaven from this troublesome earth.'

In (9), *butan* introduces a negative conditional and can be translated as 'unless', 'if not'. Even in Present-day English, *that* would not be used in this context. In (10), the subordinate clause could be analysed as a

7 The common subordinators *þær, þanon, þider*, derived from adverbs but not used as prepositions, are also used without a marker in most cases. There are only eight examples of the use of *þe* with these three subordinators in the Old English part of the *Helsinki Corpus*. Cf. Mitchell (1985, II: 258; 263; 264).

kind of noun clause governed by *secgan* 'say'; the particle *that* is natural in contexts of this kind even in Present-day English (cf. Quirk *et al.* 1985: 999). This distinction is also pointed out by Mitchell (1985, II: 819-820), with reference to Kivimaa (1966). Even more generally, Mitchell is doubtful about the subordinator character of the combination *butan þæt* and suggests that in this combination "*þæt* introduces a noun clause governed by *butan*" (1985, II: 820). In all, the number of the instances of the combination *butan þæt* is 32 in the *Helsinki Corpus*, as against several hundred of the subordinator *butan* used without *that*. In all the *butan þæt* instances the subordinator is used in contexts corresponding to example (10).

The variation between zero and *þæt* with *butan* implies that semantic context was of importance in the introduction of the marker *þæt*, although it could spread from more natural contexts to other contexts, as a result of further grammaticalisation.

The temporal or local subordinator *oþ* (on which, see Rissanen 2007) can be used either with or without *þæt*. The analysis of the combination *oþ þæt* is problematic, as *þæt* can be either a subordination marker or a demonstrative pronoun as in the combinations listed in the right-hand column of Table 1. It is most likely, however, that the *þæt* in this combination is the particle; it is in variation with the simple form of the subordinator *oþ*, and its use becomes increasingly preferred over the Old English period (Table 2).

Sub-period	*oþ* + zero	*oþ* + *þæt*/*þe*
OE2 (850-950)	31 (34)	62 (68)
OE3 (950-1050)	13 (5)	189 (75)
OE4 (1050-1150)	4 (6)	39 (58)
Total	48	291

Table 2. *Oþ* + zero and *oþ þæt*/*þe* in the Old English sub-periods of the *Helsinki Corpus*. Absolute figures (Figures per 100,000 words in brackets).

Þe is extremely uncommon with *oþ*, and only occurs a few times in Late Old English texts (example 3, above). The same is true of the combination *oþ þæt þe* (example 11). This last-mentioned fact may be regarded as another indicator of the particle character of *þæt*: if *þæt* were a demonstrative pronoun, *oþ þæt þe* should be as common as the use of *þe* in the prepositional subordinators formed with *ær*/*æfter*/*for*/*mid*/*wiþ*

+ dem. pron., listed in the right-hand column of Table 1, above, and discussed in Section 2.3 below.

(11) ðonan benioðan wuda on geryhte ut on hreodpol ðonne up on afene **oððæt ðe** se alda suinhaga utscioteð to afene (Documents 34 BIRCH HC)

'Then through the forest directly to the reed pool, then up to the river, **up to the point where** the old swine enclosure touches the river.'

The discussion above implies that subordinators going back to simple or very old fully grammaticalised compound adverbs or prepositions are used either with zero marker or *þæt.* The use of *þæt* with the adverb-based subordinators *forþ* and *nu* confirms this suggestion, although the number of Old English examples is very low:

(12) þa men of Scrobscyre [...] comon & hergodon & bærndon on Wiðreceastrescire **forð þæt** hi comon to þam porte sylfan. & woldon þa ðæne port bærnen. (A-S Chronicle 223 CHRONE2)

'the men of Shropshire [...] came and destroyed and burnt in Winchestershire **until** they come to the port itself and wanted to burn the port.'

(13) Zosimus hire to cwæð, eala min hlæfdige hu mænige gear synt **nu þæt** þu on þysum westene eardodost? (Mary of Egypt 187 DOEC)

'Zosimus said to her, "Lo, my Lady, how many years is it **that** you have lived in this wilderness?"'

There are no instances of these subordinators with the marker *þe.*

2.3. Adverbial subordinators used with zero marker or þe

Most of the adverbial subordinators which mainly have zero or *þe* as the subordination marker go back to prepositional phrases of the type preposition + oblique form of a demonstrative pronoun (*þam/þon/þy*), as in examples (14)-(19). With these subordinators, *þæt* is rare or non-existent in Old English texts.

(14) Ða cwæþ þara ðegna sum, se wæs on naman Sustenis, ær ic me sylfne ofslea mid mine sweorde, **ær þon** ic sende mine hond on þas fæmnan. (Martyrology 210 MART)

'Then one of the soldiers said, whose name was Sosthenes, "I would rather kill myself with my sword **ere** I would lay hands upon this maiden".'

(15) He ys gehaten eac Crist; be þam cwæð sum witega for fela hund gearum, **ær þan þe** he acenned wurde: (Ælfric's Letter to Sigeweard 45 LSIGEW)

'He is also called Christ, of whom some prophet spoke many hundreds of years ago, **before** he was born:'

(16) he nyste hwæt þæs soþes wæs, **for þæm** he hit self ne geseah (Ohthere 17 OHTHR2)

'He did not know what the truth was **because** he did not see it himself.'

(17) ic ondræde me **for ðam ðe** ic eom nacod, (Hept. Gen. 3 AELFOLD)

'I am afraid **because** I am naked.'

(18) þa ongan ic wundrian, for hwon wit to þam walle eodan, **mid ðy** ic on him nænige duru ne eahþyrl [...] on ænge halfe geseon meahte. (Bede 428 BEDEHE)

'Then I began to wonder why we went to the wall **as** I could not see any door or window [...] on either side.'

(19) Hælend [...] hine het to him gelædon; & **mid þy þe** he him genealæhte, he him tocwæþ, Hwæt wilt þu þæt ic þe do? (Blickling Homilies 15 BLICK2)

'Christ [...] asked the man to be led to him, and **when** the man approached him, Christ asked him, "What would you like me to do for you?"'

From the point of view of the development of subordination, the most interesting feature of these subordinators is the gradual proportional increase of the occurrence of *þe* in the course of the Old English period, as illustrated by Table 3.[8] *Þæt* is uncommon: there are no instances of it in the *Helsinki Corpus* with *ær*, 15 with *for*, and 3 with *mid.*

8 See also Mitchell's (1985, II: 529-531) notes on the variation between zero marker and *þe* with *for* + dem. pron. denoting 'explanatory reason' or 'true reason'.

Sub-period	*ær* + dem. pron.			*for* + dem. pron.			*mid* + dem. pron.		
	zero	*þe/þæt*	(% *þe/þæt*)	zero	*þe/þæt*	(% *þe/þæt*)	zero	*þe/þæt*	(% *þe/þæt*)
OE2 (850-950)	9	9	(50%)	428	139	(24%)	41	9	(18%)
OE3 (950-1050)	12	14	(54%)	268	126	(31%)	9	19	(67%)
OE4 (1050-1150)	1	13	(93%)	148	164	(53%)	1	3	(75%)

Table 3. Relative frequencies (per 100,000 words) of *ær/for/mid* + dem. pron. as subordinators in the Old English section of the *Helsinki Corpus*. (Total number of occurrences = *ca.* 1500.)

With *æfter* + dem. pron., which develops a subordinator use in the course of the Old English period, the distribution is even more marked: in 39 out of the 41 *Helsinki Corpus* instances the combination is followed by *þe* (example 20); see also Adams (1907: 211-213; Mitchell 1985, II: 347-348).

(20) Ac þa arleasan cyningas nales micelre tide, **æfter þon þe** heo þone soðfæstnisse bodan from him adrifon, þæt heo deofla bigængum freolice þeowedon.(Bede 114 BEDEHE)

'But the impious kings, a little time **after** they had driven away the preacher of the truth, freely gave themselves up to the worship of devils.'

The same is true of the combination *wiþ* + dem. pron., also a fairly late subordinator indicating condition or purpose: out of the 23 instances, 19 are used with *þe*, two with *þæt* and 2 with *gif* (examples 21-22).[9]

(21) Eala þu bisceop, to bysmore synd getawode þas earman landleoda, and me nu leofre wære þæt ic on feohte feolle **wið þam þe** min folc moste heora eardes brucan. (Ælfric Lives of Saints 318 AELIVES32)

'O bishop, the poor people have been put to shame and now I would rather that I died in battle **if that would mean that** my people could till their land.'

(22) Hu micle suiðor sculon we ðonne beon gehiersume ðæm ðe ure gæsta Fæder bið **wið ðæm ðæt** we moten libban on ecnesse. (Cura Pastoralis 255 CP)

'How much more obedient should we then be to him who is our spiritual Father **that** we may live eternally.'

9 The majority of the instances occur in recipes in which the original sense of *wiþ* 'against' is probably still traceable.

The marker *þe* is also typical of some other phrasal adverbial subordinators, such as *þa hwile þe*, which seems to have been grammaticalised fairly late in Old English. Out of the 74 instances in the *Helsinki Corpus*, only four are used without *þe* (example 23) and there are no instances with *þæt*.

(23) he ann his wife þæs 232ands æt Cylleshale [...] **þa hwile** hire dæg beo. (Charters 54 WHIT19)

'he gives his wife the land at Cylleshale [...] for **as long as** she lives.'

(24) Swa eac se lichoma bið lichoma **þa hwile þe** he his limu ealle hæfð; (Boethius 90 BOETHAL HC)

'So also the body is a body **while** it has all its limbs.'

The increasing popularity of the use of *þe* with Old English prepositional subordinators indicates the growing importance of this particle as the subordination marker, at the expense of *þæt*, probably due to the increase in the degree of the grammaticalisation of the subordinators. It also seems to provide evidence of a growing consciousness of the hierarchical arrangement of clauses, that is, the difference between coordination and subordination.

The pattern of development outlined above is, however, complicated by some adverbial subordinators, most notably by *þeah* and *to* + dem. pron. As *þeah* is a simple subordinator form, going back to an adverb, we should expect either the zero marker or *þæt* with this item, like with *siþþan, ær* or *butan*. In the majority of cases *þeah* is, indeed, used without an overt marker (example 25), but when the marker appears, it is always *þe* (example 26). This combination increases in popularity in the course of the Old English period, from 19 occurrences per 100,000 words in the period between 850 and 950 to 26 per 100,000 words in the next 100 year period. It seems that as *þe* is gaining ground as the general subordination marker, it also comes to be added to *þeah* more or less automatically, although there is no real need to mark the subordinating use of this connective. In view of the preceding discussion, this is a more likely line of development than that the simple subordinator *þeah* with zero marker would go back to an earlier *þeah þe*, as suggested in earlier studies (see Mitchell 1985, II: 709-11). It is notable that throughout the Old English period *þeah* is used without *þe* in the majority of the instances: over five hundred in the *Helsinki Corpus* as compared with around a hundred with *þe.*

(25) ealne weg hi hi ðweað, & ne beoð hie næfre clæne, **ðeah** hi ealneg wepen; (Past. Care 421 CP)
'they are washing themselves all the time and they are never clean, **although** they are always lamenting.'

(26) ða singað ðone sang [...] ðætte ða oðre gecorenan ðone song gehiran mægen, **ðeah ðe** hine swa singan ne mægen, (Past. Care 409 CP)
'they sing the song [...] so that the other elected ones may hear that song, **although** they cannot sing it.'

The unexpected feature in the formation of the subordinator *to* + dem. pron. is that, in contrast to the other prepositional subordinators discussed above (*ær/for/mid/æfter/wiþ* + dem. pron.), it is followed by *þæt* (example 27) instead of *þe* (see also Mitchell 1985, II: 245). Furthermore, no instances of this subordinator used with zero marker occur in the *Helsinki Corpus.*

(27) Hwæt sculon we nu don **to þon þæt** we mægen cuman to þæm soðum gesælðum? (Boethius 79 BOETH HC)
'What shall we now do **in order that** we might come to the true Happiness?'

It can be suggested, at least tentatively, that the indication of purpose, which is the primary meaning of the subordinator *to þam/þon þæt* 'for that purpose that', has a different semantic shape from the other prepositional subordinators discussed in this section. As with *buton þæt* in Section 2 above, the subordinate clause is perhaps analysed as a kind of noun clause which demands the linking *þæt.* It is also possible that the remarkable semantic change from the original local sense to the final sense of the adverbial *to þæt* plays a role here. The fact that the overt marker is obligatory seems to point in the same direction. In other words, while the other prepositional adverbial subordinators only need a grammaticalised and grammaticalising marker, the semantics of the purpose clause may require a link relating it to the other uses of the subordinator *þæt.* Mitchell (1985, II: 460-461) points out that all Old English subordinators indicating purpose and result have the marker *þæt* rather than *þe* and describes the clause as "in a sense explanatory". He also notes (1985, II: 472) that even the rare instances of *for* + dem. pron. + *þæt* indicate purpose or result rather than reason (see also Kivimaa 1966: 157).

3. Middle English development

The later development of the use of subordination markers with adverbial subordinators displays interesting cyclicity. In early Middle English *þe* began to lose ground and *þæt* dramatically increased in popularity. The latter could be appended to a number of subordinators which were new in the language or with which it did not occur in Old English (see e.g. Fischer 1992; Rissanen 1997; 1998). Even *if* came to be used with a following *that.* However, in Early Modern English, even this *that* gradually disappeared from most contexts and usage approached the present system of subordinators (Rissanen 1997; 1999).

4. Concluding remarks

It is obvious that the story of the overt means of indicating subordination in Old English is not a simple and straightforward matter. Attention must be drawn, among other things, to the quality and form of the adverbial subordinator, the chronology of its grammaticalisation, and to the semantics of the relationship between the main clause and the subordinate clause. The earlier the grammaticalisation and the simpler the form of the subordinator, the more likely it is to be used with zero marker or with *þæt* and the less likely to be used with *þe.* On the other hand, *þe* can be appended even to this kind of subordinator by analogy in the course of the Old English period, as in the case of *þeah þe*. The semantics of the relationship between the propositions in the main clause and the subordinate clause probably affect the choice of the marker, at least in the case of *butan* and *to* + dem. pron. It is also most likely that there were types of grammaticalised or grammaticalising subordinators for which the overt marker was *þe* and not *þæt* from the very beginning, such as prepositional subordinators formed with *ær/æfter/for/mid/wiþ* + demonstrative pronoun, which do not show the development from the marker *þæt* to *þe.*

References

Adams, A. 1907. *The syntax of the temporal clause in Old English prose* (Yale Studies in English 32).

Braunmüller, Kurt 1978. Remarks on the formulation of conjunctions in Germanic languages. *Nordic Journal of Linguistics* 1, 99-120.

Dictionary of Old English Corpus in Electronic Form. University of Michigan Press. Available from URL <http://www.press.umich.edu/webhome/healey/siteform.html>.

Fischer, Olga 1992. Syntax. In Blake, Norman (ed.) *The Cambridge history of the English language Vol. 2, 1066-1476.* Cambridge: Cambridge University Press, 207-408.

Jäger, Ernst 1923. *Die Konjunktionen 'for' und 'for that' im Englischen* (diss. Giessen).

Kivimaa, Kirsti 1966. *Þe and þæt as clause connectives in Early Middle English with especial consideration of the emergence of the pleonastic þæt.* Helsinki: Societas Scientiarum Fennica.

Kortmann, Bernd 1997. *Adverbial subordination: A typology and history of adverbial subordinators based on European languages.* Berlin and New York: Mouton de Gruyter.

Kortmann, Bernd 1998. Adverbial subordinators in the languages of Europe. In van der Auwera, J. (ed.) *Adverbial constructions in the languages of Europe.* Berlin/New York: Mouton de Gruyter, 457-561.

Kytö, Merja 1996 [1991]. *Manual to the diachronic part of the Helsinki Corpus of English Texts: Coding conventions and lists of source texts.* (3rd ed.) Helsinki: Department of English, University of Helsinki. Available from URL <http://khnt.hit.uib.no/icame/manuals/HC/>.

Mitchell, Bruce 1985. *Old English syntax* I-II. Oxford: Clarendon Press.

Rissanen, Matti 1997. Optional THAT with subordinators in Middle English. In Hickey, Raymond / Puppel, Stanislaw (eds) *Language history and linguistic modelling: A Festschrift for Jacek Fisiak on his 60th birthday* (Trends in Linguistics, Studies and Monographs 101). Berlin: Mouton de Gruyter, 373-383.

Rissanen, Matti 1998. Towards an integrated view of the development of English: Notes on causal linking. In Fisiak, Jacek / Krygier,

Marcin (eds) *Advances in English historical linguistics* (1996). Berlin/New York: Mouton de Gruyter, 389-406.

Rissanen, Matti 1999. Syntax. In Lass, Roger (ed.) *The Cambridge history of the English language Vol. 3: 1476-1776*. Cambridge: Cambridge University Press, 187-331.

Rissanen, Matti 2007. From *oþ* to *till*: Early loss of an adverbial subordinator. In Lenker, Ursula / Meurman-Solin, Anneli (eds) *Connectives in the history of English.* Amsterdam: Benjamins, 61-76.

Shearin, H. G. 1903. *The expression of purpose in Old English prose* (Yale Studies in English 18).

Shearin, H. G. 1909. The expression of purpose in Old English poetry. *Anglia* 32, 235-252.

van Dam, Johannes 1957. *The causal clause and causal prepositions in Early Old English prose*. Groningen: J. B. Wolters.

TOSHIO SAITO

The Syntactic Development of the Gerund in Early Modern English: A Survey Based on the Penn-Helsinki Parsed Corpus of Early Modern English

1. Introduction[1]

1.1. The aim of the present paper

Soon after the completion of the epoch-making *Helsinki Corpus of English Texts* (henceforth, HC), I explored the corpus and published a paper (Saito 1993) on the variant constructions of the gerund preceded or followed by its logical object in Early Modern English (henceforth, EModE). The conclusion of the paper was that in general the evidence yielded by the HC gave a reliable outline of development of the syntactic feature under investigation, proving the corpus a reliable and useful tool for diachronic studies of English. The compilers of the HC, a team led by Matti Rissanen, however, admitting that the corpus with 1.6 million words might be "too small for the purposes of many diachronic studies with past synchrony as their starting point" for the long time span of the history of English, promised to offer an expanded version in five years or so (Kytö/Rissanen 1993: 2).

The expansion with annotation of the HC was accomplished (though ultimately by other research groups) in 2004 with the completion of the *Penn-Helsinki Parsed Corpus of Early Modern English* (PPCEME, 1.7 million words), following such expanded versions as

1 I should like to express my sincere gratitude to Shunji Yamazaki and Robert Sigley for their invaluable comments and suggestions on an earlier draft, and to Junsaku Nakamura for his kind help with the chi-squared tests, and lastly but not least, to Satoru Tsukamoto for supporting me in using both the KWIC Concordance for Windows and the Treebank he developed.

the *Penn-Helsinki Parsed Corpus of Middle English, 2nd edition* (PPCME2, 1.2 million words, 2000), the *York-Helsinki Parsed Corpus of Old English Poetry* (York Poetry Corpus, 71,490 words, 2001) and the *York-Toronto-Helsinki Parsed Corpus of Old English Prose* (YCOE, 1.5 million words, 2003).

As the Penn-Helsinki Parsed Corpora of Historical English including the PPCEME, became available recently on CD-ROM,[2] I have made an attempt to explore this expanded corpus to re-examine the rise and fall of the same variant constructions of the gerund in the course of the EModE period, and in addition, to compare the data retrieved from this corpus with those from the HC to find out how far the increase in size has improved reliability and usefulness, or whether, alternatively, the original "too small" corpus proves as reliable and useful as the expanded corpus.

In this quantitative survey, the texts (260,116 words) of Period M4 (1420-1500) of the PPCME2, and the texts (1710-1779, roughly 140,000 words) out of Part B of the *Century of Prose Corpus* (COPC)[3] were examined as supplementary material to give a better perspective on the diachronic development of the constructions under investigation in EModE.

---

2 Cf. <http://www.ling.upenn.edu/hist-corpora/>. This CD-ROM (distributed in 2005) contains the PPCEME-RELEASE-1 (an expanded version of the EModE part of the HC), and the PPCME2-RELEASE-2 (an expanded version of the ME part of the HC). With the completion of the *Penn Parsed Corpus of Modern British English* (PPCMBE) in 2010, the PPCEME-RELEASE-2 became available as part of the *Penn Parsed Corpora of Historical English on CD-ROM (Version 3.0)*, which contains the PPCME2-RELEASE-3, the PPCEME-RELEASE-2, and the PPCMBE-RELEASE-1. The present survey initially used the PPCEME-RELEASE-1, but I corrected all relevant statistics in accordance with the updated wordcount summaries of the revised version (RELEASE-2) once that became available.

3 The COPC, compiled by Louis T. Milic (Cleveland State University) is a 500,000-word diachronic corpus designed for studying British prose composed or published during "The Century of Prose" (1680-1780). This corpus, which was complete and in circulation as early as in 1990, was one of the earliest English historical/diachronic corpora, but regrettably it has been unavailable since the compiler's death in 2003.

The application KWIC Concordance for Windows[4] was used to retrieve evidence from the corpora.

1.2. A brief description of PPCEME

According to the manual, the *Penn-Helsinki Parsed Corpus of Early Modern English* (PPCEME) compiled by Anthony Kroch, Beatrice Santorini and Ariel Diertani, is part of an ongoing larger project at the University of Pennsylvania and the University of York to produce syntactically annotated corpora for all stages of the history of English.

	Helsinki	Penn 1	Penn 2	Total
E1 (1500-1569)	191,737	192,661	183,397	567,795
E2 (1570-1639)	191,074	214,993	222,396	628,463
E3 (1640-1710)	171,885	188,786	180,924	541,595
Total	554,696	596,440	586,717	1,737,853

Table 1. Wordcount summary by time period and subcorpus (From the Manual).

This corpus, a trebled version of the (551,000-word) EModE part of the HC, consists of over 1.7 million words, and is divided into three sub-corpora, which the manual describes as follows:

1) The Helsinki directories, consisting of roughly 550,000 words, contain the Helsinki Corpus in parsed, POS-tagged, and unannotated form.
2) The Penn1 directories, consisting of roughly 600,000 words, contain a first supplement to the Helsinki Corpus. As far as possible, we have used material by the same authors and from the same editions as the material in the Helsinki Corpus. Where necessary (where the Helsinki Corpus contains an exhaustive sample of a text), we have added new material [...]
3) The Penn2 directories, consisting of roughly 590,000 words, contain a second supplement to the Helsinki Corpus. Again, we have tried to use material by the same authors and from the same editions as the material in the Helsinki Corpus. However, the Penn2 directories contain more new material than the Penn1 directories.

---

4 This is a user-friendly freeware concordancer developed by Satoru Tsukamoto (<http://www.chs.nihon-u.ac.jp/eng_dpt/tukamoto/kwic_e.html>), specially adapted for exploration of diachronic/historical corpora such as the Helsinki Corpus. Tsukamoto also developed the Treebank Search, a user-friendly freeware adapted for exploring the parsed texts in the Penn Historical Corpora.

The corpus is also divided into three 70-year time periods, E1 (1500-1569), E2 (1570-1639) and E3 (1640-1710), and texts are classified as representing 18 genres in E1 and E2, and 16 in E3, following the genre labels used in the HC.

Each of the texts in the corpus is available in parsed, POS-tagged, and unannotated form. The texts in unannotated form were used for the present survey. Consequently, in the present paper no mention can be made of the usefulness of the annotated forms featured in the PPCEME. In order to make a comparison between the HC and the PPCEME, the data of the former were retrieved from the texts contained in the Helsinki directories instead of the original HC in the ICAME Collection, 2nd Edition (1999).

1.3. The origins and development of the gerund

Before going into the details of results of the investigation, a brief overview[5] of the history of the gerundial constructions in question in Old English (henceforth, OE) and Middle English (henceforth, ME) will help to better understand their later development and change in EModE.

As Mustanoja (1960: 567) says, the origins and development of the gerund are one of the most controversial problems of English syntax. It seems certain, however, that the nominal gerund developed from the OE abstract deverbal noun of action in *-ing* or *-ung*. The logical object (henceforth, object) attached to it was normally expressed in the genitive case (*the book's reading*), sometimes in the accusative ((*the*) *book reading*). With the advancement of the analytic tendency in ME, the genitives began to be replaced by *of*-phrases; thus, *the book's*

5 For further details on the origins and development of the gerund, see e.g., Curme (1912), Jespersen (1909-49), Mustanoja (1960), Visser (1966), Kisbye (1970), Tajima (1985), Jack (1988), van der Wurff (1993), and more recently, Fanego (2004, 2006a, 2006b) and De Smet (2008a, 2008b). Recently, the gerund has been a topic of prolific research as part of non-finite clause complementation, so that there is ample literature addressing this syntactic change. Fanego's papers are especially informative, referring to a number of recent important papers on this syntactic feature.

reading (OE) > *reading of the book* (ca. 1200).[6] Then this analytic type came to be preceded by a determiner; hence *the reading of the book* (ca. 1200).[7]

The gerund preceded by its noun object was already rare in Late ME (henceforth, LME), but the gerund preceded by its pronoun object was still rather common.[8]

On the other hand, the nominal gerund functioning as prepositional object gradually developed a verbal character, acquiring the ability to take adverbial modifiers and also accusative objects without *of*. Thus a type with verbal character came into being: *reading the book (rapidly)* (ca. 1300).[9] As Houston (1989: 190) assumes, there was a split in the syntax of the nominal gerund into nominal and verbal gerunds in the middle of the ME period. Furthermore, there came into existence a type with mixed character, a nomino-verbal gerund: *the reading the book* (1340).[10]

Generally speaking, as the findings by Tajima (1985: 39) show,[11] in LME the nominal type *reading of the book* was the most common, gradually being caught up with by the other nominal type *the reading of the book*. On the other hand, the verbal type *reading the book* was still a minor type, though it was steadily gaining ground. The nomino-verbal type *the reading the book* was underdeveloped in LME.

---

6 The date of the earliest instances found by Tajima (1985: 61). The earliest instance cited by Visser (1966: §1120) is c1259 Ge. & Ex. 831.

7 The date of the earliest instances found by Tajima (1985: 67). The date of the earliest instance cited by Visser (1966:§1124) is c1303.

8 See Jespersen (1909-49: V. 8.41), Visser (1966: §1106), Tajima (1985: 42f).

9 The date of the earliest instance found by Tajima (1985: 74). The date of the earliest genuine instance cited by Visser (1966: §1123) is 1303.

10 This date is for the earliest instance found by Tajima (1985: 82), in which the gerund is preceded by a possessive pronoun. The instances of '*the* + gerund + object' found by Tajima (1985: 80) all date from the period 1450-1500, while the earliest instance cited by Visser (1966: §1124) is dated c1333.

11 Table II of Tajima (1985: 39) provides the following statistics:

	III (=B1)	IV(=B2)	V(=B3)	VI (=B4)
1300-1350	38.0%	24.5%	5.4%	0.5%
1350-1400	59.4%	24.9%	5.8%	0.4%
1400-1450	42.1%	24.4%	14.9%	0.4%

1.4. Variant types of the gerundial constructions

In EModE the gerund governing an object was still realized by the six variant ME constructions described in the previous section. They may be classified as follows:

A) Object-preposed ('O + V-*ing*'):

Type A1. Genitive (Pro)Noun + Gerund (e.g. *the book's reading*)

Type A2. Accusative Noun+ Gerund (e.g. *(the) book reading*)

B) Object-postposed ('V-*ing* + O'):

Type B1. Gerund + *of* + Object (e.g. *reading of the book*)

Type B2. Determiner + Gerund + *of* + Object (e.g. *the reading of the book*)

Type B3. Gerund + Object (e.g. *reading the book*)

Type B4. Determiner + Gerund + Object (e.g. *the reading the book*)

'Object-preposed' and 'object-postposed' in this classification[12] are just the *ad hoc* terms I use in the present paper. 'Determiner' is used in a broader sense, including e.g. (in)definite articles, demonstrative pronouns, indefinite pronouns, and also genitive (pro)nouns.

The B types also can be grouped more broadly as +*of* <B1, B2: nominal gerunds> vs. −*of* <B3: verbal gerunds, B4: nomino-verbal gerunds>.

---

12 In the present classification the gerunds preceded by genitive nouns or possessive pronouns functioning as their logical subjects (*John's/my reading (of) the book*) are included in Types B2 and B4, following the conventional classification. However, it may be better to classify separately gerunds with overt subjects (+S) vs. subjectless gerunds (–S). I agree with Fanego (1996, 2004, 2006), who states that the development of the former is "substantially different" from the latter. In my earlier surveys (Saito 1972, 1990) I classified B) into two types: (i) Subjectless gerund (−S): (+) *of* <Type I: *reading of the book*, Type II: *the reading of the book*> (−) *of* <Type III: *reading the book*, Type IV: *the reading the book*>; (ii) Subjectful gerund (+S): (+) *of* <Type IIb: *my reading of the book*>; (−) *of* <Type IVb: *my reading the book*>.

2. Preliminary survey

2.1. Distribution of the gerundial constructions in the PPCEME

The overall frequency of instances of the gerund with its object extracted from the PPCEME is shown in Table 2.

	Helsinki	Penn1	Penn2	Total (=PPCEME)
E1 (1500-1569)	382 (19.9)	356 (18.5)	322 (17.6)	1,060 (18.7)
E2 (1570-1639)	430 (22.5)	489 (22.7)	557 (25.0)	1,476 (23.5)
E3 (1640-1710)	572 (33.3)	710 (37.6)	623 (34.4)	1,905 (35.2)
Total	1,384 (25.0)	1,555 (26.1)	1,502 (25.6)	4,441 (25.6)

(Normed frequency per 10,000 words in parentheses); X^2 (4*df*) = 26.822, $p < 0.001$.
Table 2. Overall frequency of the gerund with object in the subcorpora in PPCEME.

First of all, the statistically significant data of this table show that the gerundial constructions under investigation occur with increasing frequency in the course of the EModE period. In E3 the gerund with its object occurs approximately 1.8 times as frequently as in E1: 1905 vs. 1060. Soon after the HC became available, this increasing tendency in the use of the gerund across the subperiods of EModE in the corpus was reported by Saito (1993), and Fanego (1996).

Concerning the tendency in LME, Tajima (1985: 39) says "the gerund with an object of its own remains infrequent until the close of the 13th century, but then occurs with increasing frequency [...], becoming remarkably common in late ME," so that it may safely be said that EModE is a period in which the gerund continues to gain ground.[13]

13 See also Houston (1989: 176f), who states that between about 1450–1650 there was a general increase in appearance of direct objects following verbal nouns. In order to comprehend this increasing tendency, it may be necessary to take into consideration the infinitive, and also *that*-clauses, both of which are functionally in rivalry with the gerund. There is ample literature referring to this complement shift. Leech *et al.* (2009: 204) summarises the findings in terms of two long-term trends in the history of English non-finite clauses, *viz.*: (i) infinitival clauses have been gaining ground at the expense of finite clauses since the late Old English period; and (ii) from the Early Modern period onwards, gerundial

The texts of M4 (1420-1500) of the PPCME2 (totaling 260,116 words) provide 254 occurrences (9.8 times per 10,000 words), and the examined texts (1710-1779) of the COPC (roughly 140,000 words) yield 675 occurrences (48.2 times per 10,000 words). It follows, therefore, that the increasing tendency continues from LME onwards to LModE, as Figure 1 visually discloses. This tendency will be further addressed in terms of the gerundial types and the text genres in the following sections.

In addition, Table 2 shows that the PPCEME as a whole yields an observed frequency approximately three times as high as observed in the HC: 4,441 (3.2) vs. 1,384 (1). This is also the case within each time period: E1 (2.8), E2 (3.4), or E3 (3.3). This higher observed frequency certainly will give the PPCEME statistically more significant and more reliable results than the HC in the coming various investigations of the gerundial constructions.

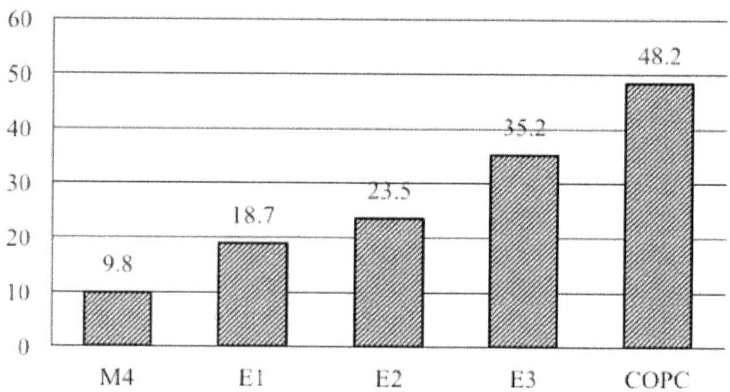

Figure 1. Increasing frequency of the gerund object from LME to LModE (per 10,000 words).

---

clauses have emerged as an additional structural option, extending their territory both at the expense of finite and infinitival clauses.

Iyeiri (2010: 7), referring to the "Great Complement Shift" propounded by Rohdenburg (2006: 159-160) analyses it as "most probably a combination of two different shifts: (a) the shift from *that*-clauses to *to*-infinitives, which the present study calls the **first complement shift**; and (b) the shift from *to*-infinitives to gerunds, which the present study calls **the second complement shift**."

On the other hand, the normed frequency of the gerundial constructions in the HC is almost the same as that in the other subcorpora, Penn1 and Penn2, as well as that in the PPCEME as a whole.[14] Thus, although it is only one third the size, the HC is nevertheless "extensive enough to show fairly reliable and consistent trends of development in a large number of topics" (Kytö/Rissanen 1993: 3-4), producing statistically significant results or at least "diagnostic" ones closely corresponding to those obtained from the expanded corpus. Such results tend to bear out Rissanen's (2000: 9) comment that, though the text extracts used in the HC are brief, "even a fairly short extract often gives a surprisingly accurate linguistic profile of the entire text".

2.2. Distribution of the six types of the gerundial constructions

Next, the distribution of the gerundial constructions in the three subcorpora of the PPCEME will be examined according to the six types, A1~A2 and B1~B4.

---

14 However, the extreme similarity of these results may not be due to the extent to which these two corpora have achieved "representativeness", but rather to the fact that, as explained in Section 1.2, the texts of Penn1 and Penn2 are mostly from material by the same authors and from the same editions as in the HC. The pairwise correlation coefficients between the corpora, calculated by means of the observed frequency in Table 2, are: +0.96 between HC and PPCEME, +0.99 between HC and Penn1, and +0.83 between HC and Penn2. Thus, the HC has a strong correlation with the Penn1 as well as the PPCEME as a whole, but it has a slightly weaker correlation with the Penn2, which contains more new material than the Penn1. It is possible that if sampling for the Penn1 and Penn2 subsets had been more independent of the initial HC text selection, less consistent results might have been observed.

Period	Subcorpus	A1	A2	B1	B2	B3	B4	Total
E1	Helsinki	9 (0.5)	4 (0.2)	116 (6.0)	134 (7.0)	109 (5.7)	10 (0.5)	382 (19.9)
	Penn1	6 (0.3)	10 (0.5)	103 (5.3)	124 (6.4)	103 (5.3)	10 (0.5)	356 (18.5)
	Penn2	4 (0.2)	2 (0.1)	105 (5.7)	116 (6.3)	82 (4.5)	13 (0.7)	322 (17.6)
	Subtotal	19 (0.3)	16 (0.3)	324 (5.7)	374 (6.6)	294 (5.2)	33 (0.6)	1,060 (18.7)
E2	Helsinki	2 (0.1)	8 (0.4)	66 (3.5)	149 (7.8)	189 (9.9)	16 (0.8)	430 (22.5)
	Penn1	11 (0.5)	4 (0.2)	64 (3.0)	150 (7.0)	242 (11.3)	18 (0.8)	489 (22.7)
	Penn2	12 (0.5)	7 (0.3)	103 (4.6)	207 (9.3)	189 (8.5)	39 (1.8)	557 (25.0)
	Subtotal	25 (0.4)	19 (0.3)	233 (3.7)	506 (8.1)	620 (9.9)	73 (1.2)	1,476 (23.5)
E3	Helsinki	6 (0.3)	7 (0.4)	18 (1.0)	86 (5.0)	352 (20.5)	103 (6.0)	572 (33.3)
	Penn1	5 (0.3)	6 (0.3)	23 (1.2)	102 (5.4)	479 (25.4)	95 (5.0)	710 (37.6)
	Penn2	2 (0.1)	3 (0.2)	23 (1.3)	106 (5.9)	415 (22.9)	74 (4.1)	623 (34.4)
	Subtotal	13 (0.2)	16 (0.3)	64 (1.2)	294 (5.4)	1,246 (23.0)	272 (5.0)	1,905 (35.2)

Table 3. Frequency distribution of the six types in the subcorpora of PPCEME (normed frequency per 10,000 words in parentheses).

Table 3 presents the frequency distribution of the gerund governing an object across the six types in the subcorpora of the PPCEME.[15] The numerical data (including both observed and normed frequencies) provide a clear picture of the rise and fall of these variant types in the course of the EModE period. Here it is to be noted that the PPCEME (=subtotals) and its subcorpora show an almost exactly parallel rise and fall of these types in the three time periods, as is visually evident from Figure 2. These results support Rissanen's (2000: 9) comment quoted in Section 2.1, and may be taken as further evidence that, as far as this

15 Where two or more gerunds are coordinated, sharing either an object, as in (a), or a determiner such as a definite article, as in (b), they are counted as two or more instances of the same type.

(a) (i) she shall then milke the Cowe boldly, and not leaue *stretching and straining of her teats* til not one drop of milke more wil come from them, (markham-e2-h) (two instances of Type B1)

(ii) but not in a Capacity of *serving and enriching his Country* any other way, (raleigh-e2-p1) (two instances of Type B3)

(b) (i) otherwise *the making, and mending of pens*, will be a very great hinderance, (brinskey-e2-p2) (two instances of Type B2)

(ii) and *the makeing and keeping such Registers* shall bee performed in such forme and methods (stat-1690-e3-p1) (two instances of Type B4)

A noun may also be coordinated with a gerundial construction, as in (c).

(c) (i) [...] the Summe of Tenne Poundes for *the Loane or Forbearinge of a Hundred Poundes* for one yere (state-1570-e2-p1) (1 instance of B2)

(ii) [...] the Duke [...] hath imagined and compassed *the Deposing and Death of the Queen's Majesty* [...] (Thoward2-e2-p2) (1 instance of B2).

stage of analysis is concerned, the HC is not "too small" to be as reliable a tool as the PPCEME, its expanded version.

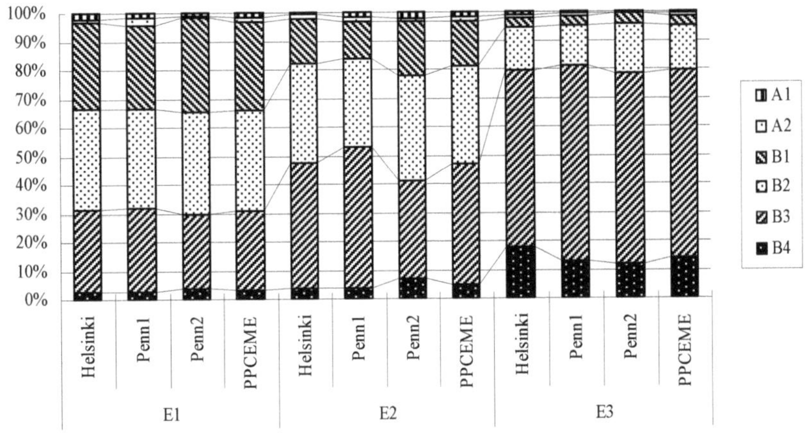

Figure 2. Distribution of the six types in the PPCEME and its subcorpora (%).

The texts of M4 (1420-1500) of the PPCME2 yield the following data: A1 (27 examples), A2 (29), B1 (121), B2 (47), B3 (26), B4 (4). The LModE texts (1710-1779) of the COPC yield the following counts: A1 (0), A2 (4), B1 (13), B2 (51), B3 (534), B4 (73).

When these findings from M4 and LModE are added to the findings from the PPCEME above, the changing distribution of the six types from the LME period down to the 18th century emerges as is seen in Figure 3. The figure clearly indicates that the quantitative expansion of the gerundial constructions continuing from ME down to LModE is mainly due to the rapidly increasing frequency of Type B3 (*reading the book*) (for further details see Section 5). Each of these trends will be illustrated with reference to retrieved examples of these variant constructions in later sections.

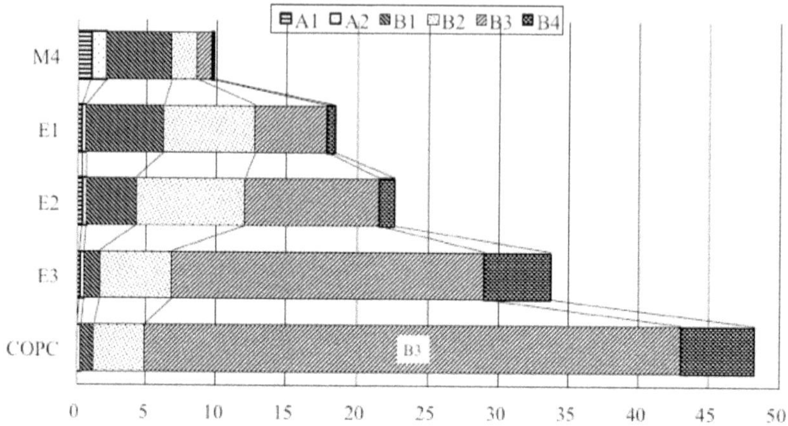

Figure 3. Rise and fall of the six types from LME to LModE (per 10,000 words).

2.3. Distribution of the gerundial constructions in terms of the prototypical text categories and the text genres

The PPCEME consists of the same text genres (which the HC calls "text types") as the original corpus: 18 genres are represented in E1 and E2; 16 in E3. In the HC these text genres are grouped into seven larger entities called "prototypical text categories" (Kytö 1993: 55), as listed below:

Statutory <STA>	---	Law <LAW>
Expository <EX>		Educational treatise <EDUC_TREAT> *
		Science, medicine <SCIENCE_MEDIC>
		Science, other <SCIENCE_OTHER>
Instruction religious <IR>	---	Sermon <SERMON>
Instruction secular <IS>		Educational treatise < EDUC_TREAT> *
		Handbook, other <HANDB_OTHER>
Narration imaginative <NI>	---	Fiction <FICTION>
Narration non-imaginative <NN>		Biography, autobiography <BIOGR_AUTO>
		Biography, other <BIOGR_OTHER>
		Diary, private <DIARY_PRIV>
		History <HISTORY>
		Travelogue <TRAVELOG>
None of the above <X>		Bible <BIBLE>
		Drama, comedy <DRAMA_COM>
		Letters, non-private <LET_NON-PRIV>
		Letters, private <LET_PRIV>
		Philosophy <PHILOSOPHY>
		Proceedings, trial <PROC_TRIAL>

**Note*: The genre 'Educational Treatise' is included within two categories, because the texts of this genre in E1 and E3 are coded as 'Instruction secular', and those in E2 'Expository.'

Furthermore, the HC provides each text with a number of parameters comprising a set of two or more values, e.g. <W='relation to spoken language': 'WRITTEN,' 'SPEECH-BASED,' 'SCRIPT'>, and <I='setting': 'FORMAL,' 'INFORMAL,' 'X'>. These parameters will help to conduct a variationist investigation. These categories and parameters are tentatively used in the present analysis, though these do not seem to have been openly adopted in the PPCEME (in that the manual's section on "Philological Information" classifies texts from new material only into text genres).

The retrieved examples of the gerundial constructions under scrutiny can be grouped into the prototypical text categories shown, along with their text genres, in Table 4.

PTC	Text Genre	E1		E2		E3		Total		**Ratio**
		Raw Freq	Normed Freq	Raw Freq	Normed Freq	Raw Freq	Normed Freq	Raw Freq	Normed Freq	E3/E1
STA	LAW	**167**	**45.1**	**202**	**54.3**	**310**	**74.8**	**679**	**58.7**	**1.7**
IS	EDUC_TREAT	159	49.1	--	--	241	55.9	400	53.0	1.1
	HANDB_OTHER	96	30.0	161	42.9	174	48.4	431	40.9	1.6
	Subtotal	**255**	**39.6**	**161**	**42.9**	**415**	**52.5**	**831**	**45.9**	**1.3**
EX	EDUC_TREAT	--	--	166	47.6	--	--	166	47.6	--
	SCIENCE_OTHER	22	10.5	41	19.9	161	44.8	224	28.9	4.3
	SCIENCE_MEDIC	23	12.0	71	32.8	--	--	94	23.0	--
	Subtotal	**45**	**11.2**	**278**	**36.0**	**161**	**44.8**	**484**	**31.6**	**4.0**
IR	SERMON	**69**	**22.5**	**51**	**16.2**	**75**	**23.7**	**195**	**20.8**	**1.1**
NN	BIOGR_OTHER	30	18.0	55	36.7	84	44.6	169	33.5	2.5
	HISTORY	49	13.7	93	29.2	140	38.8	282	27.2	2.8
	DIARY_PRIV	101	24.5	59	12.6	147	41.6	307	24.8	1.7
	TRAVELOG	36	8.2	51	11.3	42	12.8	129	10.6	1.6
	BIOGR_AUTO	22	11.7	3	7.3	11	6.2	36	8.9	0.5
	Subtotal	**238**	**15.2**	**261**	**18.2**	**424**	**30.1**	**923**	**21.0**	**19.8**
NI	FICTION	**40**	**11.1**	**42**	**10.8**	**72**	**19.2**	**154**	**13.7**	**1.7**
X	LET_NON-PRIV	63	26.1	56	32.9	140	71.3	259	42.6	2.7
	PROC_TRIAL	54	33.8	245	31.5	38	8.7	337	24.6	0.3
	LET PRIV	38	11.5	81	19.7	121	28.6	240	20.6	2.5
	PHILOSOPHY	43	13.4	37	17.0	74	25.2	154	18.5	1.9
	DRAMA_COM	18	5.5	32	8.6	75	18.6	125	11.4	3.4
	BIBLE	30	4.6	30	4.4	--	--	60	4.5	--
	Subtotal	**246**	**12.1**	**481**	**18.3**	**448**	**25.6**	**1175**	**18.3**	**2.1**
	Total	1,060	18.7	1,476	23.5	1.905	35.2	4,441	25.6	1.9

Note: All the prototypical text categories except X are arranged in descending order according to the normed frequency in column Total, and so are the text genres in their categories.
Table 4. Distribution of gerundial constructions according to prototypical text categories (PTC) and text genres in PPCEME (normed frequency per 10,000 words).

The frequency data in this table reveal that in EModE there is a wide variation in the frequency of the gerundial constructions in terms of both the prototypical text categories and the text genres.

Regarding the prototypical text categories, STA (consisting of the text genre LAW only) provides the highest frequency over the three time periods, while NI (consisting of FICTION only) shows the lowest frequency.

Among the more specific text genres, some genres (such as LAW, EDUC_TREAT, LET_NON-PRIV and HANDB_OTHER) yield a very high frequency, and some others (such as BIBLE, BIOGR_AUTO, DRAMA_COM and FICTION) a very low frequency.

According to my examination, the texts labeled as 'WRITTEN' yield a higher frequency in the use of the gerundial constructions than those labeled as 'SPEECH-BASED' and 'SCRIPT' in the E3 time period of the PPCEME: 41.8 vs. 8.0 vs. 20.8 (per 10,000 words). Additionally, 'FORMAL' yields a higher frequency than 'INFORMAL': 41.3 vs. 26.7.

LAW and LET_NON-PRIV are labeled as 'FORMAL' and 'WRITTEN', EDUC_TREAT and HANDB_OTHER as 'WRITTEN', while DRAMA_COM are labeled as 'INFORMAL' and 'SCRIPT', FICTION as 'WRITTEN' and 'INFORMAL' and BIOGR_AUTO in E3 as 'SPEECH_BASED'.

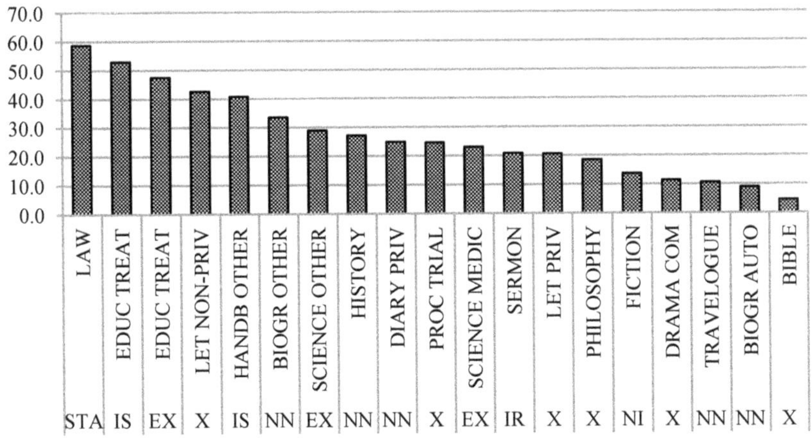

Figure 4. Distribution of gerundial constructions according to text genres (in descending order according to the normed frequency per 10,000 words listed in the Total column of Table 4).

As can be seen in Figure 4, the syntactic or stylistic association or correlation between the text genres and the prototypical text categories defined on extralinguistic criteria is not clear from the frequency data of the gerund, a syntactic feature.[16] In this figure all the genres are arranged in descending order according to the normed frequency given in the Total column in Table 4. This arrangement reveals a wide discrepancy in frequency even among genres from the same prototypical text categories, such as EX, and NN.

16 The cluster analysis for the data retrieved from the HC in Saito (1993) produced a similar result.

Diachronically, in all the text genres but two (BIOGR_AUTO, PROC_TRIAL), the gerundial constructions under scrutiny increase in frequency in the course of EModE, reflecting the general increasing tendency already noted in previous sections.[17] The column 'Ratio' in the table indicates that there is also a wide difference in the ratio of increase (the normed frequency in E3 vs. that in E1)[18] among the text genres, ranging from 4.3 times (10.5→44.8) in SCIENCE_OTHER, down to 0.3 times, i.e. decreasing (33.8→8.7) in PROC_TRIAL. Interestingly enough, the frequency and the ratio of increase do not necessarily go in parallel. For instance, LAW with the highest frequency among the genres reaches only 1.7 times as high a frequency in E3 as in E1 (45.1→74.8), which is below the average (1.9 times); on the other hand, DRAMA_COM, with a very low frequency, yields a remarkable relative increase, with an E3 frequency 3.4 times as high as in E1 (5.5→18.6).

2.4. Distribution of the variant gerundial constructions by text genre

The above evidence seems to indicate that the expansion of the use of the gerundial constructions is especially associated with genres representing informal and colloquial language. Therefore, a preliminary attempt to scrutinize the difference in frequency among the genres in terms of the variant types of the gerund will be made here in this section.

---

17 Fanego (1996: 118) says, "the use of gerunds increases considerably from the sixteenth to the seventeenth centuries, and especially in E3. Trials, Sermons, and Statutes do not share in this tendency." The discrepancy between her evidence and mine comes from the fact that her survey covers all gerunds in the selected texts (317,621 words) out of the EModE section (551.000 words) of the HC, whereas I address only the constructions of the gerund+object in the PPCEME (1.7 million words). In my data BIOGR_AUTO and PROC_TRIAL do not share in this increasing tendency, but LAW does, and marginally also SERMON. Nevalainen/Raumolin-Brunberg (1993: 65-66) suggest that corpus users should be attentive to genre drift in EModE. For example, the parameter coding for BIOGR_AUTO changes from <W: WRITTEN> in E1 and E2 to <W: SPEECH-BASED> in E3, which information helps to understand the decreasing tendency of this genre.

18 Two genres (BIBLE and SCIENCE_MEDIC) are excluded from this calculation because they lack texts in E3.

Tables A~C in Appendix 1 at the end of the present paper show the overall frequency distribution of the six variant types in relation to the text genres in the three time periods of the PPCEME. Section 2.2 has already presented a general picture of the rise and fall of the six types, in which the older types, nominal gerunds, Types A1, A2, B1 and B2 continue to lose ground over the course of EModE owing to the rapid development of a verbal gerund, Type B3 (*reading the book*). The purpose of the present section is to examine the development of Type B3 in EModE in terms of text genres, and in addition, to find out the reason why the high overall frequency observed in LAW does not occur with a correspondingly high rate of increase. Accordingly, only the data concerning Types B1~B4 in Tables A~C are used here. For this purpose I have chosen the following 9 genres from Table 4 in the previous section according to the column Ratio (E3/E1): SCIENCE_OTHER, DRAMA_COM and HISTORY out of the top group, PHILOSOPHY, FICTION and LAW out of the average group, and EDUC_TREAT, SERMON and PROC_TRIAL out of the bottom group.

Table 5 shows the distribution of the four types in the PPCEME across the genres. A study of the table along with Figure 5 shows that the history of the gerund governing a direct object in the two hundred years of EModE is that of the expansion of B3 (and also B4) at the cost of B1 and B2, but that synchronically as well as diachronically there is a considerable discrepancy in the extent of their expansion among the genres.

Period	Text genre	Object-postposed gerund				Total
		B1	B2	B3	B4	
	EDUC_TREAT	16.0	30.8	49.4	3.8	100%
	SERMON	26.1	24.6	47.8	1.4	100%
	SCIENCE_OTHER	31.8	22.7	45.5	0.0	100%
	PROC_TRIAL	11.1	42.6	38.9	7.4	100%
E1	FICTION	35.9	23.1	35.9	5.1	100%
	DRAMA_COM	50.0	8.3	33.3	8.3	100%
	PHILOSOPHY	53.7	22.0	22.0	2.4	100%
	HISTORY	37.8	46.7	13.3	2.2	100%
	LAW	39.6	45.7	12.8	1.8	100%
	E1: Mean	29.9	34.6	32.4	3.2	100%
	SCIENCE_OTHER	0.0	2.4	97.6	0.0	100%
	HISTORY	7.6	22.8	68.5	1.1	100%
	PHILOSOPHY	11.8	23.5	61.8	2.9	100%
	DRAMA_COM	7.7	23.1	57.7	11.5	100%
E2	EDUC_TREAT	7.9	32.7	56.4	3.0	100%
	SERMON	15.7	35.3	47.1	2.0	100%
	FICTION	20.0	35.0	45.0	0.0	100%
	PROC_TRIAL	14.9	36.1	40.2	8.7	100%
	LAW	38.8	42.3	14.3	4.6	100%
	E2: Mean	17.4	33.0	45.0	4.6	100%
	PHILOSOPHY	0.0	9.5	89.2	1.4	100%
	FICTION	1.4	5.6	87.5	5.6	100%
	DRAMA_COM	4.1	6.8	83.6	5.5	100%
	EDUC_TREAT	3.4	15.6	75.9	5.1	100%
E3	SCIENCE_OTHER	4.3	20.5	68.3	6.8	100%
	HISTORY	1.4	8.7	67.4	22.5	100%
	PROC_TRIAL	0.0	11.1	66.7	22.2	100%
	SERMON	0.0	24.7	65.8	9.6	100%
	LAW	6.5	27.1	44.5	21.9	100%
	E3: Mean	3.5	17.4	66.7	12.4	100%
Total		14.1	26.4	51.7	7.7	100%

Note: The genres are arranged in each time period in descending order according to the frequency (%) in column B3.

Table 5. Distribution of Types B1~B4 according to the text genres in PPCEME (%).

As expected, the genres indicating informality and orality (PHILOSOPHY, DRAMA_COM and FICTION) are ranked in the top group by percentage of B3. The text for PHILOSOPHY is an English translation of Boethius' *De Consolatione Philosophiae,* which is a dialogue described with the parameter <J: 'INTERACTIVE'>. Conversely, the <'FORMAL'> genres of

PROC_TRIAL <'SPEECH-BASED'> and SERMON <'SCRIPT'> are ranked in the bottom group. These results suggest that comparatively nominal gerunds tend to occur more frequently in 'formal' genres than in 'informal' ones, whereas verbal gerunds tend to be more frequent in 'informal' genres. Interestingly, in contrast to verbal gerunds, nomino-verbal gerunds can easily occur in 'formal' genres (for details see Section 5).

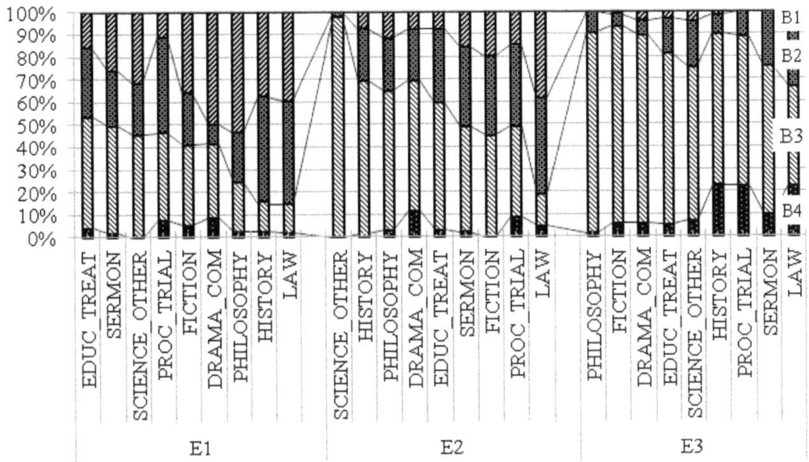

Figure 5. Distribution of Types B1~B4 across the genres in PPCEME.

The most notable feature of the data in Table 5 is that LAW yields the lowest percentage for B3 among the examined genres in all three time periods, and preserves the old nominal gerunds, B1 and B2. Therefore, this evidence proves the language of LAW to have already become old-fashioned and stilted in E3. However, LAW also shows relatively high use of B4, an emerging nomino-verbal gerund. About this characteristic of the language of LAW, Nevalainen/Raumolin-Brunberg (1993: 68) say, "As successors of the earliest national standard, fifteenth-century Chancery English, legal language and official correspondence have been regarded as representatives of the standard norm at the beginning of the sixteenth century. [...] It seems, however, that this type of official language soon lost its norm status and became a special language."

In order to investigate thoroughly the syntactic development of the gerund, it is necessary to examine more closely the relationship between the text genres and the variant types of the gerund. However, investigation at the necessary level of detail will have to be left for another paper. With the exception of one revealing result to be presented in Section 3.3.1 (in Table 13), subsequent sections will mostly investigate the gerundial constructions in question without paying attention to the distribution across text genres.

3. The position of the gerund object

3.1. Object-preposed vs. object-postposed

It was pointed out in Section 1.3 that in LME the object-preposed gerundial constructions ('O + V-*ing*') were already being replaced by the object-postposed gerundial constructions ('V-*ing*+O'). The statistical data extracted from the PPCEME in Table 6 show that in EModE the object-preposed constructions are vanishingly rare in comparison to the object-postposed constructions throughout the EModE period. The object-postposed constructions are already established in EModE as almost the only way of expressing the gerund object. Here it is to be noted that the establishment of the word order of the "actor-action-goal" construction (SVO) by the middle of the 15th century seems to have much to do with this decline of the object-preposed construction.[19]

	Object-preposed	Object-postposed	Total
E1 (1500-1569)	35 (3.3%)	1,025 (96.7%)	1,060 (100%)
E2 (1570-1639)	44 (3.0%)	1,432 (97.0%)	1,476 (100%)
E3 (1640-1710)	29 (1.5%)	1,876 (98.5%)	1,905 (100%)

$X^2(2df) = 11.899, p = 0.003$.

Table 6. Object-preposed vs. object-postposed gerundial constructions in PPCEME.

The object-preposed constructions account for 22.0% of the cases in M4 of the PPCME2, but only 0.6% in the COPC.

19 Concerning the establishment of SVO, see e.g. Saito (1974).

In Table 6 and subsequent tables, the statistical data of the PPCEME are not divided according to the three subcorpora (directories). Instead, for comparison's sake, the corresponding data in the HC (Helsinki directories) are given in Appendix 2 at the end of the present paper. (For example, Table 6′ in Appendix 2, corresponding to Table 6 here, shows that a similar pattern obtains in the HC data, but owing to the smaller sample size, the difference does not reach statistical significance.)

3.2. Object-preposed gerundial constructions

As shown in Section 1.4, the object-preposed constructions of the gerund have two types, 'Genitive (Pro)noun+Gerund' (Type A1: *the book's reading*) and 'Accusative Noun + Gerund' (Type A2: *(the) book reading*). However (as seen in Table 6 above), the object-preposed constructions are too low in frequency for any further breakdown to give conclusive results. At this level of analysis, even the PPCEME is not large enough for differences to reach significance (and HC even less so: see Tables 7′ and 8′ in Appendix 2). Accordingly, chi-squared tests on both Tables 7 and 8 below return statistically nonsignificant results. Nevertheless, the data in Table 8 is consistent with the statement by Jespersen (1909-1949: V. 8.4_1) that construction A1 "is rare in ModE and is there generally found with personal (possessive) pronouns only".

	A1	A2	Total
E1	19 (54.3%)	16 (45.7%)	35 (100%)
E2	25 (56.8%)	19 (43.2%)	44 (100%)
E3	13 (44.8%)	16 (55.2%)	29 (100%)

X^2 (2*df*) = 1.056, *p* = 0.590 (nonsignificant).

Table 7. Distribution of A1 and A2 in PPCEME.

	Noun	Pronoun	Total
E1	2 (10.5%)	17 (85.5%)	19 (100%)
E2	0 (0.0%)	25 (100%)	25 (100%)
E3	4 (30.8%)	9 (69.2%)	13 (100%)

Note: Insufficient data for a reliable chi-squared test (expected frequency < 5 for all three Noun cells).

Table 8. Distribution of A1 classified by word classes of the gerund object in PPCEME.

Type A1 and Type A2 are illustrated below:

(1) <A1> nouns as objects:

a. that Socrates meaneth not this of *childrens teaching*, but of som other higher learnyng, (asch-e1-p1)

b. When I was sent for to my *Mother's Burying*, I left him and Madam Dormer at Dinner, (oates-e3-h)

(2) <A1> pronouns as objects:

a. our Savyor Criste was lede from the howse of Pilate vnto the place of *hys Crucifying*. (torkingt-e1-h)

b. Shall we send that foolish Carion, Mist. Quickly to him, and excuse *his throwing* into the water, […] ? (shakesp-e2-p2)

c. A bill passed in both houses for raising all the militia, and for *their keeping* together for six weeks, (burnetcha-e3-p2)

(3) <A2> nouns as objects:

a. to optayne a gloryous name by feates of warre or armes, or by the meanes of *peace makyng*. (boethco-e1-p2)

b. what think we so much of enlarging fame, & *name promoting*? (boethel-e2-p1)

c. and she shall be saved in *child-bearing*, if she be found in faith and righteousness. (jetaylor-e3-p1)

These examples of A1 bring to mind Visser's remark (1946: Pt. 1. §119) that "The frequent occurrence of the construction [sc. *Their putting to death*] in More proves that it was a regular idiom in the language of his time"; but the rare occurrence of the construction in the PPCEME and the predominance of the object-postposed constructions do not seem to endorse his statement.

Regarding Type A2, it is often difficult to distinguish gerundial constructions from compound nouns, as the examples in (3) show. As Tajima (1985: 49) says, even in late ME it was "hard to decide […] on which occasions the noun and the gerund form a compound or not."

Owing to the limited data available, no further analysis of the object-preposed types of gerundial constructions will be attempted in the present paper.

3.3. Object-postposed gerundial constructions

Table 9 provides the frequency distribution of Types B1~B4 of the object-postposed gerundial constructions in the three time periods of the PPCEME.

	B1	B2	B3	B4	Total
E1 (1500-1569)	324 (31.6)	374 (36.5)	294 (28.7)	33 (3.2)	1,025 (100%)
E2 (1570-1639)	233 (16.3)	506 (35.3)	620 (43.3)	73 (5.1)	1,432 (100%)
E3 (1640-1710)	64 (3.4)	294 (15.7)	1,246 (66.4)	272 (14.5)	1,876 (100%)

X^2 (6*df*) = 869.643, $p \ll 0.001$.

Table 9. Distribution of the types of object-postposed constructions in the time periods of PPCEME.

As shown in section 1.4, the four types, B1 (*reading of the book*), B2 (*the reading of the book*), B3 (*reading the book*) and B4 (*the reading the book*) in Table 9 can be grouped into two classes: +*of* (B1 and B2, both nominal gerunds), and –*of* (B3, a verbal gerund; B4, a nomino-verbal gerund). Table 10 shows the frequency distribution of both groups of gerundial constructions.

	+*of*	–*of*	Total
E1 (1500-1569)	698 (68.1)	327 (31.9)	1,025 (100%)
E2 (1570-1639)	739 (51.6)	693 (48.4)	1,432 (100%)
E3 (1640-1710)	358 (19.1)	1,518 (80.9)	1,876 (100%)

X^2 (2*df*) = 747.609, $p \ll 0.001$.

Table 10. +*of* vs. –*of* gerundial constructions in the time periods of PPCEME.

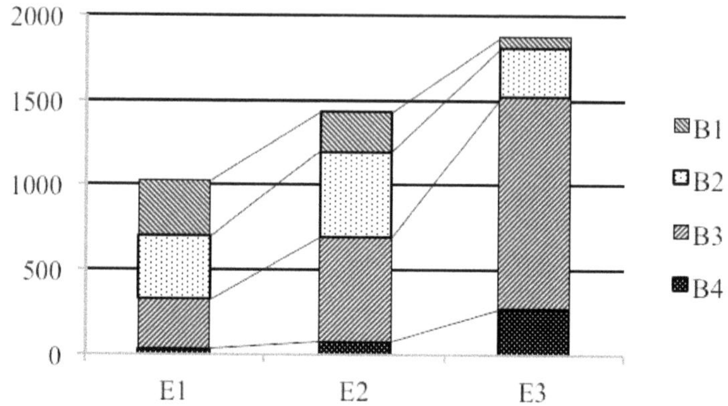

Figure 6. Distribution of the four types of object-postposed constructions in PPCEME.

The highly statistically significant trends seen in Tables 9 and 10, and graphed in Figure 6, provide a clear picture of the rise and fall of the four types of the object-postposed gerundial constructions during the EModE period. The main points of significance are as follows:

a) First of all, the history of the gerund with its object in EModE is that of rivalry between the *+of* group (nominal gerunds) and the *–of* group (verbal and nomino-verbal gerunds), the balance shifting from the former to the latter over time.
b) The nominal gerunds, Type B1 (*reading of the book*) and Type B2 (*the reading of the book*), being the prevalent types in LME, still keep that prevalence in the earliest stage of EModE, though a verbal gerund, Type B3 (*reading the book*) is already almost catching up with them. The situation in E1, the earliest time period, seems to be that Types B1 and B2 are used with almost equal frequency (31.6% and 36.5% respectively), with Type B3 only slightly behind (at 28.7%).
c) Both of these nominal gerunds, however, suffer a conspicuous setback in the later time periods. Type B1 shows an earlier fall from 31.6% in E1 to 16.3% in E2, and virtually disappears during E3.[20] On the other hand, Type B2 continues to hold ground

20 De Smet (2008a, 2008b) offers an explanation for the decline of B1 in relation to B2 and B3 along the following lines: The essential difference between B1 (*reading of the book*) and B2 (*the reading of the book*) lies in the absence or

in E2, but then records a decline of 50% in relative terms from 35.3% in E2 to 15.7% in E3.

d) The verbalization of the gerunds constantly expands during the EModE period, and the verbal type B3 (*reading the book*) gains overwhelming predominance over the nominal types in E3, being used in 66.4% of the cases.

e) Type B4 (*the reading the book*) with mixed character (both nominal and verbal) is not common during the earlier two time periods of EModE, being used in only 3.2% and 5.1% of the cases respectively. However, it gains considerable ground during E3; this phenomenon will be addressed again in the following section.

f) The increase in frequency of the object-postposed gerundial constructions from E1 to E3 is definitely due to the rapid growth and predominance of Type B3, a verbal gerund, as vividly shown in Figure 3 (in Section 2.2).

The same trends are evident in the HC data (Tables 9′ and 10′ in Appendix 2). Figure 7 graphs the figures from the HC alongside those from the PPCEME. The figure confirms the close similarity of the two corpora, which is inarguably a natural result of the PPCEME compilers' policy of expanding the HC as explained in 1.2.[21]

---

presence of the definite article, which expresses its usual function of marking referents as 'uniquely identifiable'; therefore, B1, the indefinite gerund without *the*, is functionally in competition not with B2, the definite gerund with *the*, but with B3 (*reading the book*), an emerging verbal gerund with more syntactic flexibility, so that B1 is gradually supplanted by B3 during the course of EModE, while B2 continues to be used.

Against Fanego's (2006b) claim (albeit with reference to B4) that "*the* was basically a semantically empty grammatical marker or complementizer serving to license the *ing* clause at a time when subjectless verbal gerunds in argument positions (i.e. as subjects, objects, or predicatives) were probably not yet fully acceptable", De Smet argues that "the conclusion that the definite article, as used with the gerund in the early 16th century, is not a functionally empty element can account for the historical fact that, as the verbalisation of the gerund proceeded, the use of definite gerund constructions was nevertheless maintained."

21 Correlation coefficients for observed frequencies between the HC and the PPCEME are: (E1) +0.999, (E2) +0.999, (E3) +0.996. Nishimura (2006),

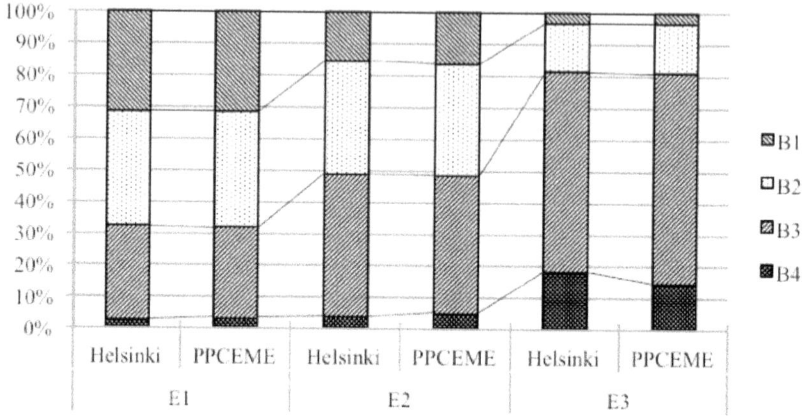

Figure 7. Distribution of the object-postposed types in PPCEME and HC (percentages).

The evidence from the COPC in Table 11 below shows that the frequency distribution of these types in the latter half of the 18th century is approaching the situation seen in Present-day English, apart from the continued presence of Type B4.[22]

---

using the PPCME2 and the PPCEME to investigate the rise and fall of the intensive adverbs *full, right,* and *very* from LME to EModE, found similarly parallel distributions of the adverbs among the three subcorpora of the PPCEME, indicating their essential homogeneity, and further corroborating Rissanen's (2000: 9) positive verdict on the HC samples (cf. Section 2.1).

22 The statistics in Saito (1972: 175f), based on H. Craik (ed. 1893), *English Prose: Selections* (Macmillan, 5 vols.), show more categorically that in the late 18th century the gerundial constructions under discussion were "polarized into two types of distinctly different character, i.e. Type II (=B2: *the reading of the book*) and Type III (=B3: *reading the book*), the balance inclining sharply toward the latter type."

Period	I [=B1]	II [=B2]	III [=B3]	IV [=B4]	Total
1501-1550	34 (27.0)	44 (34.9)	46 (36.5)	2 (1.6)	126 (100%)
1551-1600	24 (11.5)	67(32.2)	107 (51.5)	10 (4.8)	208 (100%)
1601-1650	11 (4.4)	82 (32.1)	146 (57.7)	14 (5.5)	253 (100%)
1651-1700	8 (2.3)	55 (15.4)	262 (73.4)	32 (8.9)	357 (100%)
1701-1750	6 (1.9)	25 (7.9)	277 (87.1)	10 (3.1)	318 (100%)
1751-1800	0 (0)	6 (1.7)	338 (98.3)	0 (0)	344 (100%)

Note: The +S types (<IIb> *my reading of the book*, <IVb> *my reading the book*) are excluded from these counts. In the latest period (1751-1800), only five instances are recorded for Type IVb (=B4), and none for Type IIb (=B2).

Period	B1	B2	B3	B4	Total
1710–1749	13 (3.0)	41 (9.6)	330 (76.9)	45 (10.5)	429 (100%)
1750–1779	0 (0.0)	10 (4.1)	204 (84.3)	28 (11.6)	242 (100%)

X^2 $(3df) = 14.547, p = 0.002$.

Table 11. Occurrences of gerundial constructions B1~B4 in COPC.

Concerning the decline of Type B2, Visser (1966: §1124) notes a tendency to use deverbal nouns rather than nominal gerunds in *-ing* form:

> [...] unless the aspect of duration has to be expressed, constructions of the type 'the *loss* of,' 'the *improvement* of,' 'the *realisation* of,' 'the *maintenance* of,' 'the *erection* of,' 'the *suppression* of' are nowadays preferred to constructions of the type 'the *losing* of,' 'the *improving* of,' 'the *realising* of,' 'the *maintaining* of,' 'the *erecting* of,' 'the *suppressing* of.'

The same tendency is presented by Quirk *et al.* (1985: §17.54) in the form of a "gradience" scale. This phenomenon may be seen as the ultimate result of the nominalization of nominal gerunds, in contrast to the increasing verbalization of verbal gerunds.[23]

---

23 Umesaki (1994) provides relevant statistical data on the situation in 20th-century English, using a database consisting of categories J, A and K from the LOB Corpus, and S1 and S2 from the LLC, totaling 446,000 words. She classifies the retrieved examples into the following types:
(a1) *-tion/ment** + *of* +O (e.g. *the establishment of the base*)
 * Derivative nouns except for nouns with an *-ing* suffix
(a2) Vroot+*of*+O (e.g. *the use of this machine*);
(b) V-*ing*+*of*+O (e.g. *the breaking of bridges*);
(c) V-*ing*+O (e.g. *fulfilling the role*).
Umesaki's figures for the functional distribution of these forms are reproduced below:

	(a1)	(a2)	(b)	(c)	Total
Subject	209 (25.8%)	56 (23.1%)	41 (25.6%)	12 (1.0%) + 9 (0.7%)*	327
Object	158 (15.5%)	52 (21.5%)	33 (20.6%)	114 (9.3%)	357
Complement	51 (6.3%)	28 (11.6%)	7 (4.4%)	2 (0.2%)	88
Adverbial**	317 (39.1%)	86 (36.5%)	54 (33.8%)	778 (63.3%)	1235
Postmodifier**	75 (9.3%)	20 (8.3%)	25 (15.6%)	314 (25.5%)	434
Total	810 (100%)	242 (100%)	160 (100%)	1229 (100%)	2441

*extraposition **as prepositional phrases

These results corroborate Visser's observation: Form (b) (=B2) is relatively infrequent, being supplanted by Forms (a1) and (a2). Moreover, out of 160 instances of Form (b), 154 are cases in which verbs have no other derivative form than the *-ing* suffix. N.B. even in 20th-century English, Form (c) (=B3)

These four types of gerundial constructions in the PPCEME are illustrated below:

(4) <B1>

a. and co~stantly vsed, would not onely take wholly away this butcherlie feare in *making of latines*, (asch-e1-h)

b. She, they say, is religious and discreet, and very hamsome in *dooing of any thinge*; (harley-e2-p1)

c. The best way of *propagating of them* is, in November to lay a Branch of that Years growth into the Earth, (langf-e3-h)

(5) <B2>

a. Also that the chiefest capitaines shuld be sent, with [*sic*] with them, to *the strengthening of the frontieres* of Scoteland. (edward-e1-h)

b. and that with such shouting, and applause of the vulgar sort, as if it had beene *the sacking of some hostile city*. (hayward-e2-p1)

c. and wee doe Declare that we will Signe no Letters for *the granting of any Money or Lands* or Releasing or abating any Rents (charles-1670-e3-p2)

(6) <B3>

a. I wolde god this sentence were alwaies printed in the herte of the kyng in *chosynge hys wyfe*, and in al hys officers. (latimer-e1-h)

b. which surcharge neuerthelesse is not to be remedied by *making no more bookes*, but by *making more good books*, (bacon-e2-h)

c. And be it enacted that noe Tax for *dreyneing or preserveing the said Fenns* shall at any tyme hereafter be taxed or leavyed at any other tyme (stat-1670-e3-p2)

(7) <B4>

a. Semblable ordre will I ensue in *the fourmynge the gentill wittes* of noble mennes children, (elyot-e1-p2)

b. His Purpose was to go into Flanders, and into Spain, for *the obtaining the aforesaid Money*; (raleigh-e2-h)

c. a very extraordinary thing happened, that contributed more than any other thing to *the establishing the belief* of all this evidence. (burnetcha-e3-h)

---

is largely confined to prepositional-object functions, and occurs only rarely as the subject of a clause (cf. Section 5 of the present paper).

3.4. The rivalry between Type B2 and Type B4

Concerning the rivalry of Type B2 (*the reading of the book*) and Type B4 (*the reading the book*), Visser (1966: §1124) makes the following remark:

> [...] from the beginning of the fourteenth century to the end of the nineteenth century constructions with *of* and those without *of* before the complement of a form in *-ing* preceded by *the* were used side by side – after 1500 with almost equal frequency – [...]

However, other researchers have cast doubt on the accuracy of this description. Tajima (1985: 79-80) calls it "questionable" on the grounds that the gerund governing a direct object was still in embryo in late ME; and Fanego (1996: 133-134) labels it "clearly incorrect" on the basis of data extracted from the HC. Accordingly, the purpose of the present section is to assess the validity of Visser's remark. Although these two types are preceded by a variety of determiners, Visser's copious citations are limited to examples with the definite article *the.* Therefore, only instances with *the* are retrieved here, in order to see this rivalry from the same viewpoint as Visser. The statistical evidence yielded by the PPCEME is shown in Table 12.

The tabulation does not confirm his remark, because no time period sees the two types used with "almost equal frequency." Contrary to Visser's assertion, in E1 (1500-1569) and E2 (1570-1639) Type B4 (*the reading the book*) is still very rare, in sharp contrast to Type B2 (*the reading of the book*), as Fanego (1996: 134) also points out. It is true that Type B4 gains considerable ground during E3 (1640-1710), but even in this time period, and even limiting our attention to cases with *the* as the determiner, it falls short of reaching "almost equal frequency", constituting only 37.7% of cases as opposed to 62.3% with Type B2. Data from the HC (Table 12′ in Appendix 2) shows much the same results.

	B2	B4	Total
E1 (1500-1569)	331 (94.6)	19 (5.4)	350 (100%)
E2 (1570-1639)	443 (91.3)	42 (8.7)	485 (100%)
E3 (1640-1710)	276 (62.3)	167 (37.7)	443 (100%)

X^2 (2*df*) = 183.846, $p \ll 0.001$.

Table 12. B2 vs. B4 with determiner *the* in the time periods of PPCEME.

Nevertheless, the breakdown of the statistics of these instances in E3 according to the text genres of the PPCEME reveals a great degree of textual variation within this time period, as shown in Table 13. In about one third out of the 16 text genres Type B4 is more frequent than, or almost as frequent as, Type B2. This result seems to endorse the remainder of Visser's remark, which continues as follows:

> [...] and that the choice between the two patterns was largely, if not exclusively, a question of style.

It seems therefore, that Visser's description cannot be wholly discarded as invalid; rather, "after 1500" should be replaced by "after the mid-seventeenth century."

At this level of detail, with results broken down by text category, the HC is "too small" to produce sufficient instances for conclusive results; nevertheless, it presents much the same picture (see Table 13′ in Appendix 2).

Text Genre	B2	B4	Total
Biography, other	8 (38.1)	13 (61.9)	21 (100%)
History	12 (40.0)	18 (60.0)	30 (100%)
Handbook, other	12 (52.2)	11 (47.8)	23 (100%)
Travelogue	7 (53.8)	6 (46.2)	13 (100%)
Letters, non-private	18 (54.5)	15 (45.5)	33 (100%)
Law	83 (56.1)	65 (43.9)	148 (100%)
Letters, private	14 (63.6)	8 (36.4)	22 (100%)
Science, other	32 (74.4)	11 (25.6)	43 (100%)
Diary, private	22 (75.9)	7 (24.1)	29 (100%)
Educational treatise	30 (78.9)	8 (21.1)	38 (100%)
Proceedings, trials	4 (80.0)	1 (20.0)	5 (100%)
Sermon	18 (81.8)	4 (18.2)	22 (100%)
Philosophy	7 (100)	0 (0.0)	7 (100%)
Drama, comedy	4 (100)	0 (0.0)	4 (100%)
Fiction	4 (100)	0 (0.0)	4 (100%)
Biography, autobiography	1 (100)	0 (0.0)	1 (100%)
Total	276 (62.3)	167 (37.7)	443 (100%)

Note: Genres are arranged in descending order according to the percentages of Type B4 instances.

Table 13. B2 vs. B4 (with *the*) in E3 across text genres in PPCEME.

Regarding the same rivalry in LModE, especially in the 18th century, the frequency data in Fanego (2006b: 102)[24] show that B4 (*the reading the book*) occurs more frequently than B2 (*the reading of the book*) in the early 18th century, but that B4 begins to decline in the latter part of the same century. It can be affirmed, therefore, that the time span in which B4 was widely used is much shorter than Visser asserts. Figure 8 shows the rivalry between Type B2 and Type B4 from LME (no example of B4 with *the*) through EModE down to the 19th century.

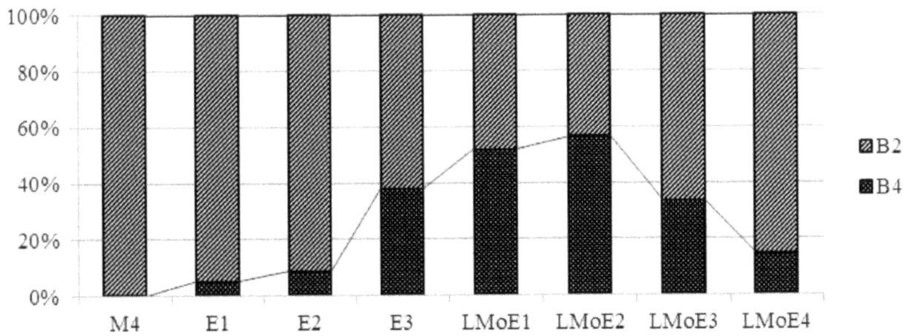

Figure 8. Rivalry between B2 and B4 (Det=*the*) from LME to the 19th century. LMoE1=1700-1726; LMoE2=1732-1757; LMoE3=1761-1797; LMoE4=1850-1879.

Concerning the decline of Type B4 (*the reading the book*), Visser (1966: §1124), citing comments from various grammarians of the 18th and 19th centuries, observes:

> The decline in frequency of the form without *of* seems to be ascribable to its being pilloried as solecistic by a number of prescriptive grammarians, who, for once, appear to have been to a large extent successful.

---

24 As part of a larger table, Fanego (2006b: 102) provides the following relevant frequency data for these two types, retrieved from a corpus of British English (1640-1879). The decline of Type B4 occurs in LModE3, coinciding with the rise of the prescriptive grammarians represented by Robert Lowth.

Period	*the* V*ing* NP	*the* N*ing of*-phrase
LModE1 (1700-1726)	29	27
LModE2 (1732-1757)	27	21
LModE3 (1761-1797)	9	18
LModE4 (1850-1879)	6	35

This observation has set off various arguments and counter-proposals as to the possible explanations of this linguistic change. For instance, Denison (1998: 271f), in support of an argument that internal linguistic factors are responsible for the decline of B4, quotes at length van der Wurff (1993), who "doubts that Visser's explanation is adequate, since the cited grammarians are not unanimously condemnatory". By contrast, Fanego (2006b) agrees with Visser that "the influence of Lowth and his fellow grammarians was no doubt crucial in bringing about the loss of hybrid gerunds [=B4]". Fanego's results (as presented in note 24) are indeed consistent with such a position; but the data available appear too limited to allow any definitive conclusion as to cause.

4. Logical subjects in gerundial constructions

4.1. The gerund with an overt subject and the subjectless gerund

The object-postposed constructions of the gerund may be classified into two groups according to the presence or absence of its logical subject (which are here referred to respectively as "subjectful" and "subjectless"), as follows:

a) +S ("Subjectful"): Constructions where the gerund is preceded by its subject, e.g. <B2> *my reading of the book*; <B4> *my reading the book*

b) –S ("Subjectless"): Constructions in which the gerund has no overt subject, e.g. <B1, B2> *(the) reading of the book*; <B3, B4> *(the) reading the book*

Table 14 shows that the first group (+S) occurs far less frequently than the second (–S) throughout the EModE period investigated.[25] The evidence from M4 of the PPCME2 and the COPC also shows a continuation of the same trend from LME down to the 18th century: 7

25 See also Fanego (2006a: 161), who notes that gerunds with an overt subject "are far less common than subjectless gerunds, both today and in earlier stages of English." Given the data, Tajima's (1985: 119) description of the gerund with an overt subject as "so common throughout all periods of English" seems untenable.

(2.8%) vs. 247 (97.2%) within M4, and 49 (7.3%) vs. 622 (92.7%) within the COPC.

	+S	–S	Total
E1 (1500-1569)	23 (2.2)	1,002 (97.8)	1,025 (100%)
E2 (1570-1639)	46 (3.2)	1,386 (96.8)	1,432 (100%)
E3 (1640-1710)	104 (5.5)	1,772 (94.5)	1,876 (100%)

X^2 (2*df*) = 122.226, $p < 0.001$.

Table 14. +S vs. –S constructions in the time periods of PPCEME.

Generally speaking, therefore, the overwhelming majority of these gerundial constructions have no overt subject, although the frequency of +S constructions does gradually increase over time. The same trend is also evident in the HC (see Table 14′ in Appendix 2).

The +S gerund has two types: <B2> *my reading of the book,* and <B4> *my reading the book.* Table 15 presents a general overview of the changes in frequency between B2 and B4 over the course of the EModE period. The former type predominates at the beginning of EModE, but its supremacy is challenged by the gradual development of the latter type. Therefore, the last period of EModE (E3) sees the firm establishment of Type B4 (*my reading the book*) as the normal one at the expense of Type B2 (*my reading of the book*).

	B2	B4	Total
E1	15 (65.2)	8 (34.8)	23 (100%)
E2	25 (54.3)	21 (45.7)	46 (100%)
E3	6 (5.8)	98 (94.2)	104 (100%)

X^2 (2*df*) = 58.836, $p < 0.001$.

Table 15. B2 vs. B4 in +S constructions in the time periods of PPCEME.

The M4 data (showing 3 vs. 4 tokens respectively) are too limited to allow any frequency comparison, but the COPC data are 1 (2.0%) vs. 47 (98.0%). This reversal in preference from E1 through E3 to LModE may be said to correspond to the expansion of Type B3 (*reading the book*) at the cost of Type B1 (*reading of the book*) and Type B2 (*the reading of the book*).[26]

The HC data (Table 15′ in Appendix 2) show a similar trend, though the sample size is insufficient to establish statistical significance.

The two +S types are illustrated below:

(8) <B2>

a. for I did learne the Reasons of *my misliking of you* M. Hare, M. Southwell, and others in the Parliament House; (throckm-e1-h)

b. therefore *your seeking of that Marriage* was for another Respect; (thoward2-e2-p1)

c. lamenting our condition, for want of good counsel and *the King's minding of his business and servants.* (pepys-e3-p1)

(9) <B4>

a. dyed for *their bryngenge vp that euell slaunder* apon it, (tyndold-e1-h)

b. You said you would prove that I knew of *the Scotish Queen's claiming the present Possession* of the Crown. (thoward-e2-p1)

c. Wherby you may the lesse Wonder of *the Indifferent Ladie's not giveing you a better answere,* and that Charles Nichols is so silent; (hoxinden-1660-e3-h)

5. Gerunds and syntactic functions

5.1. Distribution of the gerundial constructions in terms of syntactic functions

Syntactically, the gerund functions as subject (S), object (O), and complement (C), and also as prepositional object (PO), using these terms in the sense of Quirk *et al.* (1985). A closer investigation into the association of the gerundial constructions with the syntactic functions

---

26 Koma's (1987) classification of types into Nominal gerunds <Type A: *the refusing of the offer*, Type B: *refusing of the offer*> vs. Verbal gerunds <Type C: *the refusing the offer*, Type D: *(John's) refusing the offer*>, may be worth adopting, though in this case Type B should be *(John's) refusing of the offer.*

they performed in EModE reveals the situation as shown in Tables 16 and 17.

	Subject	Object	Complement	Prepositional Object	Other	Total
E1 (1500-1569)	66 (6.4)	77 (7.5)	7 (0.7)	858 (83.7)	17 (1.7)	1,025 (100%)
E2 (1570-1639)	91(6.4)	91 (6.4)	36 (2.5)	1,198 (83.7)	16 (1.1)	1,432 (100%)
E3 (1640-1710)	84 (4.5)	102 (5.4)	18 (1.0)	1,664 (88.7)	8 (0.4)	1,876 (100%)

Note: "Other" = cases out of syntactic contexts (e.g. titles, gerunds after colons, etc). X^2 (8*df*) = 49.264, $p < 0.001$.

Table 16. Distribution of gerunds according to syntactic functions in the time periods of PPCEME.

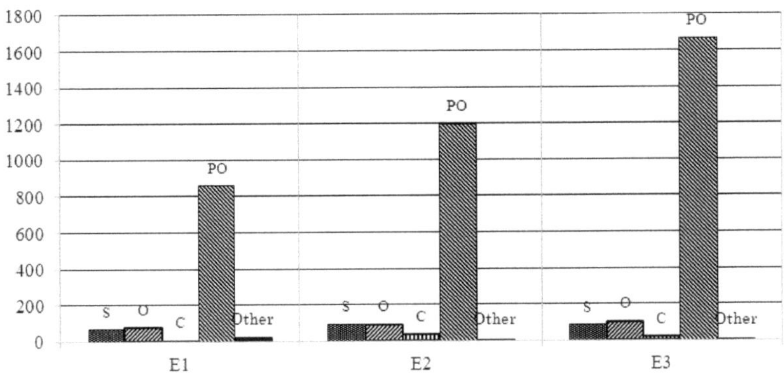

Figure 9. Gerunds according to syntactic functions in the time periods of PPCEME.

Table 16 shows that in the course of the EModE period the gerund functions as PO with overwhelmingly higher frequency than as S, O, or C, always accounting for over 80% of the cases. At the same time, the gerund as PO shows its quantitative expansion (as regards its observed frequency) over time, while the gerunds as central clause elements are infrequent and unstable throughout the period. Therefore, this also may be evidence that, as asserted by Koma (1987), Houston (1989) and others, in ME the verbalization of the gerund started where the gerund functioned as PO.[27] The HC data (Table 16′ in Appendix 2) show a similar tendency, though the sample size is insufficient to establish statistical significance.

27 The statistical data in Saito (1972, 1990, 1993) show the overwhelming predominance of the gerund as prepositional object in the EModE period. Jack (1988: 58), examining the list of instances of the gerund+object in Tajima (1985:

Now we should scrutinize the association between these syntactic functions and the variant types in EModE. Table 17 together with the two figures shows that in the course of EModE the verbal gerund, Type B3 (*reading the book*) continues to be predominant in the function as prepositional object (PO), rather than intruding into the sphere of the central clause elements (S, O, and C).[28] This is most probably because B3 lacks the initial determiner *the* which would serve as a noun-phrase marker.

On the other hand, during the EModE period, it is notable that even in E3, the nominal gerunds, especially Type B2 (*the reading of the book*), tend to hold their ground when functioning as S, O, or C. Interestingly, in E3 the nomino-verbal gerund, Type B4 (*the reading the book*) comes second in these functions as central clause elements, probably because of its nominal character denoted by the determiner (*the/my*). The same trend is evident in the HC data (see Table 17′ in Appendix 2).

Consequently, it can be concluded from these data that the quantitative expansion of the gerundial constructions pointed out in the preliminary survey of Section 2 is mainly due to the augmentation of Type B3 used as prepositional object in prepositional phrases (***in*** *reading the book*).

76-77), admits that it "does give reason to conclude that phrases comprising a gerund+object were associated with prepositional use". Fanego (2004: 9), drawing on subsequent research, is more conclusive: "as made clear by Donner (1986), Koma (1987) and Houston (1989: 181), the gerund's acquisition of direct objects started with those gerunds that were dependent on a preposition".

28 Concerning this delay in encroaching on the sphere of central clause elements (S, O and C), Fanego (2006b): 97) argues that "for a long time verbal features were found only with those prepositional gerunds", and that the verbal gerund (*reading the book*) began to function as O from the middle of the 16th century (=E1), and as S and C from the late 17th century (=E3). Therefore, I retrieved all examples labeled "IP-PPL-SBJ" (for S) and "IP-PPL-OB" (for O and C) from all the PPCEME psd texts using Tsukamoto's Treebank Search, and obtained some examples of B3 functioning as S in E1 and E2 (see Table 17), some of which are cited in (10c) below. (The Harman example could admittedly be just an IP-PPL.) Reluctance to use Type B3 gerunds as S, O, and C continues in Twentieth-century English (Umesaki 1994); see note 23.

Function	Time period	Type				Total
		B1	B2	B3	B4	
S	E1	16 (24.2)	45 (68.2)	3 (4.5)	2 (3.0)	66 (100%)
	E2	17 (18.7)	67 (73.6)	2 (2.2)	5 (5.5)	91 (100%)
	E3	6 (7.1)	36 (42.9)	10 (11.9)	32 (38.1)	84 (100%)
O	E1	14 (18.2)	56 (72.7)	4 (5.2)	3 (3.9)	77 (100%)
	E2	20 (22.0)	59 (64.8)	4 (4.4)	8 (8.8)	91 (100%)
	E3	5 (4.9)	40 (39.2)	33 (32.4)	24 (23.5)	102 (100%)
C	E1	3 (42.9)	4 (57.1)	0 (0.0)	0 (0.0)	7 (100%)
	E2	1 (2.8)	26 (72.2)	4 (11.1)	5 (13.9)	36 (100%)
	E3	1 (5.6)	4 (22.2)	3 (16.7)	10 (55.6)	18 (100%)
PO	E1	281 (32.8)	263 (30.7)	287 (33.4)	27 (3.1)	858 (100%)
	E2	186 (15.5)	350 (29.2)	608 (50.8)	54 (4.5)	1,198 (100%)
	E3	52 (3.1)	213 (12.8)	1,198 (72.0)	201 (12.1)	1,664 (100%)

Note: a) Instances of 'Other' in Table 16 are excluded from this table.
b) Separate chi-squared tests were performed on each of the function rows. Results: (S, O, C) all nonsignificant; (PO) X^2 (*6df*) = 716.383, $p < 0.001$.

Table 17. Association between syntactic functions and gerundial types in PPCEME.

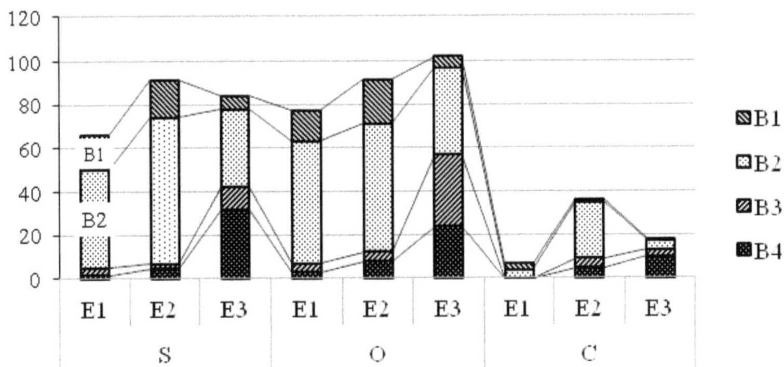

Figure 10. Association between central clause elements and the four types in PPCEME.

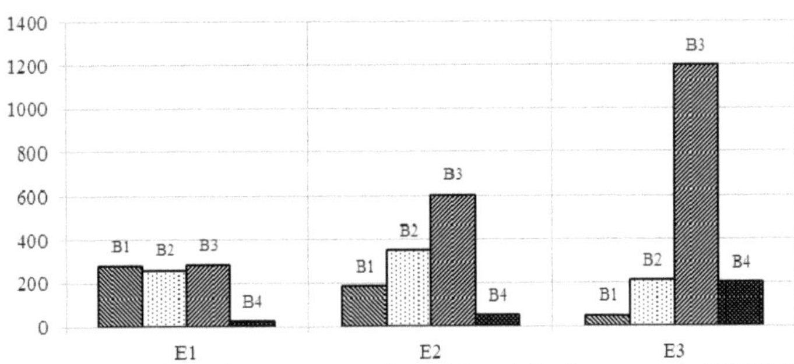

Figure 11. Association between gerunds as PO and the four types in PPCEME.

Examples of the gerund as S, O, or C are given in (10)-(12) below. For examples of the gerund as PO, see the following section.

(10) Subject

a. <B1> For *preachynge of the Gospel* is one of Goddes plough workes, (latimer-e1-p1)

b. <B2> therefore *the drinking of wine* is profitable for olde men, (turner-e1-p1)

c. <B3> Thus *feding her with frendly fantacyes*, consumed two houres and more. (harman-e1-h) / and at durge and masse contenuyd *ryngyng alle the belles* till vij at nyght. (machyn-e1-p1) / so *throwing him into the water*, will doe him a benefit. (shakesp-e2-p2) / Think you that *practising to levy War* within the Realm is not Treason? (thoward2-e2-p2) / *Slitting the bark* is an excellent additional help to most of the foresaid evils, (langf-e3-h) / and *loseing my way* made it 12 mile, (fiennes-e3-h) /And *loving these Attributes in that object*, will certainly carry us to desire them in our selves. (burnetroc-e3-p1)

d. <B4> For wher *the making felicitie* endith, there skanted is the force, & wretched makes. (boethel-e2-p2)

(11) Object

a. <B1> and thes alsoe were charged to forbeare *treating of controversyes in Religion* not to move dispute touching governement , (hayward-e2-h)

b. <B2> for thereby the Lawe doth vnderstande *the discouering of your Treasons*.(throckm-e1-h)

c. <B3> Mr M. continueth *keeping house* with his maid. (eoxinden-1660-e3-h)

d. <B4> Why, my Lord, if you deny *the raising the Power*, why should so many Men come to your House that day? (essexstate-e2-p2)

(12) Complement

a. <B1> Sumtyme ther Dwellyd Cretes, yt ys *wretyng of them* in Actibus aptor, (torking-e1-p1)

b. <B2> I tell thee the beginning of the world was *the begetting of Children* : (deloney-e2-p1)

c. <B3> In this Indictment are contained three principal Treasons, whereof the first is *imagining and conspiring the Deprivation, Death, and Destruction* of the Queen's Majesty: (thoward2-e2-p2)

d. <B4> but of all these the noblest End is *the multiplying children*, (jetaylor-e3-h)

5.2. The gerund as prepositional object

The present section provides a more detailed analysis of the data of gerunds as prepositional objects, which were found in the preceding section to be overwhelmingly predominant throughout the EModE period. Needless to say, prepositional objects together with prepositions constitute prepositional phrases: PREP+GERUND.

According to Quirk *et al.* (1985: 657), prepositional phrases have the following syntactic functions:

1) Postmodifier in a noun phrase (Adjectival): The people *on the bus* were singing.
2) Adverbial: *In the afternoon* we went *to Boston.*
3) Complementation of a verb: We were looking *at his awful paintings.*
4) Complementation of an adjective: I'm sorry *for his parents.*

Table 18 shows the further breakdown of instances of the PREP+GERUND phrase across the four syntactic functions above.

	Adjectival	Adverbial	VbC	AdjC	Total
E1 (1500-1569)	118 (13.8)	680 (79.3)	33 (3.8)	27 (3.1)	858 (100%)
E2 (1570-1639)	218 (18.2)	915 (76.4)	39 (3.3)	26 (2.1)	1,198 (100%)
E3 (1640-1710)	478 (28.7)	1,042 (62.6)	71 (4.3)	73 (4.4)	1,664 (100%)

Note: a) VbC=complementation of a verb; AdjC=complementation of an adjective.
b) X^2 (6*df*) = 107.227, $p < 0.001$.

Table 18. Distribution of PREP+GERUND across syntactic functions in PPCEME.

These figures show that the gerundial phrase in question occurs predominantly in adverbial function throughout the EModE period, though it is also rapidly increasing in adjectival function over time. The HC also shows the same trend (see Table 18′ in Appendix 2).

This statistical evidence seems to corroborate the conclusion by Koma (1987) based on the evidence from the *Paston Letters* (15th century) that in ME the gerund began to have verbal character in the context of this adverbial function.[29]

The PREP+GERUND phrase in adverbial function can be further investigated in terms of the four types of the gerundial constructions. The results are shown in Table 19.

	B1	B2	B3	B4	Total
E1	216 (32.2)	212 (31.8)	233 (34.2)	19 (2.8)	680 (100%)
E2	126 (13.8)	270 (29.5)	482 (52.7)	37 (4.0)	915 (100%)
E3	30 (2.9)	154 (14.8)	727 (69.8)	131 (12.7)	1,042 (100%)

X^2 (6*df*) = 480.623, $p << 0.001$.

Table 19. Distribution of PREP+GERUND in adverbial function across types in PPCEME.

Interestingly, in E1, all three types B1 (***in** reading of the book*), B2 (***in** the reading of the book*) and B3 (***in** reading the book*) are still attested, with almost equal frequency, though Type B3 gains predominance at the expense of Type B1 and Type B2 in the later time periods (see the same trend in Table 19′ of the HC). This statistical evidence may indicate that in ME both of these nominal gerunds as prepositional objects occurred frequently in this adverbial function, with the result that, as Koma (1987), Houston (1989) and others assume, probably under the influence of participial constructions and others, they began to have verbal character, producing a verbal gerund, Type B3: ***in** (the) reading of the book* > ***in** reading the book*. This assumption needs to be tested by solid evidence from a further investigation into ME materials.[30]

The PREP + GERUND phrase is illustrated below:

29 Koma (1987: 220f) argues that the semantic overlap between the participial construction and the *in*-phrases ('*in* + V-*ing* + *of* + Object') enabled the latter construction to acquire the verbal property of taking the direct object directly. Houston (1989: §3) also assumes that one use of the present participle – the appositive participle – influenced the development of the verbal gerund. Jack (1998), however, rejects any direct sole influence of the participle in the development of the verbal gerund, and suggests instead that a convergence of several factors including the influence of the participle brought about the verbalization.

30 Cf. Fanego's comment that "More work is still needed regarding the exact frequency of prepositional gerunds in OE and ME" (2004: §2.1).

(13) Adjectival (postmodifier in NP)

a. <B1> This is a liuely and perfite waie ***of*** *teaching of Rewles*: (asch-e1-h)

b. <B2> for the Sea and all nauigable riuers being the chiefe meanes ***for*** *the enriching of Townes and Cities*, by the reason of Traffique with forraine Nations, (jotaylor-e2-h)

c. <B3> Besides these, they would have every day some practice ***of*** *writing English* heedily, in true Orthographie; (brinsley-e2-p1)

d. <B4> I Can not heere well passe ouer this briefe note or obseruation ***of*** *the curing two seafaring men*, which trauelled a long time vpon the seas, (clowesobs-e2-p2)

(14) Adverbial

a. <B1> ***In*** *training of your horse* obserue not the number the miles, but the labour fit for your horse. (markham-e2-p2)

b. <B2> Yet ***for*** *ye further appesing of ye peoples mind*, he sent immediatli after diner in al y^e hast, one herode of armes, (moreric-e1-h)

c. <B3> Againe ***by*** *placing the Spheare* so as both the Poles may lie vppon the Horizon, you shall see the shape of the first right Sphear, (blundev-e2-h)

d. <B4> Two things have principally employd my time here ***since*** *my last kissing yr $Ma^{iy's}$ hands*; (capel-e3-h)

(15) Complementation of a verb

a. <B1> we wold not greatly care ***For*** *bursting of her huckle bone*, or *breakyng of her Chaire*, (stevenso-e1-h)

b. <B2> yet before I doe beginne to speake ***of*** *the making of the Cheese*, I will shew you how to order your Cheeselep-bag (markham-e2-p2)

c. <B3> and do use the vertue of beneficence, whiche consisteth ***in*** *counsaylinge and helpinge othe*r with any assistence in tyme of nede, (elyot-e1-pl)

d. <B4> and they were in doubt whether he would approve ***of*** *their killing the king*: (burnetcha-e3-h)

(16) Complementation of an adjective

a. <B1> Therfore ye vnpreachynge prelates, learne of the deuill to be diligent ***in*** *doing of your office*. (latimer-e1-p1)

b. <B2> The Parliament backward in raising, because jealous ***of*** *the spending of the money*. (pepys-e3-p1)

c. <B3> and then lastly to grow zealous ***of*** *doing right*, when they have no longer need to do wrong. (milton-e3-h)

d. <B4> Deare brother, I am not afraid ***of*** *y^r getting the small pox*, (mhatton-e3-p1)

6. Summary and conclusion

Concerning the diachronic changes in the use of the variant gerundial constructions in EModE, an investigation into the association between the four B types and the text genres was carried out in a preliminary survey (Section 2). This survey revealed the expansion of Type B3 (*reading the book*) among informal and colloquial genres, and also the changing status of legal language over time. Another examination of this kind was done in the section dealing with the rivalry between Type B2 (*the reading of the book*) and Type B4 (*the reading the book*) to check the validity of Visser's well-known remark. This variationist approach in terms of text genres has produced quite a revealing result, but a thorough investigation of data for the whole corpus from this viewpoint will have to be left for another paper.

As is stated in the introductory section, the present paper is focused on analyzing the gerundial constructions by the evidence extracted from the PPCEME, a triply expanded version of the HC. The evidence from the PPCEME presents a clearer picture of the rise and fall of the variant types of the gerundial constructions during the EModE period.

The total use of gerundial constructions is found to increase steadily over the EModE period, largely as a result of expansion of the object-postposed constructions, especially Type B3 (*reading the book*). By contrast, the object-preposed constructions, Types A1 and A2, already infrequent in late ME, are rare even at the beginning of the EModE period, and thereafter become rarer or obsolescent. Among object-postposed constructions, a nominal gerund (Type B1: *reading of the book*), which is the most common in ME, is still prevalent in the beginning of EModE, along with another nominal gerund (Type B2: *the reading of the book*), but starts to decline in the E2 time period. Type B2 (*the reading of the book*) is the most common at the beginning of EModE, but it also starts decreasing in frequency by the end of EModE. The verbal gerund (Type

B3: *reading the book*) expands rapidly in the middle of EModE, and by the end of the period accounts for over 65% of all the occurrences. The gerund preceded by a determiner (Type B4: *the reading the book*) also expands somewhat between the middle and end of EModE, though it then declines during the 18th century, becoming more restricted to occurrences with the subject as determiner (*my reading the book*). Thus the gerundial constructions in question are polarized roughly into two, Type B2 and Type B3, the balance inclining sharply to the latter.

Syntactically the gerund functions as prepositional object (PO) with overwhelmingly higher frequency than as a central clause element (S, O, or C) throughout the EModE period. This evidence seems to strongly support the assertion that the verbalization of the gerund started in this function during the ME period. Moreover, it is this verbal gerund (Type B3) that increases in the function as PO over time. Nevertheless, it is slow to encroach on the functions as S, O and C, where the nominal gerunds (especially B2) tend to hold ground; interestingly, the nomino-verbal gerund (B4) does encroach on the latter functions.

As for the other purpose of the present survey, the comparison of the frequency data from both the PPCEME and the HC has revealed, first of all, that the PPCEME is very highly correlated or homogeneous with the original corpus, as a natural result of the compilation policy the PPCEME compilers adopted, and also has shown that the roughly trebled corpus yields roughly three times as high an observed frequency as the HC.

One immediate consequence is that the PPCEME frequency data produces higher levels of statistical significance than the original corpus. Six out of 12 tables for the HC fail to yield significant results (Tables 6′, 7′, 8′, 15′, 16′ and part of 17′). For the PPCEME, out of the 14 data tables subjected to chi-squared tests, only two tables (Tables 7 and 8) and part of a table (S, O, C in Table 17) fail to yield any significant differences. However, Tables 7 and 8 of the PPCEME (and Tables 6′, 7′ and 8′ of the HC) deal with the disappearing object-preposed constructions, which have frequencies too low for this level of breakdown. These results mean that even the expanded 1.7 million word corpus is still "too small" to provide sufficient evidence to address such infrequent linguistic items.

These items aside, the PPCEME has proved to be a useful and reliable corpus for investigating syntactic features in the EModE period, so that the completion of this expanded corpus is indeed a blessing for diachronic corpus linguists, to say nothing of the merits of its annotated forms.

Nevertheless, the results of the comparison are consistent with Saito's (1993) conclusion that the "too small" Helsinki Corpus is still a useful and reliable tool for diachronic linguistic research. Indeed, the present survey has revealed that any one of the three subcorpora of the PPCEME is – just as Kytö/Rissanen (1993: 3-4) described the HC – "extensive enough to show fairly reliable and extensive trends of development in a large number of topics."

Appendix 1. Overall frequency tables for the six gerundial construction types in the PPCEME, by text genre

(All tables present text genres in descending order of the total normed frequency.)

Text Genre	Word Count	Type and Observed Frequency						Total	
		A1	A2	B1	B2	B3	B4	Observed Freq	Normed Freq
EDUC_TREAT	32,362	3		25	48	77	6	159	49.1
LAW	37,018	2	1	65	75	21	3	167	45.1
PROC_TRIAL	15,978			6	23	21	4	54	33.8
HANDB_OTHER	31,975			44	39	13		96	30.0
LET_NON-PRIV	24,102			14	33	9	7	63	26.1
DIARY_PRIV	41,223	4	2	38	23	32	2	101	24.5
SERMON	30,713			18	17	33	1	69	22.5
BIOGR_OTHER	16,684	1	2	8	10	8	1	30	18.0
HISTORY	35,853	2	2	17	21	6	1	49	13.7
PHILOSOPHY	32,091		2	22	9	9	1	43	13.4
SCIENCE_MEDIC	19,115	1		10	6	6		23	12.0
BIOGR_AUTO	18,725	1	1	9	6	5		22	11.7
LET_PRIV	32,993			4	24	10		38	11.5
FICTION	35,909	1		14	9	14	2	40	11.1
SCIENCE_OTHER	20,914			7	5	10		22	10.5
TRAVELOG	44,020	2	1	12	12	7	2	36	8.2
DRAMA_COM	32,517	1	5	6	1	4	1	18	5.5
BIBLE	65,603	1		5	13	9	2	30	4.6
Subtotal	567,795	19	16	324	374	294	33	1,060	18.7

Table A. Period E1 (1500-1569).

Text Genre	Word Count	Type and Observed Frequency						Total	
		A1	A2	B1	B2	B3	B4	Observed Freq	Normed Freq
LAW	37,169	2	4	76	83	28	9	202	54.3
EDUC_TREAT	34,900	1		13	54	93	5	166	47.6
HANDB_OTHER	37,514	8	2	19	70	60	7	166	44.3
BIOGR_OTHER	14,974			9	28	15	3	55	36.7
LET_NON-PRIV	17,032			3	25	26	2	56	32.9
SCIENCE_MEDIC	21,674	2	1	15	32	17	4	71	32.8
PROC_TRIAL	77,749	4		36	87	97	21	245	31.5
HISTORY	31,874		1	7	21	63	1	93	29.2
SCIENCE_OTHER	20,600				1	40		41	19.9
LET_PRIV	41,053	1	1	12	19	35	8	76	18.5
PHILOSOPHY	21,804	2	1	4	8	21	1	37	17.0
SERMON	31,546			8	18	24	1	51	16.2
DIARY_PRIV	46,988	1	1	8	13	33	3	59	12.6
TRAVELOG	45,330		2	8	17	20	4	51	11.3
FICTION	39,011		2	8	14	18		42	10.8
DRAMA_COM	37,138	3	3	2	6	15	3	32	8.6
BIOGR_AUTO	4,125			1	1	1		3	7.3
BIBLE	67,982	1	1	4	9	14	1	30	4.4
Subtotal	628,463	25	19	233	506	620	73	1,476	23.5

Table B. Period E2 (1570-1639).

Text Genre	Word Count	Type and Observed Frequency						Total	
		A1	A2	B1	B2	B3	B4	Observed Freq	Normed Freq
LAW	41,434			20	84	138	68	310	74.8
LET_NON-PRIV	19,637		1	3	20	91	25	140	71.3
EDUC_TREAT	43,087	4		8	37	180	12	241	55.9
HANDB_OTHER	35,946	5	1	4	13	135	16	174	48.4
SCIENCE_OTHER	35,932			7	33	110	11	161	44.8
BIOGR_OTHER	18,832				9	54	21	84	44.6
DIARY_PRIV	35,353		4	7	25	84	27	147	41.6
HISTORY	36,042	2		2	12	93	31	140	38.8
LET_PRIV	42,377	1	3	6	15	60	29	114	26.9
PHILOSOPHY	29,313				7	66	1	74	25.2
SERMON	31,673		2		18	48	7	75	23.7
FICTION	37,518			1	4	63	4	72	19.2
DRAMA_COM	40,423		2	3	5	61	4	75	18.6
TRAVELOG	32,795		2	1	7	32	7	49	14.9
PROC_TRIAL	43,522	1	1		4	24	8	38	8.7
BIOGR_AUTO	17,711			2	1	7	1	11	6.2
Subtotal	541,595	13	16	64	294	1,246	272	1,905	35.2

Table C. Period E3 (1640-1710).

Appendix 2. Tables for the Helsinki Corpus (HC)

The following HC data, corresponding to the tables presented in the main text for the PPCEME, were retrieved from the unannotated texts in the Helsinki directories of the PPCEME.

	Object-preposed	Object-postposed	Total
E1 (1500-1569)	13 (3.4)	369 (96.6)	382 (100%)
E2 (1570-1639)	10 (2.3)	420 (97.7)	430 (100%)
E3 (1640-1710)	13 (2.3)	559 (97.7)	572 (100%)

X^2 (2*df*) = 1.342, $p > 0.05$ (nonsignificant).

Table 6′. Object-preposed vs. object-postposed gerundial constructions in HC.

	A1	A2	Total
E1	9 (69.2)	4 (30.8)	13 (100%)
E2	2 (20.0)	8 (80.0)	10 (100%)
E3	6 (46.2)	7 (53.8)	13 (100%)

Note: Insufficient data for a reliable chi-squared test.

Table 7′. Distribution of Type A1 and Type A2 in HC.

	Noun	Pronoun	Total
E1	0 (0.0)	9 (100)	9 (100%)
E2	0 (0.0)	2 (100)	2 (100%)
E3	2 (33.3)	4 (66.7)	6 (100%)

Note: Insufficient data for a reliable chi-squared test.

Table 8′. Distribution of Type A1 classified by word classes of the gerund object in HC.

	B1	B2	B3	B4	Total
E1	116 (31.4)	134 (36.3)	109 (29.5)	10 (2.7)	369 (100%)
E2	66 (15.7)	149 (35.5)	189 (45.0)	16 (3.8)	420 (100%)
E3	18 (3.2)	86 (15.4)	352 (63.0)	103 (18.4)	559 (100%)

X^2 (6*df*) = 301.139, $p << 0.001$.

Table 9′. Distribution of the four types of object-postposed constructions in HC.

	+of	−of	Total
E1	250 (67.8)	119 (32.2)	369 (100%)
E2	215 (51.2)	205 (48.8)	420 (100%)
E3	104 (18.6)	455 (81.4)	559 (100%)

X^2 (2*df*) = 240.256, $p << 0.001$.

Table 10′. +*of* vs. −*of* in HC.

	B2	B4	Total
E1	112 (99.6)	4 (3.4)	116 (100%)
E2	138 (93.9)	9 (6.1)	147 (100%)
E3	81 (57.0)	61(43.0)	142 (100%)

X^2 (2*df*) = 89.547, *p*<0.001.

Table 12′. B2 vs. B4 (preceded by *the*) in HC.

Text genre	B2	B4	Total
Travelogue	0 (0.0)	3 (100)	3 (100%)
Letters, non-private	2 (25.0)	6 (75.0)	8 (100%)
History	4 (36.4)	7 (63.6)	11(100%)
Biography, other	1 (50.0)	1 (50.0)	2 (100%)
Handbook, other	5 (50.0)	5 (50.0)	10 (100%)
Science, other	5 (55.6)	4 (44.4)	9 (100%)
Law	29 (56.9)	22 (43.1)	51 (100%)
Letters, private	3 (60.0)	2 (40.0)	5 (100%)
Sermon	8 (66.7)	4 (33.3)	12 (100%)
Educational treatise	12 (70.6)	5 (29.4)	17 (100%)
Diary, private	5 (71.4)	2 (26.6)	7 (100%)
Drama, comedy	3 (100)	0 (0.0)	3 (100%)
Fiction	2 (100)	0 (0.0)	2 (100%)
Philosophy	2 (100)	0 (0.0)	2 (100%)
Biography, autobiography	0 (0.0)	0 (0.0)	0 (100%)
Proceedings, trials	0 (0.0)	0 (0.0)	0 (100%)
Total	81 (57.3)	61(43.0)	142 (100%)

Note: Genres are listed in descending order of the percentage of Type B4 instances.

Table 13′. B2 vs. B4 (with *the*) across text genres in E3 of HC.

	+S	–S	Total
E1	12 (3.3)	357 (96.7)	369 (100%)
E2	10 (2.4)	410 (97.6)	420 (100%)
E3	39 (7.0)	520 (93.0)	559 (100%)

X^2 (2*df*) = 13.630, *p* = 0.001.

Table 14′. +S vs. –S constructions in the time periods of HC.

	B2	B4	Total
E1	8 (66.7)	4 (33.3)	12 (100%)
E2	5 (50.0)	5 (50.0)	10 (100%)
E3	0 (0.0)	39 (100)	39 (100%)

Note: Insufficient data for a reliable chi-squared test.

Table 15′. B2 vs. B4 in +S constructions in the time periods of HC.

Period	Subject	Object	Compleme nt	Prepositional Object	Others	Total
E1	23 (6.2)	26 (7.0)	1 (0.3)	317 (85.9)	2 (0.5)	369 (100%)
E2	25 (6.0)	22 (5.2)	5 (1.2)	368 (87.6)	0 (0.0)	420 (100%)
E3	27 (4.8)	27 (4.8)	5 (0.9)	499 (89.3)	1 (0.2)	559 (100%)

Note: Insufficient data for a reliable chi-squared test.

Table 16′. Distribution of gerunds according to syntactic functions in HC.

		B1	B2	B3	B4	Total
S	E1	6 (26.1)	15 (65.2)	1 (4.3)	1 (4.3)	23 (100%)
	E2	4 (16.0)	20 (80.0)	0 (0.0)	1 (4.0)	25 (100%)
	E3	1 (3.7)	13 (48.1)	4 (14.8)	9 (33.3)	27 (100%)
O	E1	4 (15.4)	21 (80.8)	1 (3.8)	0 (0.0)	26 (100%)
	E2	8 (36.4)	11 (50.0)	2 (9.1)	1 (4.5)	22 (100%)
	E3	0 (0.0)	14 (51.9)	8 (29.6)	5 (18.5)	27 (100%)
C	E1	0 (0.0)	1 (100)	0 (0.0)	0 (0.0)	1 (100%)
	E2	0 (0.0)	4 (80.0)	1 (20.0)	0 (0.0)	5 (100%)
	E3	0 (0.0)	1 (20.0)	1 (20.0)	3 (60.0)	5 (100%)
PO	E1	105 (33.1)	96 (30.3)	107 (33.8)	9 (2.8)	317 (100%)
	E2	54 (14.7)	114 (30.0)	186 (50.5)	14 (3.8)	368 (100%)
	E3	17 (3.3)	58 (11.6)	338 (67.7)	86 (17.2)	499 (100%)

Note: (a) Table excludes category ‘Other’.
(b) S, O, C: nonsignificant; PO: X^2 (*6df*) = 266.389, $p << 0.001$.

Table 17′. Association between syntactic functions and gerundial types in HC.

	Adjectival	Adverbial	VbC	AdjC	Total
E1	43 (13.6)	249 (78.5)	13 (4.1)	12 (3.8)	317 (100%)
E2	62 (16.8)	286 (77.7)	13 (3.5)	7 (1.9)	368 (100%)
E3	142 (28.5)	319 (63.9)	17 (3.4)	21 (4.2)	499 (100%)

X^2 (*6df*) = 34.751, $p < 0.001$.

Table 18′. Distribution of PREP+GERUND across syntactic functions in HC.

	B1	B2	B3	B4	Total
E1	82 (32.9)	81 (32.5)	81 (32.5)	5 (2.0)	249 (100%)
E2	37 (12.9)	86 (30.0)	154 (53.8)	9 (3.1)	286 (100%)
E3	9 (2.8)	38 (11.9)	211 (66.2)	61 (19.1)	319 (100%)

X^2 (*6df*) = 213.707, $p << 0.001$.

Table 19′. Distribution of PREP+GERUND in adverbial function across types in HC.

References

Curme, George O. 1912. History of the English Gerund. *Englische Studien* 45, 349-380.

Denison, David 1998. Syntax. In Romaine, Suzanne (ed.) *The Cambridge history of the English language.* Vol. 4. Cambridge: Cambridge University Press, 92-329.

De Smet, Hendrik 2008a. Functional motivations in the development of nominal and verbal gerunds in Middle and Early Modern English. *Journal of English Language and Linguistics* 12, 55-102.

De Smet, Hendrik 2008b. Nominal gerunds in 16th-century English: The function of the definite article. *Folia Linguistica Historica* 28, 77-113.

Donner, Morton 1986. The gerund in Middle English. *English Studies* 67, 394-400.

Fanego, Teresa 1996. The Gerund in Early Modern English: Evidence from the Helsinki Corpus. *Folia Linguistica Historica* 17, 97-152.

Fanego, Teresa 1998. Developments in argument linking in Early Modern English gerund phrases. *English Language and Linguistics* 2, 87-119.

Fanego, Teresa 2004. On Reanalysis and Actualization in Syntactic Change: The Rise and Development of English Verbal Gerunds. *Diachronica* 21/1, 5-55.

Fanego, Teresa 2006a. Drift and the development of sentential complements in British and American English from 1700 to the present day. In Pérez-Guerra, Javier *et al.* (eds) *Selected papers from the Second International Conference on the English Language in the Late Modern Period (LMEC2), University of Vigo, 25-27 November 2004.* Bern: Peter Lang, 162-234.

Fanego, Teresa 2006b. The role of language standardization in the loss of hybrid gerunds in Modern English. In Breivik, Egil Leiv / Halverson, Sandra / Haugland, Kari (eds) *These things write I vnto thee...: Essays in honour of Bjorg Bækken.* Oslo: Novus Press, 93-110.

Houston, Ann 1989. The English Gerund: Syntactic Change and Discourse Function. In Fasold, Ralph W / Schiffrin, Deborah (eds)

Language Change and Variation. Amsterdam and Philadelphia: John Benjamins, 173–196.

Iyeiri, Yoko 2010. *Verbs of Implicit Negation and their Complements in the History of English*. Amsterdam: John Benjamins, Tokyo: Yushodo Press.

Jack, George 1988. The Origins of the English Gerund. *NOWELLE*, 12, 15–75.

Jespersen, Otto 1909-49. *A Modern English Grammar on Historical Principles*. London: George Allen & Unwin.

Kisbye, Torben 1971. *An Historical Outline of English Syntax*. Part I. Tryk: Akademisk Boghandel.

Koma, Osamu 1987. On the Initial Locus of Syntactic Change: Verbal Gerund and its Historical Development. *English Linguistics* 4, 311-322.

Kytö, Merja 1993. *Manual to the Diachronic Part of the Helsinki Corpus of English Texts*. Helsinki: Department of English, University of Helsinki.

Kytö, Merja / Rissanen, Matti 1993. General Introduction. In Rissanen, Matti / Kytö, Merja / Palander-Collin, Minna (eds) *Early English in the Computer Age: Explorations through the Helsinki Corpus*. Berlin and New York: Mouton de Gruyter, 1-17.

Leech, Geoffrey / Hundt, Marianne / Mair, Christian / Smith, Nicholas 2009. *Change in Contemporary English: A Grammatical Study*. Cambridge: Cambridge University Press.

Mair, Christian 2006. *Twentieth-Century English: History, Variation and Standardization*. Cambridge: Cambridge University Press.

Mustanoja, Tauno F. 1960. *A Middle English Syntax*. Part I. Helsinki: Société Néophilologique.

Nevalainen, Terttu / Raumolin-Brunberg, Helena 1993. Early Modern British English. In Rissanen, Matti / Kytö, Merja / Palander-Collin, Minna (eds) *Early English in the Computer Age: Explorations through the Helsinki Corpus*. Berlin and New York: Mouton de Gruyter, 53-73.

Nishimura, Hideo 2009. Intensive adverbs in PPCME2 and PPCEME (in Japanese). In Watanabe, Shinichiro / Hosoya, Yukiteru (eds) *English Philology and Corpus Studies: A Festschrift in Honour of Mitsunori Imai to Celebrate His Seventieth Birthday*. Tokyo: Shohakusha, 135-152.

Quirk, Randolph / Greenbaum, Sidney / Leech, Geoffrey / Svartvik, Jan 1985. *A Comprehensive Grammar of the English Language*. London and New York: Longman.

Rissanen, Matti 2000. The world of English historical corpora: From Cædmon to the computer age. *Journal of English Linguistics* 28, 7-20.

Saito, Toshio 1972. The Constructions of the Gerund with its Object in Early Modern English: A Preliminary Survey. *Kenkyu Shuroku*. College of General Education, Osaka University 19, 171-186.

Saito, Toshio 1974. Word Order in Late Middle English – A Statistical Survey Based on the Early Fifteenth-Century London Documents. *Essays Presented to Shiko Murakami on the Occasion of his Retirement from Osaka University*. Tokyo: Eihosha, 433-444.

Saito, Toshio 1990. The Development of the Gerund in Modern Colloquial English: With Special Reference to the Constructions of the Gerund with its Object. In Jin, Koichi *et al.* (eds), *Studies in English Philology in Honour of Shigeru Ono.* Tokyo: Nan'undo, 377-392.

Saito, Toshio 1993. The Development of the Gerund in Early Modern English: Exploring the Helsinki Corpus of English Texts (in Japanese). In Modern English Association Editorial Board (ed.), *Aspects of Modern English*. Tokyo: Eichosha, 353-375.

Tajima, Matsuji 1985. *The Syntactic Development of the Gerund in Middle English.* Tokyo: Nan'undo.

Umesaki, Atsuko F. 1994. A Corpus-Based Study of Transitive Verb Nominalisations: Nominal *-ing* Clauses and Derivative Noun Phrases. *English Corpus Studies* 1, 85-98.

Visser, Frederikus Th. 1946-56. *A Syntax of the English Language of Sir Thomas More*. Louvain: Librairie Unversitaire.

Visser, Frederikus Th. 1966. *An Historical Syntax of the English Language.* Part II. Leiden: E. J. Brill.

Wurff, Wim van der 1993. Gerunds and their objects in the Modern English period. In Marle, Jaap van (ed.) *Historical linguistics 1991*. Amsterdam and Philadelphia: John Benjamins, 363-375.

YOKO IYEIRI

The Verb *Pray* in Chaucer and Caxton

1. Introduction

In his study of imperative sentences in early Modern English, Ukaji (1978: 131) states: "imperatives are very often embedded explicitly in higher clauses as the complement of the following seven verbs: *advise, beseech, charge, command, entreat, pray,* and *say*". He pays special attention to the verb *pray* on the grounds that it "is not only most frequent but also semantically most general, compatible as it is with a wide extent of request meaning" (Ukaji 1978: 133). The following is one of his early Modern English examples:[1]

(1) Be your tears wet? yes, 'faith. *I pray*, weep not. (*King Lear*, 4.7.71)

The verb *pray* was borrowed from Old French during the Middle English period, when it was used with the full meanings 'to beseech', 'to ask', etc. (*OED* s.v. *pray*). As the above example illustrates, however, *pray* in early Modern English often functions as a mere marker to introduce imperatives. In its later development, the physical form itself was reduced. Ukaji (1978: 137-38) notes that forms like *I pray you* and *I pray* are common in Shakespeare's early plays while in his later ones forms like *Pray you, Pray, I prithee,* and *Prithee* prevail. Traugott and Dasher (2002: 254) also state that "[b]y the sixteenth century two new forms without the subject pronoun appear: *prithee*, and, without any pronoun, *pray*". The following is an example of the last form, i.e. *pray*:

(2) *Pray* be not angry, sir: I'll do my best (*The Maid's Tragedy*, 5.4.22, from Ukaji 1978).

---

1 Except where otherwise stated, all italics in quotations have been added by the author to identify wordforms of particular interest.

By the stage of this example, the verb *pray* has developed into a discourse marker with the meaning 'please'.[2] The purpose of the present paper is to investigate the process in which the discourse marker use of *pray* develops, paying particular attention to later Middle English. Whereas Ukaji (1978) gives a fairly extensive analysis of the development of *pray* in early Modern English, the Middle English period needs to be further studied. I will focus upon Chaucer and Caxton, given the existence of Akimoto's (2000) accounts of *The Paston Letters*, *The Book of Margery Kempe*, and Malory's *Le Morte D'Arthur*. Hirayama (2001) also investigates some letters of the Paston family. A more comprehensive account of the historical development of *pray* in *The Paston Letters* is presented in Iyeiri (2009), drafted later but published earlier than the present study.

2. The data of the present study

As mentioned above, the present paper probes into the use of *pray* in Chaucer and Caxton. Chaucer's texts to be studied are *Boece* and *The Canterbury Tales*, while Caxton's texts that I will investigate are *Reynard the Fox*, *Paris and Vienne*, *Blanchardyn and Eglantine*, and *Eneydos*.[3] Except for *The Canterbury Tales*, which is mostly written in

2 Other terms have been used in the literature, but the present study will follow Blake (2002: 248) in using the term "discourse marker" to describe this use of *pray*. This construction with *pray* was subsequently replaced by *please* in the later history of English; for discussion of the latter shift, see Akimoto (2000: 80) and Busse (2002: 27-32).

3 The editions I have used are: *The Riverside Chaucer*, 3rd edition, ed. Larry D. Benson *et al.* (Boston, 1987); *The History of Reynard the Fox: Translated from the Dutch Original by William Caxton*, ed. Norman F. Blake (London, 1970); *Paris and Vienne: Translated from the French and Printed by William Caxton*, ed. MacEdward Leach (London, 1957); *Caxton's Blanchardyn and Eglantine c. 1489: From Lord Spencer's Unique Imperfect Copy, Completed by the Original French and the Second English Version of 1595*, ed. Leon Kellner (London, 1890); and *Caxton's Eneydos 1490: Englished from the French Liure des Eneydes, 1483*, ed. W. T. Culley/F. J. Furnivall (London, 1890). For the analysis of Caxton's texts, I have also used the texts in the

verse, the texts in this list are all prose works. In the case of *The Canterbury Tales*, I will, when necessary, conduct separate analyses of prose (i.e. "The Tale of Melibee" and "The Parson's Tale")[4] and verse (the remaining tales).

There are both advantages and disadvantages to analysing the later Middle English period. The disadvantage is the fact that the discourse marker use of *pray* has not yet fully developed in the period, although there are a number of examples showing intermediate stages in the process. The Chaucer and Caxton texts under consideration provide no example like (2), where the verb *pray* occurs alone, i.e. without a subject or an object, accompanying an imperative sentence.

On the other hand, there is a significant advantage in dealing with the period of later Middle English. Namely, ambiguities which are likely to occur in later texts are eliminated. About examples of the following kind, Akimoto (2000: 70-71) wonders whether the pronoun *you* is the dative object of *pray* or whether it is the subject of the complement clause:

(3) I pray *you* come and lodge with me here at my place ... (Malory, 94).

Fortunately, this problem does not arise in the present analysis, although Caxton is more or less contemporary with Malory. Both in Chaucer and Caxton, subjective *ye* and dative *you* are distinguished in form, as far as can be seen in my data. As (4) and (5) below illustrate, the subject of the complement clause occurs in the form of *ye*:

(4) Dame, I prey yow that ye be nat displesed of thynges that I seye, ... ("The Tale of Melibee", 1697)

(5) For your sake than ye wene I pray yow alle that *ye* remembre hym ... (*Reynard the Fox*, 108/33-34).

Innsbruck Computer Archive of Machine-Readable English Texts (ICAMET), with the exception of *Reynard the Fox*, whose electronic text was provided by Professor Tadamasa Nishimura. I am grateful to Professor Manfred Markus, the chief compiler of the ICAMET, and to Professor Nishimura.

4 Strictly speaking, the prologue of "The Parson's Tale" is written in verse. To avoid complication, however, it is included in the former group (i.e. prose). There are only three relevant examples of *pray* in the verse part of "The Parson's Tale".

It is, therefore, usually safe to judge the form *you* as dative in this study. Still, a question remains as to whether *come* in (3) above is imperative or whether it is a bare infinitive. Although I will keep this question open for the moment, I take the view that it is most likely an imperative, as I will discuss later.

The second point I would like to raise is that the verb *pray* in the data of the present study often satisfies two major conditions to develop into the discourse marker 'please'. More specifically, a number of examples of *pray* occur with first person subjects, and in the present tense. Due to the nature of the meaning of the discourse marker at issue, *pray* needs to satisfy these conditions to become a candidate. And in the texts under analysis, there are a sufficient number of candidates available. As for the subject, around 60% or more of the relevant examples, i.e. *pray* with some sort of complement, are attested in the first person (most frequently in the form of *I pray* ...).[5] *The Canterbury Tales* (prose and verse), for instance, provides 143 relevant instances of *pray*, of which 94 (65.7%) take the first person as their subjects. Similarly, *Reynard the Fox* gives a total of 41 relevant instances, of which 26 (63.4%) occur with first person subjects. By and large, the same applies to the remaining texts as well.

To turn to the matter of tense, *pray* used with first person subjects is most frequently attested in the present tense, as shown in Table 1 below. More than 90% of the attested first-person tokens of *pray* occur in present tense; thus, *pray* with first person subjects has a clear and outstanding tendency to occur in the present tense. Words used under such conditions do not always develop into discourse markers, but at least they are ready to do so. In the following sections, I will explore the extent of the development of the verb *pray* in Chaucer's and Caxton's works under consideration. The examples treated in the present paper are limited to those followed by some sort of complement; but the term "complement" is interpreted in a broad sense (including not only *pray* followed by *that*-clauses and infinitives, but also *pray* followed by imperative and interrogative sentences).

---

5 The singular pronoun *I* predominates, but the plural *we* also occurs.

Person: / Tense: / Source:	1st person		2nd and 3rd persons	
	present	others[6]	present	others
Chaucer				
Boece	7	0	0	2
The Canterbury Tales (prose)	9	0	4	7
The Canterbury Tales (verse)	83	2	6	32
Caxton				
Reynard the Fox	21	5	2	13
Paris and Vienne	59	2	4	23
Blanchardyn	18	3	1	27
Eneydos	10	2	0	8
Totals	207	14	17	112

Table 1. The tense of *pray* in the first person and in the other persons.

3. The decline of *that*-clauses after the verb *to pray*

3.1. The overall tendency

The results of Akimoto's (2000: 70) analysis of three fifteenth-century texts suggests that the decline of *that*-clauses subordinate to *pray* indicates the beginning of the syntactic development of this verb. He gives the following table, which provides the frequencies of different complements dominated by *I pray you/thee* in *The Paston Letters*, Margery Kempe, and Thomas Malory:

6 Tenseless forms of *pray* such as infinitives, gerunds, and participles are also classified under this category, as long as they are followed by the complements defined above. To turn to tensed forms, there are a very limited number of second person subjects with *pray*. Thus, most examples in this category include third person subjects. The third person is often used in narratives, which explains the frequent occurrence of *pray* with third person subjects in the past tense.

	Paston Letters	Margery Kempe	Thomas Malory
imperative	59	38	14
þat-clauses	56	1	3
to-infinitive	9	2	4

Table 2. Frequency of complements found with *I pray you/thee* in the fifteenth century (from Akimoto 2000: 70).

The major difference between *The Paston Letters* and the other two texts is the much less frequent use of *that*-clauses (*þat*-clauses in this table) in the latter. The verb *pray* in Margery Kempe and Thomas Malory most frequently dominates, or rather introduces, imperative sentences, whereas in *The Paston Letters*, *that*-clauses (56 tokens) are almost as frequent as imperative sentences (59 tokens). Most probably, the table signals that the process of the development of *pray* was further advanced after *The Paston Letters*.[7]

Thus, the present paper, first of all, focuses upon the presence or absence of *that*-clauses dominated by *pray* in Chaucer and Caxton. Table 3 shows how frequently the same verb dominates three types of complement: (i) *that*-clauses, (ii) clauses where the conjunction *that* is simply understood, though not expressed, and (iii) infinitives and imperative sentences. *The Canterbury Tales* provides two examples (to be discussed in Section 4 below) where *pray* introduces an interrogative sentence. For convenience, these are for the moment classified under (iii), since the main purpose of this table is to show the overall extent of the decline of *that*-clauses in the literary works under discussion, including first, second, and third person subjects (or understood subjects), both in the present and in the past tenses.

7 Letters of various dates are included in *The Paston Letters*, and some of them are later in date than Margery Kempe. Thus, the comparison involves issues of style and register, as well as the matter of date.

Construction: / Source:	(i) *that*-clauses	(ii) *that* understood but not expressed	(iii) infinitives and imperatives
Chaucer			
Boece	7	0	2
The Canterbury Tales (prose)	10	0	10
The Canterbury Tales (verse)	35	7	81
Caxton			
Reynard the Fox	15	0	26
Paris and Vienne	72	0	16
Blanchardyn	40	0	9
Eneydos	15	0	5
Totals	194	7	149

Table 3. Complements of *pray* in Chaucer and Caxton.

Some illustrative examples are given below in (6)–(11):

(6) & I *praye* you that ye telle to me yf ye haue doon to me suche seruyce … (*Paris and Vienne*, 28/33-35)

(7) And thanne Palas and Eneas made sacrifyce to the goddes, & *prayed* theym that they wolde be to theym socourable. (*Eneydos*, 131/29-30)

(8) I *prey* yow to my wyl ye wole assente. ("The Merchant's Tale", 1468)

(9) The quene had pyte on hym. And *prayde* the kyng to haue mercy on hym … (*Reynard the Fox*, 35/5-6)

(10) I *praye* you to telle me the trouth of it (*Blanchardyn and Eglantine*, 128/26-27)

(11) I *pray* yow aske ye hym yf it was not thus … (*Reynard the Fox*, 95/14-15).

On the whole, *that*-clauses are relatively well-preserved in both Chaucer and Caxton, although the former is much earlier in date than the latter. It is likely that the structural development of the verb *pray* is relatively slow, or at least not very dramatic, in later Middle English. Interestingly enough, however, there are a few texts which are markedly progressive in terms of the decline of *that*-clauses, both in Chaucer and Caxton: *The Canterbury Tales* (especially tales written in verse) and *Reynard the Fox*. In fact, most examples of (iii), i.e. infinitives and imperative sentences, are attested in these two texts. In the following discussion, I will make a further detailed analysis of the uses of *pray*, exploring first, second, and third persons separately. *The Canterbury Tales* and *Reynard the Fox*, which display significant recession of *that*-clauses, will be given the greatest attention, although other texts will also be considered.

3.2. The difference between the first person and the other persons

The above accounts suggest that the development of *pray* is relatively well-advanced in *The Canterbury Tales* (especially tales written in verse) and in *Reynard the Fox*. Then, the question is whether the decline of *that*-clauses is observed particularly well in the case of first person subjects. In other words, one needs to ask whether the first person is already taking a different path from the second and third persons in *The Canterbury Tales* and *Reynard the Fox*.

The difference, however, turns out to be very slight between the first person and the other persons, as far as the extent to which the use of *that*-clauses recedes is concerned. Figure 1 shows the proportions of *that*-clauses (including the ellipsis of *that*) to the total of relevant examples of *pray* in the case of the first person, while Figure 2 gives the corresponding proportions in the case of the second and third persons:

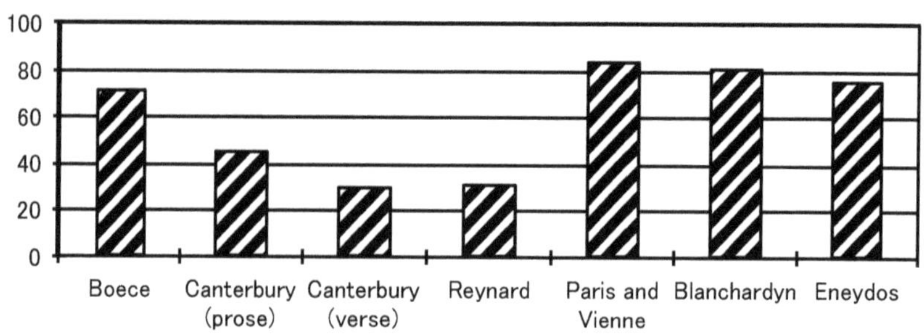

Figure 1. Proportions of first-person tokens with *that*-clauses (incl. the ellipsis of *that*) (%).

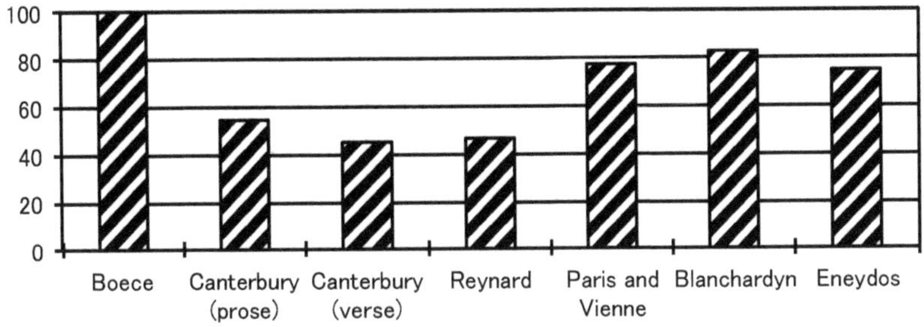

Figure 2. Proportions of second- or third-person tokens with *that*-clauses (incl. the ellipsis of *that*) (%).

Indeed, the decline of *that*-clauses is more advanced in the first person (Figure 1) than in the other persons (Figure 2), but the difference is not particularly large. Figure 2 gives the impression that *that*-clauses are especially well-preserved in *Boece* in the second and third persons. This is, however, due to the scarcity of relevant examples in this text. It gives only two for the second and third persons. Moreover, there is even a text which reveals the opposite tendency. In *Paris and Vienne*, the decline of *that*-clauses is more advanced in the second and third persons than in the first person. Here, 61 instances of the first person include 51 (83.6%) with *that*-clauses, and 27 examples of the second and third persons include 21 (77.8%) with *that*-clauses. I would surmise, therefore, that the decline of *that*-clauses is a general phenomenon which takes place with *pray* from later Middle English onwards, whether the subject of the verb is in the first person or not. In other words, the development of the discourse marker use of *pray* is more likely a result, than a cause, of the decline of *that*-clauses.

What makes the real difference between the first and the other persons is the type of complements which compete with *that*-clauses. In the case of second and third person subjects, it is predominantly *to*-infinitives that take the place of *that*-clauses. Examples include:

(12) And evere she *preyeth* hire child *to holde* his pees; ("The Man of Law's Tale", 866)

(13) neuertheles he stood and *prayd* them alle *to praye* for hym (*Reynard the Fox*, 45/12-13).

When *that*-clauses (incl. the ellipsis of *that*) are excluded, second and third person subjects in *The Canterbury Tales* (prose and verse) and

Reynard the Fox provide a total of 31 instances, of which 29 (93.5%) present *to*-infinitives. The remaining two examples are (14) and (15) below, which are most probably examples of bare infinitives.[8]

(14) Anon he *preyde* hire *strepen* hire al naked; ("The Merchant's Tale", 1958)

(15) And *prayd* me *goo* to the mare ... (*Reynard the Fox*, 58/32).

The other texts provide a total of sixteen relevant examples, all of which illustrate *to*-infinitives, as in (16):

(16) he *prayed* Edward *to wryte* to hym an ansuer wel at large of alle ... (*Paris and Vienne*, 47/14-15).

In light of the fact that a number of verbs underwent recession of *that*-clauses from later Middle English onwards (cf. Manabe 1979: 4-5; Iyeiri 2010), often leading to the expanded use of *to*-infinitives, it is only to be expected that *pray* takes the same path. For example, *forbid* is a verb of this kind. As discussed by Iyeiri (2003; 2010: 28-42), *forbid that...* is commonly encountered in Old and Middle English, but this construction dies out around the early Modern English period. In Present-day English, the same verb occurs essentially with *to*-infinitives except in such "frozen" idioms as *God forbid that I should do such a thing!* (*New English Bible*, Genesis 44:17). Two examples of *forbid* are given below. In (17), from Middle English, *forbid* dominates a *that*-clause, whereas in (18), from Present-day English, it occurs with an infinitive:

(17) In þe popes half he sede, ich *uorbede* [...] *þat* no man ne touchi þulke clerc (Robert of Gloucester [Rolles], 10369, from the *OED*)

(18) [...] it *forbids* us *to pretend* to do something which in fact cannot be done (FLOB, G52 065).

The verb *pray* with second and third person subjects also shows a decline in use with *that*-clauses, and a concomitant rise in use with *to*-infinitives.

8 Mustanoja (1960: 533) notes that the verb *pray* in Middle English "usually requires *to*, but the plain infinitive may also occur".

By contrast, the path of *pray* with first person subjects is already a different one. *To*-infinitives are evidenced, but they are restricted in frequency. There are 63 relevant examples in *The Canterbury Tales* (prose plus verse), of which only eight illustrate *to*-infinitives, as in:

(19) Thanne *preye* I thee *to rewe* upon my pyne. ("The Knight's Tale", 2382).

In *Reynard the Fox*, *to*-infinitives are slightly more frequent, but not as frequent as in the case of second and third person subjects. There are eighteen relevant examples, of which twelve show *to*-infinitives, as in:

(20) therfore I *pray* yow *to be* plesyd here wyth al (*Reynard the Fox*, 103/6).

Most of the remaining relevant examples take imperative sentences or constructions which may (or may not) be regarded as imperatives, at least in the progressive texts of *The Canterbury Tales* and *Reynard the Fox*. The path to the development of *pray* as a discourse marker with the meaning 'please' is clearly visible here. Examples like (21) and (22) below, where the imperative ending *-th* is present, are unambiguous:

(21) "I prey yow, *haveth* me nat in desdeyn, Though to this man I speke a word or two". ("The Squire's Tale", 700-1)

(22) I pray yow, *telleth* me. ("The Wife of Bath's Tale", 61).

Unfortunately, most examples occur in sequences such as (23) below. This is what Hirayama (2001: 31) classifies as "X pray Y *do*", which he identifies as the predominant form for first person subjects in *The Paston Letters*:

(23) I *prey* yow *take* the sentence of the man ("The Merchant's Tale", 2288).

This construction is ambiguous as to whether the verb is imperative or whether it is a bare infinitive. As Davis (1987: xxxvii) points out, imperatives often occur with no endings (or with *-e*) even when they are plural. Judging from the later expansion of imperative sentences along with *pray*, most examples of this kind are plausibly imperatives. Also, if the verb *pray* ever develops infinitives, it is usually *to*-infinitives rather than bare infinitives, as the above analysis of the second and third persons demonstrates.[9] Again, forms without *to* after *pray* are more likely to be imperatives than infinitives. In any case, they are, at least, examples that can be regarded as imperatives.

As long as the subject of *pray* is in the first person, the same tendency seems to persist even when the object of *pray* is *god* (often occurring with the preposition *to*, as in *to god*) instead of *thee* or *you*. Relevant examples are too scarce in *Reynard the Fox*, while *The Canterbury Tales* (prose and verse) provides thirteen cases of (iii) (i.e. infinitives and imperatives). They are all what Hirayama (2001: 31) calls the "X pray Y *do*" type, as illustrated below. None of the examples display *to*-infinitives:

(24) y pray god *kepe* you fro mysauenture [...] (*Reynard the Fox*, 45/33-34).

Here, *kepe* is most likely an imperative, although the bare infinitive interpretation cannot entirely be eliminated. The following is a clearer example of the use of an imperative after *I pray (to) God*:

(25) I prey to God so *yeve* his soule reste! ("The Clerk's Tale", 30).

Here, the existence of *so*, which often introduced imperative sentences in Middle English, leads us to the imperative interpretation.

4. The development of *pray* in *The Canterbury Tales*

As discussed thus far, the decline of *that*-clauses occurs with first person subjects and second and third person subjects alike, but the constructions adopted as replacements in these two situations differ. Most of the examples of the second and third persons without *that*-clauses reveal the use of *to*-infinitives. By contrast, the path taken by the first person is different. Some examples of first person subjects co-occur with *to*-infinitives, too, but this use is restricted in frequency.

9 My contention here differs from Visser (1963-73: §2074), who takes the bare infinitive interpretation.

Instead, a large number of relevant instances display imperatives or complements which can be regarded as imperatives. Clearly, this is a path which leads to the development of the discourse marker *pray* 'please'. The separation of the two paths is already visible in later Middle English.[10] As far as the data of the present study are concerned, *Reynard the Fox* and *The Canterbury Tales* are relatively well-advanced in terms of the development of *pray*. The present section provides some additional phenomena which are most probably related to the development of the discourse marker use of *pray* and which are evidenced particularly in *The Canterbury Tales*.

In *The Canterbury Tales*, *I (we) pray* occurs not only before the complement clauses, but also in "medial" and "final" positions, as shown in examples (26) and (27) respectively:

(26) Speketh so pleyn at this tyme, *we yow preye*, That we may understonde what ye seye. ("The Clerk's Tale", 19-20)

(27) Telle on thy tale, Manciple, *I thee preye*. ("The Manciple's Tale", 103).

Out of a total of 94 relevant instances of the first person use of *pray*, *The Canterbury Tales* provides four examples of "medial" positions and fourteen instances of "final" positions. The other texts investigated here yield only a single instance (28), which comes from Chaucer's *Boece*:

(28) "Do," quod I, "and schewe me what is thilke verray welefulnesse, *I preie the*, withoute taryinge." (*Boece*, 421/40-43).

Since the eighteen examples in *The Canterbury Tales* are all attested in verse, it is most likely that this form is, to some extent at least, as-

---

10 Hirayama gives the following scale (where "X" is the subject of *pray*, whereas "Y" is the dative object of the same verb) and considers that the verb is more and more grammaticalized as we go further down the list.
X PRAY Y *that* S + V
X PRAY *that* S + V
X PRAY Y *to do*
X PRAY Y + S + V
X PRAY Y *do*
X PRAY *do*
In my view, however, the path of the development of *to*-infinitives and that of the discourse marker use of *pray* are separate.

cribable to the metrical and rhyme schemes. At the same time, however, the example in *Boece* shows that it also occurs in prose. Certainly, the freedom in the locations of *I (we) pray* can also be considered to indicate a more advanced stage of the development of *pray*.

Here, it is relevant to mention the famous study by Thompson/Mulac (1991), which discusses the development of *I think* as an epistemic phrase.[11] They provide the following three sentences and consider that the topic of the sentences increasingly moves from the subject of the main clause to the subject of the complement clause as we go down the list. In other words, the category shift of *I think* is more advanced in (29b) than in (29a), and in (29c) than in (29b). In (29b), the conjunction *that* is deleted, and in (29c), *I think* is displaced from the original position.[12] Thus, *I think* obtains larger and larger degrees of freedom in location as we go down the list.

(29) a. I think *that* we're definitely moving towards being more technological.

b. I think *0* exercise is really beneficial, to anybody.

c. It's just your point of view you know what you like to do in your spare time *I think*.

(Thompson/Mulac 1991, italics in original)

They take the view that *I think* in (29b) and (29c) is already what they call an "epistemic phrase" and that it functions "roughly as an epistemic adverb such as *maybe* with respect to the clause it is associated with" (1991: 313). In my view, the same kind of categorical shift takes place in the process of the development of the discourse marker use of *pray*. Thus, the irregular positioning of *I (we) pray* in Chaucer's texts, particularly in *The Canterbury Tales*, is a significant feature of the development of *pray*. (26), (27), and (28) illustrate cases where *I (we) pray* is parenthetical and where the topic of the sentence is placed upon the complement clause, so that *I (we) pray* here is already a step advanced.

---

11 There is an abundance of previous studies in this field. For example, see Urmson (1952) and Brinton (2008). See also Iyeiri (2010: 119-75).

12 As Brinton (2008: 11-12) remarks, this is not the only possible approach to the development of epistemic phrases. One alternative she mentions is to assume the independent occurrence of the epistemic phrases and their later insertion into the "anchor" clause.

Incidentally, *The Canterbury Tales* is the only text that reveals the stage of (29b) in Thompson/Mulac's framework, where the conjunction *that* is deleted. Examples include:

(30)(=8) I *prey* yow to my wyl ye wole assente. ("The Merchant's Tale", 1468).

The text provides as many as seven examples of this kind, while none of the remaining texts yield any instances illustrating this construction. Although the influence of the metrical scheme cannot entirely be excluded in this verse text, examples like (30) can also be regarded as exemplifying the process of becoming a discourse marker.

Finally, *The Canterbury Tales* is again the only text that yields evidence of *pray* occurring with an interrogative sentence, as in:

(31) Why is thy lord so sluttissh, *I the preye*, And is of power bettre clooth to beye, If that his dede a ccorde with thy speche? ("The Canon's Yeoman's Tale", 636-38)

(32) What is Magnasia, good sire, *I yow preye*? ("The Canon's Yeoman's Tale", 1458).

These two are the only examples in the data presently under investigation. However, though scarce, this use of *I pray* is noteworthy in that it is again clearly parenthetical.[13] Moreover, it is performative rather than literal in meaning, functioning almost as an adverb attached to the interrogative clause. Certainly, in these examples the topic of the sentence is located in the interrogative clause.

5. Conclusion

The present paper has discussed the historical development of the uses of *pray*, by investigating a selection of writings by Chaucer and Caxton. First of all, its frequent occurrence in the present tense with first person subjects indicates that the verb already possesses inherent readiness to

13 Examples of this type are not copious in general. For more instances, see Traugott/Dasher (2002: 252-54).

develop into a discourse marker. This applies to all the texts under investigation in the present study.

As for the syntactic change that this verb experiences, Section 3 investigated the extent of the decline of *that*-clauses. Of the six texts under consideration, Chaucer's *Canterbury Tales* and Caxton's *Reynard the Fox* are more progressive than the remaining texts, in that complements other than *that*-clauses are observed to some noticeable extent in them. This is attested almost equally between *pray* with first person subjects and the same verb with second and third person subjects, although slightly more excessively in the former.

What makes the real distinction between the first person and the other persons is the type of complements which take the place of declining *that*-clauses. When the subject of *pray* is in the second or third persons, it is predominantly *to*-infinitives that develop side by side with the decline of *that*-clauses. This is in accordance with the general tendency from later Middle English to early Modern English that *that*-clauses were increasingly replaced by non-finite forms like infinitives. By contrast, *to*-infinitives are not at all common when the subject of *pray* is in the first person. Instead, *pray* is more frequently accompanied by an imperative. The tendency is particularly clear in the progressive texts of *The Canterbury Tales* and *Reynard the Fox*. Thus, *pray* with first person subjects is already taking a different path from the other persons, i.e. the path to develop into a discourse marker with the meaning 'please'.

Finally, the above discussion paid special attention to *The Canterbury Tales*, which presents some interesting phenomena in respect of the development of *pray*. The text, for example, yields eighteen cases in which *I (we) pray* occurs in clearly parenthetical positions, that is, in "medial" and "final" positions of the sentence. Outside this text, the whole sample of the present study gives only a single example of this kind in *Boece*, another Chaucerian text. Although the occurrence of these examples is, perhaps to some extent, due to the exigency of the metrical and rhyme schemes, they also display a more advanced stage of the development of *pray*, since the topic of the sentence has been shifted to the complement clause with the set *I (we) pray* functioning almost like a sentential adverb. The same applies to the deletion of *that*-clauses, which is again restricted to *The Canterbury Tales*. The final construction the above discussion treated was the use of *pray* with an interrogative sentence. Here again, the sequence *I (we) pray* functions almost like a sentential adverb attached to the interrogation. This use of *pray* is also limited to *The Canterbury Tales*.

References

Akimoto, Minoji 2000. The Grammaticalization of the Verb 'pray'. In Fischer, Olga / Rosenbach, Anette / Stein, Dieter (eds) *Pathways of Change: Grammaticalization in English*. Amsterdam: John Benjamins, 67-84.

Blake, Norman Francis 2002. *A Grammar of Shakespeare's Language*. London: Palgrave.

Brinton, Laurel J. 1996. *Pragmatic Markers in English: Grammaticalization and Discourse Functions*. Topics in English Linguistics, 19. Berlin: Mouton de Gruyter.

Brinton, Laurel J. 2008. *The Comment Clause in English: Syntactic Origins and Pragmatic Development*. Cambridge: Cambridge University Press.

Busse, Ulrich 2002. Changing Politeness Strategies in English Requests: A Diachronic Investigation. In Fisiak, Jacek (ed.) *Studies in English Historical Linguistics and Philology: A Festschrift for Akio Oizumi*. Frankfurt am Main: Peter Lang, 17-35.

Davis, Norman 1987. Language and Versification. In Benson, Larry D. *et al.* (eds) *The Riverside Chaucer*, 3rd edition. Boston: Houghton Mifflin, xxix-xlv.

Hirayama, Naoki 2001. The Language of Requests in the *Paston Letters*: The Grammaticalization and Subjectification of X PRAY Y. *Hiroshima Studies in English Language and Literature* 46, 25-43.

Iyeiri, Yoko 2003. 'God Forbid!': A Historical Study of the Verb *forbid* in Different Versions of the English Bible. *Journal of English Linguistics* 31, 149-162.

Iyeiri, Yoko 2009. The Verb *pray* in Different Letters of the Paston Family with Special Reference to its Pragmatic Use. In Watanabe, Shinichiro / Hosoya, Yukiteru (eds) *English Philology and

Corpus Studies: A Festschrift in Honour of Mitsunori Imai to Celebrate his Seventieth Birthday. Tokyo: Shohakusha, 169-183.

Iyeiri, Yoko 2010. *Verbs of Implicit Negation and their Complements in the History of English*. Amsterdam: John Benjamins.

Kerkhof, J. 1982. *Studies in the Language of Geoffrey Chaucer*. 2nd edition. Leiden: Leiden University Press.

Manabe, Kazumi 1979. *Syntax and Style in Early English: Finite and Non-finite Clauses c900-1600*. Tokyo: Kaibunsha.

Mustanoja, Tauno F. 1960. *A Middle English Syntax, Part I: Parts of Speech*. Helsinki: Société Néophilologique.

Thompson, Sandra A. / Mulac, Anthony 1991. A Quantitative Perspective on the Grammaticalization of Epistemic Parentheticals in English. In Traugott, Elizabeth Closs / Heine, Bernd (eds) *Approaches to Grammaticalization, 2: Focus on Types of Grammatical Markers*. Amsterdam: John Benjamins, 313-329.

Traugott, Elizabeth Closs / Richard B. 2002. *Regularity in Semantic Change*. Cambridge: Cambridge University Press.

Ukaji, Masatomo 1978. *Imperative Sentences in Early Modern English*. Tokyo: Kaitakusha.

Urmson, James O. 1952. Parenthetical Verbs. *Mind: A Quarterly Review of Psychology and Philosophy* 61, 480-496.

Visser, Frederik Th. 1963-73. *An Historical Syntax of the English Language*. 3 parts in 4 vols. Leiden: E. J. Brill.

SATORU TSUKAMOTO

Defining Periods of Middle English by Measuring Rates of Language Change

1. Introduction

Middle English is often referred to as a period of change. Most notably, it is a "period of levelled endings" (Sweet 1891: 211) during which most of the inflections prominent in Old English were lost. However, the fact that the English of this period is characterised more by variation than by static identifiable features makes drawing clear boundaries problematic, both around and within the period.

In consequence, most scholars draw boundaries based, not on linguistic descriptions, but instead on political or historical events. The beginning of Middle English is usually associated with the Norman Conquest of 1066. It is, however, acknowledged that this "did not suddenly put an end to [...] Old English" (Brook 1958: 42); the language changes sparked by that event took a generation or so to spread. Thus, the beginning of the Middle English period is generally placed at around 1100; but this date is chosen somewhat arbitrarily, and should not be regarded as a clear transition point.

Still less is there any clear endpoint for Middle English. The end of the period is variously identified with the introduction of printing to England in 1476 (e.g. Brook 1958), or the start of the Tudor monarchy in 1485 (e.g. Blake 1992); but again, neither of these events had any great immediate linguistic effect. For example, Brook notes that the influence of printing "became important only when the gradual spread of education increased the number of people who could read" (1958: 54). Thus, as Blake (1992: 1) comments, the political or historical events commonly used as boundary markers "may have an impact on the development of the English language in the longer term but they are hardly appropriate as guides to the dating of periods in it". (For much the same reason, Strang (1970) chooses not to rely on labels assuming some unitary "Old English" or "Middle English", and instead treats the entire history of English in 200-year periods, to allow consideration of the time span required for language changes to be completed.)

Even if we agree to maintain the conventional divisions based on English history, a problem still remains. The language changes so much during the period that it cannot easily be treated as a single entity; as Burrow/Turvile-Petre note (1992: 6), the language of "twelfth- and early thirteenth-century poets and prose writers [...] would have appeared distinctly archaic to their fourteenth-century successors". Thus the question arises of exactly how the Middle English period should be subdivided. Most descriptions, like that of Burrow/Turvile-Petre (1992), assume some division between an "early", or "archaic" Middle English, and a "late" Middle English characterised by more "innovative" features. However, Burrow/Turvile-Petre offer no further description of any criteria by which Middle English texts might be assigned to either subperiod. Meanwhile, Wright/Wright (1928: 1-2) argue instead for a three-fold division, mainly on phonological grounds, between "Early ME" (1100-1250), "Ordinary ME" (1250-1400), and "Late ME" (1400-1500).

Lass (2000) attempts to quantify the relative "archaism" of a text through quantification of ten different linguistic features: (a) root-initial accent, (b) at least 3 distinct vowel qualities in weak inflectional syllables, (c) a dual, (d) grammatical gender, (e) four vowel-grades in (certain) strong verbs, (f) distinct dative in at least some nouns, (g) inflected definite article, (h) adjective inflection, (i) infinitive suffix, and (j) person/number marking on the verb. In his system, boundaries can be defined, not politically, nor historically, but linguistically from numerical observations. In his criteria, some features are treated as binary ("full", scored as 1, versus "null", scored as 0), and others as ternary ("full" (1) versus "half" (0.5) versus "null" (0)). On this basis, Lass calculates index scores for selected reference texts of Middle English, ranging from *Orrmulum* (0.75) through *The Owl and Nightingale* (0.70), and the Kentish sermons (0.60), to Chaucer (0.35).[1]

1 Nevalainen (2006: 3) claims that "Chaucer best represents the kind of language marked as Middle English on the scale" since Chaucer's text scores at 0.35, which corresponds to the marking for Middle English on the scale by Lass (2000). One may argue what status the language in the 15th century

It should be noted, however, that this selection of texts is made not comprehensively, but rather arbitrarily; his reference texts are described as those "which I suspect most colleagues would accept as good ones" (2000: 26). It should also be noted that the value given to each variable is discrete, not continuous: the value 1 is given when a text is in "full possession of all the archaic character", 0.5 is given when it is in "a reductive modification", and 0 is given when it is in "full loss of the character" (2000: 27). His measurement is not based on the actual number of occurrences of each variable. A further limitation is that his study is based only on morphological and phonological features; syntactic variables are not considered.

The present study aims to define boundaries within the Middle English period. It adopts Lass's approach of using computable linguistic data in the analysis, and extends this to cover both morphological and syntactic features over time. It also makes use of a larger selection of texts (more than 50 texts, compared to the small number of "typical" texts in Lass's analysis). Section 2 introduces the technique applied in this analysis. Section 3 discusses the results obtained. Section 4 summarises the main conclusions.

2. Method

The objective of this research is to identify linguistic boundaries within Middle English by examining how the language changed in the period, focussing on the rates of syntactic changes that took place in the period. Changes in the rate can reveal divisions between successive segments that are obscured if the whole period is merely labelled as "Middle English". The Penn-Helsinki Parsed Corpus of Middle English, Second

---

would have, if the score of Chaucer lies at one extreme of the scale of Middle English. It is interesting to note that Lass maintains (1992: 90) that "the bulk of the fifteenth-century developments are of a piece with earlier ones, and English morphology by the 1480s is quite a lot more 'modern' looking than its phonology. […] For this reason Middle English will 'end' rather earlier in the phonological sphere than it does in the morphological […]"; hence Lass takes Chaucer as marking the end of Middle English on phonological criteria.

Edition (henceforth PPCME2) is employed here to trace chronological changes in Middle English. The corpus contains 1.3 million words coded with 90 part-of-speech tags and 57 types of phrasal markers in 55 texts.[2] Changes in these grammatical features may be considered representative of linguistic change in general. Any temporary increases observed in the overall rate of change may then be interpreted as indicating transition boundaries between slower-changing (and so, more stable) periods of English.

The following methodological steps were applied:

1) Tokens of each grammatical item were retrieved and counted in each text; the counts were then normalised for text length, to produce relative frequencies per 1000 words.
2) Grammatical items entirely absent from more than 3 texts were excluded from further analysis, on the basis that their text frequencies would be too low to produce reliable estimates for frequency differences across the entire period. This criterion eliminated 66 of the less common items.
3) Regression slopes against text date were then calculated for each remaining variable, in order to identify the variables exhibiting the most consistent, and thus the most descriptively useful, shifts (whether a decrease or an increase) over the entire Middle English period.[3]
4) Only those items with slopes (whether negative or positive) significant at $p<0.01$ were retained for investigation.[4] This criterion eliminated all grammatical items except for the 14 counts presented in Table 1 below.
5) The texts were grouped into sets representing subperiods of 50 years each.

---

2 The texts in the corpus are unevenly distributed across time periods. There are two texts in 1150-1200, 11 in 1200-1250, one in 1250-1300, one in 1300-1350, six in 1350-1400, 13 in 1400-1450, 19 in 1450-1500 and two in 1500-1550.

3 The regression slopes were calculated using R 2.8.1. The statistical test for the slope was performed using the *t*-value given for the regression model.

4 This research utilizes the linguistic items with a (positive or negative) slope value as an indicator for changes since these show the most visibly detectable signs of change. Of course, items with a levelled slope may also be involved in change.

6) The average rate of occurrence for each remaining normalised count was calculated over all of the texts representing each subperiod.
7) Finally, the difference in average frequency between each pair of successive subperiods was calculated for each feature, as a point estimate of the rate of change in that feature.

3. Results and discussion

The linear regression coefficients (i.e. the slopes of the lines describing average change over time) for the 14 variables retained are given in Table 1.[5]

Feature	Abbreviation	Slope (tokens per 1000 words per year)
Infinitive *be*	BE	+0.008859
Existential *there*	EX	+0.004071
Possessive noun	N$	–0.01734
Negation	NEG	–0.03435
Ambiguous-level nominal constituent or projection (N, N', or NP)	NX	+0.011429
Quantifier	Q	–0.034054
Present verb (including present subjunctive)	VBP	–0.06358
Noun-phrase adverb	NP-ADV	–0.018923
Second object	NP-OB2	–0.02568
Possessive noun phrase	NP-POS	–0.015515
Relative clause	CP-REL	–0.025407
Participial clause	IP-PPL	+0.007074
Subordinate clause	IP-SUB	–0.06255
Wh-prepositional phrase	WPP	+0.006219

Table 1. Slopes of the linear regression model in PPCME2.

All of these items show a significant change in frequency over the Middle English period. There is a general decline of negative forms

5 For details of the definition and coding of these features, see Taylor/Koch (1994) and Kytö (1996).

(NEG) as in (1), possessive nouns (N$, NP-POS) as in (2), quantifiers (Q) as in (3), present verb forms (VBP) as in (4), noun-phrase adverbs (NP-ADV) as in (5), second objects (NP-OB2) as in (6), subordinate clauses (IP-SUB) as in (7), and relative clauses (CP-REL) as in (8).

(1) for we *ne* mowen *nat* considere thilke ordenaunce. (CMBOETH, 452.C2.493)

(2) and thys sayde Jamys sette *the kyngys baner* agayne an howse ende (CMGREGOR, 198.1584)

(3) We schal vndirstande þat *yche* word of Godes lawe ys soth algatys, *al* gif *somme* men vndurstanden hyt falsely. (CMWYCSER, 227.64)

(4) Ich *chulle* þtt he *wite* hit ful wel, tu eke mid al. (CMJULIA, 100.72)

(5) and there was Gryfflette put to the erth *horse and man*, and Lucas the Butler *horse and man*, by kynge Brandegoris and kynge Idres and kynge Angwyshaunce. (CMMALORY, 21.651)

(6) þis *me* were leouere gef þu wel waldest to habben & to halden þe cwic þen to acwelle þe. (CMKATHE, 43.383)

(7) for in that dai God ceesside of al his werk which *he made of nougt*, that *he schulde make*. (CMOTEST, II, 1G.86)

(8) Therfor Jhesus cam in to a cite of Samarie, *that is seid Sicar*, bisidis the place, *that Jacob gaf to Joseph, his sone*. (CMNTEST, IV, 1.248)

By contrast, there are general increases of existential *there* (EX) as in (9), infinitival *be* (BE) as in (10), participial clauses (IP-PPL) as in (11), *wh*-prepositional phrases (WPP) as in (12), and ambiguous-level nominal constituents (NX) as in (13).

(9) whan the kynge of alle beestis had assemblid alle his court, / *ther* was none of them alle, / but that he had complayned sore on Reynart the foxe (CMREYNAR, 7.19)

(10) for bothe thy good name and thy conscience shulden so *be* blemysshed, were thei neuere so good. (CMAELR4, 4.107)

(11) Than sche, consyderyng *þis wondyrful chawngyng, sekyng socowr vndyr þe wengys of hyr gostly modyr, Holy Cherch*, went. (CMKEMPE, 2.15)

(12) This Joyous trouth conteyneth in itself two partyes, *In whoos declaracyon* with our lordys mercy & your suffrauce, shall stonde the some of this poore collacon. (CMFITZJA, A2R.7)

(13) Congruently also Youthe maye be namyd Nonae i. nundinae, a fayer or *market.* (CMINNOCE, 10.168)

These features represent changes that have often been noted in descriptions of the history of English. Decreases in possessive nouns and second objects are linked to the loss of morphological endings (e.g. Baugh/Cable 1978: 158-159). Replacement of *ne ... not* by *not,* and other reductions in multiple negatives, are a well-discussed feature of the development of negation (e.g. Jespersen 1924: 331-336 and Burrow/Turvile-Petre 1992: 52). Non-finite verbal forms such as infinitive and participle forms developed in this period (e.g. Fischer 1992: 313-314).

To more clearly determine the timing of these changes, an average frequency of occurrence was calculated for each variable over the texts representing each of eight successive 50-year subperiods. The results are shown in Table 2 below.

Period:[6] Feature:	1150-1200	1200-1250	1250-1300	1300-1350	1350-1400	1400-1450	1450-1500	1500-1550
BE	1.3	2.38	1.69	2.83	4.58	4.99	4.41	3.62
EX	0.25	0.45	0.28	1.72	1.0	1.09	1.4	1.93
N$	7.48	5.66	0.85	0.66	0.96	1.02	1.64	1.32
NEG	14.05	15.24	10.72	18.03	10.87	9.14	6.06	4.94
NX	0.87	0.86	0.0	1.08	2.15	1.91	4.02	2.75
Q	32.33	28.38	20.02	21.13	15.98	20.59	20.98	17.74
VBP	19.55	42.13	33.28	53.59	26.0	27.58	21.45	12.34
NP-ADV	0.89	1.41	0.28	0.27	0.61	0.74	0.59	0.58
NP-OB2	12.53	11.15	12.41	5.98	4.04	4.22	5.28	7.66
NP-POS	8.79	5.48	1.41	0.99	2.12	1.07	2.45	1.84
CP-REL	17.11	23.15	26.79	28.84	15.93	18.92	15.16	16.38
IP-PPL	0.32	1.25	0.0	0.29	1.06	1.64	3.12	2.89
IP-SUB	63.01	72.89	77.27	73.97	52.78	60.09	55.45	56.03
WPP	0.7	0.97	1.69	3.49	2.75	2.35	2.57	1.88

Table 2. Frequency of selected language features, per 1000 words, averaged across texts for 50-year subperiods of PPCME2.

6 The periods listed in Table 2 extend up to, but do not include, the closing date; e.g. "1150-1200" covers texts from 1150 to 1199.

Table 2 lists the frequencies of the 14 features, normalised per 1000 words for each text, and averaged across all texts representing each 50-year period. The features examined differ greatly in frequency; but more importantly for the purpose of this investigation, they also show considerable variation in frequency over time. These changes, however, are not the smoothly linear trends one might expect from a significant regression fit. Instead, for most features, most of the frequency movement takes place relatively suddenly (within a 50-year time span). For example, NP-OB2 has an average frequency of roughly 12 tokens per thousand words from 1150-1300, but this drops suddenly to an average of about 5 for all subsequent subperiods; and similar sudden decreases are seen for CP-REL (shifting from 28 to 15 tokens/1000w at around 1350), and IP-SUB. Conversely, sudden increases in normalized text frequencies are seen for BE (doubling from 2.5 to 5 tokens per 1000 words after 1350) and EX (which quadruples in frequency after 1300).

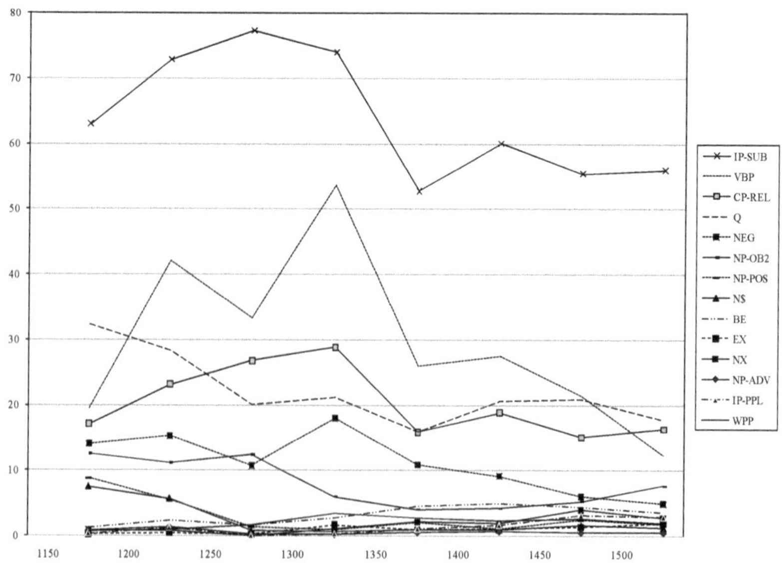

Figure 1. Average frequencies of feature occurrence in each sub-period of PPCME2.

To demonstrate some of the typical patterns of change observed in frequency of occurrence in each subperiod, figures are graphed below for four items: IP-PPL, and EX, which have the largest and second largest positive slope, and N$ and NP-POS, which have the largest and second largest negative slope. The observed frequency of each text, the expected regression line, and the average of the actual occurrence in the actual year are given in Figures 2 and 3.[7]

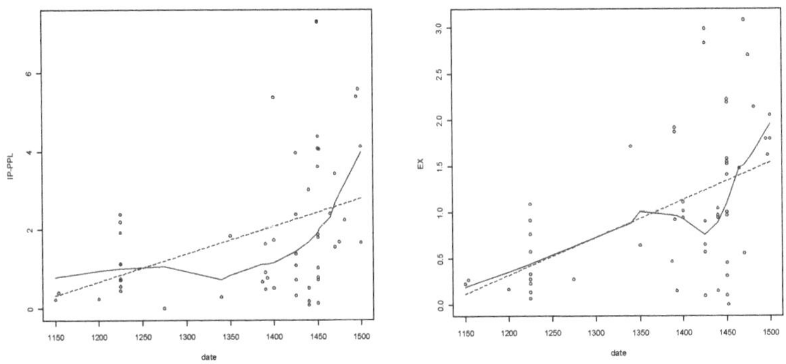

Figure 2. Scatter plots for text frequency of IP-PPL and EX against date.

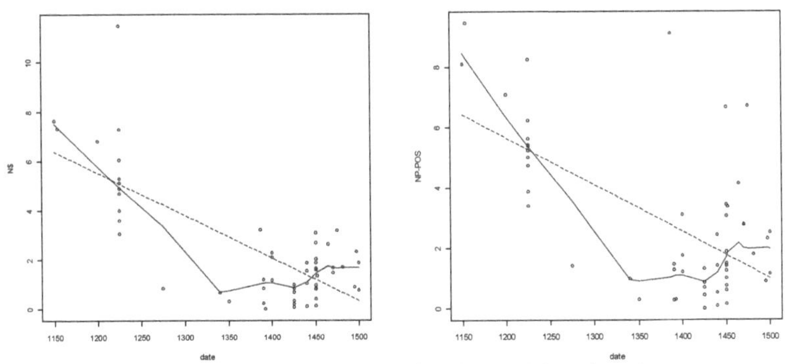

Figure 3. Scatter plots for text frequency of N$ and NP-POS against date.

The solid line in Figures 2 and 3 connects the observed average text frequencies of the feature in successive subperiods. The dotted line is the regression line obtained for the entire set of text scores (i.e., the line of best fit obtained by assuming a smoothly linear change). However, it can be seen that these two summaries of the data are not in exact agreement; for all four variables, the observed local rate of change varies over time, with a more exaggerated slope (i.e., faster change) in one time period. In fact, these graphs even exhibit an apparent change in direction of change at some time during the ME period. Against their

7 Figures 2 and 3 were obtained using graphing functions in R 2.8.1.

overall increasing trend, IP-PPL shows a temporary halt between 1300-1350, and EX shows a sudden decline between 1350-1400, while the frequency of N$ and NP-POS generally decreases over time, except for an apparent increase between 1400-1450.

One might argue from these figures that these changes of average frequency of the features may be artefacts of the relatively small amount of data provided in this corpus for some time periods. Certainly, it is true that distribution is not even through the Middle English period, as is shown by Table 3 below, which presents the dialectal distribution of the quantity of data (in terms of total wordcounts) available in each subperiod.

Dialect	East Midlands	Kentish	Northern	Southern	West Midlands	Total
1150-1200	7,390	4,316				11,706
1200-1250	123,414				116,802	240,216
1250-1300		3,546				3,546
1300-1350		48,368				48,368
1350-1400	100,009			46,874	13,020	159,903
1400-1450	157,002		188,478		68,072	413,552
1450-1500	185,919		17,661	90,046	60,741	354,367
1500-1550					66,143	66,143
Total	573,734	56,230	206,139	136,920	324,778	1,297,801

Table 3. Composition of corpus (number of words) by dialect and subperiod.

Table 3 shows that the periods 1250-1300, 1300-1350 and 1500-1550 have only a limited representation of the dialects under investigation. Nonetheless, samples for four subperiods out of eight have at least the East Midland and West Midland dialects in common; and these four subperiods are also represented by a comparably large amount of data. If early periods had a different composition of dialects compared with later subperiods, these changes could be ascribed to inter-dialectal variation. However, except perhaps over the period 1250-1350 (for which data is firstly, insufficient for very accurate estimates, and secondly, limited in dialect source) dialectal differences seem highly unlikely to make any major contribution to the observed variation. Samples for the subperiods 1200-1250 and 1350-1500 largely share the same range of dialects. It is, therefore, possible to compare at least these two subperiods and interpret the difference as indicating language change; and, if attention is focussed only on the subperiods that have dialects in common, there is still some fluctuation of frequency over time. The comparison of average frequency between these periods for N$ and NP-POS in Figure 3, for example, shows that there is a sudden change in frequency between the earlier periods and the later ones.

Moreover, the uneven dialectal distribution may be expected to be less problematic for syntactic changes than for other aspects of language change. The most noticeable differences between dialects in Middle English are "partly matters of pronunciation, partly of vocabulary, partly of inflection" (Baugh/Cable 1978: 191), with comparatively little variation in syntactic structure. Fischer (1992) maintains that (English) syntactic changes are not as sensitive to dialectal differences, and so are better suited for the detection of linguistic change:

> Methodologically, it may seem a hazardous decision to ignore dialectal variants: change often originates in variation. However, as far as we know, the major syntactic changes in Middle English period do not find their origin in dialectal variants, but are a result of morphological developments discussed above. They are common to all Middle English dialects. (Fischer 1992: 208)

On this basis, syntactic changes, as used in the present study, are assumed to be a better indicator for linguistic changes. It is, therefore, appropriate to assume that the changes in the average frequencies of the linguistic items studied here indicate changes which took place in Middle English as a whole.

To more accurately reflect the observed progress of the shifts in use over time, the observed changes were estimated for all variables by calculating the differences in average frequency between each successive pair of subperiods. The results are shown in Table 4 below, and also graphed as Figure 4. The tabulated dates indicate the boundaries between successive subperiods. For example, figures for the year "1200" in Table 4 indicate the difference between the average for the texts from 1150-1200, and that for the texts from 1200-1250. This difference is a point estimate of the rate of change in frequency of each feature at the boundary year of 1200, in units of tokens per 1000 words per 50 years.

Boundary year: / Feature:	1200	1250	1300	1350	1400	1450	1500
BE	1.08	–0.69	1.14	1.75	0.40	–0.57	–0.80
EX	0.19	–0.16	1.43	–0.72	0.10	0.31	0.52
N$	–1.81	–4.82	–0.18	0.30	0.06	0.62	–0.32
NEG	1.19	–4.53	7.31	–7.16	–1.72	–3.09	–1.11
NX	–0.01	–0.86	1.08	1.08	–0.25	2.11	–1.27
Q	–3.95	–8.36	1.11	–5.15	4.61	0.39	–3.24
VBP	22.57	–8.85	20.31	–27.59	1.58	–6.12	–9.11
NP–ADV	0.52	–1.13	–0.01	0.34	0.13	–0.14	–0.01
NP–OB2	–1.38	1.26	–6.43	–1.93	0.17	1.06	2.38
NP–POS	–3.31	–4.07	–0.42	1.13	–1.06	1.38	–0.61
CP–REL	6.03	3.64	2.05	–12.91	2.98	–3.76	1.21
IP–PPL	0.93	–1.25	0.29	0.77	0.58	1.48	–0.23
IP–SUB	9.88	4.38	–3.30	–21.2	7.31	–4.63	0.58
WPP	0.28	0.72	1.80	–0.74	–0.40	0.22	–0.69

Table 4. Observed changes in frequency between successive periods of PPCME2.

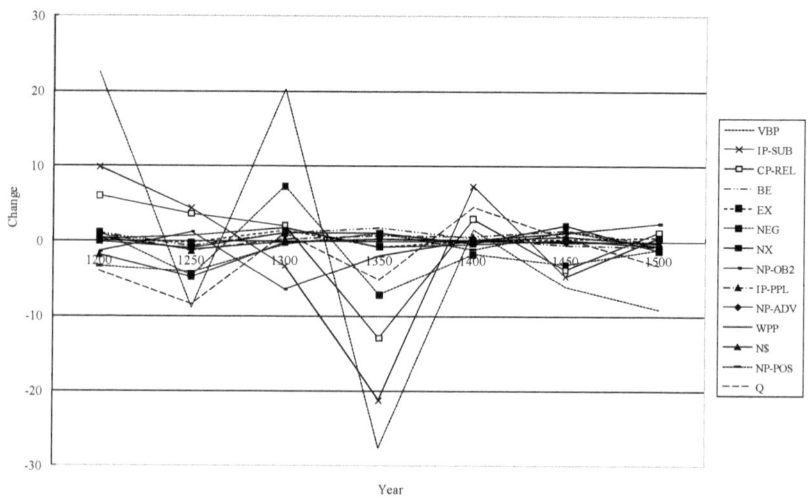

Figure 4. Observed changes in frequency between successive periods of PPCME2.

The frequency of BE shows its maximum change, rising by 1.75, at 1350. The frequency of EX has its largest absolute change at 1300, increasing by 1.43 (from 0.28 to 1.72, a large movement in relative terms). NEG also has its maximum frequency shift at 1300, jumping from 10.72 to 18.03. NP-OB2 also has a maximum frequency shift at the same time, dropping by 6.4, from 12.4 to 5.98. CP-REL and IP-SUB scores show similar sharp declines, by 12.91 and 21.2 respectively, at 1350. All of these shifts constitute relatively abrupt changes in observed frequency. Thus, for many of the features under investigation, the rate of change is not constant, but instead has a maximum associated with some time period.

The next step is to consider whether any generalisations are possible across these observed frequency shifts for various syntactic features: are there any times of particularly rapid change in Middle English grammar as a whole, which might then serve as transition boundaries within the period (separating more stable periods of slower change)? For this purpose, the maximum rate of change is more relevant than the direction of that change. Accordingly, Table 5 below identifies the dates corresponding to the maximum absolute shift in frequency for each feature in turn.

Feature	Date		Feature	Date
BE	1350		NP-ADV	1250
EX	1300		NP-OB2	1300
N$	1250		NP-POS	1250
NEG	1300		CP-REL	1350
NX	1450		IP-PPL	1450
Q	1250		IP-SUB	1350
VBP	1350		WPP	1300

Table 5. Dates corresponding to maximum changes of frequency in PPCME2.

The dates for maximum changes of frequency do not coincide exactly. It is, however, easy to observe the general trend of the data. Twelve items' maxima fall between 1250 and 1350. The largest observed changes in N$, Q, NP-ADV, and NP-POS occur at or around 1250. Around 1300, maxima are observed for EX, NEG, NP-OB2, and WPP. Maxima for BE, VBP, CP-REL, and IP-SUB fall under 1350. There are only two exceptions with maxima falling under 1450, namely NX and IP-PPL.

One may deduce from this that something significant happened in English between 1300 and 1350. It is not possible to identify one single event, since these changes involve various aspects of grammar, and operate over an extended period of time; but one tendency does emerge. The features with maxima at earlier dates are relevant to the system of noun endings marking case: N$ and NP-POS correspond to the genitive case marker, while NP-ADV is one use of the dative or accusative cases of nouns. By contrast, BE, VBP, CP-REL, and IP-SUB are related to the verbal system. Such a pattern suggests that inflectional decline in nouns was completed by 1300, and the verbal and clausal system developed after 1300. This date therefore seems associated with a shift in the linguistic focus of grammatical change.

This analysis first selected those frequent grammatical features that showed the greatest relative change in text frequency over the entire Middle English period, and then calculated the changes in text frequency between successive 50-year subperiods. Within the Middle English period of four hundred years, the rate of change is not constant. Instead, some kind of split is indicated, which allows us to specify a dividing line between early Middle English and late Middle English, whereby Early Middle English covers 1100 to 1300, and late Middle English covers 1300 to 1500.

4. Conclusion

In diachronic analysis, phonological features are commonly used as criteria for defining Middle English, as in Wright/Wright (1928). Partly as a result of the fact that inflectional endings collapse in this era, phonological changes are more easily perceived. The present analysis does not deny the necessity of examination of such aspects. However, as Fischer (1992) claims, syntactic changes are aspects of language change that show less variation by dialect, so syntactic change is better suited for use in constructing indexes to measure diachronic shift. The present analysis has applied just such an approach to observations of syntactic development in Middle English.

An attempt has been made here to identify subperiods of language change within the Middle English period. Diachronic development is observed using the Penn-Helsinki Parsed Corpus of Middle English, a corpus of 1.3 million words. Fourteen grammatical categories were selected through a regression model as showing especially marked development over the period in question. There was found to be a particularly large fluctuation in frequencies around 1300, compared to the overall occurrence of these syntactic features throughout the Middle English period. The date 1300 that lies midway in the Middle English period (which extends from 1100 to 1500), can therefore be seen as a dividing line between two subperiods: early Middle English, which exhibits changes mostly in the noun case system, and late Middle English, which mostly involves development of verbal features. The former subperiod can be characterized as a "nominal phase", and the latter as a "verbal phase", of the syntactic development of Middle English. As such, the present statistical analysis of syntactic features identifies a qualitative change in Middle English syntactic development.

References

Baugh, A. C. / Cable, T. 1978. *A History of the English Language*. 3ed. London: Routledge and Kegan Paul.

Blake, Norman 1992. "Introduction" in Blake, Norman (ed.) *The Cambridge History of the English Language II: 1066-1476*. Cambridge: Cambridge University Press. 1-22.

Brook, G. L. 1958. *A History of the English Language*. London: Andre Deutsch.

Burrow, J. A. / Turvile-Petre, T. 1992. *A Handbook of Middle English*. Oxford: Blackwell.

Fischer, Olga 1992. "Syntax" in Blake, Norman (ed.) *The Cambridge History of the English Language II: 1066-1476*. Cambridge: Cambridge University Press. 207-408.

Jespersen, Otto 1924. *The Philosophy of Grammar*. London: George Allen and Unwin.

Kroch, S. Anthony / Taylor, A. 2000. *The Penn-Helsinki Parsed Corpus of Middle English* (Manual).

Kytö, Merja 1996. *Manual to the Diachronic Part of the Helsinki Corpus of English Texts: Coding Conventions and Lists of Source Texts*. Helsinki: Department of English, University of Helsinki.

Lass, Roger 1992. "Phonology and Morphology" in Blake, Norman (ed.) *The Cambridge History of the English Language II: 1066-1476*. Cambridge: Cambridge University Press. 23-155.

Lass, Roger 2000. Language periodization and the concept "middle". In Taavitsainen, I., / Nevalainen, T. / Pahta, P. / Rissanen, M. (eds) *Placing Middle English in Context*. Berlin: Mouton de Gruyter. 7-41.
Mustanoja, T. F. 1960. *A Middle English Syntax: Part I*. Helsinki: Société Néophilologique.
Nevalainen, Terttu 2006. *An Introduction to Early Modern English*. Oxford: Oxford University Press.
Strang, Barbara M. H. 1970. *A History of English*. London: Methuen.
Sweet, Henry 1891. *A New English Grammar, Logical and Historical*. Oxford: Clarendon Press.
Wright, Joseph / Wright, Elizabeth Mary 1928. *An Elementary Middle English Grammar*. Oxford: Oxford University Press.

Section 4
Descriptions of Social and Stylistic Variation

PAM PETERS

Style and Politeness: The Case of the Personal Pronoun

1. Introduction: the English personal pronoun system[1]

The English personal pronoun system has been subject to continuous erosion over the last millennium. In Old English / Anglo-Saxon there were up to six case contrasts for all three personal pronouns, singular and plural. By early modern English (C17), the system presented only three case contrasts (nominative/accusative/genitive) for the first and third persons, singular and plural. For the second person, the contrasts available were reduced even further: the nominative/accusative and singular/plural contrasts became almost obsolete, leaving only two case contrasts (genitive/other).

The drastic reduction of the second person pronouns is usually explained in terms of pragmatic forces challenging the grammatical paradigm (Brown/Gilman 1960). With both power and solidarity at stake when referring to the other party in a verbal exchange, politeness if not deference prompts discretion in the choice of pronoun, and a neutral option is highly valued. Considerations like these allowed *you* to consolidate its position as the sole second person pronoun for both singular and plural, and to become the common case for both nominative and accusative use. Pragmatic forces can thus be seen to radically reshape the grammatical system.

Present-day variability in the use of first and third person pronouns raises similar questions. When the pronoun chosen is not the grammatically sanctioned one, are the driving forces behind that choice primarily linguistic (reflecting general, but perhaps competing, systemic or structural patterns), or are they instead sociolinguistic or

1 The contribution of my research assistant Yasmin Funk to the analysis of data presented in this paper is gratefully acknowledged.

pragmatic? Are ongoing adjustments to the pronoun system prompted by those already in place for the second person? Is there any general, ongoing trend towards a common case for all three personal pronouns? Or is the variability in pronominal form conditional, and determined by more abstract linguistic features, such as whether the pronoun is functioning as "strong" or "weak" (Quinn 2005)? Do politeness and contextual style influence the case chosen for the pronoun? Finally, to the extent that any such effects (whether linguistic or stylistic) can be identified, are they consistent, or are they more visible in some registers and varieties of English than in others (Wales 1996)? These are the questions to be addressed in the following sections.

2. Sites of pronoun variation

Continuing instability in the use of the English personal pronouns is noted in all recent grammars, including Quirk *et al.* (*Comprehensive Grammar of the English Language,* 1985), Biber *et al.* (*Longman Grammar of Spoken and Written English,* 1999), and Huddleston/ Pullum (*Cambridge Grammar of the English Language,* 2002). The *Longman Grammar* points to several known sites of variability between nominative and accusative, namely:

(a) after BE (i.e. as subject predicative complement, *It's me / It is I*);

(b) after (i.e., as a complement of) AS/THAN (*quicker than me / quicker than I*);

(c) in coordinated phrases, as first and second coordinate (*Jane and I / Jane and me / Me and Jane went shopping*); and

(d) in peripheral and nonintegrated NPs, including right- or left-dislocated pronouns (*Me, I don't agree*), and sentence fragments.

Traditional grammar required the nominative in (a) and (b), and for (c) when the phrase served in subject role. Yet while the nominative could be insisted on in writing, spoken usage was never so conforming. Plenty of evidence of construction (a) being expressed as accusative comes from the earlier C20, reported by Jespersen (1909-1949, Part VII: 251-255) and Fries (1940: 91-95). Little use of the nominative shows up in data from large British and American corpora of the late C20. "It is I" with the final pronoun is felt to be overly polite, and is used only in writing with a following relative clause (Biber *et al.* 1999: 336). In the tension between style (formal/informal) and grammatical correctness, the need for a less marked style seems to have prevailed.

Other examples, in which the nominative case is under some degree of stress (and thus "strong"), are less clear cut. In coordinate structures used as the clausal subject, the role of the nominative is somewhat unsettled, as demonstrated by the following examples (1)–(2), taken from the spoken component of ICE-AUS (described in Section 3 below), in which the struggle to find the situationally appropriate pronoun emerges in the form of speaker vacillation between several alternatives.

(1) He him him and the brood are all going to Queensland... (ICE-AUS S1A098:78)

(2) Me and Julie, me and Julie, Julie and I were first partners... (ICE-AUS S1A089: 293)

Example (1) captures a speaker trying to avoid sounding too formal – in what is presumably an informal conversation, to judge by the subsequent use of "brood" for "family". By contrast, example (2) displays the opposite kind of pronoun adjustment. Here the speaker starts with the informal accusative pronoun, and then upgrades to the grammatically more acceptable nominative – as well as exchanging the two coordinates so as to achieve the "polite" order of pronouns, with the first person placed second or last (Wales 1996: 103-106). Both examples show the speaker vacillating over the choice of pronouns, and the interplay between grammar and contextual style in the heat of conversation.

Grammatical assumptions about pronoun case are almost always based on written rather than spoken language, and explained in terms of the argument structure of the clause. As a result, there has been comparatively little attention given to grammatical specifications for the pronoun in marginal syntactic structures such as those mentioned under (d) above. Peripheral pronoun subjects requiring case selections (i.e., first and third person) in fact produce some remarkable sequences, as in (3):

(3) We're all in the same boat, just her, you and I (ICE-AUS S1A024 (A): 376)

Here the choice of the accusative *her* for the first right-dislocated pronoun suggests the postverbal effect noted by Quirk *et al.* (1985: 337). There is no attempt to secure case agreement with the preverbal *we*. Yet the final selection of nominative *I* raises other issues: agreement with the preceding *we* seems a less likely explanation than the effect of it being the final coordinate, and the need there for a "strong" pronoun (as discussed below in Section 5). The fact that, in this example, these two sites for choice in case-marking are separated by the non-case-marked *you* may have some influence in weakening any tendency to select forms that "agree" in case. Again this example provides interesting evidence of competing grammatical and discoursal forces.

Challenges to regular case selections are also posed by cleft sentences such as *It was I/me who(that)....* While older usage handbooks preferred the nominative, Wales (1996: 95f.) noted that the accusative often sounded quite acceptable. In her survey of 91 young New Zealand speakers, Quinn (2005: 134), found that although the majority preferred the accusative for both first and third person pronouns, the results for the first person (*me* and *us*) were higher (above 85%), whereas those for the third person (*him, her, them)* ranged from 62% to 78%. This suggests that there are somewhat different constraints affecting the use of first and third person pronouns. Further instability can be anticipated when the clefted subject involves coordinated pronouns, which are themselves subject to variability in terms of constructions (a) and (c) above. For example *It was X and me/I who…* One very striking example of this instability can be found in data from the Australian ICE corpus, where the dislocated subject requires a genitive, but the actual utterance was:

(4) It was *Firstname and I's celebration (ICE-AUS S1A004:23)

Again there are grammatical and pragmatic forces in contention: the discoursal need for a strong pronoun (and the preference for *I* as the second coordinate), which seem to prevail here over the regular genitive (*my)*. It is an unusual utterance from a native speaker of English. Variability between genitive and nominative pronouns is mostly associated with creole Englishes including AAVE (Williamson 1971: 506; Wales 1996), as when *spoke to they father* is used instead of "spoke to their father".

Variability between the genitive pronoun and the accusative comes up in other kinds of complex constructions, when they function as the rank-shifted subject of a gerund-participle, as in (5) and (6).

(5) It's about our working through multilateral agencies (ICE-AUS S1B-045 (A):27)

(6) I wasn't thinking about them being scared (ICE-AUS S1A-068 (B):114)

This variability between genitive and accusative derives from the traditional grammarians' long-standing difficulty with the gerund-participle construction, and the strict position taken by Webster in C18 through to Fowler in C20, that the genitive pronoun was the proper idiom (Peters 2004: 229). English writers themselves made use of both genitive and accusative, as shown by Jespersen (1909-49, Part V: 133-140); and Fries (1940: 84) found that the two were about equally represented in the "Standard English" of his corpus of American correspondence from World War I. Quirk *et al.* (1985: 1290-1) demonstrated that the gerund operates on a cline of nominality to verbality, and the case of the pronoun varies accordingly, so that the genitive correlates with the nominal end of the scale and the accusative with the verbal. Though the grammaticality of the accusative pronoun can no longer be challenged, the prescriptive voices of Fowler (1926) and of Strunk/White (1935 and later) still tended to prompt the selection of the genitive pronoun in more formal writing. Nunally (1991: 365) found traces of it in hypercorrect American speech, in *prevent that's happening*, where the demonstrative pronoun is curiously inflected under pressure from the "formality of the language situation". In British English (as represented by the BNC sampler), stylistic preference for the genitive pronoun still correlates most strongly with academic writing, and it is strongly dispreferred in spoken discourse (Lyne 2006: 46, 51). However, research on other written corpora suggests that stylistic colorings do not necessarily hold across all varieties of English. The accusative pronoun prevails across the stylistic board in Australian English (Collins/Peters 2004: 605-6), suggesting that the grammaticalization of the accusative structure is more advanced in the southern hemisphere than elsewhere.

In most of the sites of pronoun variability discussed in Section 2, ordinary usage tends towards the accusative, supporting the view that it could be the "common case" for the first and third person pronouns, as for the second. Corpus evidence used by Biber *et al.* (1999) shows that the accusative predominates in most of the variable constructions noted as (a) to (d) above. We have however noted in passing some affirmative uses of the nonaccusative, as when the first person reference occurs as second coordinate in non-subject role. The linguistic contexts of use, as well as the regional contexts, therefore call for further investigation, to examine more closely the extent of variation (regional/social/stylistic) signalled by Wales (1996) and by Quinn (2005). Fully corpus-based research supports more detailed appraisal of pronoun use in a range of linguistic and stylistic contexts, and can provide collective evidence of the directions of change in the English pronoun system.

3. Sources of data and objectives

The International Corpus of English (ICE) network of corpora is designed for regional comparisons, and for comparing spoken and written data in each variety of English (Greenbaum/Nelson 1996). It also provides some subcategorizations of speech (from private dialogue to public monologue), and thus a continuum of usage from speech to writing, by which to explore the impacts of the context of discourse on linguistic choices within. All ICE corpora are committed to the same set of discourse categories, and principles of collection, e.g. that the private conversations collected as dialogue should be those of educated speakers (operationally defined as those who had completed secondary education in the country concerned). So with comparable speakers and registers of communication, the ICE corpora from Australia (AUS), New Zealand (NZ) and Great Britain (GB) will allow us to see whether the cline of pronoun usage, from speech to writing, is much the same all those varieties of English, or whether, for example, the southern hemisphere Englishes are developing their own pronominal trends at the threshold of C21.

In what follows, ICE data will be used to profile the frequencies of fully case-marked pronouns (first and third person) in contemporary Australian, New Zealand and British English, and in three of the sites of variability identified above: (i) following *than* (in Section 4); (ii) in coordinated phrases in subject and non-subject roles (in Section 5); and (iii) preceding a gerund-participle (in Section 6). The data will be examined to see whether there are visible trends towards selecting the accusative; whether such variability as there is correlates with the medium (speech rather than writing); and whether the trend is more advanced in one regional variety than the others.

4. Pronoun choice following *than*

Comparisons articulated with *than* may be expressed through a comparative clause or phrase, because it functions as either conjunction or preposition, in traditional grammar terms:

(7) *conjunction*: He'll give you more details than I can about it (ICE-AUS S1A-001B:234)

(8) *preposition*: She can't be much older than me (ICE-AUS S1A-020A:50)

The dual role for *than* is now uncontentious, though the prepositional use seems to have become stigmatized in the later C19. The first edition of the Oxford English Dictionary (1884-1928) provides evidence of resistance to it in a remarkable note which still stands in the second edition (1989). THAN is said to appear:

> with a personal pronoun or relative pronoun in the objective case instead of the nominative (as if *than* were a preposition). This is [...] the invariable construction in the case of *than whom,* which is universally accepted in stead of *than who.* With the personal pronouns it is now considered incorrect.

In keeping with this, the citations for using *than* as a preposition stop abruptly at 1871, though they stretch back in time to the C16 and the Geneva Bible. The Oxford Dictionary's note helps to explain the traditional grammarians' reluctance to allowing *than* as anything other than conjunction, and insisting on the nominative pronoun. Even when there was no verb following, this was justified by saying that the pronoun was still the subject of an ellipted clause, thus shoring up the claims of *than* as a conjunction and not a preposition. It rationalized the use of the nominative, as in:

(9) Those more knowledgable than I about it [...] (ICE-AUS S1B-021C:143)

The combination of *than* with the accusative nevertheless continues in speech ("*more knowledgable than me...*"), as documented by Biber *et al.* (1999: 336). Its currency sets up a stylistic distinction, between the nominative (with or without following clause) as the formal selection, and the accusative as colloquial style.

In what follows, we will review the ICE corpus data on the relative frequencies of both prepositional and conjunctional uses of *than,* with and without a following clause. The table below shows the distribution of phrasal and clausal comparative constructions in ICE-AUS, ICE-NZ and ICE-GB, across the samples of dialogue, monologue and writing. What quickly emerges is that the clausal construction with a nominative pronoun as subject is by far the commonest in all three corpora. The second and third constructions (i.e. phrasal ones) are a good deal less frequent, and the clauseless nominative is indeed rare in all three corpora.

than +	dialogue (180 samples)	monologue (120 samples)	writing (200 samples)	Totals
ICE-AUS				
nom. + clause	27	19	20	66
clauseless nom.	1	1	1	3
accusative	8	1	1	10
Totals	36	21	22	79
ICE-NZ				
nom. + clause	21	10	39	70
clauseless nom.	1	0	1	2
accusative	8	0	4	12
Totals	30	10	44	84
ICE-GB				
nom. + clause	36	18	25	79
clauseless nom.	1	0	1	2
accusative	5	0	4	9
Totals	42	18	30	90

Table 1. Relative frequencies of comparative clauses and phrases in spoken and written data in three ICE corpora.

The results show clearly that conjunctive *than* (nom. + clause) is the unmarked construction for expressing comparison, used freely across the board, in dialogue, monologue and writing. This is of some interest, given the comments of Biber *et al.* (1999: 529) that comparative constructions are associated particularly with writing, as an explanatory device in academic prose, and a means of constructing the imaginative world in fiction. They found fewer comparatives in journalistic prose or conversational data from both British and American sources in the Longman corpus. Yet in this ICE data for *than*, clausal comparisons, and indeed all types of comparison, actually occur more often in dialogue in both Australian and British ICE data. Only the New Zealand data suggest more use of comparatives in written material, though the frequencies found in the 8 subcategories of writing are too small to compare effectively with the Longman data. However, the distinctiveness of New Zealand English norms begins to emerge.

Table 1 provides some useful data on the question of whether phrasal comparison with a simple pronoun is more likely to be expressed with the accusative than the nominative. The corpus frequencies show a preference for the accusative over the genitive in all three varieties of English, in keeping with Quinn's (2005: 143) survey findings. In ICE-AUS the accusative appears to be strongly associated with dialogue; yet closer inspection of the written occurrences in the three corpora shows that they are all from fiction or "nonprinted" writing (i.e. students' unpublished essays). So *than* + accusative may still be stylistically colored through its association with dialogue and informal style in all three varieties of English. The stylistic markedness of *than* + clauseless nominative is very clear from closer inspection of its rare appearances in the data – only in excerpts from public speaking (not private dialogue), and in academic discourse or formal letter writing, where communication is often highly wrought. The selection of the nominative pronoun is clearly a marked choice in spoken or written discourse, which comes across as hypercorrection (comparable to *It is I*). Huddleston/Pullum (2002: 1113) suggest that some speakers find the clauseless nominative construction "obtrusively formal", while others feel that the accusative is "obtrusively informal", and the ICE data suggest that both reactions may be there. Yet such stylistic polarization seems likely ultimately to favor the accusative. The verbless nominative is easily extended into the full comparative clause which operates across the stylistic spectrum as the ICE data show, and this allows the accusative to gain/regain ground as the complement of *than.* Such variability as there may have been in the choice of pronoun with (prepositional) *than* will be resolved in favor of the accusative.

5. Pronoun choice in coordinated noun phrases

Variability in the choice/case of pronoun in coordinated phrases is affected by multiple grammatical factors, as well as matters of style and politeness. Huddleston/Pullum (2002: 458-9) note that the nominative pronoun is unchallenged when it serves as noncoordinated subject of finite clause. Their comment foregrounds the impact of coordination on the selection of the pronoun's case, and of the syntactic role of the coordinated phrase in which the pronoun appears: whether it is the subject of finite clause, or plays a nonsubject role, e.g. as object of verb, or complement of a preposition. Although this is a primary consideration, it does not always determine the final selection, as we have seen above in Section 2.

An additional dimension of variability is whether the pronoun appears as first or second coordinate. Biber *et al.* (1999: 337) found that the accusative predominated when the pronoun was the first coordinate, though they did not cross-tabulate it with the clausal role of the NPs concerned. This is of no small importance since it affects the pronoun's proximity to the verb, and the extent to which it is susceptible to the arguments of the verb. A further issue affecting the placement of pronouns within the coordinate phrase is the polite convention noted by Quirk *et al.* (1985: 338) and Wales (1996: 103-6), which obliges the speaker to put the first person last whenever other persons (second and/or third) are referred to in the same construction. Just how far the convention still holds in British and other varieties of English, and its interface with the other selectional variables, is a matter for further investigation. The medium of discourse (spontaneous speech vs. more reflective writing) seems likely to impact on the choice of pronoun. Beyond that, the impact of more and less interactive speech (dialogue vs. monologue) is a possible factor in pronoun choice. We might expect to find a kind of stylistic gradient in the case selection for pronouns, with those used in monologic discourse tending to match those of writing rather than dialogic speech.

In order to test the range of possible variables, let us first look at the ICE-AUS data. The figures shown below in Table 2 are confined to singular personal pronouns, first and third person, because of the dearth of examples for their plural counterparts.

Clausal role of coordinated phrase	Subject			Non-subject		
	dialogue	monologue	writing	dialogue	monologue	writing
Pronouns as first coordinate: nominative						
I	0	0	0	0	0	0
he	6	2	13	0	0	0
she	1	3	2	0	0	0
Total	7	5	15	0	0	0
accusative						
me	7	0	0	6	0	6
him	2	1	0	3	2	2
her	4	0	0	1	2	0
Total	13	1	0	10	4	8
Pronouns as second coordinate: nominative						
I	40	14	34	7	0	0
accusative						
me	2	0	0	1	2	2
Total	42	14	34	8	2	2

Table 2. Data from ICE-AUS on the selection of pronouns associated with coordinate phrases.

Looking first at the data in Table 2 on pronouns occurring as *first* coordinate, we note a strong preference for the third person nominative (*he, she*) when the pronoun is in subject role, which correlates with their complete avoidance in the first coordinate nonsubject role, in all three kinds of discourse shown. That apart, we note the total absence of the first person nominative as first coordinate, which might suggest the force of the politeness convention noted above (that the first person should not be mentioned first). However the middle section of Table 2 shows that the first person accusative pronoun (*me*) is actually used more often than nominative as first coordinate in subject role, as in example (10) from dialogic speech:

(10) Me and *Forename7 got right in the front (ICE-AUS S1A-005 (Z) 234)

The accusative is also found for the third person singular in dialogue, as in (11):

(11) Her and my girlfriend might have a big bitch fight (ICE-AUS S1A-039 (B) 434)

The choice of the accusative is less regular for the third person, and clearly context-related, as the Table 2 figures show. It occurs in dialogue and very occasionally in monologue, but there are no instances in writing. The phenomenon correlates with the mode and style of discourse.

The foregrounding of the first person *me* as first coordinate, as in the first example above, still seems to violate the politeness convention mentioned above. The fact that it also violates the rules of grammatical case would explain why it seems so abhorrent to prescriptive grammarians. Yet others such as Biber *et al.* (1999: 338) note that the polite order of persons may be varied for reasons of "informational status" – e.g. in order to maintain the topic focus in conversation or narrative. Its given status fosters a weak rather than a strong pronoun (cf. Quinn 2005). It is also arguable that the use of the first person accusative (i.e. the oblique case) is a mitigating strategy against the effect of giving (impolite) priority to the first person, and readily available to speakers who are slower to find other forms of paraphrase.

Apart from that special situation, the accusative is the dominant form in all three pronouns in all three kinds of discourse for the first coordinate in nonsubject roles. This is no doubt helped by the fact that it is then often directly governed by the verb or preposition, apart from its being in "object" territory generally (Fries 1940: 90-1; Quirk *et al.* 1985: 337). The most interesting gap in the data set is the lack of monologic instances of *me* as first coordinate (whereas both *her/him* are found there). Perhaps the politeness constraint does operate here, and a sensitivity to the foregrounded self-reference. Everyday observation shows that constructions like *me and my wife* are avoided, and *my wife and myself* used instead.

The data for the *second* coordinate shown in Table 2 are confined to first person pronouns, because of the dearth of third person examples. Here the nominative *I* is very strongly preferred for the subject, no doubt because it typically appears next to the finite verb, and there is no politeness sanction against it. The two exceptions with the accusative both occur in contexts where the subject role is underspecified or challenged by other syntagmatic factors:

(12) Who's going? You and me, George. ICE-AUS S1B-075(B) 382

(13) He's happy we're going sailing on Saturday, just him and me. (ICE-AUS S1A-022 (A) 293)

Though the subject role is set up in the first example, the coordination of the first person with invariant *you* probably shields it from the nominative selection. In the second, *me* is an extraposed subject, and coordinated with accusative *him.*

The most striking departure from grammatical expectations in Table 2 is the figure for the use of *I* as second coordinate in a non-subject role. Examples can in fact be found in English writers from Shakespeare on (*Webster's Dictionary of English Usage*, 1989: 778) to ground this usage, especially when the coordinate phrase is headed by a preposition. However, data from ICE-AUS shows this use of *I* as second coordinate following both prepositions and full verbs. It is of course more frequent in dialogue; and emails and statements hot off the press may show it, when later press releases edit it out. When *The Guardian* newspaper interviewed an Australian Vice Chancellor designate in London, it quoted him (probably verbatim) as saying:

(14) This is a wonderful opportunity to join a University recognized for its innovation [...] and a chance for [my wife] and I to spend more time with our children in Australia

The statement was corrected to "a chance for my wife and me" when released by the university's own media office. The story shows how highly educated speakers may use nominative pronoun as second coordinate in nonsubject role. Huddleston/Pullum (2002: 463) comment that it is "so common in speech and used by so broad a range of speakers that it has to be recognized as a variety [*sc.* "variant"] of Standard English". We might well argue from the ICE-AUS data shown above that it has already become the standard selection: the use of the nominative as second coordinate in nonsubject roles is manifestly more common than the accusative. Grammatical correctness gives way to the pragmatic consideration of self-projection in a public interview.

These marked and unmarked patterns of pronoun use by Australians suggest that their selections are not random, but correlate with constraints over and above their position in the phrase (as first or second coordinate) and the clausal role of the phrases. Let us now compare the ICE-AUS data with that from ICE-NZ and ICE-GB – to see whether the same trends can be seen across all three varieties of English.

The data in Table 3 is arranged slightly differently from that in the previous table, so as to show the first and second coordinates in their actual order. We note first that the distribution of the nominative case is very similar in all three data sets. There is scant use of *I* as first coordinate, but plenty as second. Only the British data provides a handful of case of *I* as first coordinate, and closer inspection shows that they occur in either unscripted monologue or unpublished correspondence, i.e. in extended but unedited discourse. Two of the examples refer to *I and my colleagues:*

(15) Please could you let me know as soon as possible if you require assistance, and I and my colleagues [...] will be delighted to help. (ICE-GB W1B-019)

This *non*polite order of persons reflects the fact that the first person reference is more salient than the third in this context of communication, and no discourtesy is intended to the "colleagues". Apart from this small difference in the British use of the nominative, all three varieties show the same pattern of strongly preferring to use *I* as second coordinate, whether the coordinated phrase is in subject role or not. Thus all three varieties provide evidence of the "for my wife and I" phenomenon discussed above. It is equally evident in ICE-AUS and ICE-NZ, a little less so in ICE-GB. Its presence confirms the fact that it must indeed be regarded as the standard variant.

Clausal role of coordinated phrase	Subject		Non-Subject	
Pronoun selections	First coordinate	Second coordinate	First coordinate	Second coordinate
ICE-AUS				
nominative				
I	0	88	0	7
s/he	27	0	0	0
accusative				
me	7	2	12	5
her/him	7	0	10	0
Total	41	90	22	12
ICE-NZ				
nominative				
I	0	76	0	7
s/he	35	0	0	0
accusative				
me	18	2	8	2
her/him	5	2	5	0
Total	58	80	13	9
ICE-GB				
nominative				
I	5	63	0	4
s/he	26	1	0	0
accusative				
me	7	3	8	6
her/him	0	1	8	0
Total	38	68	16	10

Table 3. Data from ICE-AUS, ICE-NZ and ICE-GB on the selection of pronouns in coordinate phrases.

Against these marked patterns of use for the first person singular pronoun, all three data sets show that the third person nominative pronoun is still very strongly associated with the first coordinate (subject role). Whenever the nominative form is chosen, it coincides with the regular grammar of the clause.

The uses of accusative are similar across the three data sets, with some remarkable evidence of its use as first coordinate in subject role, contra strict grammatical agreement. This phenomenon is most noticeable in the data from the southern hemisphere varieties, especially ICE-NZ. In both New Zealand and Australia, *me* seems to assume the role not taken up by *I* as first coordinate, at least in dialogue. In the

ICE-GB data also, *me* serves instead of *I* in casual conversation. This dovetails with the earlier finding, that all instances of *I* as first coordinate in the British data were found in monologic or written discourse, showing complementary selections for different discourse styles. The colloquial advance of *me* into subject role in coordinate phrases is evident in all three varieties, especially in natural dialogue, but there are scattered examples in fiction as well. The tendency can also be seen for the third person pronouns in the New Zealand and Australian data, but not the British. Again we see that changes in case assignments may affect the whole set, or only the first person, depending on the variety; but in each case, the first person pronoun is clearly the most susceptible.

Interestingly, this tendency for the accusative to move into subject role in coordinated phrases goes with it being first rather than second coordinate. Some explanation for it may be found in terms of self-depreciation, as mentioned earlier. It serves to deemphasize the otherwise prominent first person by use of the oblique case, and thus – unexpectedly – may have some politeness value within the colloquial code. Huddleston/Pullum (2002: 463) call it "nonstandard", but that description might be challenged in the light of the fact that ICE corpus data was collected from "educated" speakers in all three places. In their survey of the world's Englishes, Kortman/Szmrecsanyi (2004: 1094, 1126) found it in 40 out of 46 of the varieties surveyed, and in 10 out of 11 of the L1 (native-speaker) varieties.

6. Pronoun selection with the gerund participle

The choice of pronoun preceding the gerund participle has been in contention from C18 on. Unlike the cases discussed above in Sections 4 and 5, it requires a choice between the genitive and the accusative, although here again the accusative is the less formal construction, and the unmarked choice for choice for some constructions. According to Biber *et al.* (1999: 750), the pronoun selected in NP + gerund-participle constructions is overwhelmingly accusative when following aspectual or cognitive verbs, e.g. *kept it running; saw it coming,* where the pronoun is the object of the controlling verb. Lyne (2006: 46) found this held across all three varieties of writing in her BNC data with no stylistic differentiation. But the genitive prevailed in constructions involving a preposition, after (prepositional) verbs, adjectives and nouns, where it appeared more than twice as often. These then are the constructions where variation between accusative and genitive is most likely to be seen, and so, of greatest interest to us here.

Data from ICE-AUS, ICE-NZ and ICE-GB allow us to investigate the interplay between the several parameters of variation affecting the takeup of the accusative in gerund-participle constructions, including regional variation (Collins/Peters 2004: 605-6); variation between spoken and written data (Peters 2006: 773); and the various complementary constructions in which pronouns appear with the gerund-participle mentioned in the previous paragraph. The ICE data appear in the table below, subcategorized as follows:

- complement of a prepositional verb: *complained about him being around...*
- a noun/pronoun: *the idea of me coming for a week or so*
- an adjective: *conditional on it gaining 50.1 per cent...*
- a prepositional phrase: *instead of us watching them...*

Other noteworthy instances in all three ICE corpora had the gerund-participle with preceding pronoun functioning as a clausal constituent, as:

- subject: *him leaving had nothing to do with her*
- complement to subject: *It's not me having to decide*
- complement to the predicative complement (SVCC): *It was no good us being righteous.*
- absolute construction: *Imagine what Bob would think, us talking like this.*

Uses of the gerund-participle as a clausal constituent are not very frequent, and they have therefore been tallied together in Table 4 below. They are nevertheless of some interest as another set of constructions in which the grammatical constraints on pronoun choice are unusually complex.

	ICE-AUS		ICE-NZ		ICE-GB		
	gen.	acc.	gen.	acc.	gen.	acc.	
Complement of :							Totals
prepositional verb	3	7	3	6	5	10	34
noun/pronoun	5	17	4	12	12	16	66
adjective	1	5	1	1	3	2	13
preposition	4	12	3	7	2	8	36
Clause constituent	2	8	1	8	0	5	24
Totals	15	49	12	34	22	41	
(spoken; written)	9; 6	35; 14	2; 10	25; 9	13; 9	31; 10	

Table 4. Selection of pronouns in gerund-participle constructions in three ICE corpora, in spoken and written data.

The ICE data tabled above shows that overall the accusative is the preferred case for the pronoun in all three varieties of English. In the ICE-GB data the ratio between accusative and genitive frequencies is about 2:1, whereas it is almost 3:1 for ICE-NZ and well over 3:1 for ICE-AUS. These rankings, with Australian English leading the others in its preference for accusative, confirm the earlier research on written corpus material from the three varieties and from American English (Collins/Peters 2004:606). The ICE data analysed here shows that the accusative is not felt to be too informal for the written medium, and is used there about as often as the genitive in both ICE-NZ and ICE-GB. In ICE-AUS the accusative is clearly the commoner form in both mediums. The neutralization of stylistic difference is further shown by the fact that in both ICE-AUS and ICE-GB, the genitive appears freely in spoken and written data. However this does not hold for ICE-NZ, where the data are still strongly polarized towards the use of the genitive in writing, and the accusative in speech.

Table 4 provides an overview of the various complementary roles of the pronoun + gerund-participle, and shows their relative importance. In all three corpora the noun complementation role is the most frequent of all, and contributes substantially to the overall frequency of the accusative pronoun, despite the "nominality" of the construction. The ratio of accusative to genitive is however much closer in ICE-GB than in the southern hemisphere data sets. But when the construction complements a prepositional verb, the ratio between the accusative and genitive constructions is the same across all three varieties of English (ca. 2:1). When complementing a preposition, the differences are larger for all three, though the British data actually comes out with the strongest preference for the accusative, in contrast with the result for noun complementation. When the gerund-participle stands as an actual clause constituent, it too mostly takes the accusative pronoun, in all varieties of English. This is to be expected as the neutral choice, except when it appears in subject role. Yet even there the data provide examples of the accusative construction, in conversational responses such as:

(16) Well, me being a pauper… (ICE-AUS S1A-073B 173)

Examples such as this suggest that thc accusative is becoming the default selection for the construction, and is not constrained by grammatical or stylistic factors.

In both kinds of roles, as complement to a key constituent, and as an independent constituent, the pronoun selected to go with the gerund-participle is prevailingly accusative. The traditional stylistic constraints on its use seem to have faded in all three varieties of English investigated here. There is little to show the superiority of the genitive form, except its slightly higher frequency in British data when it complements a noun. It seems therefore to be another site of pronoun variability in which the choice is being neutralized in favor of the accusative.

7. Conclusions

Further attrition of the English personal pronoun paradigm is evident in all the data discussed above. This investigation of several sites of pronoun variability has found that the accusative forms for first and third person singular pronouns are often used where they might be considered marked forms or unacceptable according to the tenets of traditional grammar. The tendency holds for the use of the accusative after prepositional *than,* as first coordinate in subject role in colloquial speech, and in the trend towards the accusative with gerund-participles, when used as complementary constructions or as independent clause constituents. However the data from those different contexts is itself partial, providing stronger evidence for default use of the accusative for the first person singular pronoun than for the first person plural or third person (singular/plural). It would therefore be premature to speak of a general trend towards making the accusative the common case (as with *you*).

An additional countertendency is the growing use of the first person nominative as second coordinate in nonsubject role, which is not found for third person pronouns. This difference between the two persons suggests that pragmatic issues are indeed at play for the first person, as does the fact that this phenomenon is particularly associated with autobiographical public statements. Pragmatic issues affecting the first person also seem to account for the fact that *me* (to a greater extent than *her/him)* can appear as the first coordinate in subject role, at least in colloquial interactions – which may be an intuitive form of compensation for violating the polite convention of not foregrounding the first person. The self-deprecating use of *me* in subject role, and "genteel" and/or self-conscious use of *I* in nonsubject role, both seem to reflect social imperatives on the speaker, in different communicative contexts. Their effects on the first person pronoun paradigm are no less radical than the neutralization of the case distinctions for the second person pronoun in early modern English. The fact that they tend in opposite directions shows that some regrammaticalization is also possible, rather than simple neutralization.

The trends identified are much the same in all three varieties of English, though the ICE data show New Zealand ahead of both Australian and British English in its use of accusative pronouns (both first and third person) as first coordinate in subject role. Australian English meanwhile is the most advanced in the use of the accusative with gerund-participles. Stylistic differentiation between the accusative and genitive constructions has faded in both Australian and British English, whereas in New Zealand the genitive is still associated with formal writing.

Some kinds of stylistic differentiation thus seem to operate more locally, whereas others, such as the sanctioning of *me* as first or second coordinate in subject role (in spoken dialogue but not monologic speech or writing), were found across all three varieties. Traditional grammar rules for the selection of nominative and accusative still prevail in edited prose throughout the English-speaking world. But where discourse is subject to the communicative priorities of the moment, pronoun case selections will be decided in accordance with the norms of style and politeness applicable to the context.

References

Biber, Douglas / Johansson, Stig / Leech, Geoffrey / Conrad, Susan / Finegan, Edward 1999. *Longman Grammar of Spoken and Written English.* London: Longman.

Brown, Roger / Gilman, Arnold 1960. The pronouns of power and solidarity. In Sebeok, Thomas A. (ed.) *Style in Language*. Cambridge: MIT, 253-76. Reprinted in Laver, John / Hutcheson, Sandy (eds) 1972 *Communication in Face to Face Interaction.* Harmondsworth: Penguin, 128-45.

Collins, Peter / Peters, Pam 2004. Australian English: Morphology and syntax. In Kortmann, Bernd / Burridge, Kate / Mesthrie, Rajend / Schneider, Edgar W. / Upton, Clive (eds) 2004, 593-610.

Fowler, Henry 1926. *A Dictionary of Modern English Usage.* Oxford: Clarendon Press.

Fries, C. C. 1940. *American English Grammar.* New York: Appleton Century Crofts.

Greenbaum, Sidney / Nelson, Gerald 1996. *The International Corpus of English.* Oxford: Oxford University Press.

Huddleston, R. / Pullum, Geoffrey 2002. *Cambridge Grammar of the English Language.* Cambridge: Cambridge University Press.

Jespersen, Otto 1909-1949. *Modern Grammar on Historical Principles,* Parts I to VII. Heidelberg: Karl Winter.

Kortmann, Bernd / Szmrecsanyi, Benedikt 2004. Global synopsis: morphological and syntactic variation in English. In Kortmann, Bernd / Burridge, Kate / Mesthrie, Rajend / Schneider, Edgar W. / Upton, Clive (eds) 2004, 1142-1202.

Kortmann, Bernd / Burridge, Kate / Mesthrie, Rajend / Schneider, Edgar W. / Upton, Clive 2004. *A Handbook of Varieties of English*. Vol. 2: *Morphology and Syntax*. Berlin: Mouton de Gruyter.

Lyne, Susanna 2006. The form of the pronoun preceding the verbal gerund. *ICAME Journal* 30, 37-53.

Nunally, Thomas 1991. The possessive with gerunds: what the handbooks say, and what they should say. *American Speech*, 66/ 4 (Winter, 1991), 359-370.

Peters, Pam 2004. *Cambridge Guide to English Usage.* Cambridge: Cambridge University Press.

Peters, Pam 2006. English usage, prescription and description. In Aarts, Bas / McMahon, April (eds) *Handbook of English Linguistics.* Oxford: Blackwell.

Oxford English Dictionary = Murray, A. / Craigie, A. (eds) 1884-1928. *New English Dictionary.* Oxford: Clarendon Press.

Quinn, Heidi 2005. *The Distribution of Pronoun Case Forms in English.* Amsterdam: Benjamins.

Quirk, Randoph / Greenbaum, Sidney / Leech, Geoffrey / Svartvik, Jan 1985. *Comprehensive Grammar of the English Language.* London: Longman.

Strunk, W. / White, E. 1935, 1959; 2ed. 1972. *The Elements of Style.* New York: Macmillan.

Wales, Katie 1996. *Personal Pronouns in Present-Day English.* Cambridge: Cambridge University Press.

Webster's Dictionary of English Usage. 1989. Springfield, Massachusetts: Merriam-Webster.

Williamson, Juanita 1971. Selected features of speech: black and white. In Williamson, Juanita / Burke, Virginia (eds) *A Various Language: perspectives on American dialects.* New York: Holt, Reinhart and Winston.

MASAHIRO HORI

Approaching Literature as a Corpus: Gender-Based Conversational Styles in Hemingway's 'Hills Like White Elephants'

1. Introduction[1]

Several researchers have argued that a corpus approach holds great promise as a new way to study the language of fiction. There are several studies in this field (Hoover 1999, Hori 2004, Stubbs 2005) and several theories supporting this approach (Louw 1993, Hoey 2005). As discussed in the "Corpus Approaches to the Language of Literature" workshops, organised by Martin Wynne of the Oxford Text Archive in conferences for Corpus Linguistics (2005) and the Poetics and Linguistics Association (2006), it is both possible, and potentially beneficial, to apply corpus-based approaches to the study of stylistics. However, the corpus approach is not a cure-all; in fact it is an approach which has some lurking pitfalls and hidden risks. In this article I would like to discuss a few such potential problems and limitations, and tentatively demonstrate a possible synthesis between quantitative and qualitative corpus-based approaches to the language of fiction. As an example of the language of fiction I will examine the differences between the conversational styles of the two protagonists, a man and a woman, in Ernest Hemingway's short story 'Hills Like White Elephants'.

1 The research on which this paper is based was funded by the Kumamoto Gakuen University Grant-in-Aid for Scientific Research, 2006.

2. Potential Problems and Limitations of Corpus Use

A first point to mention is that the data of a corpus does not always directly correspond to a native speaker's instinct for what constitutes "natural" language use. For one thing, "naturalness" is subjective, determined by amount of mental exposure rather than by (input) text frequency alone. (A collocation is more likely to be judged "natural" if it requires some additional processing, e.g. if the meaning in context is not directly predictable from the meanings of its component words in isolation, and/or if the word combination must be processed as a grammatical unit.) Moreover, there is no guarantee that text frequency in a particular corpus (however large) will accurately reflect the text frequency in the input experienced by any particular native speaker (which may show very different weightings of text types, regional varieties, or time periods). For items that may show skewed distribution by regional variety, speaker age, or register, corpus frequency may not be an accurate guide to overall frequency in the total attested use of a language. This is especially true for very low-frequency items, including many collocations. For example, according to Carter (1988: 57), *fat salary* is a common collocation but *stout book* is uncommon. However, the British National Corpus (or BNC) lists only two examples for *fat salary*, and one for *stout book*. Can the difference of one additional example possibly confirm usualness versus unusualness in collocation? Carter also lists *fat chicken* and *fat wad of notes* as familiar collocations, though the BNC does not include a single example of either. Therefore, the frequency of a collocation, even in a huge corpus of everyday language, is not always a good criterion for judging whether a combination of words is natural or unnatural.

Secondly, computer-based corpus analysis treats the same word forms as always having the same value or significance, even though some tokens may be working contextually as irony, or as metaphor. For example, in Charles Dickens's *David Copperfield*, Mr. Murdstone's *smile* in *a grave smile* (Ch. 4) and Miss Agnes's *smile* in *a pleasant smile* (Ch. 39) are counted as the same word form, yet within the context of the novel, they represent two completely different notions. The word *red* in the term *the red fox* or *the cunning red eye* used for Uriah Heep, the hypocrite, is counted as the same word form as the word *red* in young David's *my little red cheek* although the word *red* refers strictly to different colors or connotations respectively.

Thirdly, a computer program can count and organize words existing in a text, but cannot pick up an implied topic or an elided word. For example, in Hemingway's 'Hills Like White Elephants', which will be discussed in the latter part of this article, an important underlying topic identified by many scholars concerns an implicit conversation about pregnancy and abortion. However, this reading is made in the absence of any lexical items related to pregnancy or abortion.

As a result, a corpus-based approach, used in isolation, would seem incapable of recognising the most important parts of the meaning of literary texts. Thus it may not, at first sight, seem an especially promising avenue for analysis of such texts.

However, if we carefully bear these points in mind, and if we do not single-mindedly rely on the corpus to the exclusion of other information, then none of these above-mentioned points negate the value of the corpus and computer in analyzing the language and style of literature. In the next section, it will be demonstrated that an appropriate use of a literary corpus, that is, an appropriate balance between the quantitative data and a contextual interpretation based upon it, can be fruitful in the study of style in fiction.

3. Conversational styles in Hemingway's 'Hills Like White Elephants'

The remainder of this paper will take up, as a case study, an analysis of Hemingway's short story 'Hills Like White Elephants', which presents a conversation between two characters, a man and a woman who are referred to in the narration only as "the man" and "the girl"; hence these are also the names that will be used in the present paper.[2] The couple are waiting for a train to Madrid, which will arrive in forty minutes. They are discussing a serious problem, most likely a pregnancy and

2 The man is never named at all. However, the woman is at one point addressed by the man as "Jig".

possible abortion on the part of "the girl". The "white elephants" of the title signify, in metaphorical use, something representing a heavy burden of responsibility[3], but there is also some resonance here with the phrase "the elephant in the room", meaning a topic that everyone is aware of, but is unwilling to discuss. The language used by the characters is extremely ambiguous, with meanings implied rather than overtly expressed, and the pair appear to be talking at cross purposes. The present analysis will focus on the conversational styles of the characters of "the man" and "the girl" in this story, as a way of illuminating their different perspectives.

Based on the work of Lakoff (1975) and Tannen (1989, 1992), several scholars, including Smiley (1988) and Link (2004), have analyzed the differing conversational styles of the two participants and the miscommunication that results in this short story, by distinguishing the differing gendered discourse styles used. They have demonstrated, by analyzing verbs of perception, intensifying adverbs, repetition of key words, and personal pronouns, how their miscommunication is displayed in this dialogue. I would like to illustrate some previously unremarked linguistic features such as function words (e.g. *the*, *and*, *you*, *we*) made visible through the use of a corpus-oriented approach, and interpret those linguistic features in context, in light of Hoey's (2005) concept of "lexical priming" and Tannen's research on gender-based conversational styles.

3.1. Theoretical background

Hoey (2005) develops a model of collocation in terms of "lexical priming" in which "Every word is primed for use in discourse as a result of the cumulative effects of an individual's encounters with the word" (2005: 13), on the assumption that, for every word encountered,

3 The metaphor derives from the status of white elephants as rare and sacred animals in Thailand, who were not permitted to work, but who nevertheless required absolute care and attention for the duration of their long lives; the king would give such an animal as a mark of special honour – but one not always appreciated by the recipient!

"the mind has a mental concordance [...] richly glossed for social, physical, discoursal, generic and interpersonal context" (2005: 11).

In general, the study of collocation is discussed from three viewpoints: lexical collocation (or collocates), semantic collocation (or semantic prosodies), and grammatical collocation (or colligation). Hoey attempts a more in-depth analysis of collocation and puts forward the following ten claims, adding a pragmatic aspect, relevant to the discussion in the following section:

1. Every word is primed to occur with particular other words; these are its collocates.
2. Every word is primed to occur with particular semantic sets; these are its semantic associations.
3. Every word is primed to occur in association with particular pragmatic functions; these are its pragmatic associations.
4. Every word is primed to occur in (or avoid) certain grammatical positions, and to occur in (or avoid) certain grammatical functions; these are its colligations.
5. Co-hyponyms and synonyms differ with respect to their collocations, semantic associations and colligations.
6. When a word is polysemous the collocations, semantic associations and colligations of one sense of the word differ from those of its other senses.
7. Every word is primed for use in one or more grammatical roles; these are its grammatical categories.
8. Every word is primed to participate in, or avoid, particular types of cohesive relation in a discourse; these are its textual collocations.
9. Every word is primed to occur in particular semantic relations in the discourse; these are its textual semantic associations.
10. Every word is primed to occur in, or avoid, certain positions within the discourse; these are its textual colligations. (Hoey 2005: 13)

One interesting aspect of this model is that it takes account of the importance of the text in which a word or word sequence is encountered: the perceived "greatness of a literary work or the centrality of a religious text may ensure that an encounter with a word in such writings has a bigger impact on the priming" (Hoey 2005: 12) and similarly, in conversation, "words spoken by a close friend are likely to affect our primings more directly than those spoken by someone to whom we are indifferent" (2005: 12). The "textual priming" of a word in his theory also has three aspects: "textual collocations" (claim 8), "textual semantic associations" (claim 9) and "textual colligations" (claim 10). The most interesting among these three aspects is "semantic associations". This is basically the same notion as "semantic prosodies" (Louw 1993) and "semantic preference" (Sinclair 1998). When discussing the dialogue between a man and a woman in Hemingway's short story, the following sections will show that function words are also "positively or negatively primed for occurring as part of a specific type of semantic or pragmatic relation or in a specific textual pattern" (Hoey 2005: 122-23).

3.2. Quantitative approach

As groundwork for the corpus-based study of conversational style in 'Hills Like White Elephants', an initial survey was conducted of word frequencies in the story, within text representing each of the three main "voices" present (i.e., the narrative, and the characters of "the man" and "the girl"). High-frequency items showing significant differences between the two characters were identified, and compared with the distributions of the same items within the "demographically sampled" conversational data of the British National Corpus (BNC), and with gendered voices in other works of literature.

Table 1 shows the total length of text, in terms of word counts, representing each of the various "voices" present in the story. The narrative accounts for 588/1469 words, or about 40% of the total story length; about 32% is speech by "the man", and 27% by "the girl". A third character, a waitress, contributes only 17 words of speech, which is excluded from further analysis.

	Narrative	Man's speech	Girl's speech	Waitress's speech	Total
Words	588	463	401	17	1,469

Table 1. Distribution of text among "voices" in 'Hills Like White Elephants' (raw wordcounts).

Table 2 lists all words represented by 5 or more tokens, for each of the three main "voices" of the text. Alongside the raw counts are presented relative frequencies in tokens per 10,000 words.

Narrative			Man's speech			Girl's speech		
Word	Raw freq	Freq/ 10000 words	Word	Raw freq	Freq/ 10000 words	Word	Raw freq	Freq/ 10000 words
the	107	1820	*you*	31	670	*I*	23	574
and	26	442	*I*	26	562	*it*	20	499
said	26	442	*to*	20	432	*and*	17	424
girl	22	374	*it*	17	367	*we*	15	374
at	19	323	*it's*	15	324	*you*	11	274
of	19	323	*don't*	14	302	*all*	8	200
she	12	204	*the*	14	302	*do*	8	200
man	11	187	*want*	14	302	*like*	8	200
he	10	170	*do*	12	259	*me*	7	175
looked	10	170	*have*	10	216	*please*	7	175
on	9	153	*that*	10	216	*be*	6	150
table	8	136	*but*	9	194	*could*	6	150
curtain	7	119	*we*	8	173	*don't*	6	150
two	7	119	*know*	7	151	*have*	6	150
was	7	119	*all*	6	130	*then*	6	150
were	7	119	*anything*	6	130	*know*	5	125
across	6	102	*if*	6	130	*no*	5	125
woman	6	102	*with*	6	130	*the*	5	125
asked	5	85	*and*	5	108	*they*	5	125
hills	5	85	*just*	5	108	*things*	5	125
out	5	85	*perfectly*	5	108	*what*	5	125
put	5	85						
station	5	85						
through	5	85						
to	5	85						

Table 2. Types represented by 5 or more tokens for each text "voice".

As is well known, in any written text, the definite article *the* is overwhelmingly the highest frequency word, with *and* the second-highest in occurrence. The narrative in this story also shows the same tendency. However, in the speech of "the man" and of "the girl" in the text, the definite article *the* is ranked by frequency at 7th and 18th respectively.

The following table, including the instances of *you* and *we* in such contracted forms as *we'll* and *you've*, is a list of function words showing notable differences in frequency of use between speech representing "the man" and "the girl".

Character	"the man"		"the girl"	
Word	Tokens	Freq/10000w	Tokens	Freq/10000w
the	14	302	5	125
and	5	108	17	424
you	33	713	15	374
we	9	194	18	449

Table 3. Function words showing notable differences in frequency of use between speech representing "the man" and "the girl".

Table 3 demonstrates several clear differences in frequency of function words between the speech representing "the man" and "the girl" in this story. The definite article *the* occurs in speech by "the girl" with less than half the relative frequency it does in speech by "the man". A difference in the same direction is apparent in conversational data from the demographically sampled dialogues of the BNC, where *the* occurs with a frequency of 296/10000w among male speakers, but 260/10000w among female speakers.

Although at least the direction of gender difference appears consistent with differences in real usage of *the*, the extent of the difference appears somewhat exaggerated, in that, whereas use of *the* associated with "the man" is close to the relative frequency observed in the BNC conversations, the relative frequency of *the* in the speech of "the girl" is less than half that in the BNC conversations. Similarly exaggerated constructions of gender distinctions in the use of *the*, though with different overall frequencies, also appear for speech by the characters of Hamlet and Ophelia in Shakespeare's *Hamlet* (Table 4) and for the gendered narratives by the author, as opposed to the character of Esther Summerson, in Dickens' *Bleak House* (Table 5).

Thus there seem to be relatively consistent patterns in constructed gender styles, more or less reflecting differences in actual conversational styles, that have an effect on the overall frequencies of *the*. At least as regards frequency of use, Hemingway may have been responding to real differences in gender styles in constructing the contrasting voices of his characters. However, it is unclear from frequencies alone exactly why these differences occur. Accordingly, the functional use of the definite article *the* in context by each of the two characters will be examined in more detail in Section 3.3 below.

Hamlet's speech			Ophelia's speech		
Text size	Tokens	Freq/10000w	Text size	Tokens	Freq/10000w
11,732	464	395	1,190	34	286

Table 4. Frequency of *the* in Shakespeare's *Hamlet.*

We also find a gender difference in the frequency of *the* between Hamlet and Ophelia.[4] This seems to be also true of any given written text. Table 5 illustrates the frequencies of *the* in two different narratives in Dickens' *Bleak House*: the non-dialogues of the masculine author and of a feminine narrator, Esther Summerson.

Author's non-dialogue			Esther's non-dialogue		
Text size	Tokens	Freq/10000w	Text size	Tokens	Freq/10000w
100,983	6,136	607	115,204	4,634	402

Table 5. Frequency of *the* in two different narratives in Dickens' *Bleak House.*

Table 3 further shows a significant difference in frequency of *and*: "the girl" uses *and* almost four times as often as "the man". Moreover, her tokens have a different positional distribution: eight of the 17 instances of *and* occur sentence-initially, in contrast to only a fifth of the tokens attributed to "the man". While we cannot state with any precision the 'reason' for this, we can note the argument that the initial *and* of a sentence suggests "more spontaneous discourse, [...] evidencing the lack of attention to prescriptive rules of ordinary speech" (Biber *et al.* 1999: 84), and a less settled, and less logical interlocutor.

Table 6 indicates the frequency per ten thousand words of *and* in text representing the speech of male and female participants in BNC demographically-sampled conversational data.

Male	Female
208	222

Table 6. Frequency of *and* by speaker gender in BNC conversations.

The BNC data shows a difference by gender in the use of the coordinator *and* in real conversation. A similar difference is apparent between the speech of Hamlet and Ophelia in *Hamlet* (Table 7); but by contrast,

4 These data were derived from The Shakespeare Computational Stylistics Facility on PCA Online in the University of Newcastle (URL <http://www.newcastle.edu.au/centre/cllc/pcaonline/index.html>).

there is no significant difference in frequency for the gendered narratives of *Bleak House* (Table 8):

Hamlet's speech			Ophelia's speech		
Text size	Tokens	Freq/10000w	Text size	Tokens	Freq/10000w
11,732	325	277	1,190	43	361

Table 7. Frequency of *and* in Shakespeare's *Hamlet.*

Author's non-dialogue			Esther's non-dialogue		
Text size	Tokens	Freq/10000w	Text size	Tokens	Freq/10000w
100,983	3,900	386	115,204	4384	381

Table 8. Frequency of *and* in two different narratives in Dickens' *Bleak House.*

The third difference evident in Table 3 concerns the characters' use of personal pronouns. Speech by "the girl" contains more tokens of *we* than *you*, whereas the reverse is true of the speech constructed for "the man"; moreover, "the girl" shows a higher relative frequency of *we* than "the man", whereas "the man" shows a higher relative frequency of *you*. This seems consistent with Tannen's (1992) note that the singular pronoun is more direct and usual in male speech, but plural pronouns (*we, us, our*) are more indirect and common in female speech, where these serve to include the addressee and construct a shared conversational space. However, the demographically-sampled conversational data of the BNC does not show any gender difference in the relative frequencies of these pronouns (Table 9). Meanwhile, a different gender imbalance in pronoun use is seen in the speeches of the main characters of *Hamlet* (Table 10): Ophelia's speech contains higher relative frequencies of both *you* and *we* than Hamlet's speech.

Word	Male	Female
you	322	320
we	80	80

Table 9. Tokens per 10,000 words of *you* and *we* in the spoken demographic texts of BNC.

Hamlet's speech (11,732 words)			Ophelia's speech (1,190 words)		
Word	Tokens	Freq/10000w	Word	Tokens	Freq/10000w
you	228	194	*you*	32	269
we	38	32	*we*	6	50

Table 10. Frequency of *you* and *we* in Shakespeare's *Hamlet.*

The evidence presented in this section has shown that treating even a short work of fiction as a corpus can identify differences in function words that may have some meaning in distinguishing characters within that work. Comparison with the BNC suggests that in most cases, the gender differences constructed between fictional characters may be somewhat exaggerated, or more sharply differentiated, compared to differences observed in overall frequencies of usage by men and women in real conversations. The differences between the voices of the characters in Hemingway's story are also generally more marked than those between the narrative voices of *Bleak House*, or between the characters of Hamlet and Ophelia in *Hamlet*. However, in order to interpret the differences in frequency of these function words between characters' voices, it is also necessary to examine whether they are actually being used in the same way. The following section therefore presents a more detailed qualitative analysis of the use of these function words in context in the voices of the story's two protagonists.

3.3. Qualitative approach

The present section explores, in order, the use in the speech by "the man" and "the girl" of each token of *the* (Section 3.3.1), *you* (Section 3.3.2), and *we* (Section 3.3.3).

3.3.1. Textual semantic associations of the

In this section we will first turn to the use of *the* in the speech of "the man" and "the girl" in 'Hills Like White Elephants'. The examples of *the* appearing in speech by "the girl" are listed in (1):

(1) a. Especially all **the things** you've waited so long for, like absinthe.
b. I said **the mountains** looked like white elephants.
c. I just meant **the coloring** of their skin through the trees.
d. I just meant the coloring of their skin through **the trees.**
e. Then come back and we'll finish **the beer.**

All of the five tokens of *the* attributed to "the girl" occur in affirmative sentences. Four of the five tokens of *the* in the speech of "the girl" function as deixis, referring to objects physically present in the immediate surroundings (examples (1b)-(1e)). Even token (1a), which is cataphoric, referring forward to the following definition of *things*, is subsequently referenced to a specific substance present (*absinthe*). Hence the usage of *the* by "the girl" seems largely limited to concrete reference; no examples appear to have any role in establishing a wider argument.

"The man" uses fourteen examples of definite articles, as presented in (2) below.

(2) a. That's **the way** with everything
b. **The beer's** nice and cool,
c. It's really not anything. It's just to let **the air** in
d. I'll go with you and I'll stay with you all **the time**
e. They just let **the air** in and then it's all perfectly natural
f. That's **the only thing** that bothers us
g. It's **the only thing** that's made us unhappy
h. I think it's **the best thing** to do
i. We can have **the whole world**
j. Come on back in **the shade**,
k. **the train** is coming in five minutes
l. I'd better take **the bags** over to the other side of the station,
m. I'd better take the bags over to **the other side** of the station,
n. I'd better take the bags over to the other side of **the station**,

By contrast with the direct concrete reference assigned to "the girl", these tokens display a wider variety of functions. In addition to deixis as seen in (2b) and (2j)-(2n), "the man" also uses *the* with a variety of "special quantifiers" such as universals (2a, 2d, 2i), uniques (2f, 2g), or superlatives as in (2h). Such usage is more subjective, presenting the speaker's own evaluations of what is possible or desirable. This is especially obvious in the use of special quantifiers in (2f)-(2h), which present the pregnancy as "the only thing" wrong between them, and present having the abortion as "the best thing to do" to solve the problem. This usage of *the* is therefore consistent with this character's role of constructing an argument intended to persuade "the girl", by presenting his own evaluations as being given knowledge, i.e. something that would be assumed to be true by any reasonable person.

3.3.2. Textual semantic associations of you

The present section examines the use of the second person pronoun *you*. Fifteen tokens appear in speech by "the girl", as listed in (3) below:

(3) a. No, **you** wouldn't have.
b. Especially all the things **you**'ve waited so long for, like absinthe.
c. **You** started it,
d. What makes **you** think so?
e. And **you** think then we'll be all right and be happy.
f. And **you** really want to?
g, h. And if I do it **you**'ll be happy and things will be like they were and **you**'ll love me?
i. But if I do it, then it will be nice again if I say things are like white elephants, and **you**'ll like it?
j. If I do it **you** won't ever worry?
k. And once they take it away, **you** never get it back.
l. Doesn't it mean anything to **you**?
m. Yes, **you** know it's perfectly simple.
n. Would **you** do something for me now?
o. Would **you** please please please please please please please stop talking?

Of these examples, nine (3d, 3f, 3g, 3h, 3i, 3j, 3l, 3n, 3o) are interrogatives, and four (3a, 3j, 3k, 3l) occur in negative clauses. These may be seen in context either to directly disagree with statements by "the man", or to offer some less directly stated challenge to the validity of his utterances, as in (3d), in which "What makes you think so?" is not a simple enquiry, but rather, in its wider context (4), signals "I don't think you have any valid reason to think that".

(4) 'Then what will we do afterwards?'
'We'll be fine afterwards. Just like we were before.'
'What makes you think so?'

However, even the grammatically affirmative sentences such as (3c, 3e, 3m) appear to function as a signal of displeasure or complaint, constituting an accusatory or bitter echo of statements by "the man", and certainly not implying any level of agreement; (3m) at least is subsequently clearly interpreted by "the man" as disagreement (though not a disagreement he feels obliged to address seriously), as shown in the extended context provided in (5) below.

(5) 'Of course it does. But I don't want anybody but you I don't want anyone else. And I know it's perfectly simple.'
'Yes, **you know it's perfectly simple.**'
'It's all right for you to say that, but I do know it.'

The predominant use of *you* in the speech of "the girl" thus appears to be to react to, and show disagreement with, statements by "the man", by setting up an opposition of *you* = "not me".
The characters' difference in orientation is apparent even in their respective uses of *you know*. Neither character uses the phrase in its most common discourse function ("primarily to check comprehension", cf. Carter/McCarthy 2006: 108). Whereas "the girl" uses *you know* in (5) above to express contrast with what *she* believes (i.e., that the abortion is not at all as "perfectly simple" as the man might think), "the man" instead uses *you know*, in (6) below, with stress on "know", to assert that "the girl" has that knowledge, which is therefore shared between them. Thus the same expression *you know* is used in very different ways by the two characters.

(6) 'And if I do it you'll be happy and things will be like they were and you'll love me?'
'I love you now. **You know** I love you.'

"The man" uses 33 examples of *you*. Many of the contexts of use seem to be associated with some positive or compassionate meaning. For example, his tokens in affirmative sentences, listed in (7) below, position *you* = "the girl" within the context of their relationship, as an object of care and attention:

(7) a. I'll go with **you** and I'll stay with **you** all the time.
b. I love **you** now. **You** know I love **you.**
c. **You** know how I get when I worry.
d. Well, I care about **you.**
e. I'd do anything for **you.**

Even the examples in negative contexts, listed in (8) below, treat "the girl" as, in some sense, an object. The stated meaning offers every appearance of consideration, as these statements seemingly offer her the freedom of choice; however, all of these sentences are nevertheless couched in terms of what "the man" wants for her. He does not ask, nor even appear to want to know, what she actually wants.

(8) a. Well, if **you** don't want to **you** don't have to.
b. I wouldn't have **you** do it if **you** didn't want to.
c. But I don't want **you** to do it if **you** don't really want to.
d. I don't want **you** to do anything that **you** don't want to do.

e. **You**'ve got to realize [...] I don't want **you** to do it if **you** don't want to.

Thus in both the positive and negative contexts for his use of *you*, "the man" is, rightly or wrongly, constructing himself as (or, believes himself to be) a considerate partner. However, we have also seen in his use of *the* that he believes himself to be more rational than "the girl", and because of that, he does not even question whether his opinions should be a controlling influence on her (which is how "the girl" sees them, whence comes a large part of her resentment).

3.3.3. Textual semantic associations of we

As seen in Section 3.2, the first person plural pronoun *we* appears twice as often in the speech of "the girl" than in that of "the man". An examination of each token in context also reveals a wider variety of use in the voice of "the girl", with different meanings associated with referents located in different time periods (past, present and future), distinct from those present in the speech of "the man", which thus serve to reveal differences in the characters' orientations towards their relationship, as can be seen in the extended context of example (9) below:

(9) 'And **we** could have all this,' she said. 'And **we** could have everything and every day **we** make it more impossible.'
'What did you say?'
'I said **we** could have everything.'
'We can have everything.'
'No, **we** can't.'
'We can have the whole world.'
'No, **we** can't.'
'We can go everywhere.'
'No, **we** can't. It isn't **ours** any more.'
'It's ours.'
'No, it isn't. And once they take it away, you never get it back.'
'But they haven't taken it away.'
'**We**'ll wait and see.'

In (9), "the girl" systematically refers to present difficulties with, or limits on, their lives ("we make it more impossible"; "we can't [have everything / go everywhere]"), in comparison with a past history characterised by limitless freedom ("not any more"), and hints at an uncertain future

("We'll wait and see"), in contrast to the repeated insistence by "the man" that there are no problems, that "we can" do anything we want.

(10) 'I'll go with you and I'll stay with you all the time. They just let the air in and then it's all perfectly natural.'
'Then what will **we** do afterwards?'
'We'll be fine afterwards. Just like we were before.'

Therefore, her uses of *we* in these three different contexts have different semantic associations from his. That is, *we* in the past has a positive association, *we* in the present has an uncertain or uneasy association, and *we* in the future has a negative association. However, to the man, *we* in the past and also in the future (if she undergoes the operation), has only positive associations, and even in the present, *we* has mostly positive associations, with any problems regarded as minor.

Time reference for *we*	Associations for "the girl"	Associations for "the man"
Past	positive	positive
Present	negative, restricted	continuing freedom (unchanged); any problems = minor
Future	continuing uncertainty	continuing freedom (unchanged)

Table 12. Semantic associations of *we* for each character, by time reference.

4. Conclusion

As shown above, the conversational styles adopted by the characters of "the man" and "the girl" in Hemingway's short story 'Hills Like White Elephants' are quantitatively and qualitatively different even in the use of such function words as *the*, *and*, *you*, and *we*. The quantitative differences are not obvious by conventional literary analysis, even on a close reading of the text, but are clearly brought out by approaching the text as a corpus, and by making comparisons to corpus data representing actual spoken usage. However, text frequencies, and indeed, even the reference corpus frequencies, are not easily interpreted; it is not immediately clear why differences exist in gendered conversational styles, either in real speech, or in constructed fictional "voices". Such differences may provide a valuable starting point for identifying heretofore unknown or unnoticed aspects of a writer's style; but it is also necessary to interpret that usage in context. Therefore, in this article I have argued for a hybrid approach, consisting of a synthesis of quantitative (corpus-based) and qualitative approaches, to the language of fiction. This article has focused on a few specific function words in a single short story, but it seems likely that the same kind of approach may also prove useful in examining content words in a longer work such as a novel. Taking corpus linguistics in this direction will establish the usefulness of corpus-based approaches as a tool for cracking the 'code' of a story.

References

Biber, Douglas / Johansson, Stig / Leech, Geoffrey / Conrad, Susan / Finegan, Edward 1999. *Longman Grammar of Spoken and Written English.* Harlow: Pearson Education.

Carter, Ronald 1998. *Vocabulary: Applied Linguistic Perspectives* (2nd edition). London: Routledge.

Carter, Ronald / McCarthy, Michael 2006. *Cambridge Grammar of English: A Comprehensive Guide: Spoken and Written English Grammar and Usage*. Cambridge: Cambridge University Press.

Hemingway, Ernest 1987. Hills Like White Elephants. *The Complete Stories of Ernest Hemingway.* The Finca Vigia Edition. New York: Scribner / Simon & Schuster, 211-214.

Hoey, Michael 2005. *Lexical Priming: A new theory of words and language*. London: Routledge.

Hoover, David 1999. *Language and Style in 'The Inheritors'.* New York: University Press of America.

Hori, Masahiro 2004. *Investigating Dickens' Style: A Collocational Analysis*. Basingstoke: Palgrave Macmillan.

Huddleston, Rodney / Pullum, Geoffrey 2002. *The Cambridge Grammar of the English Language*. Cambridge: Cambridge University Press.

Lakoff, Robin 1975. *Language and Woman's Place*. Oxford: Oxford University Press.

Lamb, Robert 1996. Hemingway and the Creation of Twentieth-Century Dialogue. *Twentieth Century Literature* 42/ 4, 453-480.

Link, Alex 2004. Staking Everything on it: A Stylistic Analysis of Linguistic Patterns in 'Hills Like White Elephants'. *The Hemingway Review* 23, 66-74.

O'Brien, Timothy D. 1992. Allusion, Word-Play, and the Central Conflict in Hemingway's 'Hills Like White Elephants,' *The Hemingway Review* 12, 19-25.

Quirk, Randolph / Greenbaum, Sydney / Leech, Geoffrey / Svartvik, Jan 1985. *A Comprehensive Grammar of the English Language*. London: Longman.

Rayson, Paul / Leech, Geoffrey / Hodges, Mary 1997. Social differentiation in the use of English vocabulary: some analyses of the conversational component of the British National Corpus. *International Journal of Corpus Linguistics* 2/1, 133-152.

Smiley, Pamela 1988. Gender-Linked Miscommunication in 'Hills Like White Elephants'. *The Hemingway Review* 8, 2-12.

Stubbs, Michael 2005. Conrad in the computer: examples of quantitative stylistic methods. *Language and Literature* 14/1, 5-24.

Tannen, Deborah 1989. *Talking Voices: repetition, dialogue, and imagery in conversational discourse*. Cambridge: Cambridge University Press.

Tannen, Deborah 1992. *That's not what I meant: how conversational style makes or breaks your relations with others*. London: Virago Press.

MARIA STUBBE

Active Listening in Conversation: Gender and the Use of Verbal Feedback

1. Introduction[1]

Conversation consists of much more than alternating turns at talk: rather, it is a collaborative endeavour which requires participants to engage actively as both 'speakers' and 'listeners' in the sequential construction of an interaction. Listenership therefore involves much more than simply being a passive recipient of what the current speaker is saying: it means taking an active part in the ongoing construction of the interaction. This is empirically observable in the way listeners use a variety of verbal responses and non-verbal cues, as well as in the pragmatic use of silence and pauses, all of which can vary in frequency, distribution and intensity to fulfill a complex array of interactive, epistemic and social functions.

Supportive verbal feedback takes many forms, ranging from brief vocalisations such as laughter, minimal responses such as *mhmm* and *yeah* and other brief expressions of overt or implicit support or agreement, through to longer sequences of various sorts, including backchannel utterances and cooperative overlaps. Verbal feedback occurs regularly and frequently in all types of conversational interac-

---

1 The research on which this paper is based was made possible by a grant from the New Zealand Foundation for Research, Science and Technology, and was carried out during the author's tenure as research fellow with the School of Linguistics and Applied Language Studies, Victoria University of Wellington from 1996-2003. I am grateful to all those who allowed their interactions to be recorded and analysed as part of the Wellington Corpus of Spoken New Zealand English. I also thank Robert Sigley for his assistance with the statistical tests, and David Britain, Chris Lane, Janet Holmes and an anonymous referee for their useful input on earlier iterations of this work. Any errors and infelicities remain entirely my own responsibility.

tion, closely aligned with non-verbal signals such as gestures, head nods, facial expression and gaze, and is a primary resource for engaging in active listenership. At a minimum these devices serve to signal the listener's alignment with the current interactional activity, but they may also help to construct more substantive forms of involvement and affiliation between interlocutors.

Using tools from conversation analysis, interactional sociolinguistics and pragmatics, analysts of spoken discourse have developed an increasingly sophisticated understanding of how verbal listener responses function in their sequential context (e.g. Bublitz 1988; Coates 1989; Farr 2003; Gardner 1997, 1998, 2001, 2007; Jefferson 1984, 1993, 2002; McCarthy 2003; Norrick 2012; Orestrom 1983; Schegloff 1982; Schiffrin 1987; Stenström 1987, 1994; Stivers 2004, 2008; Stubbe 1994, 1998a; Ward/Tsukahara 2000, 2003; Xudong 2008). More recently, with the increasing availability of video corpora and analytic tools, the focus of interest has widened further to encompass micro-level multimodal analysis of active listenership, specifically the fine articulation between verbal responses and non-verbal cues (e.g. Carter/Adolphs 2008; Knight/Adolphs 2008; Stivers 2008).

The focus of this chapter is on gendered patterns of variation in the use of supportive verbal feedback in a sample of conversational data from the Wellington Corpus of Spoken New Zealand English (WSC).[2] The original analysis of this data was carried out between 1995 and 1998 as part of a wider-ranging study of pragmatic variation in New Zealand English discourse. An analytic framework for the classification of supportive verbal feedback in corpus data was developed by the author as part of this project (see Section 3), and was subsequently applied to a quantitative and qualitative analysis of ethnic and gender

2 The Wellington Corpus of Spoken New Zealand English consists of one million words of spoken New Zealand English, of which the conversational component is made up of speech excerpts of over 2000 words. All contributors are speakers of New Zealand English, from a range of gender, age, and social and ethnic backgrounds (Holmes/Vine/Johnson 1998). See Sigley (this volume) for an overview of the text-category makeup of this corpus.

variation in a matched sub-sample of the WSC (see Stubbe 1996; Holmes/Stubbe 1997; Stubbe 1998a).[3]

A brief overview of the relevant literature on gender and verbal feedback in conversation is provided next. The rest of the chapter exemplifies one possible approach to analysing variation in the use of complex interactive discourse variables using corpus data. Section 3 provides an updated account of the classification framework for analysing supportive verbal feedback referred to above, followed by discussion of the methods and results of the gender variation analysis in Section 4.

2. Gendered speech styles and the use of verbal feedback

Research on gender and language use in Western, English-speaking societies has consistently reported women to be generally more facilitative, cooperative conversationalists than men (e.g. Aries 1976; Coates 1996; 1998, 2003, 2004; Crawford 1995; Holmes 1995, 2006; Holmes/Meyerhoff 2003; Johnson/Meinhof 1997; Romaine 1999; Talbot 1998; Tannen 1990, 1993, 1994; Wertheim/Bailee/Corston-Oliver 1998; Wodak 1997). In particular, it has been claimed that women are more active listeners in the sense that they are more likely to use conversational strategies, including supportive verbal feedback or response tokens, which support the smooth progress of an interaction and facilitate others' opportunities to speak.

Much of the early work in this area focused on quantifiable gender differences in the use of closed sets of linguistic devices which were assumed to generically index putative 'competitive' or 'facilitative' conversational styles. To begin with, these styles were often positioned as polar opposites, though, as discussed further below, the

3 The present paper provides a more detailed account of the gender component of this previous analysis than has been published previously, including some previously unpublished results, and draws on relevant material in later publications by the author and colleagues (e.g. Stubbe 1999, 2003; Stubbe/Holmes/Vine/Marra 2001; Stubbe/Lane/Hilder/E.Vine/B.Vine/Holmes/Marra/Weatherall 2003; Stubbe/Holmes 1995, 2000; Holmes/Stubbe 1992, 2003; Holmes/Stubbe/Marra 2003).

argument was increasingly made that in reality such differences were indicative of a distributional gendered style continuum which could be drawn on by both men and women in different settings (e.g. Cameron 1995, 1997; Bing/Bergvall 1996; Stubbe *et al.* 2001; Coates 2004). This early quantitative work largely predated the era of widespread access to large computerised corpora, and thus typically involved the manual coding and counting of formally defined categories of features such as interruptions or minimal feedback tokens in relatively small, purposively collected sets of naturally occurring or elicited interactions. One marker assumed to index the more co-operative interactive style associated with women was a greater use of supportive minimal response tokens such as *mhmm*, *mm*, and *yeah.*

Many studies (though not all) reported that women tended to use more minimal responses than men to signal their involvement or to encourage others to contribute and keep talking (e.g., Dittman 1972; Fishman 1983; Gilbert 1990; Hirschman 1974; Hyndman 1985; Leet-Pellegrini 1980; Munro 1987; Nordenstam 1992; Roger 1989; Reid 1995; Strodtbeck/Mann 1956; Stubbe 1978; Zimmerman/West 1975). However, such analyses took little account of potentially confounding variables such as text and activity type or topic (see below), or of the often complex interrelationship between the range of possible forms and the different functions they can be used to perform 'online' in the local context of the discourse. These studies were also often flawed from a statistical standpoint due to the interactive nature of the variables being examined. For example, the frequency of feedback responses produced is obviously co-dependent on other variables such as the relative amount of talk produced by each speaker, and the degree to which each speaker holds the floor. It is not surprising therefore that subsequent research showed the relative frequency of minimal responses to provide at best only a very crude measure of interactional supportiveness by listeners, whatever their gender.

From the early 1980s a number of researchers using a more action-oriented or functional analytic framework began to identify patterns of gender difference in the use of open-ended categories of facilitative verbal feedback. These included sentence completions, echoes, cooperative overlapping and other longer comments or questions which appeared to indicate active listening or intense involvement. Several studies found that such responses tended to occur in less formal contexts where a 'one-at-a-time' model of turn taking (cf. Sacks/Schegloff/Jefferson 1974) is not strictly adhered to by participants. For example, Edelsky (1981) demonstrated that American women's participation in faculty meetings increased during "collaborative floor" sections of the interaction, while Nordenstam (1992: 84) reported that Swedish women talking to one another used a more varied and elaborated range of backchannel signals which were often more "emotionally charged" (e.g. *det var ju fantastiskt* – 'that's incredible'). Other researchers have observed that women often prefer collaboratively constructed "all-together-now" talk, especially when exchanging personal stories or gossiping with close friends (Coates 1989, 1998, 2004; Pilkington 1994, 1998).

Researchers also began to put forward evidence suggesting women and men may use and interpret simple minimal responses such as *mhmm* somewhat differently. For instance, Maltz/Borker (1982) claimed that men were more likely than women to interpret a simple minimal response as implying agreement, and Fishman observed that women in heterosexual couples were "particularly skilled at inserting *mms*, *yeahs*, *ohs* and other such comments throughout streams of talk rather than at the end", very precisely timed to fall between the breaths of the speaker (1983: 96). Reid Thomas (1995) noted a relationship between gender and the timing and intonation of simple minimal responses, and a tendency for women's responses to be interpreted more often than men's as meaning *I'm listening* versus *I agree*. Fellegy (1995) reported that different usage or distributional rules were assigned to minimal responses by the Anglo-American men and women in her sample: even though overall frequencies were very similar, the women spread minimal responses more evenly throughout the speaker's utterance than the men, who tended to load up their responses at the ends of syntactic units.

More recent work on language and gender has increasingly questioned the value of earlier quantitative research which was conducted predominantly within a 'gender difference' paradigm. This tended to be based on an essentialist assumption of consistent gendered differences in language behaviour, regardless of the context and purpose of the communicative event, or the locally occasioned contingencies of talk-in-interaction. Since the mid-1990s many language and gender researchers (myself included) increasingly moved away from formally based quantitative approaches to more nuanced qualitative analyses of how people use a range of interactional resources to 'perform' or construct gender identities as they talk within gendered communities of practice (e.g. Bergvall 1999; Bing/Bergvall 1996; Cameron 1997, 2003; Eckert/McConnell-Ginet 1999, 2003, 2007; Freed 2003; Holmes/Meyerhoff 2003; Holmes/Stubbe 2003; McElhinney/Mills 2007; Stubbe 1998b; Talbot 2003; Weatherall 2002).

As Cheshire (2002: 439) points out, "not all women prefer affective meanings, or speak in a cooperative speech style; and [...] those who do, do not always do so. The same applies to men and their apparent preference for referential meanings; and to (other) patterns of sex differentiation". In other words, pre-determined social categories like 'men' and 'women' are not simple homogeneous groupings, any more than other common intergroup comparisons. The reality is that the communicative behaviours observed in any particular interaction result from a complex interaction between the socio-cultural norms associated with the enactment of various social roles and identities (of which gender may not be the most salient) and other situated aspects of the encounter. The specific requirements of the context or type of talk in which speakers are engaged are likely to influence the use of particular features at least as much as an individual's 'performance' of gender or other aspects of social identity, and *intra*-sex differences in communicative behaviour are thus likely to be at least as great as any *inter*-sex differences. In so far as generalisations in terms of sex or gender are possible at all, therefore, it is important to take account of overlaps between women's and men's behaviour as well as any actual or presumed differentiation (Freed/Greenwood 1996).

The use of verbal feedback is highly contingent on the local context and the sequential organisation of the interaction at the point where it occurs. While it is impractical to micro-analyse each interaction in a corpus sample to determine the effect of context line by line, more macro-level contextual indicators such as text type have frequently been commented on in relation to gender and the use of feedback, and provide a useful starting point for exploring the part played by the discursive context. For example, Coates (1989, 1996) found that the frequency and discourse functions of feedback responses in women's conversation varied systematically according to whether the participants were engaged in "interaction-focused" talk (where no one speaker has primary responsibility for the development of the topic), or "information-focused" talk such as narrative or descriptive sequences with a single "topical speaker" (West/Garcia 1988). Coates found that in information-focused talk, listener responses were used less frequently but in specific ways, for example to signal agreement to a topic shift, or to mark active agreement with a speaker's summing up. In these text types the immediate involvement of the listener in the development of the topic is less. Moreover, narratives in particular are characterised by long turns which need to be negotiated initially by the speaker, but then require less regular localised feedback from the listener than is the case in other more dialogic text types.

The topic being discussed has also been shown to influence the degree and nature of listener involvement. For example in a New Zealand study comparing gossip and non-gossip texts, Pilkington (1994, 1998) found that, when gossiping, both sexes shifted to a relatively 'high-involvement' style, characterised in part by higher use of overtly supportive minimal responses and cooperative overlaps. However, Pilkington found that men and women were not equally likely to select the same feedback strategies, and also had different frequency baselines. For instance, when gossiping, men showed a preference for supportive minimal responses to signal high involvement, while women used more overlaps; however, the women's baseline rate of cooperative overlap use in general conversation was equivalent to that of men engaged in gossip.

Earlier research has also consistently reported that men and women tend to discuss different types of topics (Kalcik 1975; Aries 1976; Haas/Sherman 1982; Aries/Johnson 1983; James/Drakich 1993; Tannen 1990; Coates 1989, 1996, 2003). In same-sex settings men tend to focus on shared activities such as sports and hobbies, and speak less about themselves, their feelings or their relationships with others, whereas women tend to talk more often about personal feelings and interpersonal relationships, and about intimate topics and daily activities. Because such topics pose potential threats to both speaker's and listener's face, it is predictable that they would be associated with more frequent use of affectively supportive listener feedback and other addressee-oriented pragmatic devices such as *you know* which function both to encourage and support contributions by other participants in an interaction, and to convey solidarity and shared understanding. Clearly, if women talk more than men about personal topics, and if such topics as a rule generate relatively more high-involvement feedback regardless of listener gender, then it is reasonable to predict that women in a representative corpus will produce a higher proportion of explicitly supportive feedback than men (assuming otherwise comparable discourse contexts).

More recent research in this area has tended to embrace a post-modernist or social constructionist paradigm which problematises the use of predetermined 'essentialist' social categories such as gender and the decontextualised classification and analysis of linguistic features. Nevertheless, as Cameron (1995) points out, much of the earlier gender difference research was well-conceived and carefully executed, with a pattern of results that has proved to be remarkably robust over time. What has principally changed is the way in which such patterns are now interpreted. As such, this earlier body of work continues to provide a useful and relevant starting point for analysing gender patterns in corpus data, with the important proviso that the complexities of precisely how discourse features such as listener responses function in context must be taken fully into account when interpreting the results. This point is explored further in the next section.

3. Developing a workable analytic framework

This section describes a taxonomy of supportive verbal feedback devices derived from an exploratory analysis of 1800 listener responses in 22 dyadic conversations and radio interviews from the WSC (see Stubbe 1996, 1998a), and explains its underlying theoretical rationale. This analysis built on the conclusions drawn from the research reviewed above; namely, that the definition of what constitutes a supportive feedback device should include more extended feedback like cooperative overlapping and sentence completions as well as simple minimal responses, and that it would be instructive to look more closely both at the functions and patterns of placement or distribution of feedback responses in relation to patterns of variation. The resulting model was used to classify and quantify gender patterns in the use of listener feedback for the subsample analysis described in Section 4 below.

The data for the initial exploratory study came from the informal speech section of the WSC. This constitutes 75% of the overall corpus, while 50% of the corpus is private face-to-face conversations (DPC) collected using the 'friend of a friend' method. The WSC overall is roughly representative in terms of gender: women contributed 52% and men 48% of the final transcribed words, reflecting the New Zealand population balance. However, the WSC does not include representative samples from particular ethnic groups other than the indigenous Māori people. In respect to other social variables, there is a bias towards the 20-30 year age band in the DPC data category, and the conversation participants are much more likely to be university-educated than the general New Zealand population at the time (Holmes/Vine/Johnson 1998).[4] The sample analysed for the exploratory study comprised approximately 50,000 running words in total, with 44 participants representing two age bands (16-34, 40-55), two ethnic groups (36 Pakeha, 8 Māori), and an even split of men and women. Because only audio-taped data was available, non-verbal feedback was not studied.

3.1. Defining verbal feedback

Analysis in context of the 1800 listener responses identified in the exploratory analysis highlighted the sheer complexity and range of the interactional resources available to listeners. As with other complex discourse variables, listener responses are not bound to a closed set of forms, and the 'meanings' or actions performed by these utterances are, by definition, co-constructed and contingent on the local sequential context. This makes it challenging to reliably categorise these phenomena for the purposes of a variationist discourse analysis of corpus data (see also Pichler 2010).

The following excerpt from the WSC exemplifies just a few of the interactional devices listeners may draw on to actively involve themselves in a conversation while an interlocutor holds the floor, and provides some indication of the complexity with which these devices

---

4 Of individuals with completed background information sheets in WSC conversations, 32.9% had a university degree, compared with 8.5% of the New Zealand population in the 1996 census.

function interactively. It is also a canonical example of the collaborative 'high involvement' listening style often associated with women in the language and gender research of the late twentieth century, as discussed above. (Supportive verbal feedback devices are shown in bold).[5]

(1) Supportive verbal feedback

Context: A woman tells her friend about a botched hair dyeing job.

Mona: [laughs] so this is really silly 'cause the hair's white okay //they muck
it up so i end up red + in a couple of months i've got to go back\ +
Carol: /**[laughs]**\\
Carol: **[laughs]: have it str-=/**
Mona: /**=they'd strip streaks** of the red strip it right
back to white but don't do it she said don't do the whole head
Carol: **[laughs] streak it white //[laughs]**\
Mona: **/streak bits of it white**\\ and then eventually the red will grow
out and fade and the white will dominate but it's going to take months
Carol: **yeah**
Mona: that's why i want to get it back to something close to normal and i've got
my niece's wedding to go to in //december\ so i'm going to go down=
Carol: /**oh no**\\
Mona: =in posterity in the family photographs as a //redhead **[laughs]**\
Carol: /**[laughs]** \\ **oh dear** + **hmm**
Mona: still mark thinks it's lovely
Carol: **does he**=/
Mona: /=**oh yes**
Carol: **oohh** // + **oohh [quietly]: how could he:**\
Mona: /i think it's a real sexist thing i think he thinks it makes me look\\
you know a lot younger and [laughs] therefore it might make him look
a little bit younger if i'm //with him i think that's the reasoning\
Carol: /**[drawls]: oh gosh:** \\
aren't they pathetic
Mona: **[laughs] they are yes [laughs]**

(DPC283; extract from section of text not included in WSC)

In this example, Carol listens sympathetically to Mona's account of a recent disastrous visit to the hairdresser to have her hair dyed. As narrator, Mona mostly holds the floor, but Carol too is actively participating in the conversation. At appropriate points in the narrative, she laughs along with Mona (L3, L4, L7, L15); provides supportive

5 See Appendix for transcription conventions. All names used in examples are pseudonyms.

minimal responses – *yeah* (L10), *oh no* (L13), *oh dear, hmm* (L15), *oh gosh* (L23); quietly interpolates longer 'backchannel' comments – *have it str-* (L4), *oohh + oohh how could he* (L19); partially echoes Mona's words in L5 "*strip streaks ... right back to white*" with *streak it white* (L7); and asks facilitative (rhetorical) questions which function as aligning evaluations – *does he* (L17), *aren't they pathetic* (L24).

Without ever taking the floor as such, Carol thus indicates in various ways that the story has her active attention and interest, and encourages Mona to continue telling it. At the same time, the finely nuanced choices she makes about the type, placement and intensity of verbal feedback she provides add a complex layering of additional meanings. She can be heard to express her sympathy with and understanding of Mona's plight, and humorously reinforces shared aspects of their friendship and social identity (e.g. gender, age, life experience) by reflecting and extending further Mona's attitude of mock exasperation with her male partner. Mona in turn weaves reciprocal feedback to Carol into her own narrative by projecting possible completions, echoing or responding to Carol's laughter and other supportive comments, often in overlap with Carol: *they'd strip streaks* (L5), *streak bits of it white* (L8), *oh yes* (L18), *i think it's a real sexist thing* (L20), *they are yes* (L25). On hearing the excerpt, one is also struck by the rapidity and precision timing with which these various listener responses are interpolated into the stream of talk, including latched utterances[6] (L4-5, L17-18), and the echoes and overlaps deployed by both participants as they co-construct the discourse (e.g. L5-8, L19-20, L22-23).

This example highlights some important observations about verbal feedback in conversation. First, all supportive listener responses typically share a basic interactive function of aligning with the current activity (Stivers 2008) in that they "appear to ratify or otherwise contribute to the talk of a current speaker" (Zimmerman/West 1975: 104) and confirm that speaker and listener share a common frame of reference without threatening the current speaker's floor holding. Neither minimal responses nor more extended backchannels are generally

6 The term 'latched utterance' is used here in a structural sense to refer to turns which follow on with no discernible gap or intervening pause between utterances.

heard as interruptions or as separate turns at talk (Coates, 1989, 2004; Edelsky 1981; Tannen 1984).

Second, listener responses may convey several levels of meaning simultaneously: minimal responses in particular "punch above their weight" in terms of their interactional importance (McCarthy 2003). For instance, as we saw in Example 1, supportive responses can provide an explicit warrant for a long turn to continue (Coates 1989; Schegloff 1993) and may also function to pass back the floor in cases where the speaker has yielded the turn, or as a polite means of "booking" a turn at talk (Stubbe 1994). "Topicalising utterances" (West/Garcia 1988) or "news receipts" (Maynard/Frankel 2006) such as *really* or *oh yeah* play an important part in ongoing topic development and maintenance, while jointly constructed minimal response sequences are regularly used to formally close down a topic (Filipi/Wales 2003; West 2006). At a referential level, verbal feedback allows listeners to display indirectly their own knowledge or competence within the domain of action to which the topic relates. It can also indicate the listener's stance towards what is being said by indexing a wide range of epistemic meanings from relative indifference or doubt, through simple affirmation to enthusiastic interest and agreement (Bublitz 1988; Gardner 2001, 2005; Stenström 1994; Stubbe 1994). In addition, listener feedback can be used to express supportive/affiliative relational meanings, ranging from simple acknowledgment of an interlocutor's feelings to explicit expressions of sympathy, interest, surprise, or enthusiasm.

Third, the forms and functions of listener responses are not in a one-to-one relationship. Listeners have a wide range of possible feedback devices to select from, and can produce, combine and distribute these strategically in many different ways according to the context. The precise 'meaning' or interactional effect of such utterances is thus subject to conversational inference, and is highly contingent on how an interaction unfolds turn by turn.

Moreover, although feedback is a ubiquitous feature of conversation in all languages, the specific meanings that may be inferred from different forms, baseline frequencies or distribution of listener feedback and the levels or types of feedback considered appropriate in particular contexts, have been shown to vary widely across cultures (see Stubbe 1998a for a more detailed discussion). For example, the typical Finn is a silent listener by comparison with members of many other European ethnolinguistic groups: verbal feedback occurs infrequently, and interruption and overlaps are generally considered unacceptable (Lehtonen/Sajavaara 1985). Japanese speakers on the other hand are reported to have a relatively high baseline for verbal backchannelling; this has been linked to the cultural value of *omoiyari*, which places great value on the creation and maintenance of harmonious interaction (Hayashi 1988; White 1989). Xudong (2008) studied the use of listener responses in Mandarin Chinese and Australian English conversations, and found a number of differences in frequency, types and the positioning of listener responses. Chinese speakers used fewer listener responses, used more paralinguistic vocalic forms rather than lexical items, and were more likely to place their listener responses during a turn. New Zealand Māori,[7] in common with other Pacific cultures, also place great importance on the creation of involvement and solidarity in informal discourse (White/Watson-Gegeo 1990; Britain 1992); however, in contrast with Japanese interactions, Māori conversationalists place a strong reliance on non-verbal cues and implicit reference in preference to the use of explicit verbal feedback (Metge/Kinloch 1984; Britain 1992; Stubbe 1998a; Holmes/Stubbe 2000).

Finally, it is important to note that verbal feedback does not always function supportively as in this excerpt. Listeners have been reported to use both delayed feedback and minimal responses rather than full turns at talk as strategies for avoiding further participation in a conversation or to shut down discussion of a topic (Zimmerman/West 1975; Fishman 1983). Listener responses may also be used to indirectly signal impatience (Stivers 2004) and disagreement or doubt (Stubbe 1994). Bublitz (1988: 184) observes that because minimal responses such as *mm* can be inserted almost anywhere in the stream of talk, they are also an excellent device for "pretending to listen", while extended sequences of simultaneous speech may just as readily be intended (or perceived) to interrupt an interlocutor's turn as to function as a cooperative overlap or projected completion (Tannen 1990). Any analysis of

---

7 The Māori people are New Zealand's original Polynesian inhabitants, comprising about 15% of the population. *Pakeha* is a Māori word used widely in New Zealand English to refer to people of European (mainly British) descent; this is the dominant cultural/ethnic grouping in New Zealand.

verbal feedback cannot therefore rely on formal features alone but must take account of the localised contingent nature of spoken interaction.

3.2. The supportive feedback continuum

Three main dimensions of variation in how listeners provided supportive verbal feedback were identified in the exploratory analysis:

1) the *type* of feedback device (defined by lexical, paralinguistic and interactional features);
2) the *frequency* and *distribution* of feedback responses;
3) the *placement* of feedback in relation to the current speaker's utterances.

These variables were observed to interact in complex ways as resources for producing a range of meanings particular to the local discourse context. The overall conclusion was that listener responses are most appropriately characterised as a relatively open class of multi-functional utterances operating along a continuum or "backchannel gradient" (cf. Stenström 1994: 81) reflecting the nature and degree of joint involvement in the interaction,[8] the degree of explicit referential or affective support provided by the listener, and the degree of social distance or solidarity (Stubbe 1991, 1994, 1998a); see Figure 1.

---

8 More recently, Norrick (2012) has made the related observation that more "insistent" response tokens that function as assessments or challenges (e.g. *wow, really*) will often elicit further responses in their own right, unlike less "obtrusive" responses such as *uh-huh*, and proposes that listener responses could also usefully be ranked along a scale of obtrusiveness or insistency.

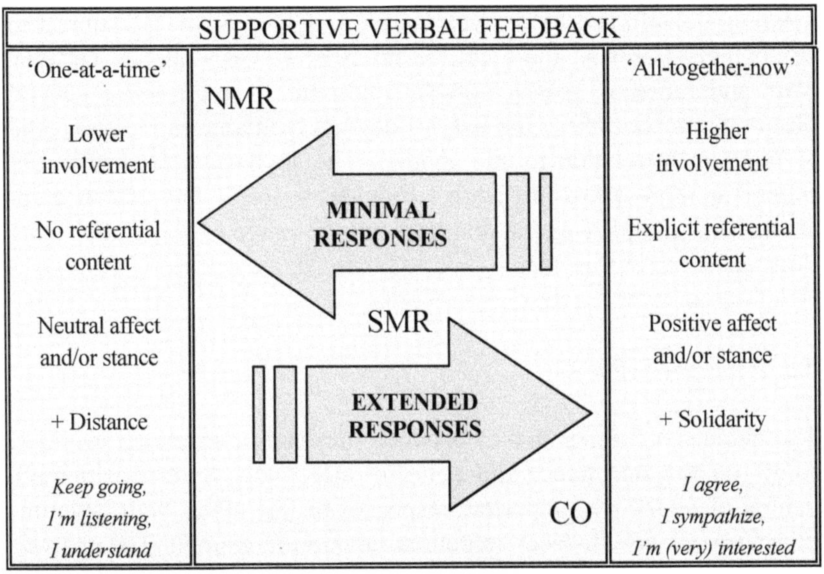

Figure 1. The supportive verbal feedback continuum.

This provides a flexible system (both culturally and situationally relative) that allows listeners to take an active role in influencing the topical development and interactional structure of a conversation, as well as to convey a wide range of social and affective meanings. Available responses range from providing the minimum amount of interactional feedback compatible with sustaining the conversation, right through to the joint construction of the discourse. At the affective and propositional levels, a listener response may simply be a neutral attention signal, or it may carry a greater or lesser degree of positive referential or affective meaning, such as confirming or agreeing with another speaker's statement of fact or opinion, or explicitly expressing empathy and interest in what is being said. Such strategies can function simultaneously to encourage and support contributions by other participants in an interaction, and to convey solidarity and shared understanding.

Listeners are thus able to vary the type, placement and distribution of the feedback responses in a way that allows them to meet their conversational goals in particular contexts. Particular devices or forms are also multi-functional, both in the sense that they can perform different actions according to the context, and also in their ability to function on more than one level simultaneously. Because the precise meaning constructed by a given feedback device is always subject to contextual inference, there can be no strict correspondence between form and function. It is nonetheless possible to make some general observations about how the various devices available to listeners tend to function in relation to one another. The supportive feedback continuum as represented in Figure 1 provides a useful way of conceptualising this complex interaction between the range of forms and functions observed in this data.

3.3. Types of feedback

The choices a listener makes between minimal or extended response forms on the one hand, and between affectively or propositionally neutral or explicitly supportive responses on the other, both have implications for how listener responses function in context. The analysis distinguished three main categories of verbal feedback: neutral minimal responses (NMRs), explicitly supportive minimal responses (SMRs) and cooperative overlaps (COs). These three types of feedback are defined and exemplified next.

3.3.1. Neutral minimal responses (NMRs)

To the left of the continuum are brief minimal responses which can be heard as interactionally supportive, but which are affectively and referentially neutral in tone. Typical functions of such neutral minimal responses might include signalling attention, understanding, a willingness to keep listening, or the negotiation of a topic shift. NMRs are basically heard as an acknowledgement or continuation signal, though they may sometimes imply a secondary meaning of tacit agreement or reserving judgement. Example (2) illustrates the kinds of responses classified as NMRs: these are drawn from a very small closed set of lexical items such as *mm*, *uh-huh*, *yeah, okay* and variants (cf. Hirschman 1974; Fishman 1983; Schegloff 1982; Jefferson 1984). They sound prosodically and lexically unmarked, are characterised by mid to low pitch, fairly level intonation and relatively low volume, and are usually placed at the boundary of a syntactic or tone unit (i.e. a transition relevance point (TRP) as defined originally by Sacks *et al.* 1974). It is quite possible for a listener to utter such neutral minimal responses more or less automatically and still appear attentive (Bublitz 1988).

(2) Neutral minimal responses (NMRs)

Context: Two male colleagues discuss a television programme.

Tama: well er the catholic bishops' conference has made statements on homosexuality and so on //and\ um have taken into account //i i know\

Eru: **/mm**\\ **/mm mm**\\

Tama: what er Māori opinion is for Māori catholics

Eru: **mm**

(DPC317: 1030-1055)

3.3.2. Supportive minimal responses (SMRs)

Along the continuum to the right are verbal responses which are still minimal in form, but which are heard as more emotionally and epistemically charged. SMRs are more differentiated in function or actions performed, expressing meanings such as sympathy, interest, surprise, and explicit or enthusiastic agreement (cf. Nordenstam 1992; Pilkington 1994, 1998; Stenström 1994; Stubbe 1994, 1998a; Reid 1995). Listeners typically achieve this by clustering several neutral minimal responses together in quick succession, or by using prosodically marked minimal response forms which can be heard as being explicitly supportive in some way. SMRs can be realised by a wide range of short utterances including explicit agreement markers and minimal responses like *mm* or *uh-huh,* which are marked paralinguistically by extended pitch span, raised voice range and higher volume and/or by rapid repetition. While SMRs also function in an aligning way as an acknowledgement or continuer, they simultaneously signal an explicitly supportive affective or positively valenced evaluative meaning of some sort along a continuum of 'strength'. Excerpt (3) provides an illustration of the forms and placement typical of this response category.

In this excerpt, Carol uses SMRs four times in quick succession to construct an affiliative stance, to demonstrate her active attention to and interest in Mona's story, and to signal her continued willingness to be in the listener role as Mona continues with her extended narrative. In L3 she expresses emphatic surprise with *oh gee*, produced in overlap. When Mona finishes her turn in L4, Carol produces *yeah* with a similar intonation contour, which constructs it as an explicitly affiliative response while at the same time functioning as a continuer. Mona then renews her narrative thread, marking the transition to the upshot of her narrative with *so*. Carol's next SMRs in L7 (*precisely ++ yeah*) and L9 (*exactly*) are designed as explicit agreements with Mona's stated position, with the positively valenced lexical choices boosted by the prosodic features, and in the case of L7, by the addition of the post-posed *yeah*.

(3) Supportive minimal responses (SMRs)
Context: Two female friends discuss a botched hair-dyeing job.

1 Mona: so whether I have to go back and get one of these colour bath things
2 //done\ every four weeks=
3 Carol: /**oh gee**\\
4 Mona: =i don't know but i- and i don't know how much that will cost
5 Carol: yeah
6 Mona: so that's the annoying thing //all i'm asking them for is a refund\
7 Carol: /**precisely** ++ **yeah**\\
8 Mona: fo- for the original amount i //spent there\ and if they're not careful=
9 Carol: /**exactly**\\
10 Mona: =i'll take them to the small claims tribunal and ask for maintenance
11 money as well

(DPC283; extract from section of text not included in WSC).

3.3.3. Cooperative overlaps

Listeners may also signal high involvement or solidarity with more extended feedback of various types, referred to here collectively as cooperative overlaps. This term, as used here, includes brief interjections, sentence completions, echoes and repetitions, through to more extended segments of simultaneous or actually overlapping speech which may include paraphrases, comments, elaborations and questions.[9] These usually align and/or affiliate with the content of the other speaker's utterance in some way, and are sometimes followed by an

9 Previous labels for this type of verbal feedback include "extended back-channels" (West/Zimmerman 1983), "non-turn-competitive incomings" (French/Local 1983), "non-floor-holding turns" (Edelsky 1981), "co-operative overlaps" (Tannen 1990), "supportive interruptive forms" (Stubbe 1991, 1994), "secondary speaker contributions" (Bublitz 1988) and "all-together-now" talk or interruptions (Coates 1989; Dunne/Ng 1994; Pilkington 1994, 1998).

indication of support from the primary speaker. Like minimal responses, cooperative overlaps seem to function along a continuum of lesser to greater involvement in the primary speaker's turn. Features such as sentence completions and echoes function much like SMRs in that they are overtly supportive, yet carry little or no independent or new referential meaning. As Example 4 illustrates, cooperative overlaps differ from minimal responses in that they are not drawn from a closed set of forms, and listeners are more involved in the joint construction of text. At the high involvement end of the scale co-operative overlapping becomes "duetting" (Coates 1991; Falk 1980) or contrapuntal talk which may appear to resemble disruptive interruptions, although participants clearly do not orient to them as such.

(4) Cooperative overlaps (COs)

Context: Two female friends discuss proposed purchase of a piece of land.

Kate: mm i mean if you put your house up here you'd be tucked away from your property +
**//you'd be tucked away from- yes it would actually i think + **

Tessa: **/it would be good for vegetable gardens and things like that round there wouldn't it +**

Kate: **yeah=/**

Tessa: **/='cause it looked like very fertile soil there**

(DPC080: 0430-0445)

3.4. Frequency, distribution and placement of feedback responses

In previous research, as noted earlier, the overall frequency of verbal feedback throughout an interaction has often been assumed to relate directly to how supportive a particular listener is being. However, the analysis of the WSC data suggested that at the macro-level at least, the overall frequency of feedback in an interaction can at best provide only a crude measure of interactive supportiveness (see also Stubbe 1994). This is because, in addition to the variability in the *type* of feedback response already discussed, both the *frequency* and *distribution* of feedback also varies both within and between particular interactions. This variation appears to correlate with a number of different factors, including the text types produced by the participants, the overall balance between participants in the roles of speaker and listener, and the nature of the topics under discussion, as well constraints imposed by the immediate discourse context.

On the other hand, at a more localised discourse level, the way in which feedback responses are distributed had much clearer functional implications in the WSC data. For example, a clustering of responses in close succession appeared to be consistent with a higher level of involvement, either at an affective level, or with some aspect of discourse structure, independently of the form of the verbal response. Thus a cluster of NMRs at a point of topic shift could indicate the listener's alignment with the current speaker taking an extended turn. By way of contrast, the more spaced out but constant and explicitly supportive feedback provided by Carol in examples (1) and (3) also suggested high involvement and explicit positive affect, but in this case for the reason that such regular feedback is not expected throughout a narrative sequence, and its presence therefore carries relatively more functional weight. Examples such as these show that it is not necessary or appropriate to use verbal feedback to the same extent or in the same way in all contexts, and that speakers are sensitive to such norms. Therefore, although a high relative rate of verbal feedback can be one indicator of conversational involvement and mutual interest, this cannot be measured in absolute terms.

In addition, minimal responses often follow a consistent pattern of precise and well-timed placement at the end of information units such as the tone group or clause (Coates 1989, Dittman/Llewellyn 1967) or at phrasal junctures in predicates (Fellegy 1992). The latter study also reported a pattern of sensitivity to semantic completion at an underlying level. Intonation plays a part too in signalling where a minimal response is expected to occur in certain text types such as narratives (Corston 1993). However, in the WSC data, as elsewhere, minimal responses also frequently occurred at non-boundary points, a phenomenon which has been associated with more active listening styles, as noted in 3.1 above. The link between the contrapuntal placement of feedback responses and the listener's degree of involvement in the conversation was seen most clearly in the case of cooperative overlaps.

4. Analysis of gender variation in WSC sub-sample

4.1. Sample and method of analysis

A sample of eight dyadic conversations (roughly 17,288 running words in total) was selected from the WSC. Each extract was approximately ten minutes in length, beginning and ending at natural topic boundaries. Age and social class were controlled in selecting the sample: all 16 participants were between 40 and 60 years old, and came from professional backgrounds. Further, the speakers in each dyad were matched for both gender and ethnicity, with two conversations representing each gender/ethnicity group (i.e. Māori men, Māori women, Pakeha men and Pakeha women), as shown in Table 1.

	Pakeha/NZ European	Māori
Male	4 (2 dyads)	4 (2 dyads)
Female	4 (2 dyads)	4 (2 dyads)

Table 1. Sample design.

In total, 905 instances of supportive interactive feedback were identified and classified as NMRs, SMRs or COs. Given the interactive nature of listener feedback, a simple comparison of individual raw scores would not allow meaningful comparisons between individuals or groups of speakers. However, because participants were matched for gender and ethnicity, it was possible to use the dyad as the statistical unit of analysis. (Nevertheless, it is important to note that this does introduce a different limitation, namely that by using only matched dyads, the patterns of interaction identified may not generalise to mixed dyads or groups.)

The raw totals and the total number of words uttered for each dyad were used to calculate the rate of feedback responses in relation to the total word count expressed as the number of occurrences per 1000 words. The proportion of each type of feedback in relation to the total number of feedback responses was then calculated for each dyad, expressed as a percentage figure. The statistical significance of differences between sets of dyad index scores representing each gender or ethnicity group was evaluated using Mann-Whitney *U* (for non-parametric, 2-sample score comparison).

The placement of minimal responses was also investigated. Minimal responses occurring at transition relevance points (i.e. potential or actual points of speaker change) were included in the count, along with the more frequent 'within-turn' or backchannel responses which are interpolated into the primary speaker's utterance. Instances of clustering of responses were noted, and in the case of 'within-turn' minimal responses, a count was done to determine the relative frequencies of responses occurring at the boundaries of syntactic units or tone groups versus those that were inserted at non-boundary points.

A macro-level analysis of the discourse structure of the eight extracts was then carried out, to check the possible influence of contextual factors such as text type and topic of conversation on the feedback patterns observed. The results of this analysis were subsequently cross-checked against the wider dataset of 22 interactions from which the sample was drawn to confirm the generalisability or otherwise of any patterns observed.

4.2. Quantitative patterns

4.2.1. Overall frequency of supportive verbal feedback responses

Table 2 shows the total rate of occurrence per 1000 words of all types of verbal feedback responses (calculated for both dyads in each gender x ethnicity category).

	Female		Male	
	Dyad	Rate	Dyad	Rate
Pakeha	PF1	60	PM1	55
	PF2	65	PM2	82
Subtotal		63		69
Māori	MF1	38	MM1	59
	MF2	34	MM2	42
Subtotal		36		51
TOTAL	Female dyads	50	Male dyads	60

Table 2. Frequency of feedback responses (all categories); tokens per 1000 running words.

In terms of gender, the overall averages for men and women were broadly comparable at 60 and 50 per 1000 words respectively overall, though the highest rate was produced by a Pakeha male dyad (PM2), with the Māori women producing by far the lowest rate of feedback.

The data also shows a clear grading of feedback rates in this sample between Māori and Pakeha, as shown in Figure 2.

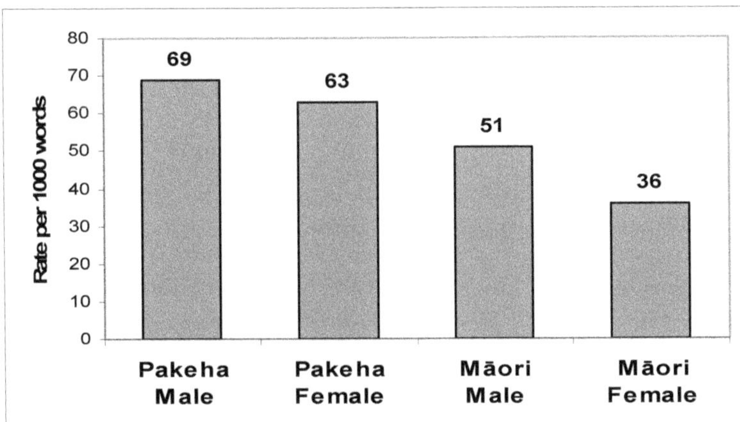

Figure 2. Verbal feedback rates by gender and ethnicity.

This pattern is consistent with previous research on cross-cultural differences, and is at least partly explained by the observation in previous research that Māori interactional norms include a lower baseline for the amount of verbal feedback considered appropriate or necessary, together with differences in the use and interpretation of pauses and silence and a greater use of indirect feedback strategies such as code switching (see Metge/Kinloch 1984; Britain 1992; Stubbe 1998a). This result nicely illustrates the pitfalls in assuming that gender or ethnicity somehow operate as unitary categories when we are analysing variation (see also Stubbe 1998a,b).

4.2.2. Distribution of different feedback types

(a) Minimal versus extended feedback (MR vs. CO)

The figures in Table 3 show that, as expected, minimal responses (NMRs and SMRs combined) accounted for the majority (74% to 88%)

of all feedback responses produced by each dyad, regardless of gender or ethnicity. However, the data also showed a small but consistent gender difference across the sample, with females tending to produce proportionately fewer minimal responses and more cooperative overlaps than males. The largest gap was between Māori women and men, but the proportions for Pakeha and Māori women were comparable and in both cases were higher than for both groups of men.

	Female		Male	
	% MR	% CO	% MR	% CO
Pakeha	74	26	80	20
Māori	77	23	88	12
Overall	75.5	24.5	84	16

Table 3. MRs and COs as a proportion of all feedback.

This pattern may well have affected the gender distribution for overall feedback rates reported above because of the way feedback responses were indexed here (namely in terms of occurrences per 1000 words). For the same reason, the figures shown in Table 3 for cooperative overlaps are probably understated by comparison with those for minimal responses, and the gender variation is therefore likely to be greater than is immediately apparent from these statistics.

(b) Neutral versus supportive minimal responses (NMR vs. SMR)

Figure 3 demonstrates that, in addition to a higher proportion of minimal responses overall, the male dyads in this sample consistently produced a higher proportion of *neutral* minimal responses (NMRs) than the female dyads, and a correspondingly lower proportion of explicitly *supportive* minimal responses (SMRs). The greatest proportion (65%) of female minimal responses comprised SMRs, whilst the reverse was true of males, for whom NMRs comprised 60% of total minimal responses.

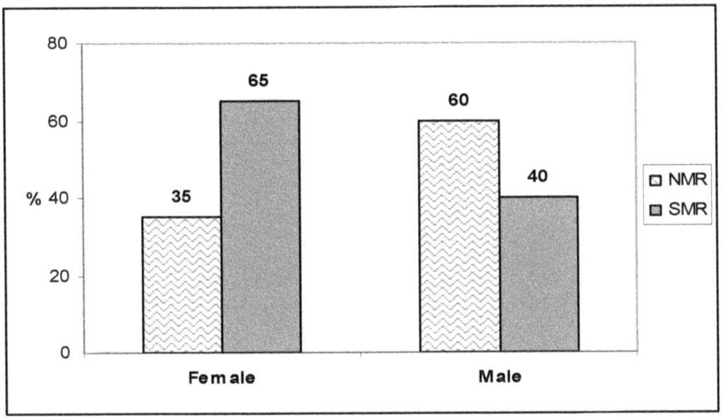

Figure 3. Proportion of minimal response types by gender.

This inverse pattern of gender variation held true across the sample, although, as shown in Table 4, the two Pakeha female dyads produced on average one third more SMRs than all other dyad pairs in numeric terms.

	Female		Male	
	Average rate per 1000 words	% total MRs	Average rate per 1000 words	% total MRs
Pakeha	30	64%	19	41%
Māori	19	68%	21	39%
Totals / Overall %	24.5	65%	20	40%

Table 4. Frequency of SMRs by gender and ethnicity.

Figure 4 plots the range of overall NMR rates for each dyad by gender and ethnicity. This clearly shows that *all* male dyads produced higher NMR rates than *all* female dyads in this sample, a result that was statistically significant ($U\,(4,4) = 0, p = 0.021$).

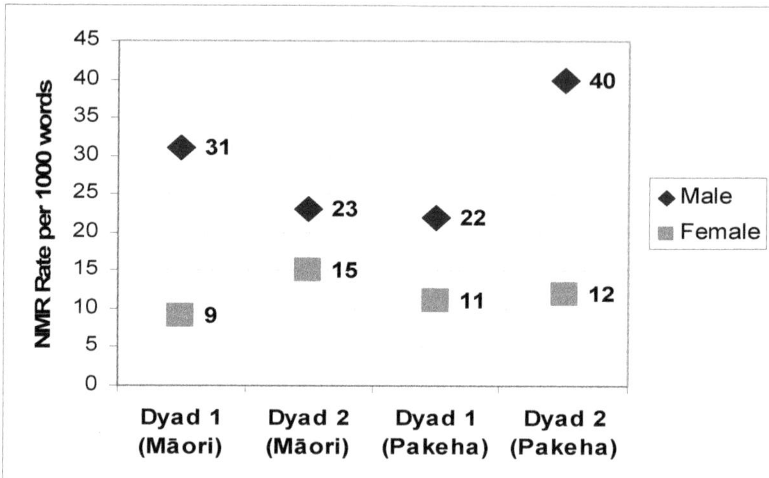

Figure 4. Range of NMR rates per dyad (by gender and ethnicity).

(c) Explicitly supportive feedback responses (SMRs vs. CO)

When SMRs and cooperative overlaps (COs) were combined into a single functional category, a much higher proportion of female feedback responses could be classified as explicitly supportive, 'high-involvement' feedback than was the case for the men. Figure 5 shows that, on average, almost three-quarters (73.5%) of the women's tokens of feedback were explicitly supportive, while just under half of the men's feedback came into this category. This result was statistically significant ($U(4,4) = 0$; $p = 0.021$).

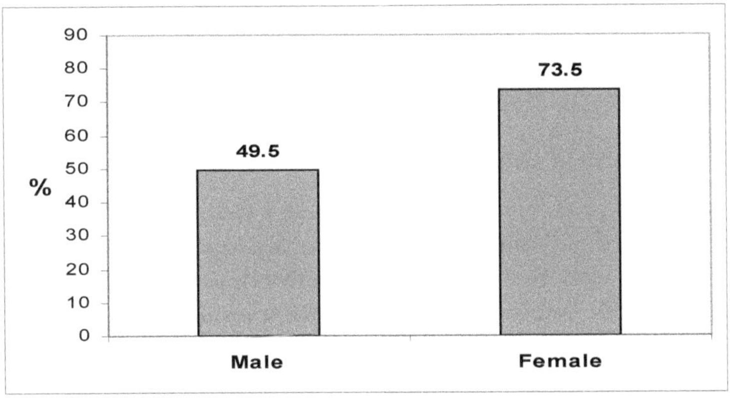

Figure 5. Proportion of explicitly supportive responses by gender.

Figure 6 clearly illustrates the interaction between gender and ethnicity in the use of explicitly supportive feedback. Overall, the tendency to use more of this type of feedback is particularly marked for the Pakeha women in the sample, as we also saw for the SMR rates shown in Table 4 above. However, because the proportions for the Māori listeners overall relative to Pakeha are slightly lower anyway, the male–female differential remains roughly equivalent for both ethnic groups.

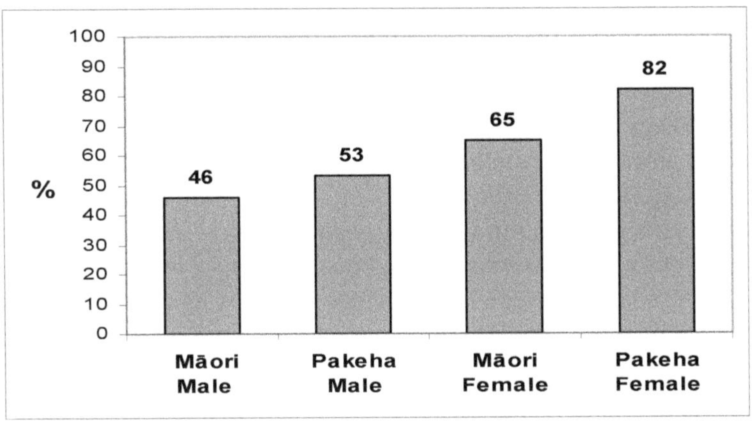

Figure 6. Proportion of explicitly supportive responses by gender and ethnicity.

To sum up, overall the women in this sample tended to use a higher proportion of both types of explicitly supportive verbal feedback. Interestingly, however, Māori and Pakeha women signalled this higher level of involvement in different ways, with the Pakeha women making proportionately greater use of SMRs, while the Māori women were more likely to use cooperative overlaps.

4.2.3. Placement of minimal responses within turns

The placement of minimal responses within a turn was the final variable to be quantified. All minimal responses which occurred within a speaker's turn were classified according to whether or not they occurred at the boundary of an information unit (a TRP/transition relevance point). Table 5 shows the proportions of within-turn minimal responses which occurred during a stream of talk, rather than at a unit boundary.

	Female	Male
Pakeha	48	24
Māori	20	25
Overall %	34	25

Table 5. Proportion of non-boundary minimal responses within utterances (% of total MR rate).

The Pakeha women placed minimal responses at non-boundary points almost half the time, and were also at least twice as likely to place minimal responses at non-boundary points compared with either the Pakeha men or the Māori listeners of either gender. At one level this result is consistent with the findings of previous research (e.g. Fishman 1983; Fellegy 1995; Coates 1991, 2004); namely, that women are more likely to place their responses throughout the stream of talk, while men are more likely to wait for the end of a syntactic unit. However, it also once more highlights the fact that gender patterns do not necessarily remain constant across other group boundaries such as ethnicity.

The analysis revealed a particularly interesting pattern in relation to the use of NMRs and SMRs in cases where a minimal response was placed throughout the stream of talk rather than at a boundary point). Figure 7 shows that regardless of gender or ethnicity, a significantly higher proportion of total MRs occurring in this environment are SMRs rather than NMRs.

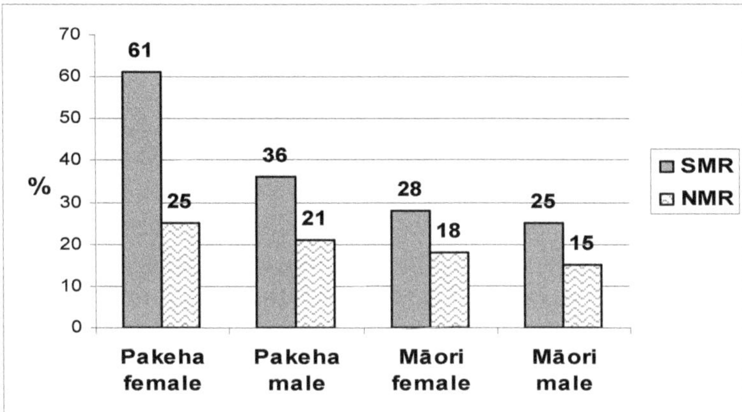

Figure 7. Proportions of NMRs and SMRs at non-boundary points.

Again, this tendency was particularly marked in the case of the Pakeha women: while just under half of their total minimal responses were placed at non-boundary points, over 60% of their SMRs occurred there. This result parallels the higher proportion of SMRs and COs used by the Pakeha women overall, and is consistent with an overall tendency for both Pakeha and Māori women to make greater use of contrapuntal responses as a feedback strategy.

4.2.4. Summary of quantitative results

The analysis revealed no significant correlation between gender and the overall frequency of supportive listener responses. However, when the results were broken down further according to the different feedback types and placement of responses within a turn, some interesting gender patterns did emerge.

First, the men produced a significantly higher rate of neutral minimal feedback than the women, and a higher proportion of their feedback overall was of the neutral and minimal response types. By contrast, a markedly higher proportion of the women's feedback responses were overtly supportive, with a correspondingly higher rate of cooperative overlaps; fewer were minimal responses, and of those, a greater proportion were supportive minimal responses in non-boundary positions. In short, the quantitative data showed a clear tendency for men to respond more neutrally and minimally, while the women's feedback included a greater proportion of responses which were both overtly supportive and more extended and contrapuntal in nature.

Second, there was a clear interaction in this data between gender and ethnicity: Māori and Pakeha interlocutors were not equally likely to use the same strategies or to produce similar rates of feedback. For example, although both Māori and Pakeha women used a greater *proportion* of overtly supportive feedback than men of either ethnicity, the Pakeha women produced such feedback at a significantly higher *rate* than the Māori women. On the other hand, the gender difference in the use of cooperative overlaps was more marked for the Māori listeners, while the Pakeha women in this sample were the most likely of all the informants to place within-turn minimal responses, particularly SMRs, at non-boundary points in an utterance.

4.3. Analysis of contextual variables

The degree of variation between dyads and *within* groups (men, women, Māori, Pakeha) in the data analysed for this study suggests that the macro-contextual factors such as text type, discourse structure (dialogic/monologic) and topic type, discussed earlier, may well have influenced the feedback patterns reported in the previous section. Accordingly, a qualitative analysis of the discourse structure of the eight extracts in the sub-sample was carried out to identify such influences. The following tendencies were evident (and were also checked against the 22-extract initial sample discussed in Section 3 above).

Firstly, in those interactions where both speakers were actively involved in topical development throughout all or most of the conversation, overall feedback rates tended to be higher relative to those for other members of the same gender or ethnic group. These interactions were also characterised by regular alternation of the role of 'topical speaker' with both speakers contributing topic content more or less equally, and by a higher proportion of opinion or problem-solving texts. Conversely, in more monologic interactions where one speaker dominated in the role of topical speaker for relatively long stretches of the discourse, and where the interaction comprised predominantly narrative and description text types, overall feedback rates for that dyad were generally lower.

Secondly, as in previous studies, the characteristics of the topic(s) being discussed also correlated with the degree and type of listener involvement. Regardless of gender, the highest rates of explicitly supportive types of feedback occurred in those conversations, or sections of conversations, where personal or sensitive topics were being discussed, especially where these involved a degree of self-disclosure or, as in gossip or opinion texts, the overt evaluation of the other person's behaviour or ideas.

These points will now be illustrated by close analysis of several extracts. This will serve at the same time to demonstrate how the analysis and interpretation of distributional patterns observed in corpus data can be enriched by taking contextual variables into account.

Example 5 is taken from an interaction between two Pakeha male speakers (Dyad PM2). This is a typical excerpt from the conversation, throughout which both speakers contributed roughly equal amounts and alternated in the role of topical speaker. The two men were colleagues in the music industry; they knew each other well and were engaged in relaxed chat about topics of mutual interest, and about which they shared a large amount of background knowledge. Their conversation included a number of work-related gossip sequences, as well as a more general sharing of 'news and views', and the excerpt illustrates how the two men both signalled their close involvement as listeners through the use of frequent precision-timed verbal feedback. (Verbal feedback responses are in bold).

(5) *Two Pakeha men discuss the staging of a modern opera.*

H: mm be interesting to see what [name of opera] is like
W: **exactly**
H: it's getting a huge amount of publicity i //suppose\ just by virtue of it=
W: /**mm**\\
H: =having been picked up by the festival
W: **yeah yeah**
H: but er but it's sort of i mean i can't help //[laughs]\ , noticing the comparison
W: /**[laughs]**\\
H: because i mean //it seems\ as if i mean it's on a similar scale and //and\=
W: /**mm**\\ /**mm**\\
H: =of course isn't it i mean //those things\
W: /**i don't know about**\\ length
it's probably quite a lot lon//ger (2) I suspect \
H: /**is it do you think mm + mm**\\

W: with chorus and
H: **yeah**
W: but i- i've never- i heard it in the last festival in that concert performance
did you
H: no i was away +//mm\
W: /**oh right**\\ and the vocal writing was um
i mean it just didn't sound as though he knew where to put in +
H: **yeah?**
W: a higher i mean a high soprano singing quite fast narrative
//about top g just absurd\
H: /**[laughs] yeah**\\

(DPC310: 0225-0320)

This dyad produced the highest overall rate of feedback of all the interactions in the sample, and the third highest rate of overtly supportive feedback. It is also the only male interaction in the sample where the topics discussed had any significant personal content, whereas three of the four female interactions did. As predicted by previous research, the dominant text types (gossip, discussion), discourse structure (dialogic) and topic types (personal, 'office politics') all correlate here with a high rate of verbal feedback, in particular explicitly supportive feedback. However, this predominantly takes the form of minimal feedback and laughter, not cooperative overlapping.

By comparison, the other Pakeha male interaction (Dyad PM1) produced a significantly lower rate of feedback and was also noticeably different in other ways. Although the speakers here also knew each other well, and the purpose of the talk too was primarily social, the nature of the topic appeared to produce a number of differences at the discourse level. Here, the participants were predominantly exchanging stories about their respective experiences with painting their houses, a far more neutral topic, which generated mainly narrative and description texts with one or other speaker holding the floor for extensive periods. In this case, the choice of topic with its associated text types and turn taking structure appears to have had a direct correlation with both the relatively low frequency of feedback, and the predominant use of neutral minimal feedback.

A contextual analysis of the two Māori female interactions (MF1 and MF2) may provide some explanation as to why these dyads produced the lowest rates of verbal feedback, both overall and relative to the other Māori interactions (see Table 2 above), while at the same time producing a higher proportion of SMRs and cooperative overlaps than any of the conversations involving either the Māori or Pakeha men. Both of these interactions involved a number of narrative sequences, and as we have seen, this text type tends to generate a lower relative rate of verbal feedback. There is also an ethnic dimension: the use of various indirect feedback devices was most marked in the interactions between the Māori women. These included supportive silences, code-switching into Māori, deferred feedback, and implicit contextualisation devices such as the "second story" phenomenon described by Sacks (Jefferson 1992) where a participant retells and or adds to an interlocutor's previous narrative (discussed in greater detail in Stubbe 1998a: 273-8). There were also, however, several extended sequences within these two interactions where the participants engaged in very active co-construction of the text, coinciding with a shift to a more emotive topic. The overall count, based on each identified instance of localised verbal feedback across the extracts as a whole, therefore downplays the actual amount of facilitative feedback going on in these two interactions; this is reflected instead in the high proportion of explicitly supportive and contrapuntal feedback in these interactions.

Finally, it is instructive to compare two interactions (MM1 and PF2) which are quite similar in terms of their overall discourse structure and with middling overall rates of feedback (59 and 65 per 1000 respectively). In both cases the participants were friends who were attempting to reach a consensus on a topic in which they had a strong interest, yet about which they had differing opinions. Both conversations took the form of animated discussions, essentially dialogic in structure, with each participant contributing very actively throughout the discussion. In both cases, neither speaker can be said to have had any special claim to expertise, except where they resorted to personal experiences to support a point. They could be observed to have strongly held opinions and supporting evidence they wished to contribute, while at the same time carefully managing the interaction to avoid making potential areas of disagreement overt. Based on previous research, in such a context we might expect a relatively high rate of verbal feedback overall, coupled with a greater incidence of explicitly supportive feedback, and indeed, both interactions provide evidence of a relatively high degree of active listener involvement. However, the way in which that involvement was enacted is quite different in each case.

In Example 6 (Dyad MM1), the two men are talking socially over morning tea at their workplace, discussing a controversial television programme about the place of homosexual men in traditional Māori society. One has seen the programme; the other has not, although he has previously talked about it at length with his wife. Throughout this interaction, one participant often took the role of primary speaker for relatively long periods, as in the example above, and although a relatively high proportion (33%) of within-turn minimal responses occurred at non-boundary points, virtually none of the feedback provided comes from the cooperative overlap category. The turn-taking organisation is thus very much of the 'one at a time' type. Secondly, less than half of the feedback in this interaction can be classified as being explicitly supportive in function. However, at a rate of 59 feedback responses per 1000 words, this interaction has a notably higher rate of verbal feedback than any of the other three Māori dyads. This interaction also does not exhibit the periodic monologues and long pauses with no feedback which seem to account most obviously for the lower feedback rates elsewhere in the Māori data (see Stubbe 1998a: 281). By comparison with more typical Māori listener behaviour, these characteristics indicate relatively active and overtly supportive listener involvement. It seems that explicit verbal feedback was a more important strategy here in achieving the required balancing act than it was in the other Māori interactions which consisted primarily of narrative and description text types, and probably functioned here largely as a negative politeness device.

(6) *Two Māori men discuss a controversial television programme.*

Tama: and they- they still need to- they- they had a right to be part of the hapu //the\ kinship //group\

Eru: /**yes**\\ /**yes**\\

Tama: um and you see the normality as i see it from where i come from in- in my community was 'cause you know we had people with that s- with those TRAITS +

Eru: **yes yes**

Tama: er they were not tre- if they were men

Eru: **mm**

Tama: they were given MEN'S work

Eru: **yes yes**

Tama: and you know [voc] and i know of a family that- that expected the- the- th- the person with those showing those tendencies to be he was made to plough
Eru: **mm**
Tama: like the other brothers
Eru: **yes**
Tama: and he was expected to milk the cows like the //other\ brothers //+ \
Eru: **/mm\\ /mm**
Tama: expected to go fencing like the others he was not given treatment other than what his gender //+\ required him to do
Eru: **/yes**
Eru: **yes yes**

(DPC317: 0325-0420)

Excerpt 7 (Dyad PF2) provides a contrasting example. This was a discussion between two women of a collection of site plans relating to a proposed joint land purchase, and provides a marked contrast in terms of feedback use. It also provides an excellent illustration of how participants can use both cooperative overlaps and non-boundary minimal responses to signal how closely they are following the other speaker's thought processes. The excerpt below is representative of the whole conversation, with the two women alternating in a series of short turns, which often overlapped.

(7) *Two Pakeha women discuss landscaping plans.*
A: and if you can make rooms vistas to the lake and all sorts of things i mean it could be just lovely couldn't it
B: or instead of having one big lake=
A: =**yes //i would have s- a chain of little ones**
B: **/you could have + a chain of** \\ ponds and a walk //among them or something like that like that a-\=
A: **/ mm yes up to about here up- up here **
B: =chain of ponds
A: **yep**
B: like that ++ with //largish trees on the-\ on the intersections of the //walks\
A: **/yes mm \\ /mm**

(DPC080: 0800-0865)

The construction of the discourse was collaborative to such an extent that it was often impossible to assign the role of topical or primary speaker to either participant, and almost 90% of the feedback provided by both participants consisted of SMRs or cooperative overlaps.

In these two cases, a relatively high rate of minimal responses signalled high involvement for the men (they were at the top of the range for the Māori participants), while the women used a different set of strategies to achieve the same interactional goal (which, as pointed out earlier, also pushed their overall frequency count down, because they used more extended and contrapuntal sequences to provide their feedback).

The contextual factors described above help to account for the within-group differences in overall rates of feedback reported above for individual dyads. It is also clear that although a high relative rate of verbal feedback is one indicator of conversational involvement and mutual interest, this cannot be measured in absolute terms. The appropriate amount, type and placement of feedback varies in a consistent fashion according to both the context, topic and structure of the interaction, as well as to the norms of the social group(s) to which the participants belong, and any patterns of gender difference must be interpreted against this complex backdrop.

5. Conclusions

5.1. Methodological issues

This chapter has highlighted several methodological issues which arise when we try to use naturalistic corpus data to analyse patterns of occurrence for a complex discourse phenomenon such as verbal feedback. These include the technical limitations and theoretical issues inherent in attempting to 'code and count' when dealing with open-ended classes of pragmatic devices, the problem of dealing in an analytically robust way with the absence of a one-to-one relationship between form and pragmatic function, and the difficulty of teasing out the complex interrelationships between the various factors that may correlate with or account for patterns of inter-group variation.

The technical issues arising from trying to apply corpus linguistic approaches to the study of discourse have been increasingly commented on by discourse and pragmatics researchers in recent years as technical progress has allowed linguistic corpora and the associated analytic tools to evolve into ever larger and more sophisticated forms. For example, Pichler argues (2010: 1) that "a uniform model of discourse variation" is needed which defines discourse variables more to more adequately take account of their flexibility and multifunctionality, and Wong/Peters are rightly critical of the way in which "borrowing of terminology and a reliance on axiomatic definition has resulted in a diverse nomenclature and an indeterminate inventory of forms" (2007: 1). These difficulties will only multiply further as corpus linguistics expands into the realm of multimodal analysis of discourse (Knight/Adolphs 2007).

In the study presented above some of these issues were addressed by looking specifically at how verbal feedback is used from a broad functional perspective, rather than by simply quantifying a limited range of forms and plotting their distribution according to a pre-determined variable such as sex of speaker, as has often been the case in the past. The approach taken here has highlighted the sheer complexity and range of the interactional resources available to listeners. As we have seen, verbal feedback devices are typically multi-functional and are characterised by a very fluid relationship between the form used and the function or action performed. Listeners can be observed to make sophisticated choices as to the type, placement and frequency of the responses they provide in a way that is tailored to the emerging discourse context. This allows them to take an active role in influencing the topical development and interactive structure of a conversation as well as to convey a wide range of social and affective meanings.

The same characteristics which make verbal feedback such a flexible resource for listeners in conversation also make the task of interpretation an extremely challenging one for the analyst. The use and interpretation of verbal feedback is heavily contingent on the local sequential environment, and what is 'appropriate' is thus constantly being (re)negotiated throughout a conversation. Moreover, various other situational and contextual factors such as topic and text type, the structure of the discourse and the relationship between the participants also correlate and interrelate in complex ways with overall rates of feedback and the particular strategies selected for use in any given interaction. Samples of corpus data cannot be expected to control for this type of variability, but such factors will nonetheless inevitably have influenced what might be expected from listeners at a given point in a conversation and therefore what they actually did and how it might be interpreted.

Close attention to the local context is the key to understanding what listeners do and why they might be doing it that way in a particular instance. Any apparent inter-group patterns of variation must therefore always be interpreted in the light of the shared contextual and interpretive frameworks demonstrably being oriented to by all participants in a conversation. In the case of the present study, both men and women were observed to use a similar set of interactive resources to indicate their degree of involvement in a conversation along a supportive feedback continuum, and they oriented to similar normative expectations in relation to other variables such as text type and topic. However, the ways in which they deployed these resources did appear to vary systematically according to both gender and ethnicity.

The somewhat different patterns for the Māori and Pakeha women and men in this study also underline the importance of not simply assuming that gender differences, or any other inter-group differences for that matter, will apply across the board: 'women' and 'men' are not homogeneous groups (cf. Coates 1989: 11) any more than people from a particular ethnic or social group. Moreover, other personal and intergroup identities are bound to interact with gender in complex ways, although it is interesting that, at least in the data analysed here, there were nevertheless certain gender patterns which seemed to cross inter-group boundaries.

The listener's interactive and relational involvement in a conversation is the concept which linked all these variables and underpinned the model of supportive verbal feedback used in the analysis of gender variation presented in this chapter. According to this model, the interactive functions of feedback can range from providing the minimum amount of interactive feedback compatible with sustaining the conversation, to significantly influencing topic and turn taking structures, right through to the joint construction of the discourse. At the propositional, relational or affective level, listener feedback may involve a quite neutral attention signal, or it may carry a greater or lesser degree of positive affective meaning, such as confirming or agreeing with another speaker's statement of fact or opinion or explicitly expressing empathy and interest in what is being said. Such strategies can function simultaneously to encourage and support contributions by other participants in an interaction, and to convey solidarity and shared understanding.

5.2. Feedback and gender

Despite the complexity of the data and the underlying pragmatics, this analysis nonetheless revealed some clear correlations between gender and patterns of feedback use. The key finding of the present study was that the males as a group provided proportionately more feedback which was both affectively neutral and minimal in form, while the females provided a significantly greater *proportion* of overtly supportive feedback, together with more extended and contrapuntal responses of various kinds. However, the actual *rates* and localised *distribution* and *placement* of feedback in this sample correlated more strongly with culturally relative norms and contextual factors such as text type and topic than with gender.

These findings are consistent with previous research which suggests that men and women (or different ethnic groups) (i) may use different strategies to achieve similar effects such as signalling greater or lesser involvement in a conversation, or conversely, may use certain ways of providing feedback to signal somewhat different meanings; and (ii) may have different baselines or starting points with respect to the amounts and types of verbal feedback which are considered appropriate in different contexts.

While at one level such observations are helpful in explaining the gender differences in listener behaviour reported here, they do not address the deeper question of why it is that women and men should have different response styles in the first place. Cameron (1995: 41) argues that differences in the ways women and men interact are socially produced, and have their roots in unequal gender relations. Thus, if women and men systematically use different discourse strategies, this is because they are engaged in fundamentally different tasks. She goes on to suggest that different verbal practices should be seen simply as one aspect of the process by which a particular community defines masculinity and femininity. Rather than seeing male and female styles as simple markers of gender identity, she concludes that "the styles themselves are produced as masculine and feminine, and that individuals make varying accommodations to those styles in the process of producing themselves as gendered subjects" (1995: 43).

Eckert/McConnell-Ginet take a similar approach in advocating that the study of language and gender should be grounded in "detailed examination of the social and linguistic activities of specific communities of practice" (1995: 469). Thus patterns of variation often emerge from the co-construction of gender and other variables such as class or ethnicity (1995: 501), and when speakers use a particular variant or speech style these do not simply reflect "a meaning already set and waiting to be recycled", but simultaneously produce a social meaning (1995: 503).

Such an approach provides a useful framework for understanding the sometimes elusive patterns of gender difference in a discourse feature as complex and variable as verbal feedback, one which typically defies attempts to find clear-cut bipolar oppositions once the data is analysed in context and in finer detail. Listeners can be observed to select from a wide range of feedback strategies in order to influence the topical development and interactive structure of a conversation, as well as to convey a range of social and affective meanings in a way that is appropriate to the local discourse context. Moreover, localised verbal feedback of the kind analysed here is only one aspect of the listener's repertoire: there are many other ways to signal conversational involvement as well. It is therefore unlikely that there is any kind of predetermined relationship between a social category such as sex/gender and patterns of feedback use. A more plausible interpretation of the gendered patterns reported in this study, therefore, is that verbal feedback functions as one of a number of interactive resources available for 'doing gender' as one aspect of identity work, in addition to its many other interactive and social meanings.

In conclusion, this study has highlighted some of the limitations inherent in using linguistic corpora to study gender variation in the use of a complex discourse feature such as supportive verbal feedback. As we have seen, the multi-functionality and highly contingent nature of listener responses makes the job of quantifying and interpreting these discourse variables in natural conversations an extremely challenging one. One way of dealing with this challenge is by combining quantitative and qualitative approaches to the data, and by taking due account of the relevant contextual variables and functional complexities in interpreting the results. In the study presented here, the verbal feedback continuum provided a unifying analytic framework to account for the complex and fluid interrelationships between the various forms and functions of supportive verbal feedback. Using a flexible analytic model such as this makes it possible to generate valuable insights into wider distributional patterns which complement more in-depth micro-analysis of smaller datasets. Notwithstanding the very real challenges, linguistic corpora therefore remain an important and useful resource for the study of interactive discourse variables.

Appendix: Transcription conventions

The conventions used in the examples in this paper are a simplified version of those developed for the Wellington Corpus of Spoken New Zealand English.

(hello)	Transcriber's best guess at an unclear utterance
?	Rising or question intonation
-	Incomplete or cut off utterance
YES	Capitals denote emphatic stress
[laughs] [softly]	Paralinguistic features or transcriber comment
+	Pause of up to one second
//... ...\	Simultaneous speech
/... ...\\	
...=	Current speaker's utterance continues onto another line
=...	
...=/	Latching (no discernible gap between utterances)
/=...	

References

Aries, Elizabeth J. 1976. Interaction patterns and themes of male, female and mixed groups. *Small Group Behaviour* 7/1, 7-18.

Aries, Elizabeth J. / Johnson, Fern L. 1983. Close friendship in adulthood: conversational content between same-sex friends. *Sex Roles* 9/12, 1183-1196.

Bergvall, Victoria L. 1999. Toward a comprehensive theory of language and gender. *Language in Society* 28, 2: 273-293.

Bing, Janet M. / Bergvall, Victoria L. 1996. The question of questions: beyond binary thinking. In Bergvall, V.L. / Bing, J.M. / Freed, A.F. (eds), *Rethinking Language and Gender Research: Theory and Practice*. New York: Longman, 1-30.

Britain, David 1992. Linguistic change in intonation: The use of high rising terminals in New Zealand English. *Language Variation and Change* 4, 77-104.

Bublitz, Wolfram 1988. *Supportive Fellow-Speakers and Co-operative Conversations: Discourse Topics and 'Recipient Action' in a Particular Type of Everyday Conversation.* Amsterdam: Benjamins.

Cameron, Deborah 1995. Rethinking language and gender studies: some issues for the 1990s. In Mills, S. (ed.) *Language and Gender: Interdisciplinary Perspectives*. London and New York: Longman, 31-44.

Cameron, Deborah 1997. Performing gender identity. In Johnson, S. / Meinhof, U.H. (eds), *Language and Masculinity.* Oxford: Blackwell, 47-64.

Cameron, Deborah 2003. Gender and language ideologies. In Holmes, Janet / Meyerhoff, Miriam (eds) *Handbook of Language and Gender*. Oxford: Blackwell, 447-467.

Carter, Ronald / Adolphs, Svenja 2008. Linking the verbal and visual: new directions for corpus linguistics. *Language and Computers* 64/1, 275-291.

Cheshire, Jenny 2002. Sex and gender in variationist research. In Chambers, J. K. / Trudgill, Peter / Schilling-Estes, Natalie (eds) *The Handbook of Language Variation and Change*. Oxford: Blackwell, 423-443.

Coates, Jennifer 1987. Epistemic modality and spoken discourse. *Transactions of the Philological Society* 1987: 110-131.

Coates, Jennifer 1989. Gossip revisited: language in all-female groups. In Coates, Jennifer / Cameron, Deborah (eds) *Women in their Speech Communities*. London: Longman, 94-122.

Coates, Jennifer 1991. Women's cooperative talk: a new kind of conversational duet? In Uhlig, C. / Zimmerman, R. (eds) *Proceedings of the Anglistentag 1990 Marburg*. Tubingen: Max Niermeyer Verlag.

Coates, Jennifer 1996. *Women Talk*. Oxford: Blackwell.

Coates, Jennifer (ed.) 1998. *Language and Gender. A Reader*. Oxford: Blackwell.

Coates, Jennifer 2003. *Men Talk*. Oxford: Blackwell.

Coates, Jennifer 2004. *Women, Men and Language. A Sociolinguistic Account of Gender Differences in Language*. 3rd edition. UK: Pearson Education.

Crawford, Mary E. 1995. *Talking Difference: On Gender and Language*. London and Thousand Oaks: Sage.

Dittmann, Allen T. 1972. Developmental factors in conversational behaviour. *Journal of Communication* 22, 404-423.

Dunne, Michael / Ng, Sik Hung 1994. Simultaneous speech in small-group conversation: all-together-now and one-at-a-time? *Journal of Language and Social Psychology* 13/1, 45-71.

Eckert, Penelope / McConnell-Ginet, Sally 1995. Constructing meaning, constructing selves. Snapshots of language, gender and class from Belten High. In Hall, Kira / Bucholtz, Mary (eds) *Gender Articulated. Language and the Socially Constructed Self*. New York and London: Routledge, 469-507.

Eckert, Penelope / McConnell-Ginet, Sally 1999. New generalizations and explanations in language and gender research. *Language in Society* 28/2, 185-201.

Eckert, Penelope / McConnell-Ginet, Sally 2003. *Language and Gender*. Cambridge: Cambridge University Press.

Eckert, Penelope / McConnell-Ginet, Sally 2007. Putting communities of practice in their place. *Gender and Language* 1/1, 27-37.

Edelsky, Carole 1981. Who's got the floor? *Language in Society* 10, 383-421. Reprinted in Tannen, Deborah (ed.) 1993. *Gender and Conversational Interaction*. Oxford: Oxford University Press.

Falk, Jane 1980. The conversational duet. *Proceedings of the 6th Annual Meeting of the Berkeley Linguistics Society* 6, 507-514.

Farr, Fiona 2003. Engaged listenership in spoken academic discourse: the case of student–tutor meetings. *Journal of English for Academic Purposes* 2/1, 67-85.

Fellegy, Anna M. 1995. Patterns and functions of minimal response. *American Speech* 70/2, 186-199.

Filipi, Anna / Wales, Roger 2003. Differential uses of *okay*, *right*, and *alright*, and their function in signaling perspective shift or maintenance in a map task. *Semiotica* 147 (Nov 2003), 429-455.

Fishman, Pamela M. 1983. Interaction: the work women do. In Thorne, Barrie / Kramarae, Cheris / Henley, Nancy (eds) *Language, Gender and Society*. Rowley, Massachussets: Newbury, 89-102.

Freed, Alice 2003. Epilogue: Reflections on language and gender research In Holmes, Janet / Meyerhoff, Miriam (eds) *Handbook of Language and Gender*. Oxford: Blackwell, 699-721.

Freed, Alice F. / Greenwood, Alice 1996. Women, men and type of talk: What makes the difference?' *Language in Society* 25, 1-26.

French, Peter / Local, John 1983. Turn-competitive incomings. *Journal of Pragmatics* 7/1, 17-38.

Gardner, Rod 1997. The listener and minimal responses in conversational interaction. *Prospect* 12, 12-32.

Gardner, Rod 1998. Between speaking and listening: The vocalisation of understandings. *Applied Linguistics* 19, 204-224.

Gardner, Rod 2001. *When Listeners Talk: Response Tokens and Listener Stance.* Amsterdam: John Benjamins Publishing Company.

Gardner, Rod 2007. The *Right* connections: Acknowledging epistemic progression in talk. *Language in Society* 36, 319-341.

Gilbert, Jane 1990. *Secondary school students talking about science: language functions, gender and interaction in small group discussions.* Unpublished MA thesis, Victoria University of Wellington.

Haas, Adelaide / Sherman, Mark A. 1982. Reported topics of conversation among same-sex adults. *Communication Quarterly* 30/4, 332-342.

Hayashi, Reiko 1988. Simultaneous talk – from the perspective of floor management of English and Japanese speakers. *World Englishes* 7, 269-288.

Hirschman, L. 1974. Analysis of assertive and supportive behaviour in conversations. Paper presented at *Linguistic Society of America* meeting, July 1974.

Holmes, Janet 1995. *Women, Men and Politeness*. London and New York: Longman.

Holmes, Janet 2006. *Gendered Talk at Work: Constructing Gender Identity Through Workplace Discourse*. New York and Oxford: Blackwell.

Holmes, Janet / Meyerhoff, Miriam 2003. Different voices, different views: an introduction to current research in language and gender. In Holmes, Janet / Meyerhoff, Miriam (eds) *The Handbook of Language and Gender*. Oxford: Blackwell, 1-17.

Holmes Janet / Meyerhoff, Miriam (eds) 2003. *The Handbook of Language and Gender*. Oxford: Blackwell.

Holmes, Janet / Stubbe, Maria 1992. Women and Men Talking: Gender-based Patterns of Interaction. In Olsson, Suzann (ed.) *The Gender Factor: Women in New Zealand organisations*. Palmerston North: Dunmore Press, 149-163.

Holmes, Janet / Stubbe, Maria 1997. Good listeners: gender differences in NZ conversation. *Women and Language* 20/2, 7-14.

Holmes, Janet / Stubbe, Maria 2003. Discourse in gendered workplaces: how do women manage it? In Holmes, Janet / Meyerhoff, Miriam (eds) *The Handbook of Language and Gender*. Oxford: Blackwell, 573-600.

Holmes, Janet / Vine, Bernadette / Johnson, Gary 1998. *The Wellington Corpus of Spoken New Zealand English: a Users' Guide*. Wellington: School of Linguistics and Applied Language Studies, Victoria University of Wellington.

Holmes, Janet / Burns, Louise / Marra, Meredith / Stubbe, Maria / Vine, Bernadette 2003. Women managing discourse in the workplace. *Women in Management Review* 18/8 (2003), 414-424.

Holmes, Janet / Stubbe, Maria / Marra, Meredith 2003. Language, humour and ethnic identity marking in New Zealand English. In Mair, C. (ed.) *The Politics of English as a World Language. New Horizons in Postcolonial Cultural Studies. ASNEL Papers 7*. Amsterdam / New York: Rodopi, 431-456.

Hyndman, C. 1985. Gender and language differences: a small study. Unpublished terms paper. Wellington: Victoria University.

James, Deborah / Drakich, Janice 1993. Understanding gender differences in amount of talk: a critical review of research. In Tannen, Deborah (ed.) *Gender and Conversational Interaction.* New York, Oxford: Oxford University Press, 281-312.

Jefferson, Gail 1984. Notes on a systematic deployment of the acknowledgment tokens 'yeah' and 'mmhm'. *Papers in Linguistics* 17/2, 197-216.

Jefferson, Gail 1993. Caveat speaker: Preliminary notes on recipient topic-shift implicature. *Research on Language and Social Interaction* 26, 1-30.

Jefferson, Gail 2002. Is 'no' an acknowledgment token? Comparing American and British uses of (+)/(–) tokens. *Journal of Pragmatics* 34, 1345-1383.

Johnson, Sally / Meinhof, Ulrike H. (eds) 1997. *Language and Masculinity.* Oxford: Blackwell.

Kalcik, Susan 1975. 'Like Ann's gynecologist or the time I was almost raped.' Personal narratives in women's rap groups. *Journal of American Folklore* 88, 3-11.

Knight, Dawn / Adolphs, Svenja 2008. Multi-modal corpus pragmatics: The case of active listenership. In Romero-Trillo, J. (ed.) *Pragmatics and Corpus Linguistics. A Mutualistic Entente.* Berlin and New York: Mouton de Gruyter, 175-190.

Leet-Pellegrini, H. M. 1980. Conversational dominance as a function of gender and expertise. In Giles, Howard / Robinson, W. Peter / Smith, P. M. (eds) *Language: Social Psychological Perspectives.* Oxford: Pergamon Press, 97-104.

Lehtonen, Jaakko / Sajavaara, Kari 1985. The silent Finn. In: Tannen, Deborah / Saville-Troike, Muriel (eds) *Perspectives on silence.* Norwood, N J: Ablex, 193-201.

Maltz, Daniel N. / Borker, Ruth A. 1982. A cultural approach to male–female miscommunication. In Gumperz, John J. (ed.) *Language and Social Identity.* Cambridge: Cambridge University Press, 196-216.

Maynard, Douglas W. / Frankel, Richard M. 2006. On diagnostic rationality: bad news, good news, and the symptom residue. In Heritage, John / Maynard, Douglas W. (eds) *Communication in Medical Care. Interaction between Primary Care Physicians and Patients*. Studies in Interactional Sociolinguistics 20. Cambridge: Cambridge University Press, 248-278.

McCarthy, Michael 2003. Talking back: 'small' interactional response tokens in everyday conversation. *Research on Language and Social Interaction,* 36/1, 33-63.

McElhinny, Bonnie / Mills, Sara 2007. Editorial: Launching studies of gender and language in the early 21st century. *Gender and Language* 1/1, 1-13.

Metge, Joan / Kinloch, Patricia 1984. *Talking past each other: Problems of cross-cultural communication.* Wellington: Victoria University Press/Price Milburn.

Munro, F. 1987. Female and male participation in small-group interaction in the E.S.O.L. classroom. Unpublished terms project. Graduate Diploma in TESOL. Sydney: Sydney College of Advanced Education.

Nordenstam, Kerstin 1992. Tag questions and gender in Swedish conversations. *Working Papers on Language Gender and Sexism*. 4/1, 69-77.

Norrick, Neal R. 2012. Listening practices in English conversation: The responses responses elicit. *Journal of Pragmatics* 44/ 5 (April 2012), 566-576.

Orestrom, Bengt 1983. *Turn-taking in English Conversations.* Lund: Liber.

Pichler, Heike 2010. Methods in discourse variation analysis: Reflections on the way forward. *Journal of Sociolinguistics* 14, 581-608.

Pilkington, Jane 1994. *Women, Men and Gossip: What's the Story?* Unpublished MA thesis, Victoria University of Wellington.

Pilkington, Jane 1998. 'Don't try and make out that I'm nice!' The different strategies women and men use when gossiping. In Coates, Jennifer (ed.) *Language and Gender: A Reader*. Oxford: Blackwell, 254-269.

Reid Thomas, Helen 1995. The use and interpretation by men and women of minimal responses in informal conversation. *Working Papers on Language Gender and Sexism* 5/1, 65-89.

Reid, Julie 1995. A study of gender differences in minimal responses. *Journal of Pragmatics* 24, 489-512.

Roger, Derek 1989. Experimental studies of dyadic turn-taking behaviour. In Roger, Derek / Bull, Peter (eds) *Conversation: an Interdisciplinary Perspective*. Clevedon, U.K.: Multilingual Matters Ltd.

Romaine, Suzanne 1999. *Communicating Gender*. Mahwah, N.J.: Lawrence Erlbaum.

Sacks, Harvey / Schegloff, Emanuel A. / Jefferson, Gail 1974. A simplest systematics for the organization of turn-taking for conversation. *Language* 50, 696-735.

Schegloff, Emanuel A. 1982. Discourse as interactional achievement: Some uses of 'uh huh' and other things that come between sentences. In Tannen, Deborah (ed.), *Analyzing discourse, text, and talk*. Washington, DC: Georgetown University Press, 71-93.

Schegloff, Emanuel A. 1993. Reflections on quantification in the study of conversation. *Research on Language and Social Interaction* 26/1, 99-128.

Schiffrin, Deborah 1987. *Discourse Markers*. Cambridge: Cambridge University Press.

Stenström, Anna-Brita 1987. Carry-on signals in English conversation. *Costerus* 59: 87-119.

Stenström, Anna-Brita 1994. *An Introduction to Spoken Interaction*. London: Longman.

Stivers, Tanya 2004. 'No no no' and Other Types of Multiple Sayings in Social Interaction. *Human Communication Research* 30/2, 260-293.

Stivers, Tanya 2008. Stance, alignment, and affiliation during storytelling: When nodding is a token of affiliation. *Research on Language and Social Interaction* 41/1, 31-57.

Strodtbeck, Fred L. / Mann, Richard D. 1956. Sex role differentiation in jury deliberations. *Sociometry* 19, 3-11.

Stubbe, Maria 1978. *Sex roles in conversation: a study of small group interaction*. Unpublished terms paper. Wellington: Victoria University.

Stubbe, Maria 1991. *Talking at cross-purposes? The effect of gender on New Zealand schoolchildren's interaction strategies in pair discussion*. Unpublished MA thesis, Victoria University of Wellington.

Stubbe, Maria 1994. What's the score? Qualitative analysis in gender research. *International Journal of Applied Linguistics* 4/1, 3-18.

Stubbe, Maria 1996. Active listening in conversation: gender and the use of verbal feedback. *Australian Linguistics Society Conference*, Canberra (July 1996).

Stubbe, Maria 1998a. 'Are you listening?' Cultural influences on the use of supportive verbal feedback in conversation. *Journal of Pragmatics* 29, 257-289.

Stubbe, Maria 1998b. Striking a balance: language, gender and professional identity. *Engendering Communication. Proceedings of the Fifth Berkeley Women and Language Conference 1998.* Berkeley: University of California Berkeley Women and Language Group (1998), 545-556.

Stubbe, Maria 1999. Research report: Māori and Pakeha use of selected pragmatic devices in a sample of New Zealand English. *Te Reo, Journal of the Linguistic Society of New Zealand* 42, 39-53.

Stubbe, Maria 2003. Taking language and gender research beyond the academy. Workshop, *Perception and Realization in Language and Gender Research: An International Conference.* COSWL/ IGALA, Michigan State University, East Lansing, Michigan, July 18-20, 2003. Available from URL <http://www.linguistics.ucsb.edu/faculty/bucholtz/conference/stubbe.html>.

Stubbe, Maria / Holmes, Janet 1995. 'You know', 'eh' and other 'exasperating expressions': an analysis of social and stylistic variation in the use of pragmatic devices in a sample of New Zealand English. *Language and Communication* 15/1, 63-88.

Stubbe, Maria / Holmes, Janet 2000. Talking Māori or Pakeha: signalling identity in discourse. In Bell, Allan / Kuiper, Koenraad (eds) *New Zealand English.* Wellington: Victoria University Press / Benjamins, 249-278.

Stubbe, Maria / Holmes, Janet / Vine, Bernadette / Marra, Meredith 2001. Forget Mars and Venus, let's get back to earth: Challenging gender stereotypes in the workplace. In Holmes, Janet (ed.) *Gendered Speech in Social Context: Perspectives from Gown & Town.* Wellington: Victoria University Press.

Stubbe, Maria / Lane, Chris / Hilder, Jo / Vine, Elaine / Vine, Bernadette / Holmes Janet / Marra, Meredith / Weatherall, Ann 2003. Multiple Discourse Analyses of a Workplace Interaction. *Discourse Studies* 5/3, 351-388.

Talbot, Mary 1998. *Language and Gender: an Introduction.* Oxford: Polity Press.

Talbot, Mary 2003. Gender stereotypes: reproduction and challenge. In Holmes, Janet / Meyerhoff, Miriam (eds) *Handbook of Language and Gender.* Oxford: Blackwell, 447-467.

Tannen, Deborah 1984. *Conversational style – analysing talk among friends.* Norwood, New Jersey: Ablex.

Tannen, Deborah 1990. *You Just Don't Understand. Women and Men in Conversation.* Australia: Random House.

Tannen, Deborah 1993. *Gender and Conversational Interaction.* Oxford: Oxford University Press.

Ward, Nigel / Tsukahara, Wataru 2000. Prosodic features which cue back-channel responses in English and Japanese. *Journal of Pragmatics* 32, 1177-1207.

Ward, Nigel / Tsukahara, Wataru 2003. A study of responsiveness in spoken dialog. *International Journal of Human–Computer Studies* 59/5, 603-630.

Weatherall, Ann 2002. *Gender, Language and Discourse*. Women and Psychology Series. East Sussex and New York: Routledge.

Wertheim, Suzanne / Bailey, Ashlee C. / Corston-Oliver, Monica (eds) 1998. *Engendering Communication. Proceedings of the Fifth Berkeley Women and Language Conference.* April 24-26, 1998. Berkeley: Berkeley Women and Language Group.

West, Candace 2006. Coordinating closings in primary care visits: producing continuity of care. In Heritage, John / Maynard, Douglas W. (eds) *Communication in Medical Care. Interaction between Primary Care Physicians and Patients.* Studies in Interactional Sociolinguistics 20. Cambridge: Cambridge University Press, 379-415.

West, Candace / Garcia, Angela 1988. Conversational Shift Work: A Study of Topical Transitions between Women and Men. *Social Problems* 35/5, 551-575.

West, Candace / Zimmerman, Don 1983. Small insults: a study of interruptions in cross-sex conversations between unacquainted persons. In Thorne, Barrie / Kramarae, Cheris / Henley, Nancy (eds) *Language, Gender and Society*. Rowley, Massachussets: Newbury, 103-118.

White, Geoffrey M. / Watson-Gegeo, Karen A. 1990. Disentangling discourse. In Watson-Gegeo, Karen A. / White, Geoffrey M. (eds) *Disentangling: Conflict Discourse in Pacific Societies.* Stanford, CA: Stanford University Press, 3-52.

White, Sheida 1989. 'Backchannels across cultures: A study of Americans and Japanese.' *Language in Society* 18/1, 59-76.

Wodak, Ruth (ed.) 1997. *Gender and Discourse*. London: Sage.

Xudong, Deng 2008. The use of listener responses in Mandarin Chinese and Australian English conversations. *Pragmatics* 18/2, 303-328.

Zimmerman, Don H. / West, Candace 1975. Sex roles, interruptions and silences in conversation. In Thorne, B. / Henley, N. (eds) *Language and Sex: Difference and Dominance.* Rowley, Massachussets: Newbury House, 105-129.

Notes on Contributors

TERUHIKO FUKAYA is a Professor of English Linguistics in the Department of Foreign Studies at Sugiyama Jogakuen University, Nagoya, Japan, where he is also Dean of the School of Cross-Cultural Studies. His current main research interests are in corpus linguistics, discourse analysis and systemic functional grammar, in particular the grammar of evaluation in English and Japanese. He has also published and presented widely on corpus-based descriptive grammar, collocation and phraseology of English, and has been a member of the JAECS steering committee for the past ten years. He is currently involved in a research project on large corpus-based studies of English constructions and their methodological accountability.

SEBASTIAN HOFFMANN is Professor of English Linguistics at Trier University. He received his doctoral degree from the University of Zurich, where he also worked for several years. Before moving to Trier, he spent three years at Lancaster University (UK) as Lecturer in English Linguistics (2006-2009). His research predominantly focuses on the application of usage-based approaches to the study of language. Recent research topics include: syntactic change, as in *Grammaticalization and English Complex Prepositions: A Corpus-based Study* (2005); tag questions; the lexico-grammar of New Englishes; and corpus linguistic methodology involving Internet-derived data. He is a co-author of BNCweb, a user-friendly web-interface to the British National Corpus, which also forms the basis for his textbook (with Stefan Evert, Nicholas Smith, David Lee and Ylva Berglund-Prytz) *Corpus Linguistics with BNCweb – A Practical Guide* (2008).

MASAHIRO HORI, Ph.D., is a Professor of English Linguistics and Stylistics at Kumamoto Gakuen University, Japan and President of Japan Association for English Corpus Studies. His research interests are in corpus-stylistic investigation of fiction in English and his ongoing collaborative research project is the production of a Digital Dickens Lexicon. His *Investigating Dickens' Style: A Collocational Analysis* (2004) was awarded Japan's Corpus Studies Association Prize for 2005. His recent books include: *English Collocations Learned through Exercises* (2011) [in Japanese]; *Introduction to Collocation Studies in English* (2009) [in Japanese]; and *Stylistic Studies of Literature: In Honour of Professor Hiroyuki Ito* (co-editor, 2009).

YOKO IYEIRI is an Associate Professor at Kyoto University. Her interests include historical linguistics, sociolinguistics and corpus linguistics. She is the author of *Verbs of Implicit Negation and their Complements in the History of English* (2010) and *Negative Constructions in Middle English* (2001). She has also edited *Aspects of English Negation* (2005), and *Middle and Modern English Corpus Linguistics: A Multi-dimensional Approach* (with Manfred Markus, Reinhard Heuberger and Emil Chamson, 2012). Her current research centres on the historical development of negation and patterns of complementation in the English language.

The late STIG JOHANSSON (1939–2010) was Professor Emeritus at University of Oslo. A pioneer in the field of English corpus linguistics, he was a founder of the International Computer Archive of Modern [and Medieval] English (ICAME), serving as coordinating secretary and *ICAME Journal* editor for 20 years. His research ranged over early comparative vocabulary studies of regional and register-based varieties (e.g. of British vs. American English, and of academic writing), through grammatical description (such as his contribution to the *Longman Grammar of Spoken and Written English*), to use of parallel corpora for translation studies. He had key roles in the development of corpora including the Lancaster-Oslo/Bergen corpus of edited written British English (LOB), the English-Norwegian Parallel Corpus (ENPC), the Oslo Multilingual Corpus, and the Norwegian component of the International Corpus of Learner English (NICLE).

GRAEME KENNEDY is Emeritus Professor of Applied Linguistics at Victoria University of Wellington. He previously held the Chair of Applied Linguistics at Victoria from 1982-2004. He graduated from Victoria with an MA (Hons) in English, and then completed a PhD at the University of California, Los Angeles in 1970. His major teaching and research interests have been in second language acquisition theory, corpus-based linguistic analysis, the grammar of English, Deaf Studies (including New Zealand Sign Language lexicography), and New Zealand English. He has served at Victoria as Director of the English Language Institute (1982-93), Director of the Deaf Studies Research Unit (1990-1998) and Director of the New Zealand Dictionary Centre (1997-2004), a joint venture between Victoria University of Wellington and Oxford University Press. He is a former Dean of Languages and Literature, and has served as Acting Dean and Pro Vice-Chancellor of the Faculty of Humanities and Social Sciences in 2003-2004. He is General Editor of *A Dictionary of New Zealand Sign Language* (1997), and *A Concise Dictionary of New Zealand Sign Language* (2002). He is co-editor (with Tony Deverson) of *The New Zealand Oxford Dictionary* (2004), and author of *An Introduction to Corpus Linguistics* (1998) and *Structure and Meaning in English* (2003).

PAM PETERS is an Emeritus Professor of Linguistics at Macquarie University (NSW, Australia), where she was for many years the director of the Dictionary Research Centre. She has a long-standing research interest in variation in English usage, and has produced a number of corpus-based reference books on variation in standard written English, including the *Cambridge Australian English Style Guide* (1995), the *Cambridge Guide to English Usage* (2004) and the *Cambridge Guide to Australian English Usage* (2007). She is a frequent participant and former board member of ICAME, and led the compilation of two computer corpora of Australian English: the Australian Corpus of English (ACE), and the Australian component of the International Corpus of English (ICE-AUS).

MATTI RISSANEN is Professor Emeritus of English Philology at the University of Helsinki. His main field of interest is corpus-based analysis of the history of English syntax and lexis, from Old English to Late Modern English. He was the leader of the project compiling *The Helsinki Corpus of English Texts* and he wrote the chapter on syntax in Volume 3 of *The Cambridge History of the English Language.* In recent years his research has been focused on the development of adverbial links and he has published a number of articles on this topic, paying particular attention to grammaticalisation and language contact.

TOSHIO SAITO (born 1933) is Professor Emeritus at Osaka University, where he took his BA, MA, and PhD, and taught English from 1971 to 1996. He was a visiting postgraduate student under Randolph Quirk at University College London in 1967-1968, and he was a visiting associate professor of English at the University of New Hampshire in 1978-1979. In 1993 Toshio Saito took the leading role in founding the Japan Association for English Corpus Studies (JAECS) with the aim of catching up to the 'explosive' development of corpus linguistics, and he served as its president for the next eight years. His research interest from the start has been in syntactic developments in transitional periods, such as from Late OE to Early ME, or from Late ME to Early ModE. On his contribution to corpus linguistics, and major works, see Geoffrey Leech's Foreword and the editors' Preface.

ROBERT SIGLEY is an Associate Professor in the Faculty of Foreign Languages at Daito Bunka University. He was a member of the team compiling the Wellington Corpus of Written New Zealand English (which formed the database for his Ph.D. from Victoria University of Wellington), and has been a participant at both ICAME and JAECS. His corpus-based research interests range over linguistically, regionally, stylistically and socially conditioned variation and change in modern English. Specific topics addressed in his previous work include variation in modern English spelling; relative pronoun choice in New Zealand English; the statistical modelling of linguistically-conditioned variation; the definition and use of stylistic continua to characterise corpus texts and help explain the distribution of specific linguistic variants; and (with Janet Holmes) the use of gender-marking terms in occupational contexts.

MARIA STUBBE is a Senior Research Fellow at the Department of Primary Health Care and General Practice, Wellington School of Medicine and Health Sciences, and a Research Associate in the Language in the Workplace Project, Victoria University of Wellington. Her research interests include studies of the different ways English is used in interpersonal communication to signal identity and maintain relationships in contexts such as the workplace. Topics covered in her research to date include variation by ethnicity and gender in the use of pragmatic devices; the use of humour as an ethnic identity marker;

gender roles in the workplace; gendered styles of management; and the construction of professional identity.

SATORU TSUKAMOTO is Professor at Nihon University (Japan). His research focuses on the history of the English language and its theoretical framework. In particular, his special interest lies in quantifying linguistic changes over time in English by using statistical methods. In "Syntactic Chronology: Dating Text in the History of English" (2004), he attempted to capture chronological linguistic trends in English in terms of the regression model. He has also developed corpus retrieval software: KWIC Concordance for Windows and Treebank Search. The former software is available for general use in corpus studies and the latter is tailored to searches in the Penn Parsed Corpora of Historical English.

SHUNJI YAMAZAKI is a Professor, and currently Vice-President, at Daito Bunka University. He received his Ph.D. from Victoria University of Wellington, New Zealand. As Vice-President of JAECS he oversaw the invitation of eminent international corpus linguists as guest speakers; he has also been a regular participant at ICAME. Specific topics addressed in his previous corpus-based research include the importance of collocations as a source of variation; the influence of the indigenous language of Maori to New Zealand English (with Graeme Kennedy); and adjective use in New Zealand English. Together with Toshio Saito and Junsaku Nakamura, he edited *English Corpus Linguistics in Japan* (2002).

Linguistic Insights

Studies in Language and Communication

This series aims to promote specialist language studies in the fields of linguistic theory and applied linguistics, by publishing volumes that focus on specific aspects of language use in one or several languages and provide valuable insights into language and communication research. A cross-disciplinary approach is favoured and most European languages are accepted.

The series includes two types of books:

- **Monographs** – featuring in-depth studies on special aspects of language theory, language analysis or language teaching.
- **Collected papers** – assembling papers from workshops, conferences or symposia.

Each volume of the series is subjected to a double peer-reviewing process.

Vol. 1 Maurizio Gotti & Marina Dossena (eds)
Modality in Specialized Texts. Selected Papers of the 1st CERLIS Conference.
421 pages. 2001. ISBN 3-906767-10-8 · US-ISBN 0-8204-5340-4

Vol. 2 Giuseppina Cortese & Philip Riley (eds)
Domain-specific English. Textual Practices across Communities and Classrooms.
420 pages. 2002. ISBN 3-906768-98-8 · US-ISBN 0-8204-5884-8

Vol. 3 Maurizio Gotti, Dorothee Heller & Marina Dossena (eds)
Conflict and Negotiation in Specialized Texts. Selected Papers of the 2nd CERLIS Conference.
470 pages. 2002. ISBN 3-906769-12-7 · US-ISBN 0-8204-5887-2

Vol. 4 Maurizio Gotti, Marina Dossena, Richard Dury, Roberta Facchinetti & Maria Lima
Variation in Central Modals. A Repertoire of Forms and Types of Usage in Middle English and Early Modern English.
364 pages. 2002. ISBN 3-906769-84-4 · US-ISBN 0-8204-5898-8

Editorial address:

Prof. Maurizio Gotti Università di Bergamo, Facoltà di Lingue e Letterature Straniere,
Via Salvecchio 19, 24129 Bergamo, Italy
Fax: 0039 035 2052789, E-Mail: m.gotti@unibg.it

Vol. 5 Stefania Nuccorini (ed.)
Phrases and Phraseology. Data and Descriptions.
187 pages. 2002. ISBN 3-906770-08-7 · US-ISBN 0-8204-5933-X

Vol. 6 Vijay Bhatia, Christopher N. Candlin & Maurizio Gotti (eds)
Legal Discourse in Multilingual and Multicultural Contexts.
Arbitration Texts in Europe.
385 pages. 2003. ISBN 3-906770-85-0 · US-ISBN 0-8204-6254-3

Vol. 7 Marina Dossena & Charles Jones (eds)
Insights into Late Modern English. 2nd edition.
378 pages. 2003, 2007.
ISBN 978-3-03911-257-9 · US-ISBN 978-0-8204-8927-8

Vol. 8 Maurizio Gotti
Specialized Discourse. Linguistic Features and Changing Conventions.
351 pages. 2003, 2005.
ISBN 3-03910-606-6 · US-ISBN 0-8204-7000-7

Vol. 9 Alan Partington, John Morley & Louann Haarman (eds)
Corpora and Discourse.
420 pages. 2004. ISBN 3-03910-026-2 · US-ISBN 0-8204-6262-4

Vol. 10 Martina Möllering
The Acquisition of German Modal Particles. A Corpus-Based Approach.
290 pages. 2004. ISBN 3-03910-043-2 · US-ISBN 0-8204-6273-X

Vol. 11 David Hart (ed.)
English Modality in Context. Diachronic Perspectives.
261 pages. 2003. ISBN 3-03910-046-7 · US-ISBN 0-8204-6852-5

Vol. 12 Wendy Swanson
Modes of Co-reference as an Indicator of Genre.
430 pages. 2003. ISBN 3-03910-052-1 · US-ISBN 0-8204-6855-X

Vol. 13 Gina Poncini
Discursive Strategies in Multicultural Business Meetings.
2nd edition. 338 pages. 2004, 2007.
ISBN 978-3-03911-296-8 · US-ISBN 978-0-8204-8937-7

Vol. 14 Christopher N. Candlin & Maurizio Gotti (eds)
Intercultural Aspects of Specialized Communication.
2nd edition. 369 pages. 2004, 2007.
ISBN 978-3-03911-258-6 · US-ISBN 978-0-8204-8926-1

Vol. 15 Gabriella Del Lungo Camiciotti & Elena Tognini Bonelli (eds)
Academic Discourse. New Insights into Evaluation.
234 pages. 2004. ISBN 3-03910-353-9 · US-ISBN 0-8204-7016-3

Vol. 16 Marina Dossena & Roger Lass (eds)
Methods and Data in English Historical Dialectology.
405 pages. 2004. ISBN 3-03910-362-8 · US-ISBN 0-8204-7018-X

Vol. 17 Judy Noguchi
The Science Review Article. An Opportune Genre in
the Construction of Science.
274 pages. 2006. ISBN 3-03910-426-8 · US-ISBN 0-8204-7034-1

Vol. 18 Giuseppina Cortese & Anna Duszak (eds)
Identity, Community, Discourse. English in Intercultural Settings.
495 pages. 2005. ISBN 3-03910-632-5 · US-ISBN 0-8204-7163-1

Vol. 19 Anna Trosborg & Poul Erik Flyvholm Jørgensen (eds)
Business Discourse. Texts and Contexts.
250 pages. 2005. ISBN 3-03910-606-6 · US-ISBN 0-8204-7000-7

Vol. 20 Christopher Williams
Tradition and Change in Legal English. Verbal Constructions in Prescriptive Texts.
2nd revised edition. 216 pages. 2005, 2007. ISBN 978-3-03911-444-3.

Vol. 21 Katarzyna Dziubalska-Kolaczyk & Joanna Przedlacka (eds)
English Pronunciation Models: A Changing Scene.
2nd edition. 476 pages. 2005, 2008. ISBN 978-3-03911-682-9.

Vol. 22 Christián Abello-Contesse, Rubén Chacón-Beltrán, M. Dolores López-Jiménez & M. Mar Torreblanca-López (eds)
Age in L2 Acquisition and Teaching.
214 pages. 2006. ISBN 3-03910-668-6 · US-ISBN 0-8204-7174-7

Vol. 23 Vijay K. Bhatia, Maurizio Gotti, Jan Engberg & Dorothee Heller (eds)
Vagueness in Normative Texts.
474 pages. 2005. ISBN 3-03910-653-8 · US-ISBN 0-8204-7169-0

Vol. 24 Paul Gillaerts & Maurizio Gotti (eds)
Genre Variation in Business Letters. 2nd printing.
407 pages. 2008. ISBN 978-3-03911-681-2.

Vol. 25 Ana María Hornero, María José Luzón & Silvia Murillo (eds)
Corpus Linguistics. Applications for the Study of English.
2nd printing. 526 pages. 2006, 2008. ISBN 978-3-03911-726-0

Vol. 26 J. Lachlan Mackenzie & María de los Ángeles Gómez-González (eds)
Studies in Functional Discourse Grammar.
259 pages. 2005. ISBN 3-03910-696-1 · US-ISBN 0-8204-7558-0

Vol. 27 Debbie G. E. Ho
Classroom Talk. Exploring the Sociocultural Structure of Formal ESL Learning.
2nd edition. 254 pages. 2006, 2007. ISBN 978-3-03911-434-4

Vol. 28 Javier Pérez-Guerra, Dolores González-Álvarez, Jorge L. Bueno-Alonso & Esperanza Rama-Martínez (eds)
'Of Varying Language and Opposing Creed'. New Insights into Late Modern English.
455 pages. 2007. ISBN 978-3-03910-788-9

Vol. 29 Francesca Bargiela-Chiappini & Maurizio Gotti (eds)
Asian Business Discourse(s).
350 pages. 2005. ISBN 3-03910-804-2 · US-ISBN 0-8204-7574-2

Vol. 30 Nicholas Brownlees (ed.)
News Discourse in Early Modern Britain. Selected Papers of CHINED 2004.
300 pages. 2006. ISBN 3-03910-805-0 · US-ISBN 0-8204-8025-8

Vol. 31 Roberta Facchinetti & Matti Rissanen (eds)
Corpus-based Studies of Diachronic English.
300 pages. 2006. ISBN 3-03910-851-4 · US-ISBN 0-8204-8040-1

Vol. 32 Marina Dossena & Susan M. Fitzmaurice (eds)
Business and Official Correspondence. Historical Investigations.
209 pages. 2006. ISBN 3-03910-880-8 · US-ISBN 0-8204-8352-4

Vol. 33 Giuliana Garzone & Srikant Sarangi (eds)
Discourse, Ideology and Specialized Communication.
494 pages. 2007. ISBN 978-3-03910-888-6

Vol. 34 Giuliana Garzone & Cornelia Ilie (eds)
The Use of English in Institutional and Business Settings.
An Intercultural Perspective.
372 pages. 2007. ISBN 978-3-03910-889-3

Vol. 35 Vijay K. Bhatia & Maurizio Gotti (eds)
Explorations in Specialized Genres.
316 pages. 2006. ISBN 3-03910-995-2 · US-ISBN 0-8204-8372-9

Vol. 36 Heribert Picht (ed.)
Modern Approaches to Terminological Theories and Applications.
432 pages. 2006. ISBN 3-03911-156-6 · US-ISBN 0-8204-8380-X

Vol. 37 Anne Wagner & Sophie Cacciaguidi-Fahy (eds)
Legal Language and the Search for Clarity / Le langage juridique et la quête de clarté.
Practice and Tools / Pratiques et instruments.
487 pages. 2006. ISBN 3-03911-169-8 · US-ISBN 0-8204-8388-5

Vol. 38 Juan Carlos Palmer-Silveira, Miguel F. Ruiz-Garrido &
Inmaculada Fortanet-Gómez (eds)
Intercultural and International Business Communication.
Theory, Research and Teaching.
2nd edition. 343 pages. 2006, 2008. ISBN 978-3-03911-680-5

Vol. 39 Christiane Dalton-Puffer, Dieter Kastovsky, Nikolaus Ritt &
Herbert Schendl (eds)
Syntax, Style and Grammatical Norms. English from 1500–2000.
250 pages. 2006. ISBN 3-03911-181-7 · US-ISBN 0-8204-8394-X

Vol. 40 Marina Dossena & Irma Taavitsainen (eds)
Diachronic Perspectives on Domain-Specific English.
280 pages. 2006. ISBN 3-03910-176-0 · US-ISBN 0-8204-8391-5

Vol. 41 John Flowerdew & Maurizio Gotti (eds)
Studies in Specialized Discourse.
293 pages. 2006. ISBN 3-03911-178-7

Vol. 42 Ken Hyland & Marina Bondi (eds)
Academic Discourse Across Disciplines.
320 pages. 2006. ISBN 3-03911-183-3 · US-ISBN 0-8204-8396-6

Vol. 43 Paul Gillaerts & Philip Shaw (eds)
The Map and the Landscape. Norms and Practices in Genre.
256 pages. 2006. ISBN 3-03911-182-5 · US-ISBN 0-8204-8395-4

Vol. 44 Maurizio Gotti & Davide Giannoni (eds)
New Trends in Specialized Discourse Analysis.
301 pages. 2006. ISBN 3-03911-184-1 · US-ISBN 0-8204-8381-8

Vol. 45 Maurizio Gotti & Françoise Salager-Meyer (eds)
Advances in Medical Discourse Analysis. Oral and Written Contexts.
492 pages. 2006. ISBN 3-03911-185-X · US-ISBN 0-8204-8382-6

Vol. 46 Maurizio Gotti & Susan Šarcević (eds)
Insights into Specialized Translation.
396 pages. 2006. ISBN 3-03911-186-8 · US-ISBN 0-8204-8383-4

Vol. 47 Khurshid Ahmad & Margaret Rogers (eds)
Evidence-based LSP. Translation, Text and Terminology.
584 pages. 2007. ISBN 978-3-03911-187-9

Vol. 48 Hao Sun & Dániel Z. Kádár (eds)
It's the Dragon's Turn. Chinese Institutional Discourses.
262 pages. 2008. ISBN 978-3-03911-175-6

Vol. 49 Cristina Suárez-Gómez
Relativization in Early English (950-1250). the Position of Relative Clauses.
149 pages. 2006. ISBN 3-03911-203-1 · US-ISBN 0-8204-8904-2

Vol. 50 Maria Vittoria Calvi & Luisa Chierichetti (eds)
Nuevas tendencias en el discurso de especialidad.
319 pages. 2006. ISBN 978-3-03911-261-6

Vol. 51 Mari Carmen Campoy & María José Luzón (eds)
Spoken Corpora in Applied Linguistics.
274 pages. 2008. ISBN 978-3-03911-275-3

Vol. 52 Konrad Ehlich & Dorothee Heller (Hrsg.)
Die Wissenschaft und ihre Sprachen.
323 pages. 2006. ISBN 978-3-03911-272-2

Vol. 53 Jingyu Zhang
The Semantic Salience Hierarchy Model. The L2 Acquisition of Psych Predicates
273 pages. 2007. ISBN 978-3-03911-300-2

Vol. 54 Norman Fairclough, Giuseppina Cortese & Patrizia Ardizzone (eds)
Discourse and Contemporary Social Change.
555 pages. 2007. ISBN 978-3-03911-276-0

Vol. 55 Jan Engberg, Marianne Grove Ditlevsen, Peter Kastberg & Martin Stegu (eds)
New Directions in LSP Teaching.
331 pages. 2007. ISBN 978-3-03911-433-7

Vol. 56 Dorothee Heller & Konrad Ehlich (Hrsg.)
Studien zur Rechtskommunikation.
322 pages. 2007. ISBN 978-3-03911-436-8

Vol. 57 Teruhiro Ishiguro & Kang-kwong Luke (eds)
Grammar in Cross-Linguistic Perspective.
The Syntax, Semantics, and Pragmatics of Japanese and Chinese.
304 pages. 2012. ISBN 978-3-03911-445-0

Vol. 58 Carmen Frehner
Email – SMS – MMS
294 pages. 2008. ISBN 978-3-03911-451-1

Vol. 59 Isabel Balteiro
The Directionality of Conversion in English. A Dia-Synchronic Study.
276 pages. 2007. ISBN 978-3-03911-241-8

Vol. 60 Maria Milagros Del Saz Rubio
English Discourse Markers of Reformulation.
237 pages. 2007. ISBN 978-3-03911-196-1

Vol. 61 Sally Burgess & Pedro Martín-Martín (eds)
English as an Additional Language in Research Publication and Communication.
259 pages. 2008. ISBN 978-3-03911-462-7

Vol. 62 Sandrine Onillon
Pratiques et représentations de l'écrit.
458 pages. 2008. ISBN 978-3-03911-464-1

Vol. 63 Hugo Bowles & Paul Seedhouse (eds)
Conversation Analysis and Language for Specific Purposes.
2nd edition. 337 pages. 2007, 2009. ISBN 978-3-0343-0045-2

Vol. 64 Vijay K. Bhatia, Christopher N. Candlin & Paola Evangelisti Allori (eds)
Language, Culture and the Law.
The Formulation of Legal Concepts across Systems and Cultures.
342 pages. 2008. ISBN 978-3-03911-470-2

Vol. 65 Jonathan Culpeper & Dániel Z. Kádár (eds)
Historical (Im)politeness.
300 pages. 2010. ISBN 978-3-03911-496-2

Vol. 66 Linda Lombardo (ed.)
Using Corpora to Learn about Language and Discourse.
237 pages. 2009. ISBN 978-3-03911-522-8

Vol. 67 Natsumi Wakamoto
Extroversion/Introversion in Foreign Language Learning.
Interactions with Learner Strategy Use.
159 pages. 2009. ISBN 978-3-03911-596-9

Vol. 68 Eva Alcón-Soler (ed.)
Learning How to Request in an Instructed Language Learning Context.
260 pages. 2008. ISBN 978-3-03911-601-0

Vol. 69 Domenico Pezzini
The Translation of Religious Texts in the Middle Ages.
428 pages. 2008. ISBN 978-3-03911-600-3

Vol. 70 Tomoko Tode
Effects of Frequency in Classroom Second Language Learning.
Quasi-experiment and stimulated-recall analysis.
195 pages. 2008. ISBN 978-3-03911-602-7

Vol. 71 Egor Tsedryk
Fusion symétrique et alternances ditransitives.
211 pages. 2009. ISBN 978-3-03911-609-6

Vol. 72 Cynthia J. Kellett Bidoli & Elana Ochse (eds)
English in International Deaf Communication.
444 pages. 2008. ISBN 978-3-03911-610-2

Vol. 73 Joan C. Beal, Carmela Nocera & Massimo Sturiale (eds)
Perspectives on Prescriptivism.
269 pages. 2008. ISBN 978-3-03911-632-4

Vol. 74 Carol Taylor Torsello, Katherine Ackerley & Erik Castello (eds)
Corpora for University Language Teachers.
308 pages. 2008. ISBN 978-3-03911-639-3

Vol. 75 María Luisa Pérez Cañado (ed.)
English Language Teaching in the European Credit Transfer System. Facing the Challenge.
251 pages. 2009. ISBN 978-3-03911-654-6

Vol. 76 Marina Dossena & Ingrid Tieken-Boon van Ostade (eds)
Studies in Late Modern English Correspondence. Methodology and Data.
291 pages. 2008. ISBN 978-3-03911-658-4

Vol. 77 Ingrid Tieken-Boon van Ostade & Wim van der Wurff (eds)
Current Issues in Late Modern English.
436 pages. 2009. ISBN 978-3-03911-660-7

Vol. 78 Marta Navarro Coy (ed.)
Practical Approaches to Foreign Language Teaching and Learning.
297 pages. 2009. ISBN 978-3-03911-661-4

Vol. 79 Qing Ma
Second Language Vocabulary Acquisition.
333 pages. 2009. ISBN 978-3-03911-666-9

Vol. 80 Martin Solly, Michelangelo Conoscenti & Sandra Campagna (eds)
Verbal/Visual Narrative Texts in Higher Education.
384 pages. 2008. ISBN 978-3-03911-672-0

Vol. 81 Meiko Matsumoto
From Simple Verbs to Periphrastic Expressions: The Historical Development of Composite Predicates, Phrasal Verbs, and Related Constructions in English.
235 pages. 2008. ISBN 978-3-03911-675-1

Vol. 82 Melinda Dooly
Doing Diversity. Teachers' Construction of Their Classroom Reality.
180 pages. 2009. ISBN 978-3-03911-687-4

Vol. 83 Victoria Guillén-Nieto, Carmen Marimón-Llorca & Chelo Vargas-Sierra (eds)
Intercultural Business Communication and Simulation and Gaming Methodology.
392 pages. 2009. ISBN 978-3-03911-688-1

Vol. 84 Maria Grazia Guido
English as a Lingua Franca in Cross-cultural Immigration Domains.
285 pages. 2008. ISBN 978-3-03911-689-8

Vol. 85 Erik Castello
Text Complexity and Reading Comprehension Tests.
352 pages. 2008. ISBN 978-3-03911-717-8

Vol. 86 Maria-Lluisa Gea-Valor, Isabel García-Izquierdo & Maria-José Esteve (eds)
Linguistic and Translation Studies in Scientific Communication.
317 pages. 2010. ISBN 978-3-0343-0069-8

Vol. 87 Carmen Navarro, Rosa Mª Rodríguez Abella, Francesca Dalle Pezze & Renzo Miotti (eds)
La comunicación especializada.
355 pages. 2008. ISBN 978-3-03911-733-8

Vol. 88 Kiriko Sato
The Development from Case-Forms to Prepositional Constructions in Old English Prose.
231 pages. 2009. ISBN 978-3-03911-763-5

Vol. 89 Dorothee Heller (Hrsg.)
Formulierungsmuster in deutscher und italienischer Fachkommunikation. Intra- und interlinguale Perspektiven.
315 pages. 2008. ISBN 978-3-03911-778-9

Vol. 90 Henning Bergenholtz, Sandro Nielsen & Sven Tarp (eds)
Lexicography at a Crossroads. Dictionaries and Encyclopedias Today, Lexicographical Tools Tomorrow.
372 pages. 2009. ISBN 978-3-03911-799-4

Vol. 91 Manouchehr Moshtagh Khorasani
The Development of Controversies. From the Early Modern Period to Online Discussion Forums.
317 pages. 2009. ISBN 978-3-3911-711-6

Vol. 92 María Luisa Carrió-Pastor (ed.)
Content and Language Integrated Learning. Cultural Diversity.
178 pages. 2009. ISBN 978-3-3911-818-2

Vol. 93 Roger Berry
Terminology in English Language Teaching. Nature and Use.
262 pages. 2010. ISBN 978-3-0343-0013-1

Vol. 94 Roberto Cagliero & Jennifer Jenkins (eds)
Discourses, Communities, and Global Englishes
240 pages. 2010. ISBN 978-3-0343-0012-4

Vol. 95 Facchinetti Roberta, Crystal David, Seidlhofer Barbara (eds)
From International to Local English – And Back Again.
268 pages. 2010. ISBN 978-3-0343-0011-7

Vol. 96 Cesare Gagliardi & Alan Maley (eds)
EIL, ELF, Global English. Teaching and Learning Issues
376 pages. 2010. ISBN 978-3-0343-0010-0

Vol. 97 Sylvie Hancil (ed.)
The Role of Prosody in Affective Speech.
403 pages. 2009. ISBN 978-3-03911-696-6

Vol. 98 Marina Dossena & Roger Lass (eds)
Studies in English and European Historical Dialectology.
257 pages. 2009. ISBN 978-3-0343-0024-7

Vol. 99 Christine Béal
Les interactions quotidiennes en français et en anglais. De l'approche comparative à l'analyse des situations interculturelles.
424 pages. 2010. ISBN 978-3-0343-0027-8

Vol. 100 Maurizio Gotti (ed.)
Commonality and Individuality in Academic Discourse.
398 pages. 2009. ISBN 978-3-0343-0023-0

Vol. 101 Javier E. Díaz Vera & Rosario Caballero (eds)
Textual Healing. Studies in Medieval English Medical, Scientific and Technical Texts.
213 pages. 2009. ISBN 978-3-03911-822-9

Vol. 102 Nuria Edo Marzá
The Specialised Lexicographical Approach. A Step further in Dictionary-making.
316 pages. 2009. ISBN 978-3-0343-0043-8

Vol. 103 Carlos Prado-Alonso, Lidia Gómez-García, Iria Pastor-Gómez &
David Tizón-Couto (eds)
New Trends and Methodologies in Applied English Language Research.
Diachronic, Diatopic and Contrastive Studies.
348 pages. 2009. ISBN 978-3-0343-0046-9

Vol. 104 Françoise Salager-Meyer & Beverly A. Lewin
Crossed Words. Criticism in Scholarly Writing?
371 pages. 2011. ISBN 978-3-0343-0049-0.

Vol. 105 Javier Ruano-García
Early Modern Northern English Lexis. A Literary Corpus-Based Study.
611 pages. 2010. ISBN 978-3-0343-0058-2

Vol. 106 Rafael Monroy-Casas
Systems for the Phonetic Transcription of English. Theory and Texts.
280 pages. 2011. ISBN 978-3-0343-0059-9

Vol. 107 Nicola T. Owtram
The Pragmatics of Academic Writing.
A Relevance Approach to the Analysis of Research Article Introductions.
311 pages. 2009. ISBN 978-3-0343-0060-5

Vol. 108 Yolanda Ruiz de Zarobe, Juan Manuel Sierra &
Francisco Gallardo del Puerto (eds)
Content and Foreign Language Integrated Learning.
Contributions to Multilingualism in European Contexts
343 pages. 2011. ISBN 978-3-0343-0074-2

Vol. 109 Ángeles Linde López & Rosalía Crespo Jiménez (eds)
Professional English in the European context. The EHEA challenge.
374 pages. 2010. ISBN 978-3-0343-0088-9

Vol. 110 Rosalía Rodríguez-Vázquez
The Rhythm of Speech, Verse and Vocal Music. A New Theory.
394 pages. 2010. ISBN 978-3-0343-0309-5

Vol. 111 Anastasios Tsangalidis & Roberta Facchinetti (eds)
Studies on English Modality. In Honour of Frank Palmer.
392 pages. 2009. ISBN 978-3-0343-0310-1

Vol. 112 Forthcoming.

Vol. 113 Mihhail Lotman & Maria-Kristiina Lotman (eds)
Frontiers in Comparative Prosody. In memoriam: Mikhail Gasparov.
426 pages. 2011. ISBN 978-3-0343-0373-6

Vol. 114 Merja Kytö, John Scahill & Harumi Tanabe (eds)
Language Change and Variation from Old English to Late Modern English.
A Festschrift for Minoji Akimoto
422 pages. 2010. ISBN 978-3-0343-0372-9

Vol. 115 Giuliana Garzone & Paola Catenaccio (eds)
Identities across Media and Modes. Discursive Perspectives.
379 pages. 2009. ISBN 978-3-0343-0386-6

Vol. 116 Elena Landone
Los marcadores del discurso y cortesía verbal en español.
390 pages. 2010. ISBN 978-3-0343-0413-9

Vol. 117 Maurizio Gotti & Christopher Williams (eds)
Legal Discourse across Languages and Cultures.
339 pages. 2010. ISBN 978-3-0343-0425-2

Vol. 118 David Hirsh
Academic Vocabulary in Context.
217 pages. 2010. ISBN 978-3-0343-0426-9

Vol. 119 Yvonne Dröschel
Lingua Franca English. The Role of Simplification and Transfer.
358 pages. 2011. ISBN 978-3-0343-0432-0

Vol. 120 Tengku Sepora Tengku Mahadi, Helia Vaezian & Mahmoud Akbari
Corpora in Translation. A Practical Guide.
135 pages. 2010. ISBN 978-3-0343-0434-4

Vol. 121 Davide Simone Giannoni & Celina Frade (eds)
Researching Language and the Law. Textual Features and Translation Issues.
278 pages. 2010. ISBN 978-3-0343-0443-6

Vol. 122 Daniel Madrid & Stephen Hughes (eds)
Studies in Bilingual Education.
472 pages. 2011. ISBN 978-3-0343-0474-0

Vol. 123 Vijay K. Bhatia, Christopher N. Candlin & Maurizio Gotti (eds)
The Discourses of Dispute Resolution.
290 pages. 2010. ISBN 978-3-0343-0476-4

Vol. 124 Davide Simone Giannoni
Mapping Academic Values in the Disciplines. A Corpus-Based Approach.
288 pages. 2010. ISBN 978-3-0343-0488-7

Vol. 125 Giuliana Garzone & James Archibald (eds)
Discourse, Identities and Roles in Specialized Communication.
419 pages. 2010. ISBN 978-3-0343-0494-8

Vol. 126 Iria Pastor-Gómez
The Status and Development of N+N Sequences in
Contemporary English Noun Phrases.
216 pages. 2011. ISBN 978-3-0343-0534-1

Vol. 127 Carlos Prado-Alonso
Full-verb Inversion in Written and Spoken English.
261 pages. 2011. ISBN 978-3-0343-0535-8

Vol. 128 Tony Harris & María Moreno Jaén (eds)
Corpus Linguistics in Language Teaching.
214 pages. 2010. ISBN 978-3-0343-0524-2

Vol. 129 Tetsuji Oda & Hiroyuki Eto (eds)
Multiple Perspectives on English Philology and History of Linguistics.
A Festschrift for Shoichi Watanabe on his 80th Birthday.
378 pages. 2010. ISBN 978-3-0343-0480-1

Vol. 130 Luisa Chierichetti & Giovanni Garofalo (eds)
Lengua y Derecho. líneas de investigación interdisciplinaria.
283 pages. 2010. 978-3-0343-0463-4

Vol. 131 Paola Evangelisti Allori & Giuliana Garzone (eds)
Discourse, Identities and Genres in Corporate Communication.
Sponsorship, Advertising and Organizational Communication.
324 pages. 2011. 978-3-0343-0591-4

Vol. 132 Leyre Ruiz de Zarobe & Yolanda Ruiz de Zarobe (eds)
Speech Acts and Politeness across Languages and Cultures.
402 pages. 2012. 978-3-0343-0611-9

Vol. 133 Thomas Christiansen
Cohesion. A Discourse Perspective.
387 pages. 2011. 978-3-0343-0619-5

Vol. 134 Giuliana Garzone & Maurizio Gotti
Discourse, Communication and the Enterprise. Genres and Trends.
451 pages. 2011. ISBN 978-3-0343-0620-1

Vol. 135 Zsuzsa Hoffmann
Ways of the World's Words.
Language Contact in the Age of Globalization.
334 pages 2011. ISBN 978-3-0343-0673-7

Vol. 136 Cecilia Varcasia (ed.)
Becoming Multilingual.
Language Learning and Language Policy between Attitudes and Identities.
213 pages. 2011. ISBN 978-3-0343-0687-5

Vol. 137 Susy Macqueen
The Emergence of Patterns in Second Language Writing.
A Sociocognitive Exploration of Lexical Trails.
325 pages. 2012. ISBN 978-3-0343-1010-9

Vol. 138 Maria Vittoria Calvi & Giovanna Mapelli (eds)
La lengua del turismo. Géneros discursivos y terminología.
365 pages. 2011. ISBN 978-3-0343-1011-6

Vol. 139 Ken Lau
Learning to Become a Professional in a Textually-Mediated World.
A Text-Oriented Study of Placement Practices.
261 pages. 2012. ISBN 978-3-0343-1016-1

Vol. 140 Sandra Campagna, Giuliana Garzone, Cornelia Ilie & Elizabeth Rowley-Jolivet (eds)
Evolving Genres in Web-mediated Communication.
337 pages. 2012. ISBN 978-3-0343-1013-0

Vol. 141 Edith Esch & Martin Solly (eds)
The Sociolinguistics of Language Education in International Contexts.
263 pages. 2012. ISBN 978-3-0343-1009-3

Vol. 142 Forthcoming.

Vol. 143 David Tizón-Couto
Left Dislocation in English. A Functional-Discoursal Approach.
416 pages. 2012. ISBN 978-3-0343-1037-6

Vol. 144 Margrethe Petersen & Jan Engberg (eds)
Current Trends in LSP Research. Aims and Methods.
323 pages. 2011. ISBN 978-3-0343-1054-3

Vol. 145 David Tizón-Couto, Beatriz Tizón-Couto, Iria Pastor-Gómez & Paula Rodríguez-Puente (eds)
New Trends and Methodologies in Applied English Language Research II.
Studies in Language Variation, Meaning and Learning.
283 pages. 2012. ISBN 978-3-0343-1061-1

Vol. 146 Rita Salvi & Hiromasa Tanaka (eds)
Intercultural Interactions in Business and Management.
306 pages. 2011. ISBN 978-3-0343-1039-0

Vol. 147 Francesco Straniero Sergio & Caterina Falbo (eds)
Breaking Ground in Corpus-based Interpreting Studies.
254 pages. 2012. ISBN 978-3-0343-1071-0

Vol. 148 Forthcoming.

Vol. 149 Vijay K. Bhatia & Paola Evangelisti Allori (eds)
Discourse and Identity in the Professions. Legal, Corporate and Institutional Citizenship.
352 pages. 2011. ISBN 978-3-0343-1079-6

Vol. 150 Maurizio Gotti (ed.)
Academic Identity Traits. A Corpus-Based Investigation.
363 pages. 2012. ISBN 978-3-0343-1141-0

Vol. 151 Priscilla Heynderickx, Sylvain Dieltjens, Geert Jacobs, Paul Gillaerts &
Elizabeth de Groot (eds)
The Language Factor in International Business.
New Perspectives on Research, Teaching and Practice.
320 pages. 2012. ISBN 978-3-0343-1090-1

Vol. 152 Paul Gillaerts, Elizabeth de Groot, Sylvain Dieltjens, Priscilla Heynderickx &
Geert Jacobs (eds)
Researching Discourse in Business Genres. Cases and Corpora.
215 pages. 2012. ISBN 978-3-0343-1092-5

Vol. 153 Yongyan Zheng
Dynamic Vocabulary Development in a Foreign Language.
262 pages. 2012. ISBN 978-3-0343-1106-9

Vol. 154 Carmen Argondizzo (ed.)
Creativity and Innovation in Language Education.
357 pages. 2012. ISBN 978-3-0343-1080-2

Vol. 155 David Hirsh (ed.)
Current Perspectives in Second Language Vocabulary Research.
180 pages. 2012. ISBN 978-3-0343-1108-3

Vol. 156 Seiji Shinkawa
Unhistorical Gender Assignment in Laȝamon's *Brut.* A Case Study of a Late Stage
in the Development of Grammatical Gender toward its Ultimate Loss.
186 pages. 2012. ISBN 978-3-0343-1124-3

Vol. 157 Forthcoming.

Vol. 158 Bárbara Eizaga Rebollar (ed.)
Studies in Linguistics and Cognition.
301 pages. 2012. ISBN 978-3-0343-1138-0

Vol. 159 Giuliana Garzone, Paola Catenaccio, Chiara Degano (eds)
Genre Change in the Contemporary World. Short-term Diachronic Perspectives.
329 pages. 2012. ISBN 978-3-0343-1214-1

Vol. 160 Carol Berkenkotter, Vijay K. Bhatia & Maurizio Gotti (eds)
Insights into Academic Genres.
468 pages. 2012. ISBN 978-3-0343-1211-0

Vol. 161 Forthcoming.

Vol. 162 Patrizia Anesa
Jury Trials and the Popularization of Legal Language. A Discourse Analytical Approach.
247 pages. 2012. ISBN 978-3-0343-1231-8

Vol. 163-166 Forthcoming.

Vol. 167 Shunji Yamazaki & Robert Sigley (eds)
Approaching Language Variation through Corpora. A Festschrift in Honour of Toshio Saito.
421 pages. 2013. ISBN 978-3-0343-1264-6

Vol. 168 Franca Poppi
Global Interactions in English as a Lingua Franca. How written communication is changing under the influence of electronic media and new contexts of use.
249 pages. 2012. ISBN 978-3-0343-1276-9

Vol. 169-171 Forthcoming.

Vol. 172 Maurizio Gotti & Carmen Sancho Guinda (eds)
Narratives in Academic and Professional Genres.
513 pages. 2013. ISBN 978-3-0343-1371-1

www.ingramcontent.com/pod-product-compliance
Ingram Content Group UK Ltd.
Pitfield, Milton Keynes, MK11 3LW, UK
UKHW021853100926
8556IPUK00020B/1205

9 783034 312646